AN AMERICAN
LEGACY

AN AMERICAN LEGACY

RACISM, NATIVISM, AND WHITE SUPREMACY

DAVID R. MORSE

ACADEMY
PRESS

Copyright © 2020 David R. Morse. All rights reserved.

No part of this publication shall be reproduced, transmitted, or sold in whole or in part in any form without prior written consent of the author, except as provided by the United States of America copyright law. Any unauthorized usage of the text without express written permission of the publisher is a violation of the author's copyright and is illegal and punishable by law. All trademarks and registered trademarks appearing in this guide are the property of their respective owners.

For permission requests, write to the author at the below address:

David R. Morse
david@newamericandimensions.com

The opinions expressed by the Author are not necessarily those held by PYP Academy Press.

Ordering Information: Quantity sales and special discounts are available on quantity purchases by corporations, associations, and others. For details, contact the author at david@newamericandimensions.com.

Edited by: Lori McFerran and Kassandra White
Cover design by: Fiaz Ahmed Irfan
Typeset by: Medlar Publishing Solutions Pvt Ltd., India

Printed in the United States of America.
ISBN: 978-1-951591-41-0 (paperback)
ISBN: 978-1-951591-42-7 (ebook)

Library of Congress Control Number: 2020912401

First edition, September 2020.

The information contained within this book is strictly for informational purposes. The material may include information, products, or services by third parties. As such, the Author and Publisher do not assume responsibility or liability for any third-party material or opinions. The publisher is not responsible for websites (or their content) that are not owned by the publisher. Readers are advised to do their own due diligence when it comes to making decisions.

The mission of the Publish Your Purpose Academy Press is to discover and publish authors who are striving to make a difference in the world. We give marginalized voices power and a stage to share their stories, speak their truth, and impact their communities. Do you have a book idea you would like us to consider publishing? Please visit PublishYourPurposePress.com for more information.

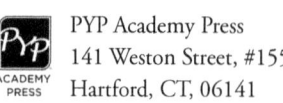 PYP Academy Press
141 Weston Street, #155
Hartford, CT, 06141

DEDICATION

I dedicate this book to my two lovely daughters, Ruby and Sophia Morse; the memories of my father, Myron "Mike" Morse, and my sister, Laura Morse Forest; my mother, Zee Morse, sister Karen Morse King, husband, Jimmy Chee, and the Simons family, Tom, Cynthia, Jerame, and Thomas.

CONTENTS

Introduction xi

PART 1 WHITE AMERICANS 1

1 | The Anglo-Saxons 7
2 | The Irish and Germans 15
3 | The Italians and Jews 29
4 | The Integration of White Folks 45
5 | Cracks in the White Wall 55

PART 2 AFRICAN AMERICANS 65

6 | Slavery and the Idea of the "Superior" Caucasian Race 69
7 | Jim Crow and the Great Migration 79
8 | From Civil Rights to Sister Souljah 91
9 | The Beginning and End of "Post-Racial America" 107

PART 3 HISPANIC AMERICANS 127

10 | Conquests 131
11 | Cheap Labor and Mob Violence 145
12 | Double Standards 155

13 | The Birth of the Illegal Immigrant 171
14 | Immigration Reform in Theory, Deportations in Practice 185

PART 4 ASIAN AMERICANS 197

15 | Exotic Orientals and Chinese Immigrants 201
16 | The Gentleman's Agreement with Japan 217
17 | East Indians and Filipinos 229
18 | From Allies and Aliens to Model Minority 245

PART 5 RACE, SCIENCE, AND CLASSIFICATION 263

19 | Early Racial Thinking, Social Darwinism, and Eugenics 267
20 | Modern Genetics and Anthropology Take Hold 277
21 | The Rise of the Human Genome 297
22 | Racial Classification and the U.S. Census 309

PART 6 WHERE ARE WE NOW? WHERE ARE WE GOING? 321

23 | A New Racial Divide? 323
24 | Race, Economics, and Society 333
25 | The Present, The Future 343

Bibliography *363*
Index *383*
Hire David to Speak *397*
Other Books *399*
Listen to the Race Talk *Podcast* *401*
About the Author *403*

INTRODUCTION

Racism is as old as America itself. It was with us at the start. And it haunts us today. Ever manifesting in new, often violent ways, it infects our national consciousness, like a cancer. While we have come far as a nation, we have yet to free ourselves from the yoke of our country's original sin, slavery, and the seemingly endless practices that were invoked to keep Blacks and other people of color down. Whether we look at the genocide of Native Americans, Jim Crow and segregation, the mass detention and deportations of Hispanics, or Chinese Exclusion and the internment of Japanese Americans in concentration camps, race in America is not a pretty picture.

I write this less than two weeks after the ungodly murder of George Floyd, a 46-year-old African American man, by police, on May 25, 2020, in Minneapolis. The incident began when a store owner called 911, saying someone had tried to pass a counterfeit bill. Arriving on the scene, police arrested Floyd, who was parked across the street, and video surveillance cameras show a compliant man being led away from his car in handcuffs. Minutes later, in a cell phone video seen around the world, former police officer Derek Chauvin kneels on Floyd's neck as Floyd repeatedly says, "I can't breathe" and "I'm about to die." When Chauvin finally removes his knee, Floyd's body is limp and unresponsive. A bystander is heard saying, "They just killed him." Floyd was taken to a hospital, where he was pronounced dead. According to a police statement, one that makes no mention of Floyd being pinned to the ground by Chauvin, Floyd was in "medical distress."

Just 12 hours earlier, in New York City's Central Park, a White woman, Amy Cooper, called 911 and told the dispatcher that an African American man was threatening her. A bird-watcher, Christian Cooper, who is no relation to Amy, had simply asked her to leash her dog, a requirement of the area they were in. As can be seen on the video that Mr. Cooper recorded on his phone, Ms. Cooper warns that she is "going to tell [police] there's an African American man threatening my life." Two days later, Amy Cooper's employer, the investment firm Franklin Templeton, fired her for racism, and Ms. Cooper apologized publically. However, the damage had been done. Ms. Cooper had consciously and deliberately conjured up an image that has been used and abused since the days of slavery: namely that of a White woman being threatened or harmed by an African America man. Ms. Cooper drew on her White Privilege, by putting Mr. Cooper's blackness at the center of her threat.[1]

Three months earlier, on February 23, Ahmaud Arbery, a 25-year-old Black man was shot to death in southeast Georgia while jogging. Three White men, Travis McMichael, his father, Gregory McMichael, and a third man, their neighbor William Bryan, stalked and killed him for allegedly committing some robberies in the area. Mr. Arbery was killed just three days before the anniversary of the 2012 killing of Trayvon Martin, an unarmed African-American teenager whose confrontation with a Florida neighborhood watch captain, George Zimmerman, helped ignite the Black Lives Matter (BLM) movement. For months after the shooting death of Arbery, no arrests were made; until on May 5, the McMichaels were charged with murder and aggravated assault – two days after a graphic video of the shooting of Mr. Arbery became public. Bryan was charged two weeks later.

While African American men are the most common victims of police shootings, Black women are by no means immune. The world found this out on March 13, when Louisville police officers, search warrant in hand, used a battering ram to burst into the apartment of Breonna Taylor, a 26-year-old emergency room technician. According to reports, police heard that a man suspected of selling drugs had used Taylor's apartment to receive packages, and they convinced a judge to issue a "no-knock warrant," allowing police to enter without warning and without having to identifying themselves as law enforcement.[2]

The police stated that they knocked on the door and announced themselves, though multiple neighbors said that neither assertion was true. When they entered, Taylor's boyfriend, Kenneth Walker, who says he thought someone was breaking into the apartment, fired a shot and hit an officer in the leg. Police then fired over 20 rounds, killing Taylor, who was hit eight times. Walker was arrested and charged with the attempted murder of a police officer. There were no drugs found, and neither Taylor nor Walker had a criminal history.[3]

Taylor's murder sparked outrage, but it took the world watching the savagely brutal lynching of George Floyd by police to spark national, indeed global, protests. In cities across the United States, tens of thousands of people took to the streets to express their outrage and sadness. In many cases, peaceful protests descended into nights of looting and vandalism, which triggered a draconian, military response by police, egged on by President Donald Trump.

I write this knowing that as a White man, I can go for a jog in my very White neighborhood in Scottsdale, Arizona, and I am not going to be shot just because of my race, my color. I am less likely to get pulled over, and if I am, I'm careful, but it doesn't enter my mind that I might find myself gasping for air minutes later. It's called White Privilege, the luxury of not having to think about my race unless that is something I choose to do. It's the result of both historic and enduring racism, and as a White person, I benefit from it every time I leave my house.

Whites like me, however, are on the numerical decline, as America fulfills its destiny of becoming a minority-majority country. According to projections, soon after the year 2040, non-Hispanic Whites will make up less than half of the U.S. population. Largely driven by immigration from Latin America and Asia, our country is undergoing a demographic revolution. As a student of history, I ask myself, where is America headed? It's not an easy question to answer.

With such startling change, America, specifically White America, needs to realize that White folks and people of color live in two different worlds. One is a world of privilege; the other exists under the shroud of systematic racism. If we are to come together, if we are ever going to eradicate the evil that besets out country, we need to acknowledge this. We need to embrace the rallying cry from the 1976 movie, *Network*: "I'm as mad as hell, and I'm not going to take this anymore!"

Quite literally, Americans live in two different worlds: one inhabited by Whites and the other by people of color. In an analysis of segregation patterns in metropolitan areas, sociologists John R. Logan and Brian J. Stults found that the typical White American lives in a neighborhood that is 77 percent White. African Americans were less likely to live in neighborhoods surrounded by co-ethnics, but the segregation numbers are still high: the typical African American lives in a neighborhood that is 48 percent black. While Logan and Stults did find a trend toward "increasing diversity," they note that Whites tend to live with other Whites, and minorities tend to live with minorities.[4]

An alarming change in recent decades has been the incarceration of young, African American males. Black men are, compared to other groups, far more likely to be imprisoned. According to Pew Research, in 2018 there were 2,272 inmates per 100,000 Black men, compared with 1,018 inmates per 100,000 Hispanic men, and 392 inmates per 100,000 White men. Among those ages 35 to 39, about one in 20 Black men were in state or federal prison (5,008 inmates for every 100,000 Black men in this age group).[5] Michelle Alexander, author of *The New Jim Crow*, writes, "The United States imprisons a larger percentage of its black population than

South Africa did at the height of apartheid. In Washington D.C. it is estimated that three out of four young black men can expect to serve time in prison."[6]

At the same time, there are indications that anti-black racism is on the rise. One study by professors at Stanford, the University of Chicago and the University of Michigan found that the proportion of voters answering questions with "explicit anti-black attitudes" increased to 51 percent in 2012 from 48 percent in 2008. They found a corresponding decrease among those expressing "pro-black attitudes," to 42 percent from 47 percent. Although Republicans were more likely than Democrats to express racial prejudice in the questions measuring explicit racism – 79 percent among Republicans compared with 32 percent among Democrats – an implicit test, designed to measure unconscious attitudes, found little difference between the two parties. Said Jelani Cobb, a professor of African-American studies, "We have this false idea that there is uniformity in progress and that things change in one big step. That is not the way history has worked. When we've seen progress, we've also seen backlash."[7]

Hispanics have been the unwilling recipients of another type of racism, a kind of xenophobia, largely directed at immigrants and heavily fueled by the U.S. president. Latin American and Caribbean nationals make up 97 percent of deportees, and some scholars have argued that detention and deportation are the 21st century corollaries of mass incarceration. Like incarceration, in the case of detention, there is big money to be made, and it's often the same companies that are incarcerating and detaining. According to Tanya Golash-Boza, Professor of Sociology at the University of California Merced, between 2008 and 2014 Corrections Corporation of America (now rebranded as CoreCivic) spent $10 million on lobbying related to immigration detention and immigration reform, and its annual profits increased from $133 million to $195 million during that time.[8] Despite indications that levels of mass detention might be leveling off, we have seen horrific images of detention centers during the Trump administration. These images showed detainees, very often children without their parents, kept like caged animals, not to mention a drowned father cradling his dead daughter and a lone mother defending herself against an armed Border Patrol Agent, with a horrified toddler at her side.

Asian Americans, often assigned the epithet of "model minority," a label that only facilitates racial division, are frequently stereotyped as being math whizzes or "perpetual foreigners." Since the outbreak of the Covid-19 pandemic, there has been a surge in the harassment of Asian Americans. According to Stop AAPI Hate, the leading aggregator of incidents against Asian Americans during the pandemic, more than 1,100 physical and verbal attacks against Asian Americans have been documented between late March and the end of May in 2020. In one, an Asian American child was pushed off her bike at a park. In another, a family at a grocery store was spat

INTRODUCTION

on and accused of causing coronavirus. For others, including one Japanese restaurant owner, the harassment has come in the form of vandalism.[9]

Although intermarriage, a key measure of what sociologists call social proximity, has increased in recent years, we are anything but a racial melting pot. While the number of Hispanics and Asians marrying people of other races is relatively high – 27 percent in the case of Hispanics and 29 percent in the case of Asians – the percentage of Whites and African Americans who marry outside the race is much lower, at 11 percent and 18 percent, respectively.[10] Some scholars have speculated that we are moving from a country of Whites and non-Whites to a country of Blacks and non-Blacks, with Blacks getting left at the bottom. As upsetting as this may be, as the coming pages reveal, there is both historical and sociological evidence that this may indeed be the case.

Most Americans would agree that we are far from the days of Jim Crow segregation, with its chain gangs, lynchings, and signs "No Coloreds Welcomed Here." However, many sociologists have argued that in its place has emerged a more subtle type of racism, what Eduardo Bonilla-Silva calls "color-blind racism." In his research, while Bonilla-Silva found that while most Whites outwardly proclaim that they don't see color, their statements are often prefaced with "Well, I'm not racist, but…"

In political terms, color-blind racism plays itself out in issues, such as affirmative action, the debate over immigration reform, and the questions over how governmental funds should be allocated. In simplistic terms, colorblindness can be thought of as the debate between Democrats and Republicans, liberals and conservatives, or advocates of an activist or laissez-faire fiscal policy. However, on many levels, it is a polemic in which Whites and non-Whites are frequently on opposing sides.

Whites are anything but a monolithic group of people. Neither, however, are non-Whites. While there are similarities between Blacks and Hispanics, ranging from inequities in income, housing, educational attainment, higher levels of incarceration, and disparities in healthcare, in other ways, there are vast differences. African Americans arrived in this continent in chains, and following the brief period of Reconstruction after the Civil War, faced *de jure* segregation in the South and *de facto* segregation in the North. By contrast, relatively few Hispanics now residing in the United States can trace their ancestry here before the 1970s. (There are exceptions. Some Hispanics, many in San Antonio for example, trace their lineage to Spain, as far back as the 16th century and well before the English began settling Jamestown.) In 1970, there were about 9 million Americans of Spanish-speaking descent; today, there are close to 60 million.

The relative recentness of most Hispanic and Asian immigration raises important sociological questions. Will these groups assimilate into the American mainstream, as did the so-called ethnic Whites of the 19th and early 20th centuries (the Irish, Italians, Jews, and Slavs, not to mention the Germans, whose descendants continue to comprise the largest non-Anglo group in the United States)? Will their mother language fluency diminish or disappear with coming generations? Will they adopt more anglicized customs, attitudes, and behaviors as they acculturate? Will they gradually be included under the umbrella of White Privilege?

In the case of African Americans, the issue of assimilation is irrelevant since most can trace their ancestry in America back for centuries. Though discrimination in employment and in public institutions has been illegal since 1964 and at the polls since 1965, Black and White Americans remain separate and unequal. Conservatives, even some African-American conservatives, blame the situation on culture, citing the high incidence of unwed mothers, a propensity toward criminality, a lack of initiative, or a sense of entitlement and reliance on government subsidies. They conjure up images of the Cadillac-driving welfare queens and young bucks buying T-bone steaks with food stamps, phrases famously attributed to President Ronald Reagan. They criticize liberals for dwelling on structural socio-economic factors and playing the "race card." White liberals, on the other hand, often underplay the effects of the lingering and sometimes opaque, sometimes overt racism that so many African Americans face. As the 2020 murders of Breonna Taylor, George Floyd, and Ahmaud Arbery attest, no African American is immune to racism.

In this book, I contend that our national obsession with race has a long history, beginning with the enslavement of Africans and the genocidal treatment of Native Americans. However, the despicable and inhuman treatment of these two groups, while representing the most egregious cases of intolerance, were hardly exceptional cases in our national experience. Rather, Americans have consistently and predictably excoriated immigrants who were considered to be different than the mainstream, whenever they arrived in large numbers or attempted to integrate mainstream society, as we are witnessing today. Perhaps with future generations, the words of writer James Baldwin, who envisions a country in which we are all simply "Americans" and are connected as such, will be realized:

I think that what we really have to do is to create a country in which there are no minorities – for the first time in the history of the world. The one thing that all Americans have in common is that they have no other identity apart from the identity which is being achieved on this continent ... The necessity of Americans to achieve an identity is a historical and a present personal fact and this is the connection between you and me.[11]

INTRODUCTION

NOTES

1. Cobb, Jelani. "The Death of George Floyd, in Context." *The New Yorker*, May 28, 2020. https://www.newyorker.com/news/daily-comment/the-death-of-george-floyd-in-context.
2. Oppel Jr., Richard A. and Derrick Bryson Taylor. "Here's What You Need to Know About Breonna Taylor's Death." *The New York Times*, June 5, 2020. https://www.nytimes.com/article/breonna-taylor-police.html.
3. North, Anna. "The Police Shooting of Breonna Taylor, a Black Woman Who Was Killed in Her Apartment, Explained." *Vox*, May 19, 2020. https://www.vox.com/2020/5/13/21257457/breonna-taylor-louisville-shooting-ahmaud-arbery-justiceforbre.
4. Logan, John R. and Brian J. Stults. "Racial and Ethnic Separation in the Neighborhoods: Progress at a Standstill." Project US2010, December 14, 2010.
5. Gramlich, John. "Black Imprisonment Rate in the U.S. Has Fallen by a Third Since 2006." *Pew Research Center*, May 6, 2020. https://www.pewresearch.org/fact-tank/2020/05/06/black-imprisonment-rate-in-the-u-s-has-fallen-by-a-third-since-2006/.
6. Alexander, Michelle. The New Jim Crow: Mass Incarceration in the Age of Colorblindness. (New York, NY: The New Press, 2012), 6.
7. "AP Poll: Majority Harbor Prejudice against Blacks," October 27, 2012. https://www.yahoo.com/news/ap-poll-majority-harbor-prejudice-against-Blacks-073551680--election.html.
8. Golash-Boza, Tanya. "The Parallels between Mass Incarceration and Mass Deportation: An Intersectional Analysis of State Repression." *Journal of World-Systems Research*, Vol. 22, No. 2, 484–509.
9. Zhou, Li. How the Coronavirus is Surfacing America's Deep-Seated Anti-Asian Biases." *Vox*, April 21, 2020. https://www.vox.com/identities/2020/4/21/21221007/anti-asian-racism-coronavirus.
10. Livingston, Gretchen and Anna Brown. "Intermarriage in the U.S. 50 Years After Loving v. Virginia." *Pew Research Center*, May 18, 2017. https://www.pewsocialtrends.org/2017/05/18/intermarriage-in-the-u-s-50-years-after-loving-v-virginia/.
11. Baldwin, James. *Nobody Knows My Name*. (New York, NY: Random House Vintage, 2013), Kindle Edition.

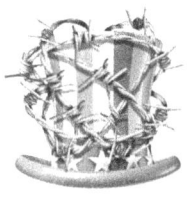

PART 1

WHITE AMERICANS

EARLY in his 2016 U.S. presidential campaign, Republican candidate and billionaire real estate mogul, Donald Trump, won popular support promising to build a wall along the Mexican border, throw the Mexicans back, and ban Muslim immigration. Just weeks prior to the Republican Party National Convention, Trump tweeted a graphic superimposing Democratic nominee, former Secretary of State Hillary Clinton, and a bright red six-pointed star resembling the Star of David stamped on a bed of cash. Donald Trump won the Republican presidential nomination.

In support of Trump, self-described "race realists" popped up on conservative talk radio, television, and the internet, decrying Blacks for "playing the race card" and accusing President Barack Obama of policies favoring Blacks to the detriment of Whites. Said one Long Island housewife in a *New York Times* interview, "Everyone's sticking together in their groups, so White people have to, too."[1]

Just three weeks into Trump's presidency, in the middle of Black History Month, a survey from Public Policy Polling was released that showed something very interesting beyond the survey topline, which revealed that Americans were evenly split on impeaching Trump. Even more fascinating was that 46 percent of Trump supporters would like to have a White History Month. Never mind that there is a Polish-American Heritage Month and an Italian-American Heritage Month (both in October) and an Irish-American Heritage Month (in March), which, for the most part, celebrate histories of groups of White people. There is even a Confederate History Month (in April). Still these Trump supporters feel left out; apparently, nobody is celebrating the contributions that Whites have made to the nation.[2]

White supremacist writer and activist, Richard Spencer, whose nonprofit National Policy Institute dedicates itself to "the heritage, identity, and future of people of European descent in the United States," boasted that Trump was "bringing identity politics for White people into the public sphere in a way no one has." A social media data mining company analyzed one week of Trump's retweets and found nearly one third of those tweeting followed one or more of 50 popular self-identified White nationalist Twitter accounts.[3]

Many analysts suggest that the declining importance of Whites in the U.S, at least in terms of numbers, and its apparent correlate, racial resentment, gave rise to Trump's popularity and a "zero sum game" over race.[4] In June 2016, the Census Bureau unveiled its population estimates. Over the prior four years, non-Hispanic Whites saw their share of the nation's voting-age population fall from 66.6 percent to 64.6 percent.[5] A study by political scientist Marc Hetherington in 2016 found that well over a third of Republicans, a nearly 90 percent White party, could be classified as "racially resentful," with nearly a quarter considered "very resentful" about race. "It is not surprising," Hetherington wrote, "that a candidate who is well known for questioning President Obama's citizenship and suggested that a Black Lives Matter protester at one of his rallies be 'roughed up' and said that black youths have 'never done more poorly' because 'there's no spirit' would be attractive to a party that these days is dripping with racial resentment." Such was not always the case. In 1986, White Republicans and Democrats did not differ in their racial attitudes, and their survey scores were nearly identical: only about twelve percent of Democrats and nine percent of Republicans fell into the same "racially resentful" category.[6]

Former President Richard Nixon stoked White racial resentment against African Americans to gain the support of southern White voters. Some political historians suggest Nixon's "southern strategy" inevitably spawned Donald Trump. *New Republic*'s Senior Editor, Jeet Heer, wrote, "Trump's popularity with voters who are racist and nostalgic for the Confederacy mark him out not as a 'cancer,' but as someone who is cagily updating a script created by the conservative movement and shaped by Republican candidates for decades now."[7]

THE 2016 ELECTION

There was plenty of race-baiting during the administration of President Barack Obama. Indeed, for some, the idea of an African-American man in the White House, with a Muslim-sounding name no less, drove them crazy. But much of that racial animus was underground, shielded away from public discourse and polite company. It took Donald Trump to energize and embolden those who believed in White power. Before even taking office, Trump appointed Steve Bannon, former head of Breitbart News, a website replete with anti-Semitic, racist garbage and the go-to publication for the alt-right – the sanitized term for White nationalists or White supremacists – to be the chief strategist of the president-elect, who ran in the Republican Party, the party started in 1860 with Abraham Lincoln. Bannon is a hero for White supremacists. House Minority Leader Nancy Pelosi tweeted: "There must be no sugarcoating the reality that a White nationalist has been named chief strategist for the Trump administration." Senate Minority Leader Harry Reid, on the Senate floor, ripped into Bannon, warning that we must not normalize having such a person as one of the most powerful people in the country.

And it was not just Bannon. Less than two weeks after the election, Trump announced that former General Michael Flynn would be his National Security Advisor – a position that doesn't need confirmation – and that his Attorney General would be Alabama Senator Jeff Sessions. These were two very troubling choices. Flynn was known as a hothead and as someone who is difficult to work with, and, most disturbingly, he had been consistent in his attacks on Islam, calling Islam a "cancer."[8] Flynn lasted only 24 days in the position. Sessions, though having served for 20 years in the U.S. Senate, was blocked from being a federal judge in the 1980s for a series of racially charged comments. The Congressional Black Caucus and the NAACP denounced this choice, but Sessions was confirmed by a clubby Senate, despite his racial baggage. (Sessions resigned at the president's request in November 2018.)

Then there was Trump transition spokesman, Kris Kobach, who floated the idea of the new administration using ID cards for Muslims. He was excoriated by Megan Kelly for using the policy of Japanese internment during World War II as "precedent." And this was on Fox News, the conservative network. In fact, many principled conservatives raised the red flag about the new administration's lack of good optics vis-à-vis race. In the days immediately following the election, Conservative radio host, Charlie Sykes, on the public radio politics show "Left, Right, and Center" said in no uncertain terms that, yes, Trump was filling his inner circle with racists.

Some saw the racism and liked it. The KKK and the American Nazi Party were ecstatic, praising the choice of Bannon. The former wizard of the KKK, David Duke, loudly proclaimed his admiration for Trump during the campaign and now says that Bannon is "basically creating the ideological aspects of where we're going."

Other analysts believe Trump's campaign fed on Whites' fear of losing majority status. Author Robin DiAngelo, Professor of Multicultural Education at Westfield

State University in Massachusetts and Affiliate Associate Professor of Education at the University of Washington in Seattle, describes a phenomenon she calls "White Fragility," a state in which "even a minimum amount of racial stress becomes intolerable," triggering a range of emotions – including anger, fear, and guilt. She concludes that "should White Americans (on average) respond to the changing demographics by becoming more politically conservative, the U.S. political landscape is likely to become increasingly racially polarized."[9]

As president, after only one week in office, Trump issued an Executive Order (E.O.) banning people from seven predominantly Muslim countries. This E.O. was decried by even conservative legal scholars as, at best, sloppily written, and at worst, completely unconstitutional. It sparked angry and large protests around the country, which lasted for weeks, and added to the speculation among many Trump detractors that the President was operating from a position of racism and xenophobia, rather than national security. They pointed out that refugees, who would be denied entry under the order, are already being thoroughly vetted and that no refugee had committed an act of terrorism on U.S. soil.

I think it's fair to say that most Trump voters may not have gravitated to him because of the overt racial overtures. They had other wants, like a ground war against ISIS or lower taxes or a conservative Supreme Court. But regardless, they were okay with the racism. And the change they wanted – what they heard from Trump, whether he said it or not – was the restoration of White power.

Since the killing of George Floyd, it is clear that the next few years will keep race – specifically, White Privilege – front and center. I can only hope that what emerges is a clearer understanding of the multicultural make-up of the United States. Before that happens, if that happens, we may have to witness with horror an energized White nationalism and some of the ugliest and most divisive rhetoric we've seen in decades. While so many individuals are now articulating, indeed demanding, a vision of equality and inclusion for people of color, those who support the thinking of people like Donald Trump and who are unconscious to the harm of racism are not likely to have a change of heart overnight. They will most likely become even more loud and aggressive about their misguided beliefs. This has been a pattern throughout White American history, as we shall see.

NOTES

1. "For Whites Sensing Decline, Donald Trump Unleashes Words of Resistance," *The New York Times*, July 13, 2016. http://www.nytimes.com/2016/07/14/us/politics/donald-trump-White-identity.html?ref=todayspaper&_r=0.

2. "Americans Now Evenly Divided on Impeaching Trump Public Policy Polling," February 10, 2017. http://www.publicpolicypolling.com/main/2017/02/americans-now-evenly-divided-on-impeaching-trump.html.
3. For Whites Sensing Decline, Donald Trump Unleashes Words of Resistance." *The New York Times*.
4. Norton, Michael I. and Samuel R. Sommers. "Whites See Racism as a Zero-Sum Game That They Are Now Losing." *Perspectives on Psychological Science*, May 2011, Vol. 6, No. 3, 215–218.
5. U.S. Census Bureau. "Population Estimates." http://www.census.gov/popest/.
6. "Donald Trump's Surprising Success with Southern Evangelicals." *The Cook Political Report*, February 26, 2016. http://cookpolitical.com/story/9309.
7. Heer, Jeet. "How the Southern Strategy Made Donald Trump Possible." *New Republic*, February 18, 2016. https://newrepublic.com/article/130039/southern-strategy-made-donald-trump-possible.
8. "Donald Trump National Security Adviser Mike Flynn Has Called Islam 'a Cancer,'" *ABC News*, November 18, 2016. http://abcnews.go.com/Politics/donald-trump-national-security-adviser-mike-flynn-called/story?id=43575658.
9. DiAngelo, Robin. "White Fragility," *International Journal of Critical Pedagogy*. Vol. 3, No. 3, 2011, 54.

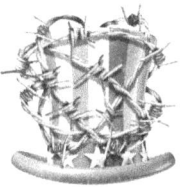

1

THE ANGLO-SAXONS

NATIVISM, a kind-of political "first come, first served" resentment toward the latest wave of immigrants, haunts American history with periods of demographic change fueling fear, anger, and resentment. Benjamin Franklin expressed open hostility to immigrant Germans whose growing numbers threatened his beloved Pennsylvania colony. In 1798, the Federalist Party's Alien and Sedition Acts extended the five-year citizen residency requirement by nine additional years to plug the perceived political threat of radical immigrants seeping in from France and Ireland. Northeastern nativists decried the Irish Catholic immigration surge of the 1830–50's until quieted by the Civil War. Well into the twentieth century, slogans like "No Irish Need Apply" (later, "No Wops Need Apply), "Rum, Romanism and Rebellion," and, later, "The Chinese Must Go" and "Japs Keep Moving," proved nativism's on-stage presence; only the players switched roles.

From the 1840's to 1920, German Americans were mistrusted because of their German-language schools, their attachment to their native tongue over English, and their neutrality in World War I. In the 1890–1920 era, nativists campaigned for immigration restriction, focusing their attention on Jews, Italians, Slavs, and other groups largely hailing from Southern and Eastern Europe. Writes Peter Schrag, "In almost every generation, nativists portrayed new immigrants as not fit to become real Americans: they were too infected by Catholicism, monarchism, anarchism, Islam, criminal tendencies, defective genes, mongrel bloodlines, or some other alien virus to become free men and women in our democratic society."[1]

In his Pulitzer Prize-winning book, *The Uprooted*, historian Oscar Handlin famously declared: "Once I thought to write a history of the immigrants in America. Then I discovered that the immigrants were American history."[2] Immigration has been central to the narrative of American exceptionalism. A fundamental part of this national ethos is the idea that the United States is a refuge of liberty and a land of opportunity,[3] As wrote Emma Lazarus, whose words are enshrined in the Statue of Liberty:

> *Give me your tired, your poor,*
> *Your huddled masses yearning to breathe free,*
> *The wretched refuse of your teeming shore.*
> *Send these, the homeless, tempest-tossed to me,*
> *I lift my lamp beside the golden door!*[4]

Throughout its history, America considered itself a nation of White Anglo-Protestants, what political scientist Eric Kaufman called the "national ethnic group."[5] Indeed, English settlers were the numerically largest group from the Jamestown settlement of 1607 until the American Revolution, though America was anything but ethnically homogenous. About 12 percent of the colonists were Scottish and Scot-Irish, 10 percent were German, and there were smaller numbers of French, Irish, and Welsh; 19 percent were of African ancestry, most of whom were slaves. The English stock itself comprised distinct migrations of people from different parts of England, each with their varied customs, motivations, and values. As historian Rudolph J. Vecoli noted, the motto "E Pluribus Unum" – Out of Many, One – reflected not reality, but rather an "aspiration" that the colonies would merge into a single state.

According to historian David Hackett Fischer, after 1629, successive waves of immigrants left their distinctive marks on American culture. In terms of regional differences among Americans, these marks survive today. While each group spoke English, was largely Protestant, and took pride in possessing British liberties, each differed from the other in terms of its religious domination, social ranking, gender makeup, spoken dialect, and worldview. By 1775, these British segments and their corresponding cultures firmly established themselves in the American colonies.[6] Out of these groups rose a distinctly Anglo and Protestant American identity.

The first wave of immigrants arrived between 1629 and 1640. These English Puritans largely fled religious persecution in England's eastern counties and settled in Massachusetts. Most traveled in nuclear families, were of the middle ranks of

English society – yeomen, husbandmen, artisans, craftsmen, and merchants –, and had high rates of literacy. Religion was the only reason for emigration, as the Puritans sought, in the words of John Winthrop, to be "as a City upon a Hill." They dressed in drab, "sad" clothing. They tended to settle in towns modeled after those of eastern England. Their villages combined crops enclosed by fields and farm animals, reminiscent of Suffolk and Norfolk.[7]

The second immigrant wave was that of cavalier gentlemen. They arrived in Virginia, from southern and western England, and settled along the shores of the Chesapeake Bay. Vastly different from the egalitarian society of the Puritans, an upper class elite, comprised of the sons of barons, knights, and the rural gentry of England, ruled Virginia with their aristocratic families' connections. Servants and laborers stood in marked contrast to these rulers. Some were recruited from the lower rural and agrarian ranks of English society, and others paid their passage to America. Profoundly conservative, the Virginian elites retained a deep longing for what they referred to as the "Old Dominion" of the motherland, thinking of themselves as "cultural exiles in a distant land." Not surprisingly, hierarchies and vast inequalities permeated Virginian society.[8]

The third wave consisted of Quakers, who largely hailed from the North Midlands of England. Both New England and Virginia enacted laws requiring their banishment. Anglicans confined or whipped many Quakers for refusing to attend Anglican services or pay tithes. While religious persecution drove most Quaker emigration from England, they embraced a utopian vision, "to show Quakerism at work, freed from hampering conditions." Highly libertarian, they believed in the sanctity of property, austerity, liberty, and worldly asceticism; marriage outside of the sect was strictly forbidden. While initially cultural pluralists, beginning around 1750, Quakers in America began an inward and more radical turn and developed ideas of pacifism, withdrawal from politics, and an increasingly severe discipline.[9]

The fourth wave, a group Fischer calls the Borderers, consisted of simple farmers, laborers, and semi-skilled craftsmen, many fleeing the famine of the England-Scotland border counties, as well as Northern Ireland. Most owned no land of their own and worked as tenants and under-tenants. Often referred to as "Ulster Irish" or "Northern Irish," they are better known in today's parlance as the "Scots-Irish." In reality, they were a "mixed medley," belonging to different religious denominations. Mostly Presbyterian, a significant number belonged to Baptist, Methodist, or other evangelical sects, tracing their ancestry beyond England, Ireland, and Scotland to Celts, Germans, and Scandinavians. Often dressed in outlandish clothes, the Scots-Irish bore strange-sounding names and spoke English with peculiar accents. They encountered derisive discrimination when they arrived just a few years before the fledgling country gained its independence, and most moved toward the interior, populating the highlands of Appalachia, and, in the nineteenth century, the backlands of Arkansas, Missouri, Oklahoma, and Texas.[10]

A group unexamined by Fischer, but nonetheless important, shaped its American identity from its immediate roots, not in Europe, but in the brutal slaveholding society based in Barbados, the oldest and richest colony in British America. Its culture would take root in the Deep South, spreading throughout South Carolina, Georgia, Mississippi, Alabama, the Louisiana Delta, eastern Texas, Arkansas, Western Tennessee, north Florida, and the southeast parts of North Carolina. Historian Colin Woodward wrote that the Deep South based its culture on "radical disparities in wealth and power, with a tiny elite commanding total obedience and enforcing it with state-sponsored terror." While in the northern Cavalier colonies, Whites outnumbered slaves about 1.7 to 1, in the Deep South, owing to exceedingly high slave mortality rates, which made it necessary to import massive numbers of Africans, slaves outnumbered Whites by as many as five to one. A firmly entrenched caste system developed, with a rich White elite at the top, poor Whites well below, and Blacks, excluded from any kind of social discourse with all Whites, at rock bottom, though forced sexual relations by White men on black slave women was "perfectly acceptable." Greatly outnumbered by slaves, the planters lived with constant fear of revolt, and the Deep South fostered an increasingly militarized and repressive society.[11]

Finally, the Dutch colony of New Netherlands followed a very different trajectory than the English colonies. Characterized by a legacy of ethnic, religious, and cultural diversity, the Dutch settlement of New Amsterdam became a hodgepodge of people from different regions, including French-speaking Walloons, Swedes, English, Norwegians, Germans, Scotch-Irish, and African slaves. Practicality best characterized the province, where religious tolerance reflected not only a recognition of New Netherland's diversity, but also the need to pursue moderate policies in order to promote trade and profits. In the words of historian Frederick Jackson Turner, "This region of many nationalities, creeds, and industries became ... a more characteristically democratic region than any of the others. Tolerance of difference of opinion was pronounced, and, in the course of time, individualism and lack of social control became marked features."[12]

Each of these disparate societies, with their concomitant folkways, cultures, and worldviews, came to dominate their respective regions and, later, other regions. The Scots-Irish moved into greater Appalachia and, ultimately, northern Texas; the Barbados slaveholders came to dominate the Deep South; and the New England Yankees spread into upstate New York and lower Canada. In the late 18th and early 19th centuries, with the construction of canals, Yankees settled along the banks of the

1 | THE ANGLO-SAXONS

Ohio River and beyond, in Illinois, Indiana, Iowa, and Missouri, founding cities like Cincinnati, St. Louis, and Chicago. As settlers moved, their cultures travelled with them. Friction between anti-slavery Yankees and Deep South slaveholders erupted into violence in Kansas and Western Missouri between 1854 and 1861 and ultimately led to the Civil War.[13]

Despite its great diversity, sociologist Steven Steinberg argues that at the time of American independence, in terms of culture, the population was still "remarkably homogenous."

> Even those non-British settlers had important cultural affinities to the English majority. Most had their origins in Northern or Western Europe, though this was barely noticed until there was an influx of groups from more diverse backgrounds a century later. Of greater and more immediate significance was the fact that as many as 99 percent of the colonists were Protestant … the claim that the nation was founded by White Anglo-Saxon Protestants is reasonably accurate.[14]

Clearly, by the American Revolution, contemporaries held the idea of a singular American identity. In a 1782 series of essays entitled *Letters from an American Farmer*, the French immigrant, J. Hector St. John de Crevecoeur, posed the question "What, then, is the American, this new man?" His answer:

> He is an American, who, leaving behind him all his ancient prejudices and manners, receives new ones from the new mode of life he has embraced, the new government he obeys, and the new rank he holds.… Here individuals of all races are melted into a new race of man, whose labors and posterity will one day cause great changes in the world. Americans are the western pilgrims.[15]

In the early days of the Republic, many Americans upheld Crevecoeur's theme of severing old roots and amalgamating immigrants into the spirit of a new people. George Washington said, "The bosom of America is open … to the oppressed and persecuted of all Nations and Religions," and "by an intermixture with our people, they, or their descendants, get assimilated to our customs, measures, and laws: in a word, soon become one people." John Adams admonished a visitor that immigrants must "cast off the European skin, never to resume it. They must look forward to their posterity rather than backward to their ancestors." Said novelist Herman Melville,

"You cannot spill a drop of American blood without spilling the blood of the whole world. On this Western Hemisphere all tribes and people are forming into one federal whole."[16]

The impact of the first Anglo settlers would ultimately reach the Pacific shores and form the bedrock of our current national identity and culture, though regional differences highlight each group's disparateness, as manifest in the form of today's Red States and Blue States.

NOTES

1. Schrag, Peter. *Not Fit for Our Society: Nativism and Immigration*. (Berkeley, CA: University of California Press, 2010), 4.
2. Handlin, Oscar. The Uprooted: The Epic Story of the Great Migrations that Made the American People." (Boston, MA: Little, Brown and Company, 1973), 3.
3. Genova, Nicholas D. eds. Daniel Martinez HoSang, Oneka LaBennett, and Laura Pulido. "Racial Formation in an Age of Permanent War," in *Racial Formation in the Twenty-First Century*. (Berkeley, CA: University of California Press, 2012), 252.
4. Lazarus, Emma. 1883, The New Colossus. http://www.libertystatepark.com/emma.htm.
5. Kaufmann, Eric. "American Exceptionalism Reconsidered: Anglo-Saxon Ethnogenesis in the 'Universal' Nation, 1776–1850," *Journal of American Studies*. Vol. 33, 1999, 437.
6. Fischer, David Hackett. *Albion's Seed: Four British Folkways in America*. (Oxford, England: Oxford University Press, 1989), 783.
7. Ibid., 151.
8. Ibid., 368.
9. Ibid., 424.
10. Ibid., 603.
11. Woodard, Colin. American Nations: A History of the Eleven Rival Regional Cultures of North America. (New York, NY: Penguin Books, 2012), 79.
12. Turner, Frederick Jackson. ed. Kerwin Lee Klein. "The Development of American Society" (1908), in *Frontiers of Historical Imagination: Narrating the European Conquest of Native America, 1890–1990*. (Berkeley, CA: University of California Press, 1999), 139.
13. Barone, Michael. *Shaping Our Nation: How Surges of Migration Transformed America and Its Politics*. (New York, NY: Crown Forum, 2013), 70.

14. Steinberg, Stephen. *The Ethnic Myth: Race, Ethnicity, and Class in America.* (Boston, MA: Beacon Press, 2001), 8.
15. de Crèvecoeur, J. Hector St. John. *Letters from an American Farmer.* (Carlisle, MA: Applewood Books, 2007), 54.
16. Schlesinger, Jr., Arthur *The Disuniting of America: Reflections on a Multicultural Society.* (New York, NY: W.W. Norton & Company, Inc., 1998), 30.

2

THE IRISH AND GERMANS

IN THE MID-1840S, great numbers of Irish Catholics and Protestant Germans began arriving on American shores, jeopardizing the vision of a unified nation. Driven by the devastating Irish potato famine of the 1830s and 1840s and by discrimination at the hands of their English overlords, 1.3 million Irish Catholics arrived on American shores in the decade between 1846 and 1855; another half million arrived in each of the next four decades. Germans immigrated in even larger numbers: about one million for five successive decades, other than the decade of the Civil War. These three million Irish and five million Germans enormously impacted a mid-19th century country of only 38 million people. While the Irish settled in northeastern cities, the Germans moved on to rural areas in what was then called the "Northwest": Wisconsin, Iowa, Minnesota and the Dakotas.[1] For the first time, but certainly not the last, large numbers of immigrants who were not Protestant from the British Isles beset the United States.

THE IRISH

In 1840, only 5 percent of Americans lived in cities with a population greater than 100,000. In contrast, most Irish Catholics arriving in America settled in cities. Upon landing in the port cities of Boston, New York, and Philadelphia, most remained, while the more adventuresome moved inland to work on railroad or canal construction or in mining country, like northeastern Pennsylvania.² In the cities, already settled countrymen exploited the newcomers. The Irish "runners" of New York met 30 to 40 arriving ships each day to hustle them off to run-down boarding houses, where Irish landlords greedily snatched what little money they had. Most Irish Catholics eventually settled in the tenements and tarpaper shacks typical of 19th century urban America.

In these crime-ridden Irish neighborhoods, sewers flowed into the streets, and tuberculosis, cholera, and alcoholism ravaged the communities. In Boston, for example, during the 1840s, an Irish immigrant could expect to live only 14 years after his arrival. Many turned to crime, and the prisons bulged with Irish occupants. Historian Lawrence J. McCaffrey notes that between 1856 and 1863, Irish inmates comprised at least half of the inmates in the Boston House of Correction. "Many Irish women drank and brawled like men," he wrote. "Their children roamed the streets engaging in mischief and petty crime."³ McCaffrey continues:

> Americans had never before experienced a foreign influx so big and of such distressing a quality. To be called "Irish" was not much better than to be called "nigger"; racist commentary made little distinction. In some respects, descriptions of the 19th century Irish ghetto anticipated those of today's black ghetto. But there was no palliative welfare state, no sense among other Americans of collective responsibility for the plight of the underclass.⁴

Domestic service provided quintessential, suitable work for young, single Irish women. In 1900, at least sixty percent of Irish immigrant women worked as domestic servants; over forty percent of the nation's servants were Irish-born. "Bridget" or "Biddy" symbolized the American servant class, and like her male counterpart "Paddy," myriad jokes and cartoons portrayed her as "ignorant" and "stupid," as well as "defiant," "insolent," and "impertinent." Yet, with access to the intimate lives of middle-class Protestant households, Biddy bridged the social gap to the Irish working class.⁵

Countless accounts of bloody brawls between men from different Irish counties document the Irish worker's reputation for rioting and fighting. In 1853, the militia quelled a battle among Irish railroad workers in Somerset, Ohio, following an Irishman's eviction from a circus performance for smoking a pipe. That same year, riots erupted along a Pacific Railroad construction line over a labor foreman's election. Yet, historian Carl Wittke argues that "not all the trouble was due to the Irishman's belligerent temperament, his love of the bottle, or his belief that contentiousness is the spice of life." Rather, while the organized labor movement struggled in its infancy, intolerable labor conditions incited much of the rioting. For example, in 1840, a riot broke out in New York City when Irish aqueduct laborers' daily wages dropped from $1.00 to $0.75; similar occurrences provoked by wage cuts erupted on the Illinois Central, the Buffalo and State Railroad, the Steubenville and Indiana, and other railroad lines. The "Molly Maguires" inflicted the most notorious reign of terror in the anthracite coal regions of Pennsylvania. Though charges of kidnapping and murder resulted against the perpetrators, the *Boston Pilot* blamed the inadequate pay, "murderous neglect of ventilation," and "rancid provisions" imposed on the Irish coal miners.[6]

Inevitably, native-born Americans struck back against the Irish. They disdained Irish anti-social behavior and squalid living conditions, though Catholicism provoked the most outrage, and native hostility took on a decidedly religious tone. In 1835, New York City saw the founding of the Native American Party, followed by a number of anti-Catholic periodicals and organizations in New York and New England. Samuel F.B. Morse, the father of the telegraph, and Lyman Beecher, a Presbyterian minister and father of Harriet Beecher Stowe, joined the nativist voices. Morse decried the Catholic monarchies of Europe, especially Austria, for sending "shiploads of Roman Catholic emigrants, and for the sole purpose of converting us to the religion of popery." Beecher accused Europeans of subverting the Protestant ethos of American democracy by flooding the country with Catholics. According to historian Nell Irvin Painter, it was considered "tragic that poor Catholics could vote and hold office just like White men. In New York City and many other Northeastern cities, bourgeois voices joined those of Morse and Beecher in deploring 'the very scum and dregs of Human nature' and the 'low Irishmen' who decided on election outcomes."[7]

By the 1850s, Catholic-hating, nativist organizations abounded. In 1834, a mob burned the Ursuline Convent in Charlestown, Massachusetts. In 1844 Philadelphia, a mob of 600 nativists burned St. Michael's and St. Augustine's churches to the ground and torched many Irish residences. The ensuing riots lasted three days, killing thirteen and wounding fifty. In Pittsburgh, an 1850 mayoral candidate running on the "People's and Anti-Catholic" ticket won the election. By the mid-1850s, clubs of the nativist Order of United Americans flourished in sixteen states. The Supreme Order of the Star-Spangled Banner and the American Party ranked among the most institutionalized vehicles for anti-Catholic racism. Labeled "Know-Nothings," American Party members replied "I know nothing" when questioned about their order. The orders required that members be born in the United States of native-born parents and that husbands of Catholic women could not join. In 1854, Know-Nothing candidates swept elections throughout urban New England, including the state of Massachusetts. The party fielded a presidential candidate in 1856, former President

Millard Fillmore, who captured about 800,000 votes, over one-fifth of those cast nationwide. Although the party split into rival sections on the eve of the Civil War and ultimately disappeared by about 1860, its phenomenal influence served as a platform for the mass of Americans disaffected by the unprecedented inflow of foreigners.[8]

Many felt that the immigration waves of the mid-1840s threatened democratic institutions and the Anglo-Saxon race. Europeans joined predictions of unsavory newcomers ultimately unraveling American society. In his 1855 essay, *The Inequality of Human Races*, Comte de Gobineau described an America overwhelmed by "the most degenerate races of olden day Europe. They are the flotsam of all ages: Irish, cross-bred German and French, and Italians of even more doubtful stock."[9] In his book *How the Irish Became White*, Noel Ignatiev writes that Irish arrivals to America were "thrown together" with Blacks, on jobs and in neighborhoods. Sexual encounters between the two, particularly between Black men and Irish women, were frequent. However, not all interactions were sexual. In New Orleans, Irish lived in the Black district; Irish grocers frequently traded alcohol for stolen sugar and flour brought to them by slaves. The minstrel stage also brought together Irish and Blacks. In 1844, New York's Five Points district, which attracted both races and sexes to its saloons, cockpits, dance halls, and theaters, featured a dance contest between the Irish champion, "Master" John Diamond and the African American, William Henry Lane, known as "Juba."[10]

According to Ignatiev, it was unclear at the time whether or not the Irish were "white." Since the first Congress's 1790 law excluded non-Whites from naturalization, many questioned whether the Irish were eligible for citizenship. He writes:

> Coming as immigrants, rather than as captives or hostages, undoubtedly affected the potential racial status of the Irish in America, but it did not settle the issue, since it was by no means obvious who was "white." In the early years, Irish were frequently referred to as "niggers turned inside out"; the Negroes, for their part, were sometimes called "smoked Irish."[11]

Before the Civil War, apart from the suffrage granted the Irish because of their White skin, very little social difference existed among the Irish and free Blacks. In a popular quip of the time, a Black man complained, "My master is a great tyrant. He treats me as badly as if I was a common Irishmen."[12] The Irish became known as "Paddies," and phrases such as "Paddy Doyle" (a jail cell), "in a Paddy" (in a rage), and "Paddyland" (Ireland), entered the vernacular, though only the term "Paddy

Wagon" remains in common parlance. Historian Nell Irvin Painter observed that no shortage of popular cartoons reinforced the Paddy stereotype: "Frequently apelike, always poor, ugly, drunken, violent, superstitious, but charmingly rascally, Paddy and his ugly, ignorant, dirty, fecund, long-suffering Bridget differed fundamentally from visual depictions of sober, civilized Anglo-Saxons."[13]

When the Irish were not being compared to Blacks, they were cast as their own unique racial category, one that frequently contained unsavory references to "Irish character." Often referred to as Celts, the Irish were described as "low-browed," "brutish," and "simian," characterized by a unique set of physical characteristics that included skin and hair color, facial type, and physique. Describing the "Celtic physiognomy," in 1851, a *Harper's Weekly* article remarked on "the small and somewhat upturned nose [and] the black tint of the skin." The Massachusetts State Board of Charities attributed Irish people's pauperism to their "inherited organic imperfection, vitiated constitution, or *poor stock*."[14] Writes Ignatiev:

> To be acknowledged as white, it was not enough for the Irish to have a competitive advantage over Afro-Americans in the labor market; in order for them to avoid the taint of blackness, it was necessary that no Negro be allowed to work in occupations where Irish were to be found. Still better was to erase the memory that Afro Americans had ever done these jobs.[15]

Not content to share the lowest rung of the social ladder with Blacks, Irish Americans joined the southern-led Democratic Party in enormous numbers. By the mid-1840s, most Irish actively opposed abolition, as well as other reforms, such as women's rights, limits on slavery's expansion, and restraints on alcohol consumption. The Transcendentalist minister, Theodore Parker, charged the Irish with retarding social progress with their low standard of living and anti-progressive view. The political activity of the Irish convinced many nativist Unionists that the entire democratic process was being stymied by these newcomers "who voted as a solid phalanx." In Boston, nativists argued that men "fresh from the bogs of Ireland" were "led up to the desk like dumb brutes, their hands guided to make a straight mark" at the polls. The "Irish party," wrote Carl Wittke, "seemed to be growing faster than the native born voting population," alarming no small number of Americans.[16]

With the Civil War, the perceived racial differences between Whites became less important when compared to that between Whites and Blacks. In 1863, J.H. Van Evrie wrote, "Irishmen, Germans, Frenchmen, etc., come here, settle down, become citizens, and their offspring born and raised on American soil differ in no appreciable or perceptible manner from other Americans.... [But the Negro is] as absolutely and specifically unlike the American as when the race first touched the soil and first breathed the air of the New World."[17]

Irish antipathy toward Blacks erupted that year in the so-called "draft riots" in New York and other Northeastern cities. Mobs, consisting of mostly Irish Americans protesting the Civil War draft, attacked African Americans in what became race riots. Still, the Irish did their part in the war. Nearly forty exclusively Irish regiments fought on the Union's side, and their valiant battlefield performance mitigated much anti-Irish sentiment.[18]

As the century wore on, the country transitioned into the Industrial Age and demanded cheap labor. The arrival of non-English speaking Italian and Eastern European immigrants later in the century helped push the Irish up from the bottom rung, socially and economically. Still, the Irish in America made very uneven progress. Many entered the ranks of skilled labor, concentrating in the building, plumbing, and plastering trades; others entered the Civil Service, particularly the Post Office, fire departments, and police departments. Many single Irish women worked in the oppressive mills and factories of New England and the Midwest. On the whole, progress crawled for many Irish Americans. Not until World War II would they make "the great leap forward into the American mainstream."[19]

By the end of the 19th century, Irish men, as well as Jews, played leadership roles in the trade union movement and in politics, where the Irish showed a particular knack. Political machines emerged in New York as early as the 1830s, and in the period before the Civil War, Boss William Tweed perfected a citywide organization riddled with corruption. Writes historian James R. Barrett:

> No symbol is more central to Irish American mythology than the big-city political boss ... The Irish turned some of their earliest networks, based in volunteer fire units and street gangs (and often it was difficult to distinguish between the two), into political assets ... As political machines reemerged nationwide in the 1890s, the continuing Irish grip on them was striking, given the dramatic transformation in city populations.[20]

By 1890, political machines dominated half of the nation's twenty largest cities, and the Irish controlled most of them.[21] In 1880, New York's Tammany Hall elected its first Irish-Catholic mayor, William Grace. Irish influence soared when Al Smith became the Democratic presidential candidate in 1928 and peaked when John F. Kennedy was elected president. In the words of Daniel P. Moynihan:

It was the last hurrah. He, the youngest and newest, served in a final moment of ascendancy. On the day he died, the President of the United States, the Speaker of the House of Representatives, the Majority Leader of the United States Senate, the Chairman of the National Committee were all Irish, all Catholic, all Democrats. It will not come again.[22]

THE GERMANS

It was not the yoke of second-class citizenship and the lack of religious freedom that drove Germans to American shores, as in the case of the Irish, but rather the quest for democracy, a passion nurtured in the European Revolutions of 1848, an unsuccessful struggle to remove outdated feudal structures and create independent nation-states. Many called themselves "Forty-Eighters" and, fleeing the autocracy of the German states, boarded steamships heading for New York, Philadelphia, and Baltimore. Unlike the Irish, most Germans moved inland, away from port cities, with New York and Philadelphia being notable exceptions. They headed to destinations such as Cincinnati and St. Louis, the two largest inland cities in 1860, each with a 27 percent German-born population. By that time there were also large German populations in Chicago, Louisville, Cleveland, Detroit, and especially Milwaukee, with a population of 35 percent born in Germany. However, unlike the Irish, many Germans, accustomed as they were to farming, settled in rural areas, such as central Missouri, Iowa, and Wisconsin, which established a bureau to encourage immigration from Germany; beginning in the 1870s, large numbers, along with Scandinavian immigrants, moved into Minnesota and the Dakotas.[23]

The Germans in the Midwest built stone houses similar to what they had left behind, constructed German Catholic and Lutheran churches, and transplanted their newspapers, theaters, singing societies, and beer gardens, keeping alive the traditions they had brought with them. Most had strong anti-slavery views and were sympathetic to the Republican Party; though as beer drinkers, they opposed a movement toward temperance that had emerged. A large part of the Republican Party's decision to nominate Abraham Lincoln for president in 1860 was to appeal to German votes, as he was opposed to both the nativism of the Know-Nothings and skeptical about temperance. Without German support, according to political analyst Michael Barone, Lincoln would not have been elected president.[24]

Germans also encountered nativism in America – they were denounced for their clannishness, infidelity, and socialism –; however, it was much less than the hostility directed at the Irish who bore the brunt of most of the rhetoric and violence.

Yet as Wittke notes, the Germans were no less critical of the "native Americans" who deprecated them:

> Germans were equally aggressive and intolerant in expressing their contempt for native American "barbarians" and "Methodists," and some of the freethinking Forty-Eighters viciously attacked all religion and all churches, and espoused a political and economic radicalism which won them the reputation of being "red Republicans" and "foreign anarchists." Thus the German leadership attacked Puritan bigotry, and the native Americans retaliated with the charge that in German communities, with their beer and band music and picnics, the Sabbath was being turned "into a saturnalia."[25]

Because of the friction between Germans and native-born Americans, hostility fueled as much by their own leaders as by American nativism, Germans in America became a culturally isolated group. As a result, many naturalized German-Americans "ceased to be Germans in any political sense, but also never became wholly American." However, despite this apparent contradiction, the "forces of Americanization" were steadily at work in bringing about the assimilation of these German immigrants and their children.[26]

One of the reasons that Germans fared better than the Irish is that while the Irish were placed into the category of being racially inferior "Celts," Germans were considered to be "Anglo-Saxons," and in the racial thinking of the late 19th and early 20th centuries, Anglo-Saxon was considered to be a race descended from a branch of a "freedom-loving, noble race of Germanic peoples." In 1899, for example, William Z. Ripley, published an exhaustive book, *The Races of Europe*, in which, after examining the cephalic index (head shapes), height, and pigmentation of countless specimens, he concluded that there were three European racial types: the Teutonic, characterized by a long head, light hair, aquiline nose and blue eyes; Alpine or Celtic, possessing a round head, chestnut hair, a broad nose and hazel-gray eyes; and the Mediterranean, with a long head, dark brown or black hair, broad nose, and dark eyes. In a 1902 lecture, he warned of the "complete submergence" of Anglo-Saxon Americans that would result from the "forcible dislocation and abnormal intermixture" of European races, combined with the low Anglo-Saxon birthrate.[27]

One indicator of the relative acceptability of Germans, especially when compared to the Irish, was the large number of not only private but public German-speaking schools that were established. As historian Roger Daniels observes, beginning in

2 | THE IRISH AND GERMANS

1839, several states, the first being Pennsylvania and Ohio, passed laws enabling – and in some cases, requiring – instruction in German when parents requested it. In Cincinnati, there were parallel systems set up: one teaching in English and the other in German; in 1850, the school board officially recognized the right of students to receive instruction in either language. In St. Louis, a bilingual curriculum was established with the objective of attracting German-American children to the public school system, though all advanced subjects were taught in English.[28]

Prolific in numbers, Germans were the largest ethnic group arriving to the United States in all but three of the years between 1854 and 1894. By the end of the 19th century, more than 5 million Germans arrived on American shores, and this number was augmented by another 2 million during the 20th century. Rather than coming in a single wave, German immigration numbers were fragmented, reflecting conditions in Germany, as well as the United States. Between 1866 and 1873, German immigration accelerated, a response to a European depression, Bismarck's wars in the 1860s, and importantly, Congressional passage of the 1862 Homestead Act, which granted free land to settlers. Numbers dropped during the American depression between 1873 and 1879, rose sharply in 1882, and fell again during the U.S. depressions in the late 1880s and 1893. By that time, an improved economy in Germany provided greater opportunities, and fewer Germans felt compelled to leave.[29]

Life for Germans in America dropped, however, in 1914, with the outbreak of World War I, and anti-German sentiment reached a fever pitch in 1917 when the United States entered the war. Suddenly, German-Americans found themselves the objects of scorn and mistrust as a wave of "100 percent Americanism" gripped the country, and Germans in the United States were accused of being part of a "vast Pan-German plot to Prussianize America." Germans, both foreign and American born, were now forced to defend their loyalty against the verbal and physical abuses of the nativists. "Teutonism" was denounced and German-Americans were called "Huns." Anything German was attacked. Super-patriots sought to eliminate the music of Beethoven, Bach, and Mozart from orchestras and school curricula; sauerkraut became "liberty cabbage"; hamburgers became "liberty steaks"' the card game pinochle was called "liberty," and German measles was renamed "liberty measles." States banned the teaching of the German language in private and public schools alike. The number of German publications fell from 613 in 1900 to 234 in 1920. The Missouri Synod Lutheran Church switched heavily from German to English services. The National German-American Alliance was dissolved in April 1918.

Though only 1,200 German citizens were imprisoned in 1917, a German was lynched in Collinsville, Illinois, and a jury acquitted the perpetrators after only twenty-five minutes of deliberations. Barone writes, "Vandalism, tarring and feathering, and arrests for unpatriotic utterances were common. In addition, another German cultural institution, the beer garden, was threatened with extinction by the advance of the prohibition movement during the war ... Thus during just two years, Americans effectively suppressed many of the outward expressions of German-American culture."[30] Writes Wittke, the son of a German immigrant, "The crisis of 1914–18, as far as the German-Americans were concerned, threatened to prove far more dangerous than the attack of the nativists of the middle 19th century."[31] Melvin G. Holli, an expert on ethnic Chicago, agrees:

> The war damaged German ethnic, linguistic, and cultural institutions almost beyond repair. What little survived came under a final blight, the "shadow of the Swastika" in the 1930s and World War II which extinguished the few smoldering embers of 19th century German ethnicity.... No Lazarus-like resurrection seems to be in the offering.[32]

While the treatment of German-Americans during World War II was less hostile, certainly not coming close to the abuses visited on Japanese-Americans, all resident aliens from Japan, Germany, and Italy encountered severe restrictions once the United States entered the war, and in December 1941, a succession of proclamations declared them to be alien enemies. In January 1942, all alien enemies were required to re-register, obtain new identification certificates, and carry them at all times. According to Daniels, there were nearly 17,000 enemy aliens arrested between December 1941 and June 1945, including 7,000 Germans, 6,000 Japanese, and 3,600 Italians.[33] Despite the high numbers of Germans, however, clearly there was a hierarchy, with Japanese at the bottom and Italians at the top. Daniels quotes an anecdote recalled by Francis Biddle, Attorney General during the war, about a conversation with President Roosevelt:

> "How many Germans are there in the country?" he [Roosevelt] asked. "Oh, about 600,000," I told him. [Daniels notes that elsewhere in his memoirs Biddle writes that there were 300,000.] "And you're going to intern all of them," he said ... "Well, not quite all," I answered. "I don't care so much about the Italians," he continued. "They are a lot of opera singers, but the Germans are different, they may be dangerous."[34]

2 | THE IRISH AND GERMANS

While the identity of German-Americans has faded into a distant cultural identification, the impact of German immigrants is clearly evident in the fabric of what we now consider to be American. Some German contributions are easy to pinpoint – sauerkraut, apple pie (strudel), the Christmas tree, Santa Claus, and the national penchant for beer. However, the German influence on life in the United States runs much deeper. German immigrants in Wisconsin, for instance, launched the first kindergarten, based on the kindergartens of Germany, and German-Americans were leaders in the call for universal education. While the names of the many German-American industrialists are best remembered today – John Bausch, Henry Lomb, Henry Steinway, John Studebaker, Henry J. Heinz, William Boeing, Levi Strauss, and Oscar Mayer, to name a few – German immigrants and their offspring also left a strong mark on American politics, carrying on the reformist legacy of their Forty-Eighter forbearers. In the late 19th and 20th centuries, there emerged the Progressive movement in Wisconsin, the Farmer-Labor Party in Minnesota, and the Non-Partisan League in North Dakota – all attempts to provide security and freedom from exploitation by giant corporations for ordinary people.

Despite the deep footprint that German-Americans left on American soil, their assimilation into the mainstream is nearly complete. As Wittke lamented in 1942:

> The German-language press is rapidly dying. Most German churches have long since given up their services in the German language, and German societies of every description find it increasingly difficult to maintain their membership. The second- and third-generation immigrant stock know little of the language of their fathers and grandfathers. The process of Americanization goes on relentlessly, and the more naturally it proceeds, the more effective it is likely to be ... In several decades more, the cultural heritage of the German immigrant stock will have been absorbed into a composite Americanism.[35]

Today, Germans make up the largest ethnic-origin group in the United States. In 2009, according to the American Community Survey, nearly 51 million Americans claimed German ancestry, well above those claiming Irish (37 million), Mexican (32 million), English (28 million), and Italian (18 million) descent. Still, for most German-Americans, their identification with German culture is either symbolic or a distant memory. The same survey showed only 1.1 million Americans speak German at home, compared to the 35.5 million who spoke Spanish.[36]

NOTES

1. Barone, 12.
2. Ibid., 122.
3. McCaffrey, Lawrence J. "Irish America." *The Wilson Quarterly*, Vol. 9, No. 2 (Spring 1985), 79.
4. Ibid., 80.
5. Barrett, James R. *The Irish Way: Becoming American in the Multiethnic City.* (New York, NY: The Penguin Press, 2012), 123.
6. Wittke, Carl. *We Who Built America: The Saga of the Immigrant.* (New York, NY: Prentice-Hall, Inc., 1948), 138.
7. McCaffrey, 135.
8. Painter, Nell Irvin. *The History of White People.* (New York, NY: W. W. Norton & Company, 2011), 142.
9. Comte de Gobineau, Arthur. "Essay on the Inequality of Human Races," in Jacobson, 44.
10. Ignatiev, Noel. *How the Irish Became White.* (New York, NY: Routledge, 1995), 40.
11. Ibid., 49.
12. Ibid., 42.
13. Painter, 141.
14. Jacobson, Matthew Frye. Whiteness of a Different Color: European Immigrants and the Alchemy of Race. (Cambridge, MA: Harvard University Press, 1999), 48.
15. Ignatiev, 112.
16. Wittke, Carl. *The Irish in America.* (Baton Rouge, LA: Louisiana State University Press, 1956), 116.
17. Van Evrie, J.H. *The Negro and Negro Slavery.* (New York, NY: Van Evrie and Horton, 1863), 52, in Jacobson, 44.
18. Ibid., 81.
19. Ibid., 85.
20. Barrett, 197.
21. Ibid.
22. Glazer, Nathan and Daniel P. Moynihan. Beyond the Melting Pot: The Negroes, Puerto Ricans, Jews, Italians, and Irish of New York City. (Cambridge, MA: The MIT Press, 1970), 287.
23. Barone, 137.
24. Ibid., 139.
25. Wittke, Carl. "German Immigrants and Their Children, "*Annals of the American Academy of Political and Social Science.* Vol. 223, Sep., 1942, 87.

26. Ibid., 88.
27. Painter, 212.
28. Daniels, Roger. Coming to America: A History of Immigration and Ethnicity in American Life. (New York, NY: HarperPerennial, 2002), 159.
29. Dinnerstein, Leonard and David M. Reimers, *Ethnic Americans: A History of Immigration*. (New York, NY: Columbia University Press, 1999), 22.
30. Barone, 153.
31. Wittke, "German Immigrants," 89.
32. Holli, Melvin.G. "German-American Ethnic Identity from 1890 Onward: The Chicago Case." *The Great Lakes Review*, Vol. 11, No. 1 (Spring 1985), 9.
33. Daniels, 87.
34. Biden, Francis. In Brief Authority. (Garden City, NY: Doubleday, 1962), 207, in Daniels, 87.
35. Barone, 151.
36. 2009 American Community Survey, U.S. Census Bureau. https://www.census.gov/compendia/statab/2012/tables/12s0052.pdf.

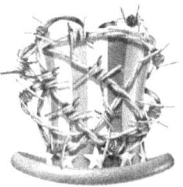

3

THE ITALIANS AND JEWS

THE LAST GREAT WAVE of White immigration occurred at the turn of the 20th century when more than 23 million immigrants, mostly from Eastern, Southern, and Central Europe, arrived between 1880 to the early 1920s. By 1910, America's population was 14.7 percent foreign born. It had been that high before, reaching 14.4 percent in 1870 and 14.8 percent in 1890. It is tricky to say before then, as the U.S. Census only began recording nativity statistics in 1850, though the Scots-Irish migration was likely just as high.[1] However, with this new immigration wave, there was a significant break with the past. Unlike many of the Irish, most spoke no English. Unlike the Germans, most settled in cities, particularly in the East. Significantly, according to the racial thinking of the day, most were "non-white." Much ado was made about the "swarthy" complexion of the Italians and the odd facial features of the Jews who hailed from Eastern Europe. Not surprisingly, a nativist fury resulted, as Americans railed at their un-assimilability and racial inferiority.

One of the reasons for the shift in emigration was that the German economy had developed and was providing jobs for an increasing number of people while Ireland's population "simply dried up," falling to half the pre-famine level of 1841. What drove the new immigrants was the promise of opportunity, as the surge in immigration coincided with years of massive industrial expansion in America and a growing demand for unskilled labor. Additionally, a great number of the Eastern Europeans arriving were Jews, victims of the relentless pogroms in Tsarist Russia in the first years of the 20th century. Also, the journey to America suddenly became economically feasible, as railroads connected the far reaches of Europe with port cities and competition among steamship lines made overseas travel much cheaper than it had been.[2]

Soon after the new immigrants began arriving in large numbers, in 1882, Congress enacted the first general immigration law – it had passed the Chinese Exclusion Act less than three months earlier – which placed a head tax on those arriving by steamship. Additionally, a more formidable change occurred in 1891, when Congress, increasingly concerned about immigration, established federal control over immigrants. In 1892, Ellis Island opened, operated by the newly established Bureau of Immigration. As Daniels notes, "A little more than a century after the founding of the republic, during which more than 16 million immigrants had entered the country, the United States finally had an immigration service."[3] For the U.S. government, the timing was opportune as the number of aliens processed at Ellis Island went from 2 million in the 1890s to 6.3 million in the first decade of the century and 3.8 million in the five years that followed.[4]

Of the immigrants arriving during those years, Italians represented the largest ethnic group, more than any other ethnicity entering America in such a short period of time, though as many as half may have returned to Italy. Most arrived from southern Italy and nearly all arrived at Ellis Island; over half remained within 100 miles of the island. By 1920, there were almost 400,000 Italian immigrants living in New York City, representing nearly a quarter of the Italian foreign born. While about half lived in Manhattan, usually below Washington Square, more than a third settled in Brooklyn, and few ventured beyond the Northeast. In 1970, two-thirds of Italian-Americans still lived in the region. Most of the immigrants were young men, largely illiterate, who came in search of employment as unskilled workers. However, there were women, too, many of whom worked in New York's rapidly expanding garment industry. Nearly all were Catholics, though not frequent churchgoers, as many shunned the Irish-dominated Catholic Church in America.[5]

Life in the Italian enclaves of New York City came to resemble the villages of southern Italy from whence they had come, albeit transferred to an urban environment. As sociologist Nathan Glazer writes:

> From the beginning, the village-mindedness of the Southern Italians was striking to American observers. When the immigrants settled in the blocks of New York or in the small industrial communities around the city, they tended to congregate with others from the same province or even village. Illiteracy seriously hampered

the development of these diverse settlements into a single ethnic group, for differences in dialect, which in turn engendered mutual suspicion, tended to endure in the absence of widespread written communication.[6]

For the Italian immigrants, wages were low, and the living conditions in the crowded New York tenements were harsh. Italians usually sent their children to work at an early age; according to Daniels, just after World War I, about 90 percent of Italian-American girls over fourteen were working. Few Italian teenagers attended high school, and Italian boys were frequently found working on the streets as musicians and acrobats.[7] At the same time, their parents frequently toiled at brutal menial jobs, often in construction, and they were frequently misused by a class of leaders, the *padroni*, bosses, usually immigrants or second generation Americans, who acted as middlemen between immigrant workers and employers. Writes Glazer:

> In the early days, when Italians were the laborers and building workers of New York, they worked in groups under a leader from the same village, or someone known to the group. These were *padroni*, who … often exploited the workers. Their contracts with employers gave them far too much of the workers' return, they lied in describing jobs, and the workers had no redress. In any case, the workers – illiterate, fearful of government, and docile before men of prominence – did not dream of bringing the *padroni* to justice.[8]

Like the Italians, the Ellis Island Jews tended to not venture far from New York – about 70 percent stayed in the city, at first crowding into five and six story tenements on the Lower East Side but moving beyond to areas east of the Bowery and south of Houston East. By 1910, there were some 540,000 Jews living in one and a half densely packed square miles on the Lower East Side, which, according to Barone, might have represented the highest population density in the world at the time. The streets were filled with pushcarts and peddler stalls, horse-drawn carts, and workers carrying piles of cloth and clothing. There were synagogues, ritual baths, and Yiddish theaters. The neighborhoods were organized by *landsmanshaftn*, organizations made up of people from one's home village or town in the Old Country, which offered life insurance, sickness and death benefits, burial plots, training in English, and assistance in finding employment, usually in garment factories. Voluntary organizations were numerous. When the subways opened, beginning in 1906, Jews moved in huge numbers to Brooklyn and the Bronx, especially Brownsville and Flatbush in Brooklyn and the Grand Concourse in the Bronx, which became predominantly Jewish neighborhoods. Outside of New York, similar communities sprang up on Chicago's West Side, in South Philadelphia, Cleveland, Baltimore, Pittsburgh, St. Louis, Detroit, and in the case of my own family, the Boston communities of Roxbury, Dorchester, and Mattapan, which in so many ways resembled the *shtetlekh*, or small Jewish villages, they had left behind in Eastern Europe.[9]

According to Daniels, in 1920, about half of all American Jews lived in New York, where they comprised about a quarter of the city's population. Like the Italians, they were members of the working poor and crowded into filthy ethnic enclaves ridden with crime and disease. Most lived in five- and six-story tenements, often without hot water and with one toilet per floor. One 1908 survey showed that in half of these rooms three or four people slept in one room, and a quarter of the rooms slept five or more. These conditions were typical in most large city Jewish neighborhoods at the time. While many worked in New York's garment industry, about a fifth worked in retail, in work ranging from pushcart vendors and peddlers to proprietors of stores.[10] My great-grandfather, an immigrant from Romania, worked in Boston as a junkman, collecting and reselling Jewish people's castaway items on his horse drawn cart; my maternal grandfather, from the Ukraine, owned a few modest shoe stores. By contrast, my paternal grandfather, who was born in Boston, was a policeman, a job that paid next to nothing. When he was promoted to sergeant, it was big neighborhood news, a rare accomplishment for a Jew on a police force that was almost entirely Irish.

In Boston, the Jewish population multiplied eightfold, during the decades of the 1880s and 1890s, from only 5,000, most of whom were German Jews, to 40,000, the vast majority from Eastern Europe. Prior to that time, most Bostonians knew very little about Jews. Writes Jonathan D. Sarna, "They heard about them more than they actually saw them, and they puzzled over how to reconcile the historically stereotyped 'mythical Jews,' found in their books with the real Jew, the proverbial 'Jew next door,' who seemed altogether different." The poet Oliver Wendell Holmes, father of the Supreme Court justice, admitted that he grew up with the idea that Jews "were a race lying under a curse for their obstinacy in refusing the gospel," whose principle function "seemed to be to lend money, and to fulfill the prediction of the old prophets of their race." When the late 19th century Jewish influx began, for Boston's Brahmins, old-fashioned anti-Semitism, with its medieval roots, transformed into a fear that the Jews, along with the other "new immigrants," were overrunning the city and imperiling their "race, their country and their way of life."[11]

Yet the new Jewish immigrants and their children were largely impervious to the disdain by which they were regarded by the Brahmins. For them, Boston was a balkanized community, with the Irish in South Boston, the Italians on the North End,

3 | THE ITALIANS AND JEWS

and the Jews in the South End of town. Journalist Theodore H. White, who is Jewish, recalled living in an enclave surrounded by "very tough Irish – working-class Irish" during his youth in the 1920s. The local library was in an Irish area, and his "first fights happened en route to the library" to get books. "Pure hellishness divided us," he recalled.[12] Nat Hentoff, in his autobiography, *Boston Boy*, relates an incident nearly identical to one that my father, who grew up in Dorchester's Franklin Park neighborhood, would often tell.

> One evening, three friends and I are walking through large, dark Franklin Park on the way to a dance at the Hebrew school. Coming toward us are four bigger boys. When they are close enough, it is clear they are not Jewish. And since they are not Italian, they are Irish. Their leader swaggers up to me and asks – what else? – "Are you Jewish?" Since there are other members of my tribe with me … I nod. "You got a light," he asks. As I go to my pocket, I look down, and a stone, a huge stone, smashes into my face. Or so it feels. The shock and pain are such that it takes a few moments for me to taste the blood and feel the space where, a second ago, there had been a tooth. Their leader, rubbing his fist with satisfaction, waits for a revengeful lunge and is not surprised when it doesn't come. So few of these kikes fight back. And he and his sturdy companions move on guffawing.[13]

Discrimination against Jews was endemic in America well into the 1950s, and they were largely kept out of the higher ranks of corporate America, prestigious law firms, the faculties of Ivy League universities, and prestigious clubs. American anti-Semitism reached a crescendo during the Red Scare of 1917–1919, when Jews were widely assumed to be part of a Bolshevik conspiracy. A leading Jewish antagonist was Henry Ford, whose magazine, the *Dearborn Independent*, launched a relentless campaign implicating Jews in an international conspiracy, and "internationalism" became an anti-Semitic epithet. "I know who makes wars," he once said. "The international Jewish bankers arrange them so they can make money out of them. I know it's true because a Jew … told me."[14]

Italians were frequently labeled as "Wops" (*WithOut Papers*), "Dagos," "Guineas," a term which linked them to Blacks, and "Greasers," an appellation pairing them with Mexicans, and their "swarthiness" was constantly invoked as a marker of their racial inferiority and non-whiteness. Writing of the crime stories that proliferated in Chicago's newspapers during the 1920s, Thomas A. Guglielmo notes that the dark skin of Italians was frequently emphasized, thereby making them seem all the more racially distinct and dangerous. In describing the tight police security at gang leader Antonio Lombardo's funeral in 1928, the *Chicago Tribune* wrote that "Chicago policemen rubbed against dark skinned mourners seeking the feel of a pistol." When reporting on the murder of a gang chieftain in November 1924, the *Chicago Daily News* described the assailants as "swarthy" and thus "probably Italians." Writes Guglielmo:

> Al Capone was constantly portrayed in books, magazine articles, pulps, and movies as having a "dark" or "swarthy" complexion. When he appeared in court in 1929 in Philadelphia on charges of having concealed a weapon, the *Chicago Daily News* noticed that his "face, which is rather dark, assumed a dull reddish hue."[15]

Italians were frequently described as savage, sometimes simian, and accounts often linked them to "the stiletto, the Mafia, the deed of impassioned violence." A piece in the *Baltimore News* declared of Italians, "The disposition to assassinate in revenge for a fancied wrong is a marked trait in the character of this impulsive and inexorable race." Historian John Higham writes:

> Every time a simple Italian laborer resorted to his knife, the newspapers stressed the fact of his nationality; the most trivial fracas on Mulberry Street caused a headline on "Italian Vendetta." The stereotype conditioned every major outburst of anti-Italian sentiment in the 1890s. The distinctive nativism which swarthy *paesani* experienced took the guise of social discipline applied to alleged acts of homicide.[16]

The massive inflow of Italians and Jews, paired with the lesser but significant immigration of Slavs and Poles, and in the West, Chinese, Japanese, and Mexicans, led to the thinkers of the early 20th century to denounce what they viewed as "race suicide," and they constructed new theories, which contrasted the "new immigrants" with those already established whose whiteness was taken for granted. Edward Ross, a popular and distinguished sociologist, published an article in 1901, "The Causes of Racial Superiority" in the prestigious *Annals of the American Academy of Political and Social Science*, decrying the "masses of fecund but beaten humanity from the hovels of far Lombardy and Galicia," adding that "from Croatia and Dalmatia and Sicily and Armenia, they throng to us, the beaten members of beaten breeds ... Slovaks and

Syrians ... as undersized in spirit, no doubt, as they are in body."[17] Francis Amasa Walker, president of M.I.T. and former superintendent of the 1870 and 1880 censuses, developed a theory that contact with inferior races caused lower births rates among the native born. He believed that while the Irish had joined the realm of whiteness, the "ignorant and brutalized peasantry from the countries of eastern and southern Europe" would weaken "American standards" with a "contact so foul and loathsome." Invoking the allegedly superior historical accomplishments of the northern European race, he concluded that "Centuries are against them, as centuries were on the side of those who formerly came to us."[18] Rather than compete with cheap foreign labor, Walker argued, Americans chose to reduce the size of their families, rather than lower their standard of living. Walker was far from being an outlier. President Theodore Roosevelt implored American mothers to have more children, and according to Higham, popular magazines published over 35 articles between 1905 and 1909 dealing directly with the topic of "race suicide."[19]

The most extreme advocated a comprehensive system of government-sponsored eugenics to weed out America's undesirables, a movement inspired by England's leading Darwinian scientist, Sir Francis Galton, and this narrative became intimately tied to fears about degenerate immigrants. Through his research, Galton had determined that the way to improve society was to better the "inborn qualities" of humans, and he began to propagandize a campaign of promoting the breeding of the best and restricting the reproduction of the worst. His eugenicist theories soon gained ground in America.[20] Charles Benedict Davenport, for example, a professor at Harvard and the University of Chicago, agreed that heredity, not environment, was the source of America's ills, and in 1922, his Eugenics Record Office offered a model for the compulsory sterilization of those deemed to be "degenerate." Virginia passed the first such law in 1924, stating, "heredity plays an important part in the transmission of insanity, idiocy, and imbecility, epilepsy, and crime." The law was not repealed until 1974.

While Davenport's eugenics programs never gained widespread acceptance – they fell especially out of favor during the 1930s when Nazi eugenics programs were exposed – they presented plenty of fodder for nativists. According to historian Nell Irvin Painter, in 1894, the Immigration Restriction League put degenerate families and immigrants into the same category, declaring, "The same arguments which induce us to segregate criminals and feebleminded and thus prevent their breeding apply to excluding from our borders individuals whose multiplying here is likely to lower the average of our people." Beginning in the 1890s, federal laws toughened to keep out "'lunatics,' 'idiots,' people likely to become public charges, the insane, epileptics, beggars, anarchists, 'imbeciles,' feeble-minded and persons with physical or mental defects which might affect their ability to earn a living."[21]

Another influential figure linking "degenerates" with immigrants at the time was Henry H. Goddard, a pedagogue who pioneered in America the use of intelligence testing in schools. In 1912, Goddard published a book, *The Kallikak Family*, based on the results of his study of the offspring of Deborah Kallikak, the first link in a family that included no shortage of illegitimate children and "sexually immoral persons, mostly prostitutes." He warned, "There are Kallikak families all about us," and "no amount of education or good environment can change a feeble-minded individual into a normal one." In 1917, at the behest of the Commissioner of Immigration, he produced a report on the state of immigrants. Among his conclusions:

- The intelligence of the average third class immigrant is low, perhaps of moron grade....
- Each test taken by itself seems to indicate a very high percentage of defectiveness. There is no exception to this....
- The immigrants of recent years are of a decidedly different character from the earlier immigration ... It is admitted on all sides that we are getting now the poorest of each race ... of every 1,000 Polish immigrants all but 103 are laborers and servants.
- 83 percent of the Jews, 80 percent of the Hungarians, 79 percent of the Italians, 87 percent of the Russians were feebleminded. 60 percent of the Jews were morons.[22]

Likely the most influential work of the time was *The Passing of the Great Race*, written by Madison Grant, a lawyer, eugenicist, and ardent conservationist. The book, written in 1916, though it became most popular during the early 1920s, traces the development of the "European races." In a scathing polemic, Grant extolls the virtues of the Nordic race and excoriates other inferior races in America, which he blames on a "pathetic and fatuous belief in the efficacy of American institutions and environment to reverse or obliterate immemorial hereditary tendencies." Decrying the immigration of his time, Grant wrote:

> These immigrants adopt the language of the native American; they wear his clothes; they steal his name; and they are beginning to take his women ... and while he is being elbowed out of his own home, the American looks calmly abroad and urges on others the suicidal ethics which are exterminating his own race.
>
> One thing is certain: in any such mixture, the surviving traits will be determined by competition between the lowest and most

primitive elements and the specialized traits of Nordic man; his stature, his light colored eyes, his fair skin and blond hair, his straight nose, and his splendid fighting and moral qualities, will have little part in the resultant mixture.... From the point of view of race it [is] better described as the "survival of the unfit."²³

Grant recommended that America undertake a systematic approach to "race improvement" by eliminating "the least desirable elements in the nation by depriving them of the power to contribute to future generations." This "system of selection," he argued, would rid society of "those who are weak or unfit – in other words, social failures" enabling "us to get rid of the undesirables who crowd our jails, hospitals, and insane asylums." He continues:

> The state through sterilization must see to it that his line stops with him, or else future generations will be cursed with an ever increasing load of victims of misguided sentimentalism. This is a practical, merciful, and inevitable solution of the whole problem, and can be applied to an ever widening circle of social discards ... and extending gradually to types which may be called weaklings rather than defectives, and perhaps ultimately to worthless race types.²⁴

Organized labor never supported an outright immigration ban on the new immigrants, as they did with Asians, and while White ethnics had more access to unionized work than did African Americans, they tended to be relegated to an "in-between" status of being neither colored nor white. Unions referred to Italians as the "White Chinese" and "padrone coolies," while new immigrants as a group were labeled as "White Coolies." Such attitudes, writes historian David Roediger, in essence, "acknowledged and questioned new immigrant whiteness at the same time, associating 'lesser' Whites with non-Whites...." However, as mechanization made real the possibility that craft skills could be replaced by unskilled labor, the unions reluctantly changed tactics, and in the early 20th century, "got into the business of organizing and Americanizing new immigrant workers."²⁵

One voice of dissension to rise above the clamor surrounding the alleged racial inferiority of the new immigrants was German-born anthropologist Franz Boas, often called the "father of American anthropology." In his 1911 book, *The Mind of Primitive Man*, Boas pointed to the achievements of Native Americans and Africans to refute claims that Whites stood at the top of the racial pyramid. "It is certainly conceivable," he writes, "that there may be other civilizations ... which are of no less value than ours, although it may be impossible for us to appreciate their values without having grown up under their influence."[26] He stated in his conclusion, "All races have contributed in the past to cultural progress in one way or another, so they will be capable of advancing the interests of mankind, if we are only willing to give them a fair opportunity." According to anthropologist Herbert Lewis, one of Boas' chief accomplishments was to call into question the accepted view of "race," instead demonstrating the effects of environment, particularly, socio-economic conditions, on the achievements of different populations.[27] However, it would not be until the 1930s that Boas' imprint would be felt on the American mainstream, when *Time*, in a 1936 cover story on Boas, called his book the "*Magna Carta* of race equality."

Still, in the first quarter of the century, nativism had the upper hand. In 1907, in response to a growing political and social concern over immigration, the U.S. government created the United States Immigration Commission, known as the Dillingham Commission. Under the leadership of Vermont Senator William Paul Dillingham, the President, the Speaker of the House, and the President of the Senate each appointed three of its nine members. In 1911, the Commission produced its 41-volume report, which concluded that the new immigrants were inferior in education and genetic ability to those who had come earlier. Among its recommendations was the intelligence testing of immigrants and the "limitation of each [race] arriving each year to a certain percentage of that race arriving during a given period of years." While the report was not acted upon at the time, in 1917, Congress passed, with certain exemptions, a literacy requirement for immigrants over the age of sixteen, despite President Woodrow Wilson's veto. The idea of restricting immigration to all but earlier immigrants would be taken up in the strict immigration laws of 1921 and 1924.

During World War I, immigration fell to a simmer; when factoring in those who had left the country, net inflows were just over 150,000 in 1916. Yet the drop in immigration did little to extinguish nativist zeal. During the war, xenophobia was high, and the federal government's disregard for civil liberties was extreme. Cries calling for "One Hundred Percent Americanism" were ubiquitous, and "hyphenated Americans," particularly German-Americans, were denounced. Former President Theodore Roosevelt declared, "We of America form a new nationality! ... Either a man is an American and nothing else, or he is not an American at all."[28] President Calvin Coolidge wrote in *Good Housekeeping* that he favored "the right kind of immigration," declaring that America had become a "dumping ground" and that there were "racial considerations too grave to be brushed aside for any sentimental reasons." Coolidge added, "Biological laws tell us that certain divergent people will not mix

3 | THE ITALIANS AND JEWS

or blend.... The Nordics propagate themselves successfully. With other races, the outcome shows deterioration on both sides."[29]

Additionally, the 1920 census revealed that America had become more urban than rural, with a majority of population growth being driven by the industrial cities of the North and Upper Midwest. In response, a conservative coalition in Congress successfully stalemated the congressional reapportionment process for a decade, marking the only time in American history that this did not occur after a census. In the thinking of the day, urban meant immigrants, and shortly after the census was made available, Congress passed legislation to apply an immigration quota based on national origin, setting levels at 3 percent of the size of each nationality as reported in the 1910 census, capping immigration at approximately 350,000 annually. However, new legislation was on its way. In 1924, The Johnson-Reed Act, known as the National Origins Act, passed, setting a limit on European immigration at 165,000. Using the year 1890 as a baseline, the quota for Polish immigrants was set at 6,000 and for Italians at 4,000. The Act ignored non-Europeans in the quotas, eliminating immigration quotas from the Western Hemisphere, thereby keeping the door open for Mexican workers in the Southwest.[30] Writes Daniels:

> The importance of the 1924 act is hard to overemphasize.... In 1924, it was a foregone conclusion that there would be a permanent restriction of immigration.... Fears about job-stealing and the lowering of the standard of living by immigrants willing to work cheap were still shaping the national mood. The nation was also gripped by xenophobia and a rejection of Europe. Most important, perhaps, was the beleaguered feeling of so many old-stock Protestant Americans. Immigrants and their non-Protestant cultures, they felt, represented a serious and sustained challenge to American values.... No other issue so completely encapsulated the spirit of the decade as immigration restriction did.[31]

One of the questions, which much of White America is still asking, was about how easily immigrants and their children would "Americanize." According to Roediger, the immigration restrictions actually "softened anti-immigrant racism," as the dire predictions of immigrants "swamping" the United States no longer had any basis. For their part, European immigrants, particularly women, pursued citizenship with a fervor – an option not yet available to non-Whites –, and their children, born in the United States, were beginning to lose contact with the culture and language of their parents. Roediger writes that, "ironically, even as the 1924 legislation made the new immigrants the victims of racism, it also encouraged them to see the advantages of whiteness and to seek it with greater zeal."[32]

By the early 1920s, a new view of American society emerged, that of the "melting pot," a term first coined in a play by the same name, written by Jewish immigrant Israel Zangwill in 1923. In the play's final scene, its hero David declares:

> There she lies, the great Melting Pot ... Celt and Latin, Slav and Teuton, Greek and Syrian, black and yellow.... Yes, East and West, and North and South, the palm and the pine, the pole and the equator, the crescent and the cross-bow, the great Alchemist melts and fuses them with his purging flame! Here shall they all unite to build the Republic of Man and the Kingdom of God.[33]

Zangwill's vision came to be embraced by native-born Americans who saw the "foreignness" of the new immigrants as a social problem unparalleled in American history. In order to ameliorate it, they turned to the public schools to assimilate their children, "to teach them the English language, to prepare them for citizenship, and to incorporate them into the structure of American society as rapidly as possible."[34] Ellwood P. Cubberley, one of the nation's leading educators, expressed these goals in 1909:

> Our task is to break up these groups or settlements, to assimilate and amalgamate these people as a part of our American race, to implant in their children, so far as can be done, the Anglo-Saxon conception of righteousness, law and order, and popular government, and to awaken in them a reverence for democratic institutions and for those things in our national life which we as a people hold to be of abiding worth.[35]

However, ethnic identity dies hard. While the new immigrants generally accepted – indeed embraced – that their children would be raised as Americans, they tended to resist the process of complete Americanization. They built networks of religious and ethnic institutions as a countervailing force, in order to maintain cultural traditions. Catholic immigrant groups built extensive parochial school systems, and Jews formed Hebrew and religious schools, which children attended after their public school classes. Additionally, agencies, such as the network of International Institutes, were formed to promote immigrant education and aid in the adjustment of ethnic

3 | THE ITALIANS AND JEWS

immigrants to urban America. For example, the 1935 constitution of the Boston International Institute states:

> The purpose of this organization shall be to provide a center for information, service, education, and assembly for the use of people of all nationalities; to develop international fellowship and understanding; to consider and promote the welfare of our foreign population as a whole and as a matter of social concern; to specialize in problems of the foreign born; to maintain contact with the social forces within nationality communities; to cooperate with other social agencies primarily interested in cultural, civic and economic welfare; to preserve and stimulate an interest in racial cultural values; to assist the older and newer citizenry in their orientation.[36]

By the 1930s, a new vision of American identity was beginning to emerge, a "cultural pluralism," a term coined in the second decade of the century by the Jewish philosopher, Horace M. Kallen, which differed markedly from the assimilationist rhetoric of his time. Kallen believed that cultural diversity and national pride were not incompatible and that ethnic and racial differences strengthened America. In his 1915 paper "Democracy versus the Melting Pot," Kallen wrote:

> As they grow more prosperous, and "Americanized," as they become free from the stigma of "foreigner," they develop group self-respect: the "wop" changes into a proud Italian, the "hunky" into an intensely nationalistic Slav. They learn, or they recall, the spiritual heritage of their nationality. Their cultural abjectness gives way to cultural pride and the public schools, the libraries, and the clubs become beset with demands for texts in the national language and literature.[37]

In the paper's conclusion, Kallen compares his vision of cultural pluralism with a symphony, a single entity in its totality, yet composed of individual instruments, each with its own, unique sound:

> Thus "American civilization" may come to mean the perfection of the cooperative harmonies of "European civilization," the waste,

the squalor, and the distress of Europe being eliminated – a multiplicity in a unity, an orchestration of mankind. As in an orchestra, every type of instrument has its appropriate theme and melody in the whole symphony, so in society each ethnic group is the natural instrument, its spirit and culture are its theme and melody, and the harmony and dissonances and discords of them all make the symphony of civilization.[38]

One to take up Kallen's call in the 1930s was Lewis Adamic, a Slovenian immigrant and journalist. Adamic thought that a new conception of America was required, which recognized that America was not an Anglo-Saxon country and that the children of immigrants should not expect to become Anglo-Saxons. Writing in 1946, he declared:

Too many of us still consider our human diversity a deplorable handicap. Too few see that it is our chief asset.... Too few realize in what Whitman rejoiced in 1845: that we Americans are a people of peoples swept together by the passion for a better life – for the chance to cease being worm and become man. In that fact lies our greatest source of inspiration and power.[39]

America was, he contended, borrowing from the words of Walt Whitman, a "nation of nations," and that a sense of ethnic pride was imperative in order to overcome a sense of cultural inferiority.

NOTES

1. http://www.census.gov/population/www/documentation/twps0081/twps0081.html.
2. Barone, 172.
3. Daniels, Roger. Guarding the Golden Door: American Immigration Policy and Immigrants Since 1882. (New York, NY: Hill and Wang, 2004), 29.
4. http://www.nps.gov/elis/forteachers/upload/Statistics.pdf.
5. Daniels, Coming to America, 188.
6. Glazer and Moynihan, 186.
7. Daniels, Coming to America, 196.
8. Glazer and Moynihan, 190.
9. Barone, 187.

10. Daniels, Coming to America, 226.
11. Sarna, Jonathan D. ed. by Johnathan D. Sarna and Ellen Smith. "The Jews of Boston in Historical Perspective," in *The Jews of Boston*, Combined Jewish Philanthropies of Greater Boston, 1995. http://www.brandeis.edu/hornstein/sarna/americanjewishcultureandscholarship/Archive6/TheJewsofBostoninHistoricalPerspective.pdf.
12. White, Theodore H. *In Search of History: A Personal Adventure*. (New York, NY: Harper and Row Publishers, 1978), 28.
13. Hentoff, Nat. Boston Boy: Growing up with Jazz and Other Rebellious Passions. (New York, NY: Knopf, 1986), 21, quoted in Sarna.
14. Higham, John. *Strangers in the Land: Patterns of American Nativism, 1860–1925*. (New Brunswick, NJ: Rutgers University Press, 2002), 263.
15. Guglielmo, Thomas A. White on Arrival: Italians, Race, Color, and Power in Chicago, 1890–1945. (Oxford, England: Oxford University Press, 2003), 86.
16. Higham, 83.
17. Ross, Edward A. "The Causes of Racial Superiority," *Annals of the American Academy of Political and Social Science* 18, 1901, 89, in Walker, 252.
18. In David R. Roediger, Working Toward Whiteness: How America's Immigrants Became White. (New York, NY: Basic Books, 2005), 65.
19. Higham, 136.
20. Ibid., 139.
21. Painter, 280.
22. Ibid.
23. Grant, Madison. *The Passing of the Great Race or The Racial Basis of European History*. (Ostara Publications, 2011), 46.
24. Ibid., 29.
25. Roediger, 82.
26. Boas, Franz. *The Mind of Primitive Man*, (New York, NY: Macmillan, 1931), 208.
27. Ibid.
28. Roosevelt, Theodore. "Fear God and Take Your Part," (New York, 1916), pp. 141, 136, in Rudolph J. Vecoli, "The Significance of Immigration in the Formation of an American Identity," *The History Teacher*, Vol. 30, No. 1 (Nov., 1996), 19.
29. Coolidge, Calvin. "Whose Country is This?" *Good Housekeeping*, Vol. 72, No. 2, February 1921.
30. Prewitt, Kenneth. What Is Your Race? The Census and Our Flawed Efforts to Classify Americans. (Princeton, NJ: Princeton University Press, 2013), 73.

31. Daniels, *Guarding the Golden Door*, 49.
32. Roediger, 149.
33. Zangwill, Israel. *The Melting Pot*. (New York, NY: The Macmillan Company, 1923), 144.
34. Mohl, Raymond A. "Cultural Pluralism in Immigrant Education: The International Institutes of Boston, Philadelphia, and San Francisco, 1920–1940," *Journal of American Ethnic History*, Vol. 1, No. 2 (Spring, 1982), 36.
35. Callahan, Raymond E. *Education and the Cult of Efficiency: A Study of the Social Forces That Have Shaped the Administration of the Public Schools* (Chicago, 1962), 15, in Mohl, 36.
36. Mohl, 44.
37. Kallen, Horace M. "Democracy versus the Melting Pot: A Study of American Nationality." *The Nation*, Feb. 25, 1915. http://thenewschoolhistory.org/wp-content/uploads/2013/10/kallen_democracyvmeltingpot.pdf.
38. Ibid.
39. Adamic, Loius. "A Nation of Nations." *Pi Lambda Theta Journal*, Vol. 24, No. 4, (May, 1946), 139.

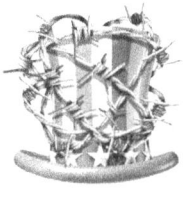

4

THE INTEGRATION OF WHITE FOLKS

DESPITE Kallen's vision of a pluralistic society, the Great Depression of the 1930s led to the emergence of a strong national culture that began to undermine ethnic barriers. President Franklin D. Roosevelt, who assumed office in 1933, sought young, liberally minded lawyers during the New Deal years, and Jews joined the Administration in large numbers, driven as much by a desire to effect social change as by an ambition fueled after being shunned by the most prestigious law firms. Writes historian Leonard Dinnerstein, the problem in Washington was "too many Jews, not too few."[1] Additionally, as so many Americans, found themselves enmeshed in the throes of poverty, differences between ethnicities and classes began to diminish. When the Depression pushed theaters to seek a broader market, old neighborhood movie houses closed, and working class, ethnic people were more likely to see movies alongside middle class, Anglo-Saxon patrons in the larger theaters that sprung up. A desire to penetrate broader markets led to the growth of national brands and chain stores, and the result was a homogenization of consumers and further diminishing of ethnic boundaries.[2] The 1930s were a period of great transition, representing a kind of halfway point between assimilation and pluralism. Of the period, historian Richard Weiss writes:

> The most ardent assimilationist had to recognize the fact of ethnic variety, however attenuated it had become. By the same token,

the most ardent pluralist had to acknowledge that the retention of cultural diversity could not preclude a substantial conformity to general American norms.[3]

Perhaps most significantly, as the second generation, and increasingly, the third generation, came of age, intermarriage between ethnics became more frequent, and Old World languages were losing ground. By 1940, while the majority of second generation Americans still tended to marry co-ethnics – 65 percent of Italians, 55 percent of Poles, and 41 percent of Russians –, foreign language usage was well on the decline. The 1940 census was the first to measure the "mother tongue" of Americans, and among Whites, English was reported as the mother tongue by 78.6 percent, German by only 4.2 percent, Italian by 3.2 percent, Polish by 2.0 percent, Spanish by 1.6 percent, Yiddish by 1.5 percent, and French by 1.2 percent. No other single foreign tongue was reported by as much as 1 percent of the total White population. Writing in 1949, social scientist Clyde V. Kiser concluded:

> If there are no drastic changes in our immigration laws, the foreign-born Whites will continue to decrease in America and proportionate importance. The children and grandchildren of the foreign-born Whites will probably become less and less distinguishable from the descendants of the early White settlers. In view of common social attitudes it is not to be expected that a similar assimilation of the colored groups will occur in the foreseeable future.[4]

With the advent of the Depression and mass unemployment in the country, immigration from Europe came to a virtual standstill, dropping from a total of 241,000 immigrants in 1930, to 23,000 three years later. From 1931 to 1940, only 528,000 immigrants entered the United States, yielding an annual average of only 53,000. World War II brought another barrier to the movement of immigrants. From a Depression peak of 83,000 in 1939, the number of immigrants fell to 24,000 in 1943; during the war, the number of immigrants averaged only 40,000 per year.[5] After the war, avenues for emigration from Eastern Europe, now under the domain of the Soviet Union were blocked, and Western Europe began to seek workers to rebuild its shattered economies. The economic growth triggered by the Marshall Plan created a strong demand for labor, and countries, like Germany, France, Britain, Belgium, and the Netherlands, not only stopped sending migrants abroad, they became

4 | THE INTEGRATION OF WHITE FOLKS

immigration destinations themselves. As sociologist Douglas S. Massey notes, "The era of mass European migration to the United States was finally and decisively over."[6]

The United States emerged from World War II with the strongest economy in the world, and the growth that followed in the next 20 years was unprecedented. The GNP in 1947 was $231 billion; it rose to $398 billion in 1955, $504 billion in 1960, and $977 billion in 1970.[7] As the economy grew, the government strove to build an American middle class by developing programs that encouraged young men to go to college and married couples to buy houses in the suburbs. The 1944 Serviceman's Readjustment Act, better known as the GI Bill of Rights, extended benefits to 16 million GIs, including preferential hiring, financial support during the job search, small loans for starting up businesses, and low-interest home loans; it also paid college tuition and living expenses, and the nearly 8 million GIs who took advantage of this stimulated the greatest wave of college building in American history. However, GIs were not the only group to benefit from the federal government's largess. The Federal Housing Administration (FHA) and Veterans Administration provided low down payment, low-interest, long-term loans to young buyers, and the National Defense Highway Act of 1941 authorized the federal government to fund a national highways system, making suburbs and automobile commuting a way of life for millions of Americans.[8]

These government programs created the means for millions of working-class Americans to rise into the middle-class. However, benefits were largely limited to Whites, and ultimately, they had the effect of exacerbating, rather than narrowing, the socio-economic differences between Blacks and Whites. The reason for this was partly political. The House of Representatives Committee on World War Legislation, for example, which crafted the GI Bill, was chaired by John Rankin of Mississippi, an unabashed racist, who succeeded in ensuring that responsibility for implementation of the bill was left to states and localities, making it susceptible to Jim Crow laws in the South. However, entrenched racist attitudes in the North also played a part in assuring that the "affirmative action" of the times was to benefit only Whites. Writes Ira Katznelson of the GI Bill: "There was no greater instrument for widening an already huge racial gap in postwar America. [The] combination of entrenched racism and willful exclusion either refused [Blacks] entry or shunted them into second-class standing and conditions.... The playing field never was level. Just as ethnic barriers between Whites were taking a tumble, providing a government-sponsored pathway out of ethnic enclaves, these same programs served to ensure the division of Americans into two worlds, one black, one white."[9]

As an example of how racism combined with politics to excise Blacks from government programs, Social Security, as passed and signed by President Roosevelt in

1935, excluded most Blacks, who as farmworkers or domestics, were not included in the program. At its inception, 65 percent of Blacks and between 70 and 80 percent in the South fell outside its scope. It was not until 1954, when Republicans controlled the White House, the Senate, and the House of Representatives, and southern Democrats finally lost much of their power, that these exclusions were eliminated. Even then, notes Katznelson, African Americans were not able to catch up since the program required at least five years of contributions before benefits could be obtained. "Thus," he writes, "for the first quarter century of its existence, Social Security was characterized by a form of policy apartheid, something neither Roosevelt nor his study commission had advocated."[10] As Gunner Myrdal observed in his landmark study of 1944, *An American Dilemma*:

> The economic situation of Negroes in America is pathological. Except for a small minority enjoying upper or middle class status, the masses of American Negroes, in the rural South and in the segregated slum quarters in Southern and Northern cities, are destitute. They own little property; even their household goods are mostly inadequate and dilapidated. Their incomes are not only low but irregular. They thus live from day to day and have scant security for the future.[11]

With the passage of the GI Bill after the war, Black access to White colleges and universities was either restricted or extremely limited and black colleges were overcrowded. As many as 15,000 black veterans could not gain entry and an estimated 50,000 additional African Americans might have sought admission had there been sufficient space.[12] No black college had a doctoral program or a certified engineering program. One study showed that of veterans born between 1923 and 1928, 28 percent of Whites but only 12 percent of Blacks enrolled in college.[13] Blacks were also systematically shut out of the suburban housing boom. They were regularly denied access to loans granted by the GI Bill since the ultimate decision on whether to loan a veteran money rested with banks; the Veterans Administration only guaranteed loans. In the vast majority of cases, financial institutions refused to approve loans to African-Americans. For example, in New York and in the northern New Jersey suburbs, fewer than 100 of the 67,000 mortgages insured by the G.I. bill supported home purchases by non-Whites.[14]

Racist lending practices were encouraged by the FHA, which grew out of the Home Owners' Loan Corporation (HOLC), a government-sponsored entity established in 1933 as part of Roosevelt's New Deal. At the time, half of the nation's mortgage debt was in default, and Roosevelt saw mortgages on single-family homes as forming the "backbone of the American financial system." In its first year, HOLC provided loans on more than a million mortgages and saved 10 percent of homes from foreclosure. However, as Roediger notes, a pillar of the New Deal's strategy was to bring business groups into the national planning process, and the HOLC eagerly sought the advice of real estate industry leaders and appraisers, who were acutely concerned with what they perceived to be a direct relationship between property values and the racial homogeneity of neighborhoods.[15] The result was the development of an elaborate neighborhood rating system, called "redlining," which was inherited by the FHA, whereby the highest value (green) was placed on all White middle class neighborhoods and the lowest value (red) was hung on racially non-White or mixed working-class neighborhoods.

Urban historian Kenneth Jackson describes the system in more detail:

> The first and best grade (green) areas were described as new, homogenous, and "in demand as residential locations in good times or bad." Homogeneous meant "Americans of the better class," and not Jewish, black, or immigrant sections. The second grade (blue) went to "still desirable" areas that had "reached their peak," but were expected to remain stable for many years. The third grade (yellow) neighborhoods were "definitely declining" because of age, obsolescence, or change of style. "Having seen their better days," such yellow-colored sections were "within such a low price or rent range as to attract an undesirable element." Finally, the fourth grade (red) or "hazardous" areas were those "in which the things taking place in [yellow] areas have already happened." Black neighborhoods were invariably rated [red], as were any areas characterized by poor maintenance, poverty, or vandalism.[16]

Redlining warned banks not to lend there, and the FHA would not insure mortgages in such neighborhoods, making it virtually impossible for African-Americans to borrow money for home-improvement or purchase. Because the system was secret, it took the Civil Rights Movement to make these practices public. Of the racism that the FHA enabled, Charles Abrams wrote in 1955:

> A government offering such bounty … could have required compliance with a nondiscrimination policy. Or the agency could at least have pursued a course of evasion, or hidden behind the

screen of local autonomy. Instead, FHA adopted a racial policy that could well have been culled from the Nuremberg laws. From its inception FHA set itself up as the protector of the all-white neighborhood. It sent its agents into the field to keep Negroes and other minorities from buying houses in White neighborhoods.[17]

The FHA played an enormous role in promoting segregation. For instance, it actively promoted restrictive neighborhood covenants, which before World War II prohibited sales of homes to Jews and Catholics, as well as African-Americans. Even after these covenants were outlawed by the Supreme Court in 1948, FHA underwriting manuals continued to insist on racially homogenous neighborhoods. The result was the effective exclusion of African Americans from the suburbanization that was gripping the White working class.[18] An article in *Harpers* describes the situation of one Black GI: "On his way to the base each morning, Sergeant Smith passes an attractive air-conditioned, FHA-financed housing project. It was built for service families. Its rents are little more than the Smiths pay for their shack. And there are a half a dozen vacancies, but none for Negroes."[19]

Because of these FHA policies, the vast majority of federally insured mortgages went to middle-class suburbs, resulting in a near complete disinvestment in largely black urban neighborhoods. As an example, an analysis of the mortgage insurance activity in the suburban county of St. Louis compared to the city of St. Louis found that during the 1950's, when tens of thousands of tract homes were built in the suburbs, the disparity between city and suburb assistance was startling: by 1960, almost 63,000 loan guarantees had been made in the county in contrast to only 12,000 in the city. In terms of dollars, the county received $559 million or $794 per capita, while the city received $94 million or $126 per capita. In other words, the suburbs of St. Louis received about six times as much assistance from FHA as did the city.[20] The study concludes that "the net effect of the FHA-VA mortgage insurance efforts was to facilitate the movement of white, middle-class families out of the [urban] core at the same time that public housing projects were institutionalizing the high-rise slum in the center of the city."[21]

Still, there was more at work besides the availability of affordable housing that drove Whites to live in the suburbs. As Guglielmo observes in his study of Italians in Chicago, many began to move when their older ethnic neighborhoods began to "change"; in other words, when "even the smallest number of African Americans entered these areas." The in-migration of Blacks during the war was explosive, and black neighborhoods, prevented from expanding because of residential restrictions, began to "burst at the seams." The result was that many African Americans increasingly crossed the color lines and settled into largely Italian neighborhoods. Guglielmo writes:

> Disturbed by these population shifts, many Italians moved fast. One woman from the Near North Side recalled that in the 1930s "The Blacks started moving in there and we had to get out, because it – I don't know – it smelled so." Similarly, an Italian man from the West Side remembered that "the reason we get out of there [was that] it was getting black. Understand? It was getting black." An Italian woman from Harmer Street put it most succinctly: she moved from the neighborhood in 1944 because "The black people that were … in that neighborhood were very bad." Given these attitudes, it can hardly be coincidental that virtually every area into which large numbers of Italians moved … had minuscule African-American populations.[22]

According to historian Rudolph Vecoli, when the United States entered the Second World War in December 1941, ethnic politics took a radical new turn. Cultural differences were subordinated to the common purpose of winning the war, and then, to containing the threat of communism. Deviations from what were viewed as the American norm were seen as "suspect" and even "subversive." Vecoli writes that "unqualified loyalty was once again made the hallmark of Americanism." In the 1950s, the postwar economic boom seemed to validate the "triumph of a homogeneous, middle-class society," which emphasized "consensus as the genius of the American political tradition." At the same time, the perspective of American history changed. The prevailing view was that Americans had always agreed on basic values, and differences of class and ethnicity were downplayed as having been the source of conflicts in the past.[23]

Perhaps nothing exemplified white, middle-class suburban conformity more than the post-war Levittowns, communities of 900- to 1,000-square-foot houses, developed by Bill Levitt and his company, Levitt and Sons, with FHA and VA guaranteed loans, in Long Island, and later in Pennsylvania, New Jersey, and Puerto Rico. In her book *How Jews Became White Folks*, anthropologist Karen Brodkin describes the typical Levittowners:

> Most … looked just like my family. They came from New York City or Long Island; about 17 percent were military, from nearby Mitchell Field; Levittown was their first house, and almost everyone

was married. Three-quarters of the 1947 inhabitants were White collar, but by 1950 more blue collar families had moved in, so that by 1951, "barely half" of the new residents were White collar.... By 1960 ... almost one-third of Levittown's people were either foreign-born or, like my parents, first-generation U.S. born.[24]

Not surprisingly, nearly all Levittowners were White. In fact, as late as 1960, out of 15,741 houses and 65,276 people, only 220 Levittowners were nonwhite. In 1958, at a press conference to open his New Jersey development, Levitt announced that he would not sell to a Black buyer; there had been a White riot when a Black family moved into his Pennsylvania Levittown a few years earlier. However, he was sued, as the state of New Jersey prohibited discrimination in federally subsidized housing, and he was ultimately persuaded to integrate.[25] In his notable 1967 work, *The Levittowners*, sociologist Herbert Gans, described the racial homogeneity he encountered while conducting his research:

> The one element missing on most Levittown blocks ... is the presence of Negro families. Although young Negro women came from nearby Burlington to work as maids, there were only two Negro families in the three neighborhoods built before Levittown's integration, and about fifty in the three built since then. Most Levittown children are unlikely to see any Negroes around them and will not have real contact with them until they enter junior high school.[26]

Ultimately, the governmentally sanctioned segregation of those with Black and White skin, a societal trend toward conformity, and the dissolution of ethnic barriers led to the creation of a firmly rooted White identity, one that would have a lasting legacy.

NOTES

1. Dinnerstein, Leonard. "Jews and the New Deal." *American Jewish History*, Vol. 72, No. 4, (June 1983), 464.
2. Butsch, Richard. "American Movie Audiences of the 1930s," *International Labor and Working-Class History*. No. 59, (Spring, 2001), 111.
3. Weiss, Richard. "Ethnicity and Reform: Minorities and the Ambience of the Depression Years," *The Journal of American History*. Vol. 66, No. 3 (Dec., 1979), 578.

4. Kiser, Clyde V. "Cultural Pluralism," *Annals of the American Academy of Political and Social Science*. Vol. 262, Reappraising Our Immigration Policy (Mar., 1949), 128.
5. Massey, Douglas S. "The New Immigration and Ethnicity in the United States," *Population and Development Review*. Vol. 21, No. 3 (Sep., 1995), 636.
6. Ibid., 637.
7. Barone, Michael. Our Country: The Shaping of America from Roosevelt to Reagan. (New York, NY: The Free Press, 1992), 197.
8. Brodkin, Karen. *How Jews Became White Folks and What That Says About Race in America*. (New Brunswick, NJ: Rutgers University Press, 2004), 46.
9. Katznelson, Ira. *When Affirmative Action Was White: An Untold History of Racial Inequality in Twentieth-Century America*. (New York, NY: W.W. Norton & Company, 2006), 121.
10. Ibid., 42.
11. Myrdal, Gunnar. *An American Dilemma, Volume 1: The Negro Problem and Modern Democracy*. (Piscataway, NJ: Transaction Publishers, 1995), 205.
12. Katznelson, 132.
13. Ibid., 133.
14. Ibid., 140.
15. Roediger, David R. *Working toward Whiteness: How America's Immigrants Became White*. (New York: Basic Books, 2005), 227.
16. Jackson, Kenneth T. "Federal Subsidy and the Suburban Dream: The First Quarter-Century of Government," *Records of the Columbia Historical Society*. Washington, D.C., Vol. 50, (1980), 421–451.
17. Abrams, Charles. *Forbidden Neighbors: A Study of Prejudice in Housing*. (Port Washington, NY: Associated Faculty Pr Inc, 1955), 214.
18. Brodkin, 49.
19. Brodkin, 48.
20. Jackson, 435.
21. Ibid., 448.
22. Guglielmo, 148.
23. Vecoli, Rudolph J. "Return to the Melting Pot: Ethnicity in the United States in the Eighties," *Journal of American Ethnic History*. Vol. 5, No. 1 (Fall, 1985), 10.
24. Brodkin, 45.
25. Ibid., 47.
26. Gans, Herbert J. *The Levittowners: Ways of Life and Politics in a New Suburban Community*. (New York, NY: Vintage Books, 1969), 169.

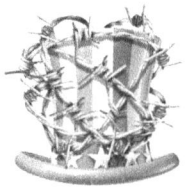

5

CRACKS IN THE WHITE WALL

IN THE 1960s, liberation movements, fueled by the war in Vietnam, urban ghetto riots, and student demonstrations, brought Blacks, Chicanos, Native Americans, women, and gays out of the shadows and introduced the idea of diversity to the White male-dominant, culture.

Writes Vecoli, "With loss of faith in the American Creed and loss of confidence in the Anglo-American establishment, the essential pluralism of the society manifested itself. The lid was off, and all those groups which felt oppressed, stifled, excluded from power and history asserted themselves." The children of the last wave of immigrants were still largely blue-collar, and they were resentful of the stigmatization suffered by their parents because of the new social policies, which seemed to favor Blacks and other minorities. Vecoli continues:

> To the "White ethnics" it appeared that black demands were directed at "their" schools, "their" jobs, and "their" neighborhoods, and that they were being forced to compensate Blacks for a history of oppression in which they had had no part. Because of this "backlash," they were denounced as "fascist pigs" and racists. By the 1970s, "White ethnicity" had been rediscovered by foundations, government agencies, and universities as a problem to be addressed."[1]

In April 1969, *New York* magazine writer Pete Hamill captured the essence of White ethnic resentment in an article titled "The Revolt of the White Lower Middle Class":

> Here comes the murderous rabble: fat, well-fed, bigoted, ignorant, an army of beer-soaked Irishmen, violence-loving Italians, hate-filled Poles, Lithuanians and Hungarians (they are never referred to as Americans). They are the people who assault peace marchers, who start groups like the Society for the Prevention of Negroes Getting Everything (S.P.O.N.G.E.), the people who hate [New York City Mayor] John Lindsay and vote for George Wallace, presumably because they believe that Wallace will eventually march every black man in America to the gas chambers, sending Lindsay and the rest of the Liberal Establishment along with them. Sometimes these brutes are referred to as "the ethnics" or "the blue-collar types." But the bureaucratic, sociological phrase is White Lower Middle Class. Nobody calls it the Working Class anymore.[2]

Countless Whites were resentful of demands made by minorities on the government. They were outraged by what they saw as the expansion of the welfare rolls resulting from Johnson's Great Society. Unemployment was high, particularly in the construction trades, and many White blue-collar workers were struggling to get by. They saw government as being on the side of minorities, ignoring the plight of working Whites.

In May of 1970, thousands of construction workers in New York City demonstrated their frustration by organizing "hard hat rallies." Wearing their construction helmets and waving American flags, the workers marched almost daily throughout the month, proclaiming their support of Nixon's policy in Vietnam. Prodded by the "Black Pride" movement in the early 1970s, there was heightened ethnic consciousness among Whites, and buttons and bumper stickers, such as "Kiss me, I'm Irish," "Ukrainian is Beautiful," and "Slovak Power," proliferated. Alex Haley's seminal book *Roots* gave force to genealogy, and pilgrimages to Ireland, Sicily, and Israel became standard fare for Whites in search of their family background. In academia, Black Studies programs fueled a movement for "ethnic studies," and in 1972, Congress established the Ethnic Heritage Studies Program, which declared that its purpose was to "afford students opportunities to learn about the nature of their own cultural heritage, and to study the contributions of the cultural heritages of the other ethnic groups of the Nation." Writes Vecoli, "For the first time, the federal government affirmed the positive value of understanding about the differing and unique contributions to the national heritage made by each ethnic group."³

In 1971, Michael Novak, a third-generation Slovak American, published *The Rise of the Unmeltable Ethnics*, a highly controversial but popular book, which became a manifesto for the White ethnic movement. It was, in large part, a response to the Civil Rights Movement and the growing vocalism of non-Whites, whom Novak saw as cornering the market on claims to having been oppressed. Novak declared the 1970s to be the "decade of the ethnics," and he praised family-centered ethnic Catholics, whom he compared to sterile and classist WASPS. The book spoke directly to the anxiety and anger of groups that felt they were missing out, despite the decades of discrimination and exclusion they had suffered. Quoting a Chicago worker, Novak wrote:

> The liberals always have despised us. We've got these mostly little jobs, and we drink beer and, my God, we bowl and watch television, and we don't read. It's goddamn vicious snobbery. We're sick of all these phony integrated TV commercials with these upper-class Negroes. We know they're phony. The only time a Pole is mentioned, it's to make fun of him. He's Ignatz Dumbrowski, 274 pounds and 5-foot-4, and he got his education by writing into a firm on a matchbook cover. But what will we do about it? Nothing, because we're the new invisible man, the new whipping boy, and we still think the measure of a man is what he does and how he takes care of his children and what he's doing in his own home, not what he thinks about Vietnam.⁴

In 1980, Ronald Reagan was elected president in a kind of "counter-reformation," and a reassertion of "traditional" American values, opposing such issues as affirmative action, abortion, gay rights, gun control, and the Equal Rights Amendment. A "crusading moralism" took hold, which manifested in pressures toward conformity to conservative ideas and values. Part and parcel of this movement was what Vicoli calls a voltafaccia from the ethnic revival of the seventies to a return to a melting pot mentality of the 1950s. Historian John Higham proclaimed in 1982 that "the ethnic revival is over, and an era in ethnic studies has come to an end."

By 1980, most of the offspring of early twentieth century immigrants were either third- or fourth-generation Americans, and as a result of extensive intermarriage, they were increasingly of mixed origins. Over half of those reporting Polish, Russian,

Czech, or Hungarian ancestry in the 1980 census were of mixed parentage; and the rate of intermarriage was 60 percent for women of Italian and Russian origin, 70 percent for Polish women, 83 percent for Czech women, and 88 percent for Hungarian women. White Americans began to lose contact with their immigrant origins. They stopped regularly consuming ethnic foods, experienced little or no discrimination, and were largely uninvolved and uninterested in ethnic politics. They were unlikely to be members of any ethnic social or political organization and tended not to live in ethnic neighborhoods. Though tens of millions of White Americans identified ethnically, the percentage calling themselves "American" or "nothing at all" was rising.[5]

Though Jews lagged behind in terms of intermarriage, an idea that was anathema to those of my parents' generation, in 1990, the National Jewish Population Survey found that 52 percent of American Jews who had married in the previous five years had chosen non-Jewish spouses. However, as historian Eric L. Goldstein notes, there followed "a flurry of community mobilization that showed just how worried many American Jews were" about the new trend, and philanthropists spent millions on programs to send unaffiliated college-aged Jews to Israel in order to bolster their Jewish identity.[6] Despite that more than half of American Jews denounced opposition to intermarriage as "racist," a 2001 survey by the American Jewish Committee revealed that a plurality – 40 percent – said that "being a part of the Jewish people" was the most important aspect of their identity.[7]

By 1980, sociologists were coming to proclaim that ethnicity, at least for Whites, was fading away. Gans wrote that all that remained would be a "symbolic ethnicity," a "nostalgic allegiance to the culture of the immigrant generation, or that of the old country; a love for and a pride in a tradition that can be felt without having to be incorporated in everyday behavior."[8] Though acknowledging that people "may even sincerely desire to 'return' to these imagined pasts" and realize intellectually that they cannot go back, they may still make the choice to retain it as part of their identities. Writing in 1979, Gans predicted that "if present societal trends continue ... symbolic ethnicity should become the dominant way of being ethnic by the time the fourth generation of the new immigration matures into adulthood, and this in *turn* will have consequences for the structure of American ethnic groups."[9] Two years later, sociologist Richard D. Alba observed the precipitous increase in interethnic and interfaith marriage among White Catholics, and concluded that ethnic identity was in its "twilight." He wrote:

> Ethnicity appears to be nearing twilight among the Catholic ethnic groups whose forebears immigrated to the United States in the nineteenth and early twentieth centuries. And it is a twilight which

may never turn into a night.... But the Catholic ethnic groups, so prominent a feature of the American social landscape for the better part of this century, seem destined as groups to recede into the background, at the same time that many Americans descended from these groups, still tinged by the ethnicity of their ancestors, move into the social heartland of America.[10]

Beginning in the 1980s and taking on full steam in the 1990s, there emerged a new field, "Whiteness Studies," in which scholars attempted to answer such questions as: What does it mean to be White? How has whiteness emerged historically? What is the role of law in defining who is White? How has whiteness been linked to White Privilege? Is confronting whiteness a necessary step in order to bring about social change?[11] Though the questions were not new – W.E.B. Dubois and James Baldwin raised them decades earlier – according to CNN, in 2012, there were dozens of colleges and universities that offered courses in the field. Frequently used as textbooks were Noel Ignatiev's *How the Irish Became White*, Nell Irvin Painter's *The History of White People*, and David Roediger's *The Wages of Whiteness*. Ignatiev, a fellow at Harvard's W.E.B. DuBois Institute, founded the journal *Race Traitor*, which proclaims, "The key to solving the social problems of our age is to abolish the White race, which means no more and no less than abolishing the privileges of the White skin. Until that task is accomplished, even partial reform will prove elusive, because White influence permeates every issue, domestic and foreign, in U.S. society."[12] Speaking in 1997, at the University of Berkeley, Ignatiev declared:

> Whiteness is not a culture. There is Irish culture and Italian culture and American culture – the latter ... a mixture of the Yankee, the Indian, and the Negro (with a pinch of ethnic salt); there is youth culture and drug culture and queer culture; but there is no such thing as White culture. Whiteness has nothing to do with culture and everything to do with social position. It is nothing but a reflection of privilege, and exists for no reason other than to defend it. Without the privileges attached to it, the White race would not exist, and the White skin would have no more social significance than big feet.[13]

According to Matt Wray, a sociologist at Temple University and co-editor of the book *White Trash: Race and Class in America*, "To be White is to be culturally broke. The classic thing White students say when you ask them to talk about who they are is,

'I don't have a culture.' They might be privileged, they might be loaded socioeconomically, but they feel bankrupt when it comes to culture…"[14] Perhaps the reason for this is that in our society, White has become "ubiquitous," to use the words of Toni Morrison, "the unacknowledged norm."[15]

However, in the era of Donald Trump there appears to be an affirmation of White identity, one that in many ways is different from that of the 1960s and 1970s, and other periods in our history. Rather than being an articulation of "ethnic" pride, the rise of Trump and his normalizing of bigotry gives White Americans (at least many who support him) a sense of identity, one they feel may be slipping away. The result, as evidenced by the appeal of Trump's call to "make America great again," is a nostalgic backsliding in attitudes on race among White Americans. White anger based on perceived cultural changes that benefit Blacks and Hispanics seems to be the primary force driving race relations today. It's not an encouraging trend.

One 2015 survey, conducted by the Public Religion Research Institute, paints the landscape in a dispiriting yet predictable way. When answering whether they agree or not that discrimination today against Whites has become as big a problem as discrimination against Blacks and other minorities, 43 percent of Americans agreed. More than half (53 percent) told pollsters American culture and "way of life" have mostly changed for the worse since 1950. The age of respondents was 18 and up, so we can assume that a significant portion of respondents was not alive in the 1950s. But the nostalgia for the 1950s was largely limited to White Americans. Sixty percent of Black Americans and 54 percent of Latinos said American culture has mostly changed for the better since the 1950s.

It is doubtful that White Americans long for big cars with tail fins, but Blacks and Latinos definitely do not. It is not fair to presume that White Americans prefer segregated public facilities and banks that would not loan money to minorities, that they miss the days of redlining neighborhoods or the public lynching of Blacks. It is unlikely that White Americans think Jim Crow was a great cultural achievement. I like to think that the stark reality of old-time racism would make most of today's Americans shudder.

However, not only do White Americans feel nostalgic for a time that they never experienced, they're more likely to be angry about their plight today. A 2016 survey commissioned by NBC and *Esquire*, showed that Whites and Republicans are the angriest Americans. In a response to the question "About how often do you hear or read something in the news that makes you angry?" 73 percent of Whites said they get angry at least once a day, in contrast to 66 percent of Hispanics and 56 percent of Blacks. Seventy-seven percent of Republicans also said they get angry at least once a day, compared to 67 percent of Democrats. *Esquire* concludes:

"Indeed, despite having what many would consider a more legitimate case for feeling angry, black Americans are generally less angry than Whites. Though they take great issue with the way they are treated by both society in general and the police in particular, Blacks are also more likely than Whites to believe that the American dream is still alive."[16]

Circling back to more PRRI survey results, half of White Americans – including 60 percent of the White working class – told researchers that discrimination against Whites has become as big a problem today as discrimination against Blacks and other minorities. Not surprisingly, fewer Latinos (29 percent) and Black Americans (25 percent) agreed. Whites feel the sting of discrimination, even though on every measure of quality of life – overall health, infant mortality, median household earnings, and retirement savings– they fare far better than Black and Hispanic Americans.[17]

Simply put, discrimination against Whites is illusory. But the intensity of their perceived victimization is chilling. What has changed since the 1950s for Whites? Their cultural dominance has slipped. They are aware that America has become a multicultural society, and for the most part, they don't like it. Latinos are gaining influence. Black Lives Matter has become a force to be reckoned with, and millions of Whites don't like it.

Charles Pierce eloquently summed up the reasons for the seemingly nonsensical sense of victimization White Americans feel:

> Now, though, thanks to 50 years of steady drum-beating about how it was in the 1960s in which the country began to slide into decline, and how it was in the 1960s that the power drained away from You in the direction of Them, a culture of victimization has arisen despite all the data proving that the victims in question have not been victimized at all, at least not in comparison to their fellow citizens, anyway. What has victimized them are economic and trade policies that have drained the country of decent paying jobs, the decline of organized labor, and a lot of sleight-of-hand political jibber-jabber that continues to this day. It's just easier to get people to blame each other. And that's what's coming to a head in the country now.

The decline of White cultural dominance and, verifiably, the decline of economic stability for White Americans, as Pierce says, "curdles into a rage that lashes out blindly at all the wrong targets."[18] Those wrong targets are Black and Hispanic Americans and, increasingly and frighteningly, Muslim Americans.

Throughout the first term of his presidency, Trump has continued his racist rhetoric, which seems to appeal so very much to his base. In 2019, the Brookings Institution concluded that Trump's racist rhetoric had led to an increase in violence in America and found "substantial evidence that Trump has encouraged racism and benefitted politically from it."[20] A 2018 study found that "racist resentment and anti-immigrant sentiments proved to be important determinants of a Trump vote.[21] Another study found that "Trump's rhetoric and rallies served to heighten White identity and increase the perceived threat facing White Americans," while counties which hosted a Trump rally saw a 226 percent increase in hate-motivated incidents.[22]

In the summer of 2020, as America faces protests, looting, and a threat by President Donald Trump to employ federal troops to squelch the cries for justice following the police murder of George Floyd, it remains to be seen if we are in the midst of a turning point or if we will continue to be a country saddled by White Privilege and racial division. As I write these words and the world looks on our race problem in horror, the future does not look promising. It may very well be that this nation is going to be, for some time to come, a racial powder keg.

NOTES

1. Vecoli, "Return to the Melting Pot." 12.
2. Hamill, Pete. "The Revolt of the White Lower Middle Class," *New York Magazine*. April 14, 1969, http://nymag.com/news/features/46801/.
3. Vecoli, "Return to the Melting Pot." 12.
4. Novak, Michael. *The Rise of the Unmeltable Ethnics: Politics and Culture in the Seventies*. (New York, NY: Macmillan Publishing, Inc., 1973), 71.
5. Massey, Douglas S. "The New Immigration and Ethnicity in the United States," *Population and Development Review*. Vol. 21, No. 3 (Sep., 1995), 640.
6. Goldstein, Eric L. *The Price of Whiteness: Jews, Race, and American Identity*. (Princeton, NJ: Princeton University Press, 2006), 232.
7. Ibid., 238.
8. Gans, Herbert J. "Symbolic Ethnicity: The Future of Ethnic Groups and Cultures in America," *Ethnic and Racial Studies*. Vol. 2, No. 1, 1979, 9.
9. Ibid., 16.
10. Alba, Richard D. "The Twilight of Ethnicity among American Catholics of European Ancestry," *Annals of the American Academy of Political and Social Science*. Vol. 454, March 1981, 97.

11. Andersen, Margaret L. Eds. Ashley W. Doane and Eduardo Bonilla-Silva, "Whitewashing Race: A Critical Perspective on Whiteness," in *White Out: The Continuing Significance of Racism*. (New York, NY: Routledge, 2003), 22.
12. http://racetraitor.org/.
13. Ignatiev, Noel. "The Point Is Not to Interpret Whiteness But to Abolish It," Talk given at the Conference "The Making and Unmaking of Whiteness." University of California, Berkeley, April 11–13, 1997, http://racetraitor.org/abolishthepoint.pdf.
14. Hsu, Hua. "The End of White America?" *The Atlantic*, January/February 2009. http://www.theatlantic.com/magazine/archive/2009/01/the-end-of-white-america/307208/.
15. Andersen, 24.
16. "American Rage: The Esquire/NBC News Survey," *Esquire*. January 3, 2016, http://www.esquire.com/news-politics/a40693/american-rage-nbc-survey/.
17. Public Religion Research Institute.
18. "The Powder Keg: The Seething Racial Resentment of the Obama Era Is Of An Altogether Different Kind," *Esquire*. November 24, 2015, http://www.esquire.com/news-politics/politics/news/a39987/america-race-powderkeg/.
19. "KKK, American Nazi Party Praise Trump's Hiring of Bannon," *The Hill*. November 14, 2016, http://thehill.com/blogs/blog-briefing-room/305912-kkk-american-nazi-party-praise-trumps-hiring-of-bannon.
20. Williamson, Vanessa and Isabella Gelfand. "Trump and Racism: What Do the Data Say." The Brookings Institution, August 14, 2019, https://www.brookings.edu/blog/fixgov/2019/08/14/trump-and-racism-what-do-the-data-say/.
21. Hooghe, Marc and Ruth Dassonnevill. "Explaining the Trump Vote: The Effect of Racist Resentment and Anti-Immigrant Sentiments," *American Political Science Association*. July 2018, 528–34.
22. Feinberg, Aval, Regina Branton, and Valerie Martinez-Ebers. "Counties That Hosted a 2016 Trump Rally Saw a 226 percent Increase in Hate Crimes," *The Washington Post*. March 22, 2019, https://www.washingtonpost.com/politics/2019/03/22/trumps-rhetoric-does-inspire-more-hate-crimes/.

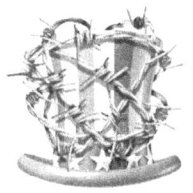

PART 2

AFRICAN AMERICANS

ON THE EVENING of November 4, 2008, President-elect Barack Hussein Obama, flanked by his wife, Michelle, and his daughters, Malia and Sasha, took the stage at Chicago's Grant Park in front of tens of thousands of people, many who shouted "Yes we can!" It was his first address to the nation after winning a decisive victory to become the nation's first African-American to ascend to the highest elected office in the nation. This was no ordinary election, and it had been clear, ever since Obama won the Iowa caucuses, that race would be a key factor.

For many, the election was a symbol of a 400-year struggle, not just for dignity and human rights, but to be fully honored as an essential part of the American quilt.

For some pundits at the time, the election of Barack Obama was the dawning of the age of a post-racial United States. Some imbued the phrase post-racial with different meanings. A common argument was that if Americans can elect a Black man to be president, then the nation has truly arrived and can move on from the racial divisions that have burdened us all. Our national stain has been wiped clean.

Another theory went like this: Obama himself is post-racial. Technically he is biracial, with an African-American father and a White mother (from Kansas), grew up in Hawaii, and spent years in Indonesia. So, the theory goes, he transcends all races and, therefore, may have been, despite his skin color, so above race, so unable to be pinned down to a race, despite those who desperately wanted to pin him down, that Americans saw him not as a Black man, but a man for all races. During the 2008 campaign's waning hours, Jim Hoagland wrote in the *Washington Post*:

> Barack Obama has succeeded brilliantly in casting his candidacy – indeed, his whole life – as post-racial. Even before the votes have been cast, he has written a glorious coda for the civil rights struggle that provided this nation with many of the finest, and also most horrible, moments of its past 150 years. If the results confirm that race was not a decisive factor in the balloting, generations of campaigners for racial justice and equality will have seen their work vindicated.[1]

During the campaign, Obama did not emphasize his race or race in general. Even as controversy surrounded comments made by Obama's pastor, Reverend Jeremiah Wright, threatened to derail his candidacy, Obama gave, in Philadelphia, one of the best speeches of his life, one that many called his "race speech." Still, even then, the speech retained an ample helping of post-racial motif.

> I have brothers, sisters, nieces, nephews, uncles and cousins, of every race and every hue, scattered across three continents, and for as long as I live, I will never forget that in no other country on Earth is my story even possible.[2]

Every race and every hue, just like America. Obama, in his introduction to Americans four years earlier, as a keynote speaker at the Democratic National Convention in 2004, said:

> There is not a White America and a black America and a Latino America and an Asian America. There is the United States of America.[3]

It was a brilliant speech, one that cast Obama as a candidate who would transcend race from the start. He couldn't have won without doing so.

In the summer of 2009, when Harvard University professor Henry Louis Gates, a Black man, was arrested in Cambridge, Massachusetts for trying to break and enter his own home, it brought racial profiling back to the national attention. Obama felt pressure to weigh in: "I think we know separate and apart from this incident is that there's a long history in this country of African Americans and Latinos being stopped by law enforcement disproportionately. That's just a fact."[4]

That, plus eight years of some ugly racism, both cloaked and overt, from Obama's detractors, showed that, for a non-White President, still, there's no such thing as non-racial or post-racial.

And then came Ferguson. And Black Lives Matter, a movement that began as a hashtag in 2012, which began capturing what African Americans had been claiming for decades. That they were over-policed, over-profiled, and sometimes murdered. The videos, subsequent protests, and high profile killings of unarmed black men started to reach middle White America with a vengeance.

This growing consciousness, however, has provoked an opposite (though not equal) reaction, like former New York City Mayor Rudy Giuliani defending why the police profile African American men:

> Be very careful of those kids in the neighborhood and don't get involved with them because, son, there's a 99 percent chance they're going to kill you, not the police. And we've got to hear that from the black community. And what we've got to hear from the black community is how and what they are doing among themselves about the crime problem in the black community.[5]

The idea that cops *must* have had a good reason to detain, tackle, tase, arrest, or kill a Black man is a pervasive attitude in White America. But, thanks again to video cameras and social media, the attitude is becoming less pervasive.

So here America stands, in 2020, and we are still awash in bigotry. George Floyd. Ahmaud Arbery. Breonna Taylor. Looting. A president threatening to stifle protests with federal troops and ordering federal law enforcement officers to fire rubber bullets and chemical gas at peaceful protesters outside the White House. Is it 1968 all over again?

No. The riots of the late 1960s unleashed destruction from which some cities never fully recovered. Watts 1965, 34 dead, over 1,000 injured. Detroit 1967, 43 dead, over 1,000 injured. Newark 1967, 26 dead, almost 1,000 injured. The last comparable riot was in Los Angeles, in 1992, in which 55 people died. When we measure civil disorder, political breakdown, assassinations, and death tolls, there is no comparing the late 1960s in the U.S. with today.

However, the divide between police and African-American communities has to decrease. A growing part of White America sees the bias going on and is learning that being an African American man is dangerous, due to the actions of some police officers. And they're starting to understand that the racist biases of those police officers are deep-seated, indeed common, in America.

NOTES

1. "The "Post-Racial Election," *The Washington Post*, November 2, 2008. http://www.washingtonpost.com/wp-dyn/content/article/2008/10/31/AR2008103103360.html.
2. "Barack Obama's Speech on Race," *The New York Times*, March 18, 2008. http://www.nytimes.com/2008/03/18/us/politics/18text-obama.html?_r=0.
3. "Transcript: Illinois Senate Candidate Barack Obama," *The Washington Post*, July 27, 2004. http://www.washingtonpost.com/wp-dyn/articles/A19751-2004Jul27.html.
4. Carbad, Devon W. and Mitu Gulati, *Acting White?: Rethinking Race in "Post-Racial" America*. (Oxford, England: Oxford University Press, 2015), 98.
5. "Rudy Giuliani: Black Fathers Need to Teach Kids 'The Real Danger to Them is not the Police,'" *The Washington Post*. July 11, 2016, https://www.washingtonpost.com/news/post-nation/wp/2016/07/10/rudy-giuliani.

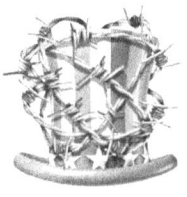

6

SLAVERY AND THE IDEA OF THE "SUPERIOR" CAUCASIAN RACE

THE ISSUE of slavery rarely comes up in everyday conversation. To have enslaved 12.5 million Africans and shipped them off to the New World is so abhorrent, so grotesque to our modern sensibilities, so opposed to our view of who we Americans are as a people, that it is much easier to avoid the issue. Many Whites consider the mere mention of the word to be divisive, if not potentially explosive. But if we are to ever have an honest dialogue about race, it is a subject that demands being addressed, a story that needs to be recounted.

During the 16th century, the Portuguese established many of the practices for transporting slaves by ship that would be employed across the Americas for the next 300 years. Writes historian David Brion Davis:

> The conditions on transatlantic slave ships ... were probably too horrible to fully convey in human words. The density of packing slaves in the decks between a ship's bottom hold and main deck far exceeded the crowding of indentured servants or even Irish prisoners shipped to the British Caribbean. The males, especially, had to lie like spoons locked together, with no real standing room above them, surrounded by urine and feces, with little air to breathe.

> One would need to turn to the suffering of slaves in ancient Greek silver mines or to the victims of Nazi death camps to find worse or roughly equivalent examples.¹

The first record of slavery in the future United States was in August of 1619, a year before the arrival of the Mayflower, when about 20 people from the Ndongo kingdom, in present-day Angola, arrived in Jamestown.² The Ndongans had been kidnapped by a band of African marauders allied with the Portuguese slave traders on the Atlantic coast at Luanda. They had been part of a larger group heading to Mexico and were taken to Virginia after English privateers captured their Portuguese slave ship.

By 1661, the General Assembly of Virginia legalized slavery; in 1662, it declared that all children born of a slave mother were slaves. In 1691, Virginia passed its first anti-miscegenation law, which forbade intermarriage, declaring that "whatsoever English or other White Man or woman being free shall intermarry with a negroe, mulatto, or Indian man or woman bond or free shall within three months after such marriage be banished and removed from this dominion forever."³ In 1705, with the development of the "slave codes":

> Slaves had no standing in the courts: they could not be a party to a lawsuit; they could not offer testimony, except against another slave or free black; and their irresponsibility meant that their oaths were not binding. Thus, they could make no contracts. The ownership of property was generally forbidden them, though some states permitted slaves to have certain types of personal property. A slave could not strike a White person, even in self-defense; but the killing of a slave, however malicious the act, was rarely regarded as murder. The rape of a female slave was regarded as a crime but only because it involved trespassing.⁴

In the early decades of 17th-century America, there were few differences between Black and White servitude; the terms "slave" and "servant" were used synonymously, and the power of the master over both was nearly total. However, there gradually emerged something new in the conception of the Black servant – the view that he or she did not belong to the community of Christian, civilized Europeans. Historian George M. Fredrickson writes that the enslavement of Africans could be "rationalized as a missionary project," just as had been done with the indigenous people of the Americas. According to Fredrickson: "Skin color probably had relatively little to do with it, except as a means of identification or possibly as an indication of racial Otherness that made it psychologically easier to treat them with the brutality that the slave trade often necessitated."[5]

However, in the view of historian Winthrop D. Jordan, color certainly played a role. The English, he notes were most intrigued by the blackness of Africans, and travelers "rarely failed to comment upon it."[6] Color set the stage for the perception that there was a profound sense of difference between Blacks and Whites, which "seemed to set the Negro apart." According to Jordan:

> Virtually every quality in the Negro invited pejorative feelings. What may have been his two most striking characteristics, his heathenism and his appearance, were probably prerequisite to his complete debasement. His heathenism alone could never have led to permanent enslavement since conversion easily wiped out that failing.
>
> If his appearance, his racial characteristics, meant nothing to the English settlers, it is difficult to see how slavery based on race ever emerged, how the concept of complexion as the mark of slavery ever entered the colonists' minds …
>
> [However], blackness itself did not urge the complete debasement of slavery. Other qualities – the utter strangeness of his language, gestures, eating habits, and so on – certainly must have contributed to the colonists' sense that he was very different, perhaps disturbingly so.[7]

There was also the religious rationale for enslaving Africans, based on the myth of the Curse of Ham, the founder of Canaan in the book of Genesis. Ham, the son of Noah, drew the wrath of God when he saw his father in a naked and drunken state and, according to some commentaries, laughed at his father's shameful condition. As a result, God uttered the words "Cursed be Canaan; a servant of servants shall he be unto his brethren.[8] The story was likely used by the ancient Hebrews to justify their subjugation of the Canaanites. However, among medieval Arabs importing slaves from East Africa to the Middle East, Ham was believed to be the ancestor of Africans, and the result of the curse was a blackening of the skin. This myth easily found its place in Europe and, later, among American slaveholders looking for a biblical justification of slavery.[9]

By the late 17th century, the idea of racial differences, whereby human beings were understood to possess discrete physical types and unequal moral and intellectual capacities, had been fairly well established. Racial categories were, by no means, universal. In Spanish and Portuguese America, an intricate system of racial classification developed, and compared with the British and French, the Spanish and Portuguese were much more tolerant of racial mixing, an attitude that was encouraged by a shortage of European women. They recognized a wide range of racial gradations, including Black, mestizo, quadroon, and octoroon. By contrast, the United States adopted a rigid two-category system of racial categorization in which any person with black blood was to be considered a "negro."[10]

It seems ironic that at the height of the Enlightenment, and with it the widespread acceptance of the idea of human egalitarianism and meritocracy, that the idea of a superior "Caucasian race" took hold. However, the Enlightenment brought with it the assumption that science offered answers to all that could be pondered, and thinkers in the emergent field of ethnography sought to explain and justify inequalities brought on by the end of feudalism, as well as slavery and the European colonization of Asia, Africa, and the Americas. According to science historian, Kenan Malik, it is not race that gives rise to inequality but inequality that gives rise to race.[11]

By the late 18th century, texts citing black inferiority based on studies of human anatomy and physiology proliferated. One such author, an English surgeon and member of the Royal Society, Dr. Charles White, was fascinated by what he saw as the downward progression of skull capacity, with Europeans possessing the most ample skulls, followed by Asians, American Indians, Blacks, "orang-outans," and monkeys. Writes Jordan:

> The Negro's skull, [White] announced, had a smaller capacity than the European's. The Negro possessed longer arms, thicker skin, rancor smell, shorter lifespan in earlier maturation, larger breasts, and "gibbous" legs. Negroes excelled Europeans, on the other hand, in certain areas where apes excelled man – seeing, hearing, smelling, and memory.[12]

The idea of black inferiority had become firmly entrenched by the time of the American Revolution. But the irony of fighting for independence while holding Blacks as slaves was not missed by all. Mrs. John Adams, for example, wrote her husband in 1774, "It always appeared a most iniquitous scheme to me to fight ourselves for what we are daily robbing and plundering from those who have as good a right to freedom as we have."[13] Others, such as Thomas Jefferson, had a complex relationship with slavery. Historians now accept that he had a long-term relationship with Sally Hemings, a slave at Monticello, and justifying the Revolution, he condemned the British for sponsoring the slave trade to the colonies. In 1778, under his leadership, Virginia banned importing slaves. As president, Jefferson led the effort to criminalize the international slave trade that took effect in 1808. Yet his musings in his *Notes on the State of Virginia*, written in 1781, reveal a fascination with the physical differences of Blacks as compared to Whites:

> The first difference which strikes us is that of colour. Whether the black of the negro resides in the reticular membrane between the skin and scarf-skin, or in the scarf-skin itself; whether it proceeds from the colour of the blood, the colour of the bile, or from that of some other secretion, the difference is fixed in nature, and is as real as if its seat and cause were better known to us …?
>
> Besides those of colour, figure, and hair, there are other physical distinctions proving a difference of race. They have less hair on the face and body. They secrete less by the kidnies, and more by the glands of the skin, which gives them a very strong and disagreeable odour. This greater degree of transpiration renders them more tolerant of heat, and less so of cold, than the Whites.[14]

As the "peculiar institution" took hold, leaders of the enlightenment looked to science to explain away the barbarism happening in front of their eyes. Two distinct theories emerged. The first, called monogenesis, held, that humans were of a single origin, as proclaimed in the Old Testament; the second, polygenesis, postulated that different human "species" came into being independently. Polygenesis would not take hold in the United States until much later, by about the mid-19th century, when an "American School of Ethnology" brought "scientific" evidence to support the claim that the nation's three main races, Whites, Blacks, and Native Americans, belonged to very different and unequal species. Writes Franklin:

> All slaves belonged to a degraded, "inferior" race; and, by the same token, all Whites, however wretched some of them might be, were superior. In a society where race was so important, the Whites at the lowest rung could satisfy themselves because they could identify themselves with the most privileged of the community.[15]

The idea of inferiority grew as a direct response to demands for emancipation, particularly when suffrage was extended to all White males, and there was a need to make White domination and Black subservience seem "natural and unavoidable."[16] A staunch observer of the early Republic was Alexis de Tocqueville, a Frenchman and ardent believer in democracy; his book *Democracy in America*, written in 1835 with a second edition published in 1840, offers a penetrating glimpse of America's racial situation. Writing of the "three races," he observes:

> Among these widely differing families of men, the first that attracts attention, the superior in intelligence, in power, and in enjoyment, is the white, or European, the MAN pre-eminently so called, below him appear the Negro and the Indian.... Both of them occupy an equally inferior position in the country they inhabit; both suffer from tyranny; and if their wrongs are not the same, they originate from the same authors.[17]

The idea of emancipation struck both fear and repugnance in the hearts of Whites. A staunch belief in Black inferiority made Whites, particularly in the South, recoil at the prospect of co-mingling with Blacks, and their revulsion was fortified by the fear that Blacks nurtured deep vengefulness that would make them a dangerous presence. The idea of a race war was ubiquitous in the minds of both Northerners and Southerners, and some Whites, including Jefferson, speculated on the possibility of combining emancipation with the colonization of Blacks outside the United States.[18] As Jefferson put it, it would be impossible "to incorporate the Blacks into the state" because of "deep-rooted prejudices entertained by the Whites; ten thousand recollections by the Blacks of the injuries they have sustained; the real distinctions nature has made; and many other circumstances will divide us into parties, and produce convulsions, which will probably never end but in the extermination of one or the other race."[19]

A half-century later, Tocqueville wrote of the deep foreboding that Whites had toward emancipation. He presciently observed:

> If I were called upon to predict the future, I should say that the abolition of slavery in the South will in the common course of things, increase the repugnance of the White population for the Blacks. I base this opinion upon the analogous observation I've already made of the North. I have remarked that the White inhabitants of the North avoid the Negroes with increasing care in

proportion as the legal barriers of separation are removed by the legislature; and why should not the same result take place in the South? In the North, the Whites are deterred from intermingling with the Blacks by an imaginary danger; in the South, where the danger would be real, I cannot believe the fear would be less.[20]

The legal status of Blacks was settled in 1857 by the United States Supreme Court in the case of *Dred Scott v. Sandford*. Scott had been a slave who had lived in the free state of Illinois and the free territory of Wisconsin before moving back to Missouri, where he was enslaved. He appealed to the Supreme Court in hopes of obtaining his freedom. The Court, led by Chief Justice Roger B. Taney, declared that all Blacks – slaves as well as free – could not be American citizens and, therefore, had no standing to sue in federal court, based on the reasoning that the framers of the Constitution had assumed that Blacks had "no rights which the White Man was bound to respect." Abolitionists were enflamed, as there was no denying that slavery was based on anything other than an insidious racism.[22]

When the Civil War ended in 1865, 4 million African Americans were free, and among the most pressing needs of the government, apart from mending the social and economic fabric of a nation that had been ripped asunder, was what to do with them. In 1865 and 1866, Southerners began to take charge and instituted a series of Black Codes that bore a marked similarity to the Slave Codes extant before the war. When it became evident that President Andrew Johnson was going to sanction White rule in the South, Republicans in the north were outraged, which ultimately led to his impeachment on February 24, 1868. The end result was passage of the Reconstruction Act of 1867, one of the most dramatic changes in American history. As a result, there were Black members of Congress, lieutenant governors, sheriffs, prosecuting attorneys, and even an interim governor, C.C. Antoine, who served 43 days in Louisiana in 1873 when his predecessor was removed from office. Teachers came from the North in large numbers to teach Blacks, and the Freedmen's Bureau assisted former slaves by supplying medical services and supplies, establishing schools, and leasing land to former slaves at affordable price. Significantly, the 14th Amendment, ratified in 1868, wrote equal citizenship for all people born in the United States, except non-taxed Indians, into the Constitution.[21]

Writes author Douglas A. Blackmon, "The destruction of slavery in the Civil War … made more transparent the fundamental question of whether Blacks and Whites could ever cohabit peacefully – of whether American Whites in any region could recognize African-Americans as humans.[22] Segregation remained the norm, even at the highest echelons of Black society. Historian Douglas R. Egerton writes, "So common was racial exclusion from elegant hotels, that when Sarah Wall Langston, the future [Black] congressman's mixed race wife, returned to Manhattan from Haiti and was escorted to a dinner table by the ship's captain, White guests assumed she was Cuban. Her husband heard two well-to-do women speculating as to her ethnicity, and when one insisted that Sarah was Black, the other remarked: 'Why, they wouldn't let a Nigger into this hotel and into the dining room.' "[23]

NOTES

1. Davis, David Brion. *Inhuman Bondage: The Rise and Fall of Slavery in the New World*. (Oxford, England: Oxford University Press, 2008), 91.
2. Painter, Nell Irvin. *Creating Black Americans: African-American History and Its Meanings, 1619 to the Present*. (Oxford, England: Oxford University Press, 2006).
3. Law Library of Congress. http://memory.loc.gov/ammem/awhhtml/awlaw3/slavery.html.
4. Franklin, John Hope and Alfred A. Moss, Jr. *From Slavery to Freedom: A History of African Americans*. (New York, NY: McGraw-Hill, Inc., 1994), 124.
5. Fredrickson, George M. *Racism: A Short History*. (Princeton, NJ: Princeton University Press, 2002), 29.
6. Jordan, Winthrop D. *The White Man's Burden: Historical Origins of Racism in the United States*. (Oxford, England: Oxford University Press, 1974), 3.
7. Jordan, Winthrope D. *White Over Black: American Attitudes toward the Negro, 1550–1812*. (New York, NY: W. W. Norton & Co Inc., 1977), 97.
8. Genesis, 9:20–27.
9. Fredrickson, *Racism: A Short History*, 43.
10. Jordan, Winthrop D. "Historical Origins of the One-Drop Rule in the United States," *Journal of Critical Mixed Race Studies*. Vol. 1, No. 1, 2014.
11. Malik, Kenan. *The Meaning of Race: Race, History and Culture in Western Society*. (New York, NY: New York University Press, 1996) 39.
12. Jordan, *The White Man's Burden*, 199.
13. Franklin, John Hope. "The Two Worlds of Race: A Historical View," *Daedalus* 140:1. (Winter, 2011), 35.
14. Jefferson, Thomas. *Notes on the State of Virginia*. (New York, NY: Penguin Classics, 1998), 246.
15. Franklin, John Hope. "Slavery and the Martial South," *The Journal of Negro History*. Vol. 37, No. 1 (Jan., 1952), 51.
16. Frederickson, *Racism: A Short History*, 79.

17. Tocqueville, Alexis de. *Democracy in America*. (Chicago, IL: University of Chicago Press, 2012), 223.
18. Fredrickson, George M. *The Black Image in the White Mind: the Debate on Afro-American Character and Destiny, 1817–1914*. (Middleton, CT: Wesleyan University Press, 1987), 3.
19. Jefferson, 245.
20. Tocqueville, 244.
21. Ibid, 239.
22. Walter Johnson, "No Rights Which the White Man Is Bound to Respect," *Boston Review*, September 27, 2017, http://bostonreview.net/law-justice/walter-johnson-no-rights-which-white-man-bound-respect.
23. Blackmon, Douglas A. *Slavery by Another Name: The Re-Enslavement of Black Americans from the Civil War to World War II*. (New York, NY: Anchor Books, 2009), 20.

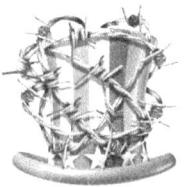

7

JIM CROW AND THE GREAT MIGRATION

IN THE END, Reconstruction was to die a regrettable death. White Southerners were pardoned, restraints were relaxed, and legislation repealed. By the mid-1870s, Republicans were losing their taste for protecting Black rights. Secret societies, the most treacherous being the Ku Klux Klan, sprang up in the South, establishing a reign of terror in parts of the South, assaulting and murdering local Republican leaders, destroying Black crops, houses, and barns, and whipping and lynching many Blacks for voting Republican, or to ensure that they did not vote Republican. Although federal marshals and U.S. troops brought to trial scores of Klansmen, the North's commitment to Blacks had rapidly deteriorated. Many felt that the South should solve its own problems. Additionally, the reports of corruption among Reconstruction officials led many Northerners to the conclusion that Reconstruction had been a mistake, especially as Southern Whites became bolder and more organized, patrolling polling places, ostensibly to ensure "fair, peaceful, and Democratic elections." Increasingly, more Blacks refrained from voting, and political power changed from Republican to Democratic hands.[1]

The final blow to Reconstruction sprang from the hotly contested presidential election between Democrat Samuel J. Tilden and Republican Rutherford B. Hayes. Although Tilden appeared to have won – he garnered 184 electoral votes to Hayes's 165 –, there were twenty electoral votes disputed among four states. An informal deal was struck in the Compromise of 1877, which awarded all 20 electoral votes to Hayes.

In return for the Democrats' acquiescence in Hayes's election, the Republicans agreed to withdraw federal troops from the South. A brief and shining moment in America's history had come to an end.

With the withdrawal of federal troops, Southern Whites proclaimed that "no simian-souled, sooty-skin, kink-curled, blubber-lipped, prehensile-heeled, Ethiopian gorilla shall pollute the ballot box with his leprous vote." With brutal force, literacy requirements, and "grandfather clauses," which restricted voting only to male persons whose fathers and grandfathers were eligible to vote prior to the passage of the Fifteenth Amendment on February 3, 1870, which gave Blacks the right to vote. However, the South was not alone. As the idealism of the Civil War died and racist theories took hold even more strongly than during the time of slavery, Northern newspapers, magazines, and advertisements consistently referred to African-Americans as "nigger, niggah, darkey, coon, pickaninny, mammy, aunt, uncle, buck light-complected-yaller man, yaller hussy."[2]

Once Blacks were disenfranchised, there was no stopping the rise of White supremacy. In 1870, Tennessee enacted laws against the intermarriage of races. Five years later, it adopted the first "Jim Crow" law. Beginning in 1883, Blacks were banned from White hotels, barbershops, restaurants, and theaters. Soon most Southern states had laws requiring separate schools.[3]

On June 7, 1892, in New Orleans, Homer Plessy took a seat in the Whites-only section of a train run by the East Louisiana Railroad railway on a train bound for Covington, Louisiana. When he refused to vacate his seat, the train was stopped, and he was arrested immediately by a detective working for the railway company. In the case, Judge John H. Ferguson ruled that Plessy was guilty for refusing to leave his seat. Four years later, the case made it to the United State Supreme Court. In a landmark decision, *Plessy v. Ferguson*, the Court ruled by a vote of seven to one that state laws requiring racial segregation in public facilities were constitutional under the doctrine of "separate but equal."[4]

Author Isabel Wilkerson vividly describes what it was like to live as a Black person in the Jim Crow South:

> There were days when Whites could go to the amusement park and a day when Blacks would go, if they were permitted at all. There were White elevators and Black elevators (meaning the freight elevators in back); White train platforms and colored train platforms. There were White ambulances and colored ambulances to ferry the sick, and White hearses and colored hearses for those who didn't survive whatever was wrong with them. There were

7 | JIM CROW AND THE GREAT MIGRATION

White waiting rooms and colored waiting rooms in any conceivable place where a person might have to wait for something, from the bus depot to the doctor's office….

Throughout the South, the conventional rules of the road did not apply when a colored motorist was behind the wheel. If he reached an intersection first, he had to let the White motorist go ahead of him. He could not pass a White motorist on the road no matter how slow the White motorist was going and had to take extreme caution to avoid an accident because he would likely be blamed no matter who was at fault. In everyday interactions, a Black person could not contradict a White person or speak unless spoken to first. A Black person could not be the first to offer to shake a White person's hand.[5]

One of the great minds to emerge during this dark period was that of W.E.B. Dubois, a celebrated sociologist, historian, and a prolific author, whose life spanned the years 1868 to 1963. In 1905, he founded the Niagara Movement, a precursor to the National Association for the Advancement of Colored People (NAACP), which called for Blacks to be granted true suffrage, equal economic opportunities, the abolition of all distinctions based on race, and the recognition of the basic principles of human fellowship. Although American racism was Dubois' primary focus – he strongly protested lynching, Jim Crow laws, and discrimination in education and employment –, his cause included people of color everywhere, particularly Africans and Asians in their struggles against colonialism and imperialism. In his essay, *The Study of the Negro Problem*, published in 1898, Dubois wrote:

> So far as the Negro race is concerned, the Civil War simply left us face to face with the same sort of problems of social condition and caste which were beginning to face the nation a century ago. It is these problems that we are today somewhat helplessly – not to say carelessly – facing, forgetful that they are living, growing social questions whose progeny will survive to curse the nation, unless we grapple with them manfully and intelligently.[6]

Yet Dubois' most famous work undoubtedly is his treatise *The Souls of Black Folk*, written in 1903, where he presciently declared that "the problem of the twentieth century is the problem of the color-line." In it, he offers a telling glimpse of rural African-American life with a description of Dougherty County, Georgia, poignantly depicting the legal system and tenant farming system as being only slightly removed from slavery. Importantly, he introduces two concepts that describe the quintessential Black experience in America – the concepts of "the Veil" and "double-consciousness"–, ideas that ring eerily true today. The Veil suggests the inability of Whites to see Blacks as "true" Americans and how Blacks themselves internalize this blindness. Double consciousness refers to the ability of Blacks to see the world through their own eyes, as well as through the eyes of Whites. He writes:

> It is a peculiar sensation, this double-consciousness, this sense of always looking at one's self through the eyes of others, of measuring one's soul by the tape of a world that looks on in amused contempt and pity. One ever feels his twoness – an American, a Negro; two souls, two thoughts, two unreconciled strivings; two warring ideals in one dark body, whose dogged strength alone keeps it from being torn asunder.... He simply wishes to make it possible for man to be both a Negro and an American, without being cursed and spit upon by his fellows, without having the doors of Opportunity closed roughly in his face.[7]

In one of the book's most moving passage, Dubois mourns the loss of his baby son and wonders if his son is not better off dead than growing up in a world dominated by the color-line:

> All that day and all that night there sat an awful gladness in my heart – and my soul whispers ever to me saying, "Not dead, not dead, but escaped; not bound but free." No bitter meanness now shall sicken his baby heart till it dies a living death, no taunt shall madden his happy boyhood ... Well sped, my boy, before the world had dubbed your ambition insolent, had held your ideals unattainable, and taught you to cringe and bow. Better far this nameless void that stops my life than a sea of sorrow for you.[8]

One of the most prevalent images to appear in the early 20th century was the idea of Black men as sexual predators, an image with deep roots in slavery, which persists to the present. According to Fredrickson, racist propaganda, which represented Black males as "raving beasts lusting after White women," was used to rationalize the practice of lynching. Executions of Black men grew increasingly brutal as time went on, and by the early 20th century, victims were likely to be tortured to death rather than simply killed.⁹

In January 1909, Senator William H. Milton of Florida introduced a bill to ban intermarriage, which though ultimately tabled, listed the following as "evidence" that Blacks were members of an inferior race:

- Abnormal length of arms, averaging 2 inches more than the Caucasian.
- Projection of the jaw at a facial angle of 70°, as against 82° for Caucasian.
- Average weight of brain, for gorilla 20 ounces, Negro 35 ounces, European 45 ounces.
- Full black eyes with black iris and yellowish sclerotic coat.
- Short, flat stub nose, depressed at base, broad at the extremity, dilating nostrils, and concave ridge.
- Thick protruding lips showing in a red surface.
- Exceedingly thick cranium enabling him to butt with a head and resist blows that would break an ordinary European skull. Correspondingly weak lower limbs, broad flatfoot, divergent and sometimes prehensile big toe and projecting heal.
- Complexion brown or blackish, due to abundance of coloring matter.
- Short black hair and distinctly woolly.
- Thick epidermis, admitting a peculiar rancid odor.
- Frame of medium height and sometimes out of perpendicular.
- The early ossification of the skull.[10]

By World War I, the full and equal participation in all aspects of American society had been systematically barred, and in the South and parts of the North, Blacks and Whites lived in separate worlds. In the South, Blacks were segregated by law in the public schools while those in the North were sent to predominantly Negro schools. Racist "Sambo" images proliferated in advertisements and games. During the war, note Henry Louis Gates Jr. and Cornel West, "No African-American could serve in a position of authority over White soldiers, or fight by their sides; no Black could participate in professional baseball, the national pastime … Black Americans were routinely lynched with impunity. 'Separate but equal' was the institutional law of the South and the *de facto* law of the land … The future of the race, at the turn-of-the-century, looked rather bleak indeed."[11]

Black soldiers returning from the war were lynched by hanging and burning, often while still in their uniforms. The Ku Klux Klan warned Blacks that they must respect the rights of Whites "in whose country they are permitted to reside." Racial conflicts swept the country, and as a response, Marcus Garvey's Universal Negro Improvement Association, which advocated settling in Africa, grew from a handful of members to an organization numbering in the hundreds of thousands. Writes John Hope Franklin, though Africa was of interest to only a few, membership symbolized a way to "indicate their resentment of the racial duality that seemed to them to be the central feature of the American social order.[12]

THE GREAT MIGRATION

From 1915 until about 1930, the first "Great Migration" of African Americans from the South to the North, transformed the face of America, particularly in cities. In 1914, the cotton market collapsed as U.S. merchants were unable to export goods to Europe due to World War I. Thousands of farmers in the South, Black and White, went out of business. At the same time, the Southern cotton crop was devastated by a boll weevil infestation. Adding insult to injury, the mechanization of agriculture reduced the demand for unskilled Black labor. This coincided with the rise of northern manufacturing and a demand for cheap labor, a need that was exacerbated by the entry of the United States in the war. As a result of these factors and the oppressive conditions of Jim Crow segregation, several million African Americans left their homes and families to begin new lives in the North.

In a letter to the *Chicago Defender*, one reader wrote of her reasons for migrating to the North:

> After twenty years of seeing my people lynched for any offense from spitting on the sidewalk to stealing a mule, I made up my mind that I would turn the prow of my ship towards the part of the country where the people at least made a pretense of being civilized ... When a man's home is sacred; when he can protect the virtue of his wife and daughter against the brutal lust of his alleged superiors; when he can sleep at night without the fear of being visited by the Ku Klux Klan because of refusal to take off his hat while passing an overseer, then I will be willing to return to Mississippi.[13]

Author Richard Wright, who himself moved to Chicago in 1927 as part of the first Great Migration, wrote:

7 | JIM CROW AND THE GREAT MIGRATION

> Perhaps never in history has a more utterly unprepared folk wanted to go to the city; we were barely born as a folk when we headed for the tall and sprawling centers of steel and stone. We, who were landless upon the land; we, who had barely managed to live in family groups; we, who needed the ritual and guidance of institutions to hold our atomized lives together in lines of purpose; we, who have known only relationships to people and not relationships to things; we who had never belonged to any organizations except the church and burial societies; we, who had our personalities blasted with 200 years of slavery and had been turned loose to shift for ourselves – we were such a folk as this when we moved into a world that was destined to test all we were, that threw us into the scales of competition to weigh our mettle.[14]

Although there were no Jim Crow laws in the North, the migrants found social conditions there to be little different from what they were fleeing in the South. Although the "etiquette" of Jim Crow was absent, many facets of Northern life were highly discriminatory toward Blacks, and the treatment they received was often just as humiliating and brutal as anything they had known in the South. According to historian Jerrold M. Packard:

> Sadly, if predictably, the Blacks who surged into the North cities changed White Northerners' perception of these communities' racial equations, leading Whites to see what had before been a "stable" situation as now a "problem." Not only were the new black migrants dramatically less educated than those who lived in the north, they were suddenly viewed as rivals for the low-paying jobs held by poorly educated Whites and, even more dangerously, were sometimes suspected as potential strikebreakers. The result was vastly increased racial tension in the North, more discrimination and racism, and all too often, racial disturbances leading to rioting and mass murder.[15]

The percentage of Blacks living in the north increased from 11 percent in 1910 to 23 percent in 1940. Still, as Barone writes, "What is remarkable about the period from the Civil War to World War II is not how many Southern Blacks and Whites moved to the North, but how few did." One factor was that southern plantation owners were desperate to maintain their supply of cheap labor, and they did everything in their power to discourage Blacks from heading north. Countless Blacks were arrested near train stations for vagrancy and put in jail.[16] Still, it would take World War II to spur the second great migration. Massive increases in defense production, as well as the military draft implemented in 1939, created a tremendous need for labor. Unemployment, which had never fallen below 16 percent during the Great Depression and had reached as high as 22 percent, fell to 5 percent in 1942 and between 1 and 2 percent during the war. Yet the Northern pull was more than economic. It offered an escape from Jim Crow and what had been decades of violence, degradation, and humiliation. Northern migration came to be seen as an "exodus," and the North was a "promised land." Black newspapers and magazines, such as the *Chicago Defender* and *Ebony*, "portrayed an abusive South and inviting North." In their hands, the North became a place where:

> ... Blacks were treated as equals, for Black men were not referred to as "boy" or "uncle," where a taboo that they could enter Whites' homes only by the back door was unheard of. Blacks could shake hands with Whites in the north, they could ride with them in the front of buses, they could wait in lines without being shunted to the back, and they could eat at restaurants with Whites and carouse in nightclubs with them, too. They would be free as well from the constant threat of violence, violence that was sanctioned by those who rule the community if they fail to live up to the unwritten code.[17]

Perhaps nothing could have catalyzed African-American resistance to Jim Crow more than the Second World War. Nearly a million served in the segregated armed forces. Yet interaction with Whites was frequent, and often non-servile in nature. Black veterans expected to return to a country whereby the old standards of White supremacy and Black submissiveness would dissolve, and their service had enabled the NAACP to press for the courts and legislature to end racial discrimination. Indeed, progress had begun even before the war. In the 1938 Supreme Court case *Gaines v. Missouri*, the 8-1 decision delivered by Chief Justice Charles Evans Hughes ruled that states providing a school to White students had to provide in-state education to Blacks as well and called for the admission of Lloyd Gaines to the University of Missouri law school.[18]

However, the North proved to be anything but the Promised Land. Whites were "willing to see Blacks among people generally in stores and shops, and movie theaters, even in restaurants, though not so much in swimming pools or parks."[19] A riot took place in Detroit in June 1943 after a fight between Blacks and Whites broke out at an amusement park on Belle Isle, an island in the Detroit River. By the time President Roosevelt sent in federal troops, rioting had gone on for three days, hundreds had been injured, and 34 people had died, 25 of whom were African American, a majority shot by police.[20]

In June 1941, A. Philip Randolph, the head of the all Black Brotherhood of Sleeping Car Porters, threatened an "all out" March on Washington of tens of thousands of Blacks "to shake up White America." Randolph had founded the porters' union in 1925 when railway unions did not accept Blacks as members. He built an organization of disciplined, literate members who traveled around the country and advocated civil rights. Following Randolph's threat, President Franklin D. Roosevelt issued Executive Order 8802, which created a Fair Employment Practices Committee to eliminate racial discrimination in government hiring. Randolph canceled the march. Yet although the new federal agency did increase the number of Blacks working in federal jobs, the government could not regulate private employers or labor unions.

It was not until July 1948, that President Harry S. Truman, under pressure from Randolph and the NAACP, issued Executive Order 9981, which abolished racial discrimination in the armed forces and eventually led to the end of a segregated military. Remarked Roy Wilkins, Editor of *The Crisis*, the official magazine of the NAACP, "Negroes did not need us at the NAACP to tell them that it sounded pretty foolish to be against park benches marked JUDE in Berlin, but to be for park benches marked colored in Tallahassee Florida." Wilkins wrote in his autobiography, "Negroes were not being sent to any concentration camps, of course, but what a thing to be thankful for."[21]

The Swedish social scientist, Gunnar Myrdal, in his 1944 masterpiece, *An American Dilemma: The Negro Problem and Modern Democracy*, employed research, statistics, and hundreds of interviews with Black People, in order to describe nearly every facet of early twentieth-century Black life. The book was extremely influential, selling over 100,000 copies in 25 printings by 1965, and highlighted the profound conflict between American race relations and the American belief in justice for all. For Myrdal, as the title suggests, the problem was not with Blacks, but rather with Whites, who created the horrendous structural conditions and intractably racist attitudes that Blacks faced, which kept them in a position not that far removed from slavery. "The American Negro problem," writes Myrdal, "is a problem in the heart of the American. It is there that the interracial tension has its focus. It is there that the decisive struggle goes on…. The 'American Dilemma' … is the ever raging conflict between, on the one hand, the valuations preserved on the general plane which we shall call the 'American Creed,' where the American thinks, talks, and acts under the influence of high national and Christian precepts, and, on the other hand ... economic, social, and sexual jealousies."

Myrdal presented a glimpse of Black America to Whites that so many had been blind to. He writes that because of Whites', particularly Northern Whites', lack of intimate contact with Blacks, stereotypes abounded, which led to the view that Blacks are "different" or "peculiar." Writing of Black speech, for example, Myrdal observed that:

> To the Northern White Man ... the speech of the Negro seems unusual. In fact, the "Negro dialect" is an important cause of the Northern Whites' unconscious assumption that Negroes are of a different biological type from themselves. The present writer found many Northern Whites who were amazed when they learned that Negroes could and did speak perfect English. It is not realized that the so-called "Negro dialect" is simply a variation of the ordinary Southern accent which so many Northerners like so well.... There is absolutely no biological basis for it; Negroes are as capable of pronouncing English words as perfectly as Whites are.[22]

Writing of the rampant segregation that he found and the justifications he heard from Whites, Myrdal's observations could just as easily have been taken from so-called colorblind Whites in the 21st century. "I have heard few comments made so frequently," he writes, "and with so much emphasis and so many illustrations as the one that 'Negroes are happiest among themselves' and that 'Negroes really don't want White company but prefer to be among their own race.'" He concluded that "segregation and discrimination are forced upon the Negroes by the Whites [by the] one sidedness of their application. Negroes are ordinarily never admitted to White churches in the South, but if a strange White Man enters a Negro church, the visit is received as a great honor."[23]

A telling story of urban life in the north for Blacks, specifically in Chicago's south side, is *Black Metropolis: A Study of Negro Life in a Northern City*, by John Gibbs St. Clair Drake and Horace Cayton. First published in 1945, the book was the product of years of collaboration between sociologists at the University of Chicago and survey researchers of the New Deal. In the book's original introduction, Richard Wright comments:

7 | JIM CROW AND THE GREAT MIGRATION

To know that a seemingly normal, ordinary American is capable of such brutality implies making a judgment about the nature and quality of our everyday American experiences which most Americans simply cannot do. For, to admit that our individual experiences are of so low a quality in nature as to preclude the deep, organic satisfactions necessary for civilized, peaceful living, is to condemn the system that provides his experiences. It will be but natural for this honest question to be asked by both Whites and Blacks: If the racial scene depicted here is true, if the points of view presented here are valid, if the meetings deduced here are real, then why have we not been told all this before?[24]

NOTES

1. Ibid., 253.
2. Cherniavsky, Michael. "Review of 'The Negro in American Life and Thought: The Nadir, 1877–1901,'" *Political Science Quarterly*. Vol. 70, No. 2, Jun., 1955, 300.
3. Franklin and Moss, 262.
4. *Plessy v. Ferguson*, 163 U.S. 537, http://chnm.gmu.edu/courses/nclc375/harlan.html.
5. Wilkerson, Isabel. *The Warmth of Other Suns: The Epic Story of America's Great Migration*. (New York, NY: Vintage Books, 2011,) 56.
6. Dubois, W.E.B. "The Study of the Negro Problems," *The Annals of the American Academy of Political and Social Science*. Vol. XI, Jan., 1898, 6.
7. Dubois, W.E.B. *The Souls of Black Folk*. (New York, NY: Open Road Media, 2014), 2.
8. Ibid., 100.
9. Frederickson, 5.
10. Logan, Rayford W. *The Betrayal of the Negro: From Rutherford B. Hayes to Woodrow Wilson*. (Cambridge. MA: Da Capo Press, 1997), 365.
11. Gates, Jr., Henry Louis and Cornel West. *The African American Century: How Black Americans Have Shaped Our Country*. (New York, NY: The Free Press, 2000), xii.
12. Franklin, John Hope. "The Two Worlds of Race: A Historical View," *Daedalus* 140:1. (Winter, 2011), 45.
13. Arnesen, Eric. *Black Protest and the Great Migration: A Brief History with Documents*. (New York, NY: Bedford/St. Martin's, 2003), 188.

14. Wright, Richard. *12 Million Black Voices: A Folk History of the Negro in the United States*. (New York, NY: Viking Press, 1941), 93.
15. Packard, Jerrold M. *American Nightmare: The History of Jim Crow*. (New York, NY: St. Martin's Griffin, 2003), 111.
16. Barone, Michael. *Shaping Our Nation: How Surges of Migration Transformed America and Its Politics*. (New York, NY: Crown Forum, 2013, 194/
17. Ibid., 214.
18. Packard, 212.
19. Barone, 214.
20. Ibid.
21. Buckley, Gail Lumet. *American Patriots: The Story of Blacks in the Military from the Revolution to Desert Storm*. (New York, NY: Random House, 2001), 258.
22. Myrdal, Gunnar. *An American Dilemma, Volume II: The Negro Problem and Modern Democracy*. (New York, NY: Harper and Row, 2003), 965.
23. Ibid., 575.
24. Wright, Richard, An American Dilemma, xxvii.

8

FROM CIVIL RIGHTS TO SISTER SOULJAH

IN THE EARLY 1950s, the NAACP brought class action lawsuits on behalf of Black schoolchildren to compel school districts to let Black students attend White public schools. In the most important of these suits, *Brown v. Board of Education of Topeka*, Oliver Brown, a Black parent, claimed that Topeka's racial segregation violated the Constitution's Equal Protection Clause because the city's Black and White schools were not equal to each other and never could be. The federal district court ruled that Topeka's segregated public schools were equal enough to be constitutional under the *Plessy* ruling. Brown appealed to the Supreme Court. On May 17, 1954, Chief Justice Earl Warren read the court's decision. "We come then to the question presented: Does segregation of children in public schools solely on the basis of race, even though the physical facilities and other 'tangible' factors may be equal, deprive the children of the minority group of equal education opportunities? We believe it does."[1]

Assimilation into the White mainstream was hardly the goal of all African Americans of the time. As historian Manning Marable notes, "It would be a mistake to equate the battle against Jim Crow with a cultural affinity for the aesthetics and social norms of the Anglo-Saxon."[2] One non-integrationist movement was the Nation of Islam, born in Detroit during the Great Depression, whose first prophet was a peddler, W.D. Ford, who was succeeded by his chief lieutenant, Elijah Muhammad. After being imprisoned briefly during World War II for resisting the draft, Muhammed began efforts to recruit the most oppressed members of African-American society whom the Black churches and civil rights organizations had largely ignored: the convicts, dope addicts, pimps, delinquents, prostitutes, and the unemployed. Among them was a pimp and small-time criminal near-orphan from the ghettos of New York City and Boston, Malcolm Little, who after leaving prison in 1952, assumed the last name "X" in a symbolic repudiation of the "White Man's name."[3]

During the 1950s, the makings of the Civil Rights Movement took hold with a force that could only temporarily be stifled by Southern Whites. On December 1, 1955, Rosa Parks sparked the Montgomery bus boycott when she refused to vacate her seat on the middle of the bus. Four days later, at a meeting held to dramatize the boycott, Martin Luther King, Jr. declared:

> There comes a time when people get tired. We are here this evening to say to those who have mistreated us so long that we are tired of being segregated and humiliated, tired of being kicked about by the brutal feet of oppression. We have no alternative but to protest. For many years we have shown amazing patience. We have sometimes given our White brothers the feeling that we like the way we were being treated. But we come here tonight to be saved from that patience that makes us patient with anything less than freedom and justice.[4]

Montgomery galvanized Blacks and countless Whites into fighting against a system that was increasingly viewed as intolerable. In 1957, when Arkansas Governor Orval Faubus defied a federal court order and ordered the National Guard to prevent nine Black students from entering all-White Central High School in Little Rock, President Eisenhower federalized the Arkansas National Guard. In 1960, four Black college students in Greensboro, North Carolina sat at a segregated lunch counter at a Woolworth five-and-dime store, thus sparking a movement of "sit-ins" and "freedom rides" throughout the South. In 1961, when James Meredith was refused admission at the University of Mississippi, a federal court ruled that he had the legal right to enroll and attend classes. Mississippi Gov. Ross Barnett called for resistance and asked a statewide television audience to join in opposing the federal government's policy of "racial genocide." Violence broke out on September 30, 1962, the day before Meredith was to enroll; two people were killed and many others injured. In the end, several hundred federal marshals and troops were sent in. On August 28, 1963, as several hundred thousand marchers gathered in front of the Lincoln Memorial, King delivered his now famous "I Have a Dream" speech. Yet the ire of White Southerners was kindled. Just two weeks later, the 16th Street Baptist Church in Birmingham was bombed, killing four girls attending Sunday school.

In a speech broadcast live on national television and radio on June 11, 1963, President John F. Kennedy unveiled plans to pursue a comprehensive civil rights bill in Congress. He stated, "This nation, for all its hopes and all its boasts, will not be fully free until all its citizens are free." Kennedy compellingly argued:

> The heart of the question is whether all Americans are to be afforded equal rights and equal opportunities, whether we are going to treat our fellow Americans as we want to be treated. If an American, because his skin is dark, cannot eat lunch in a restaurant open to the public, if he cannot send his children to the best public school available, if he cannot vote for the public officials who represent him, if, in short, he cannot enjoy the full and free life which all of us want, then who among us would be content to have the color of his skin changed and stand in his place? Who among us would be content with the counsels of patience and delay?[5]

By 1963, Martin Luther King Jr. had become the moral and political leader of millions, Black and White. As Marable notes, millions read his books and articles, his speeches were memorized, and he had become one of the three or four most influential people in the world. In 1964, he was honored with the Nobel Peace Prize.[6] At the same time, Malcolm X, who was highly critical of the Civil Rights Movement, was rising to prominence. He labeled Black democrats "chumps," dubbed the 1963 March on Washington as "The Farce on Washington," and called 1964, the year Lyndon Johnson was running for reelection, "the year of the ballot or the bullet." As his prominence grew, so did his rift with Elijah Muhammad, and in March 1964, less than a year before his assassination, he left the Nation of Islam. Writes Marable, "It is difficult for historians to capture the vibrant essence of Malcolm X, his earthy and human character, his position as a revolutionary teacher for a generation of young militants, his total love for the dispossessed.… His rhetoric, more so than even King's, was almost hypnotic upon Black audiences."[7] Years later, Malcom's words remain laden with power; during his "Ballot or the Bullet" speech, arguably his most famous, he declared:

> I'm not a Republican, nor a Democrat, nor an American, and got sense enough to know it. I'm one of the 22 million Black

victims of the Democrats, one of the 22 million Black victims of the Republicans, and one of the 22 million Black victims of Americanism. And when I speak, I don't speak as a Democrat, or a Republican, nor an American. I speak as a victim of America's so-called democracy.

You and I have never seen democracy; all we've seen is hypocrisy. When we open our eyes today and look around America, we see America not through the eyes of someone who has enjoyed the fruits of Americanism, we see America through the eyes of someone who has been the victim of Americanism. We don't see any American dream; we've experienced only the American nightmare. We haven't benefited from America's democracy; we've only suffered from America's hypocrisy.[8]

Following Kennedy's assassination, President Johnson took the mantle, and on July 2, signed the Civil Rights Act of 1964. The act banned discrimination in places of public accommodation, discrimination by employers on the basis of race, color, religion, national origin, and sex on the basis of hiring, and allowed government agencies to withhold federal money from any program permitting or practicing discrimination. On June 4, 1965, Johnson delivered a stirring speech during his commencement address at Howard University, in which he declared the need for jobs, decent homes, welfare and social programs, and care for the sick. Johnson passionately argued:

> ... Freedom is not enough. You do not wipe away the scars of centuries by saying: "Now you are free to go where you want, and do as you desire, and choose the leaders you please." You do not take a person who, for years, has been hobbled by chains and liberate him, bring him up to the starting line of a race and then say, "You are free to compete with all the others," and still justly believe that you have been completely fair. Thus it is not enough just to open the gates of opportunity. All our citizens must have the ability to walk through those gates. This is the next and the more profound stage of the battle for civil rights. We seek not just freedom but opportunity. We seek not just legal equity but human ability, not just equality as a right and a theory but equality as a fact and equality as a result ... To all of these fronts – and a dozen more – I will dedicate the efforts of the Johnson Administration.[9]

Two months later, on August 6, Johnson signed the Voting Rights Act of 1965, which enabled millions of previously disenfranchised African Americans in the South to vote. Less than a week later, the Los Angeles community of Watts exploded. In a week of looting, fires, and violence, 34 people had been killed, more than 900 injured, and 4,000 arrested.[10] Over the next four years, cities in the North and Midwest were engulfed in uprisings in Black neighborhoods, including Newark and Detroit in 1967, and throughout the country, following the assassination of Martin Luther King, Jr., on April 4, 1968. While most Blacks viewed the riots as "spontaneous outbursts brought on by years of discrimination and mistreatment," White reaction was divided. In a survey of 15 northern cities in 1968, the authors found that about a third saw the riots as "largely unjustified" and "conspiratorial assaults on law and order led by criminal, demagogue, or other undesirable elements – assaults that should be met first by firm police action."[11]

More divisive were White perceptions of the "Black Power Movement" that took on full force in the late 1960s, fueled by the rhetoric of Stokely Carmichael and Hubert "Rap" Brown. In 1967, The Black Power Conference in Newark called for "portioning of the United States into two separate independent nations, one to be a homeland for White and the other to be a homeland for Black Americans." In 1966, Oakland radicals Huey Newton and Bobby Seale founded the Black Panther Party for Self Defense, which Marable called "the most influential revolutionary nationalist organization in the United States."

The Black Panther movement employed Marxist-Leninist rhetoric to argue that economic exploitation was the primary cause of Black second-class citizenship; its most prominent spokesperson, Eldridge Clever, declared that the choice before America was "total liberty for Black people or total destruction for America." The Black Panthers wore Afros, black leather jackets, dark sunglasses and black berets, and carried guns in public, calling for full employment, decent housing, Black control of their own communities, and an end to repression and police brutality." According to historian Andrew Hartman, FBI Director J. Edgar Hoover, in a 1970 report written for President Nixon, declared that the Black Panthers were "the most active and dangerous Black extremist group in the United States;" they were the target of 233 of 295 counterintelligence operations aimed at Black political groups during the era.[12]

A 1967 poll reveals just how divided Americans were by the Black Power Movement. When Detroit White residents were asked what the phrase "Black Power" meant to them, 81 percent of Whites interpreted the phrase negatively, usually taking it to mean Black rule over Whites; by contrast, 42 percent of Blacks interviewed had a favorable impression of the movement, with many viewing the slogan as "another call for a fair shake for Blacks or a rallying cry for Black unity."[13]

However, it was not just Black Power that divided America. In 1968, the National Advisory Commission on Civil Disorders, better known as the Kerner Commission, which had been appointed by Johnson to investigate the causes of the 1967 race riots, concluded: "Our nation is moving toward two societies, one Black, one White – separate and unequal." According to the report:

> Race prejudice ... now threatens to affect our future. White racism is essentially responsible for the explosive mixture which has been accumulating in our cities since the end of World War II.... Pervasive discrimination and segregation in employment, education and housing ... have resulted in the continuing exclusion of great numbers of Negroes from the benefits of economic progress. The Black ghettos are where segregation and poverty converge on the young to destroy opportunity and enforce failure. Crime, drug addiction, dependency on welfare, and bitterness and resentment against society in general and White society in particular are the result ... [There is] a widespread belief among Negroes in the existence of police brutality and in a "double standard" of justice and protection – one for Negroes and one for Whites.[14]

During the presidential campaign that year, Richard Nixon rode a wave of division, fueled by urban unrest and polarization over the war in Vietnam. He appealed to the "silent majority," a calculated move to lure discontented Southern White and Northern working class and suburban Whites into the Republican Party, one articulated by the book penned by Nixon's political advisor, John Phillips, *The Emerging Republican Majority*. Using what has come to be known as "dog whistle politics," what legal scholar Ian Haney López describes as "coded racial appeals that carefully manipulate hostility toward non-Whites," Nixon asserted in October 1972, during his bid for reelection, that "there is no reason to feel guilty about wanting to enjoy what you get and get what you earn, about wanting your children in good schools close to home, or about wanting to be judged fairly on your ability."[15] The Republican Party, said Nixon, "understood that the United States represented "the land of opportunity, not the land of quotas and restrictions."[16]

Nixon became an ardent opponent of busing and its goal of school integration, a hot button in the 1970s, apparently following the advice of his counselor for urban affairs, Daniel Patrick Moynihan, who in a widely criticized memo recommended to the president "the time may have come when the issue of race could benefit from a period of benign neglect. The subject has been too much talked about."[17] Moynihan, a Democrat and sociologist who had served as assistant secretary of labor in both the Kennedy and Johnson administrations, was a surprising choice for Nixon as his urban affairs guru. However, part of his appeal may have been his 1965 report, "The Negro Family: The Case for National Action," in which he argued that the lack of African American social and economic progress could be blamed on single-mother families and a destructive vein in ghetto culture that could be traced back to slavery and Jim Crow discrimination. While well intentioned – he drew widely on the work of Black scholars. such as E. Franklin Frazier –, Moynihan was widely condemned for ignoring structural inequality and "blaming the victim."

Ironically, in 1970, Nixon implemented the "Philadelphia Plan," the first federal affirmative action program, designed to integrate all-White construction trade unions. Yet when the plan hindered Nixon's courtship of White blue-collar workers, he backtracked, and his patchy support allowed bureaucrats to apply their own standards, with limited success.[18] The lack of progress, indeed backsliding on racial issues during the Nixon Administration, prompted *Newsweek*, in 1973, to publish a special issue entitled "Whatever Happened to Black America?" According to the article, "The great surge that carried racial justice briefly to the top of the nation's agenda in the 1960s has been stalemated by war, economics, the flameout of the old civil rights coalition, and the rise to power of a New American Majority. Blacks and their special problems have gone out of fashion in government, politics, and civil concern...."[19]

WELFARE QUEENS, DOG WHISTLE POLITICS, AND RACE BAITING

The post-Civil Rights era of the late 20th century is notable for its lack of legislative efforts to encourage equality, even during Democratic presidential administrations. In the larger society there was a pushback against quotas, busing and other affirmative action measures. Politicians on the Right used the term "affirmative action" as a cudgel, a pejorative spat out in anger. Democrats, on the other hand, came under criticism from African-American leaders who saw them as taking the Black vote for granted without giving them much to vote for.

It was Richard Nixon who used the Southern Strategy to mobilize resentful Whites to vote Republican in the wake of the Civil Rights Act. But Republican presidents and candidates after Nixon used dog-whistle politics to stir up White animosity against African Americans, effectively scapegoating Blacks, covertly and sometimes overtly, for their lack of success, which was often attributed to Black "handouts."

During his unsuccessful presidential primary campaign in 1976 against President Gerald Ford and later as president, Reagan frequently employed dog whistle politics. As a candidate, Reagan repeatedly referred to a fictitious "Chicago welfare queen" with "80 names, 30 addresses, 12 Social Security cards [who] is collecting veteran's benefits on four non-existing deceased husbands." He would then add, "And she's collecting social security; she's got Medicaid, getting food stamps, and she is collecting welfare under each of her names. Her tax-free cash income alone is over $150,000."[20] He also made frequent references to food stamp programs, which were supposedly helping "some young fellow ahead of you to buy a T-bone steak" while "you were waiting in line to buy hamburger." In the early days, he used the phrase "strapping young buck" in lieu of "young fellow," a derogatory Southern term used to describe a strong Black man. Writes López, Reagan's "racially coded rhetoric and strategy proved extraordinarily effective when he won the presidency in 1980." Illustrating the "power of race in the campaign," the defection rate was 34 percent among Democrats who believed "civil rights leaders were pushing too fast." Additionally, 71 percent of those who felt "the government should not make any special effort to help [Blacks] because they should help themselves" voted for Reagan.[21]

In September 1982, President Ronald Reagan declared at a National Black Republican Council dinner, "Our critics to the contrary, the poor and disadvantaged are better off today than if we had allowed runaway government spending, interest rates and inflation to continue ravaging the American economy."[22] In truth, Reagan, who had campaigned against the excesses of "big government," including affirmative action and mandatory busing, gutted federal programs targeting urban poverty, declaring of Johnson's War on Poverty that "poverty had won."[23] During his presidency and that of his successor, George H.W. Bush, anti-poverty spending plummeted to levels on a par with the mid-1960s, before Johnson began his Great Society, leaving millions of poor Blacks to fend for themselves.[24] As the eminent sociologist William Julius Wilson notes in his book *More than Just Race: Being Black and Poor in the Inner City*, Reagan began a trend of sharp spending cuts to cities, dramatically reducing federal dollars available for urban mass transit, economic development assistance, social service grants, education, and public service jobs, and job training. According to Wilson, the federal contribution to city budgets was 17.5 percent in 1977, falling to 5.4 percent in 2000.[25]

Sometimes the race baiting was ugly and highly effective. In the 1988 campaign, then Vice-president George H.W. Bush ran a notorious ad against his opponent, Massachusetts Governor Michael Dukakis. The ad blamed Dukakis for the actions of a felon, a Black man named Willie Horton, who stabbed a man and repeatedly raped his girlfriend. Horton was on furlough from prison, and Dukakis had vetoed a measure that would have made convicted murderers ineligible for furlough. Though the ad never mentioned race, it featured a mug shot of Horton, over which a voice declared: "Dukakis not only opposes the death penalty, he allowed first-degree murderers to have weekend passes from prison. Despite a life sentence, Horton received 10 weekend passes from prison." Over mug shots of Horton and an image of his arrest, the voiceover continues: "Horton fled, kidnapped a young couple, stabbing the man, and repeatedly raping his girlfriend." The ad concludes: "Weekend passes: Dukakis on crime." The ad clearly garnered its desired result. Bush went from lagging in the polls to taking the lead, as 12 percent of the electorate switched from Dukakis to Bush. In the words of one historian, "No campaign ever turns on one issue, but no one – *no one* – who followed the campaign believes George Bush had any more devastating ally than the homicidal Black rapist Willie Horton."[26]

In her now-famous essay in the October 5, 1998 issue of *The New Yorker*, Nobel Prize–winner Toni Morrison, called Bill Clinton "our first Black president." Clinton was, wrote Morrison, "Blacker than any actual Black person who could ever be elected in our children's lifetime. After all, Clinton displays almost every trope of Blackness: single-parent household, born poor, working-class, saxophone-playing, McDonald's-and-junk-food-loving boy from Arkansas." Referring to the public revulsion over the President's adultery scandal, Morrison continued in the article:

> The message was clear: "No matter how smart you are, how hard you work, how much coin you earn for us, we will put you in your place or put you out of the place you have somehow, albeit with our permission, achieved. You will be fired from your job, sent away in disgrace, and – who knows? – maybe sentenced and jailed to boot. In short, unless you do as we say (i.e., assimilate at once), your expletives belong to us."[27]

The appellation stuck, and it would be another ten years before an actual African American, Barack Obama, would be elected to the nation's highest office.

As journalist DeWayne Wickham makes clear in his book, *Bill Clinton and Black America*, a collection of articles and interviews with a wide array of African Americans, one of the reasons for Clinton's popularity was his absolute comfort with Black folks. In an account of a dinner he hosted for the president, White House correspondent Bill Douglas recalls:

> When Clinton arrived for the dinner, he walked into the living room, which was filled with a lot of Black artwork, and he headed for a poster I got from France of the Paris Opera's version of *Porgy and Bess*. It was of a Black man holding up a White woman with an ample butt. He said, "I like this." … This was a soul food

dinner. We had fried chicken, catfish. We had chitlins ... he piled them high on his plate, slapped on about half a bottle of hot sauce and just sucked them up. He knew how to eat them. He had corn bread on the side. He dipped a little corn bread in the hot sauce, and he was just gnawing on those chitlins. He served himself. I just looked at him in amazement because I don't eat the stuff.[28]

Wickham notes that an August 1998 poll found that Clinton's approval rating among African Americans, 93 percent, was higher than that of Jesse Jackson, who garnered 89 percent. Four months later, when the House of Representatives voted for impeachment, his approval rating with Blacks was a solid 91 percent, 20 points above that of Whites. When he left office in January 2001, his approval rating rose to 93 percent among Blacks, while dropping to a low of 62 percent among Whites.[29]

When Clinton declared his candidacy, in October 1991, Republicans had occupied the White House for all but one term since 1968. He campaigned as a "New Democrat" who was not beholden to Black interests, a mainstream Democrat who could win over voters from both parties. Though naturally sympathetic toward Blacks, in order to win the election, Clinton needed to show that he was tough on drugs, crime, and welfare. In his characteristically reconciliatory style, he declared:

> For 12 years, Republicans have tried to divide us – race against race – so we get mad at each other and not at them. They want us to look at each other across a racial divide so we don't turn and look to the White House and ask, "Why are all of our incomes going down? Why are all of us losing jobs? Why are we losing our future?[30]

His opportunity to show his mettle came early in the campaign, in January 1992, when, as governor of Arkansas, he flew to Little Rock to personally oversee the execution of a mentally impaired African-American man, Ricky Ray Rector, denying him a last minute pardon. Rector was convicted and sentenced to death in November 1982 for the shooting death of a police officer and another murder that occurred two days earlier. After shooting the policeman, Rector turned the gun on himself, destroying part of his brain. "He is, in the vernacular, a zombie," said his attorney Jeff Rosenzweig before the execution. "His execution would be remembered as a disgrace to the state." Rosezweig accused Clinton of using the execution solely for political gain. "My personal opinion is that in his heart of hearts he's against the death penalty," Rosenzweig said. "In my opinion, this is a very easy way to show you're tough on crime."³¹ Clinton reputedly stated, "I can be nicked a lot, but no one can say I'm soft on crime."

Clinton got another moment during the election to distance himself from perceptions that he was too closely aligned with Blacks when the Los Angeles riots occurred in May 1992. On May 13, rapper Sister Souljah was quoted in the *Washington Post* as saying, "If Black people kill Black people every day, why not have a week and kill White people?" This was said during a panel discussion at a meeting dealing with ways to empower Black youth called "The Youth Summit," hosted by Rev. Jesse Jackson's Rainbow Coalition. In what would come to be known as a "Sister Souljah moment," a calculated denunciation of an extremist position or special interest group in order to get votes, Clinton appeared before the Rainbow Coalition and declared, "If you took the words, 'white' and 'Black' and you reversed them, you might think [White supremacist] David Duke was giving that speech." Clinton had twisted Souljah's remarks; her remarks continued with:

> In other words, White people, this government, and that mayor were well aware of the fact that Black people were dying every day in Los Angeles under gang violence. So if you're a gang member and you would normally be killing somebody, why not kill a White person? Do you think that somebody thinks that White people are better, or above and beyond dying, when they would kill their own kind?³²

Jackson was outraged by Clinton's statement and responded that Clinton "was actually talking to the TV audience. He was not talking to the people who were there. He was using the people who were there as a platform to spread his message … purely to appeal to conservative Whites by containing Jackson and isolating Jackson." Clinton, in turn, played up the schism with Jackson, getting votes in the process, such as the Philadelphia electrician who said, "The day he told off that fucking Jackson is the day he got [mine]."³³

During his presidency, in what Michelle Alexander, in her book *The New Jim Crow: Mass Incarceration in the Age of Colorblindness*, calls "part of a grand strategy … to appeal to the elusive White swing voters," Clinton endorsed a federal Three Strikes law, funneling $30 billion dollars into the "war on crime" and mandating life sentences for some three-time law offenders, which according to Alexander, "resulted in the largest increase in federal and state prison inmates of any president in American history." As part of his "One Strike and You're Out" initiative, which replaced Aid to Families with Dependent Children (AFDC), Clinton made it easier for federally assisted public housing projects to exclude anyone with a criminal record, "an extraordinarily harsh step in the midst of a drug war aimed at racial and ethnic minorities." Writes Alexander, "… 90 percent of those admitted to prison for drug offenses in many states were Black or Latino, yet the mass incarceration of communities of color was explained in race-neutral terms, an adaptation to the needs and demands of the current political climate. The New Jim Crow was born."[34]

Clinton, perhaps in an act of political jujutsu, tried to bury the Welfare Queen meme. He did so by "ending welfare as we know it" by signing the Personal Responsibility and Work Opportunity Reconciliation Act, which imposed a five-year limit on welfare assistance and a permanent ban on welfare and food stamp eligibility for anyone convicted of a felony drug offense, including marijuana. It may not have been a coincidence that he signed this in August of 1996, less than three months before the election. In protest, Mary Jo Bane and Peter Edelman, both assistant secretaries at the Department of Health and Human Services, resigned. Said Edelman to his staff, "I have devoted the last 30-plus years to doing whatever I could to help in reducing poverty in America. I believe the recently enacted welfare bill goes in the opposite direction."[35] Edelman would write in 2012, "40 percent of the women who left welfare during that period ended up without either a job or cash assistance, and nearly half of those ended up without any other support mechanism."[36]

Clinton left behind a mixed legacy on race and racial relations. To his credit, when he took office in 1993, he chose five African Americans to his cabinet, the largest number of Blacks ever appointed by a new president: Mike Espy as Secretary of Agriculture; Ron Brown as Secretary of Commerce; Hazel O'Leary as Secretary of Energy; Jesse Brown as Secretary of Veteran Affairs; and Lee Brown as Drug Czar (at that time, though no longer, a cabinet position). Over eight years, he appointed four more. Additionally, on June 14, 1997, he announced Executive Order 13050 and the establishment of "One America in the 21st Century: The President's Initiative on Race," declaring, "Today, I ask the American people to join me in a great national effort to perfect the promise of America for this new time as we seek to build our more perfect union … That is the unfinished work of our time, to lift the burden of race and redeem the promise of America." The committee, chaired by historian John Hope Franklin, and its report offer a penetrating documentation of racial problems in America along with recommendations for a public education campaign and guidelines to help communities discuss how to heal racial and ethnic divisions. Still, a strong argument can be made that Clinton went too far to appeal to swing voters, by backing excessively tough anti-crime and welfare reform bills that were deeply injurious to African Americans and Hispanics.[37]

NOTES

1. Text of Brown v. Board of Education of Topeka, 347 U.S. 483, http://www.law.cornell.edu/supremecourt/text/347/483.
2. Marable, Manning. *Race, Reform, and Rebellion: The Second Reconstruction and Beyond in Black America, 1945–2006.* (Jackson, MS: University Press of Mississippi, 2007), 52.
3. Ibid., 54.
4. Sitkoff, Harvard and Eric Foner. *The Struggle for Black Equality, 1954–1992.* (New York, NY: Hill and Wang, 1993), 45.
5. Kennedy, John F. "Radio and Television Report to the American People on Civil Rights." http://www.presidency.ucsb.edu/ws/?pid=9271.
6. Marable, 75.
7. Ibid., 85.
8. X, Malcolm. "The Ballot or the Bullet" Speech, delivered April 12, 1964 in Detroit. http://www.cis.aueb.gr/Besides%20Security/TALKS/TALKS-10-X%20(The%20Ballot%20or%20the%20Bullet).pdf.
9. Johnson, Lyndon B. Commencement Address at Howard University: "To Fulfill These Rights," June 4, 1965. http://www.lbjlib.utexas.edu/johnson/archives.hom/speeches.hom/650604.asp.
10. Hine, Darlene Clark, William C. Hine, and Stanley Harrold, *African Americans: A Concise History.* (Upper Saddle River, NJ: Pearson Education, 2012), 544.
11. Schuman, Howard, Charlotte Steeh, Lawrence Bobo, and Maria Krysan, *Racial Attitudes in America: Trends and Interpretations.* (Cambridge, MA: Harvard University Press, 1997), 33.
12. Hartman, Andrew. *A War for the Soul of America: A History of the Culture Wars.* (Chicago: The University of Chicago Press, 2015), 20.
13. Schuman, Howard, Charlotte Steeh, Lawrence Bobo, and Maria Krysan, 33.
14. "Report of the National Advisory Commission on Civil Disorders," National Advisory Commission on Civil Disorders (*The Kerner Report*), 1967. http://faculty.washington.edu/qtaylor/documents_us/Kerner%20Report.htm.
15. López, Ian Haney. *Dog Whistle Politics: How Coded Racial Appeals Have Reinvented Racism and Wrecked the Middle Class.* (Oxford: Oxford University Press, 2014), ix.
16. Nixon, Richard M. "Radio Address on the Philosophy of Government," October 21, *1972, Public Papers of the Presidents of the United States: Richard M. Nixon, 1972.* (Bel Air, CA: Library Reprints, 2007), 998.

17. Kotlowski, Dean J. *Nixon's Civil Rights: Politics, Principle, and Policy*. (Cambridge, MA: Harvard University Press, 2002), 173.
18. Kotlowski, Dean J. "Richard Nixon and the Origins of Affirmative Action," *The Historian*. Volume 60, Issue 3, 1998, 523.
19. *Newsweek*, February 19, 1973, 29, cited in Schuman, Steeh, Bobo, and Krysan, 36.
20. "'Welfare Queen' Becomes Issue in Reagan Campaign," *New York Times*. Feb. 15, 1976.
21. López, 58.
22. Reagan, Ronald. "Remarks at a National Black Republican Council Dinner," September 15, 1982. http://www.presidency.ucsb.edu/ws/?pid=42989.
23. Sharkey, Patrick. *Stuck in Place: Urban Neighborhoods and the End of Progress toward Racial Equality*. (Chicago, IL: The University of Chicago Press, 2013), 38.
24. Massey, Douglas S. *Categorically Unequal: The American Stratification System*. (New York, NY: Russell Sage Foundation, 2007), 170.
25. Wilson, William Julius. *More Than Just Race: Being Black and Poor in the Inner City*. (New York, NY: W.W. Norton and Company, 2010), 39.
26. López, 106.
27. Morrison, Toni. *The New Yorker*, October 25, 1998. http://www.newyorker.com/magazine/1998/10/05/comment-6543.
28. Wickham, DeWayne. *Bill Clinton and Black America*. (New York, NY: The Ballantine Publishing Group, 2002), 78.
29. Ibid., 1.
30. Clinton, Bill. "Remarks Announcing Candidacy for the Democratic Presidential Nomination," October 3, 1991. http://www.presidency.ucsb.edu/ws/?pid=77817.
31. "The 1992 Campaign: Death Penalty; Arkansas Execution Raises Questions on Governor's Politics," *The New York Times*, January 25, 1992. http://www.nytimes.com/1992/01/25/us/1992-campaign-death-penalty-arkansas-execution-raises-questions-governor-s.html.
32. "The 1992 Campaign: Racial Issues; Rapper, Chided by Clinton, Calls Him a Hypocrite," *The New York Times*, June 17, 1992. http://www.nytimes.com/1992/06/17/us/the-1992-campaign-racial-issues-rapper-chided-by-clinton-calls-him-a-hypocrite.html.
33. López, 108.
34. Alexander, Michelle. *The New Jim Crow: Mass Incarceration in the Age of Colorblindness*. (New York: The New Press, 2012), 56.

35. "Two Clinton Aides Resign to Protest New Welfare Law," *The New York Times*, September 12, 1996. http://www.nytimes.com/1996/09/12/us/two-clinton-aides-resign-to-protest-new-welfare-law.html.
36. Edelman, Peter. *So Rich, So Poor: Why It's So Hard to End Poverty in America*. (New York, NY: The New Press, 2012), 87.
37. *One America in the 21st Century: The Report of President Bill Clinton's Initiative on Race*. (New Have, CT: Yale University Press, 2009).

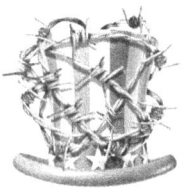

9

THE BEGINNING AND END OF "POST-RACIAL AMERICA"

SOCIOLOGIST Howard Winant writes, "The 2008 election was the first to have a viable Black candidate, but it was hardly the first U.S. election to be about race. In fact, every national election is about race."[1] Yet there was also something different about 2008, in that the candidacy, and ultimately the election, of Barack Obama brought with it a new, albeit erroneous narrative of African-American progress, one with the story line that once and for all, America overcame its racism and was able to elect a Black president. Articulating the fictitious narrative, Fredrick Harris writes: "Though it may have taken a long time for American society to change – over 250 years from slavery to citizenship with fully designated legal rights – the American economic and political order was flexible enough to accommodate the descendants of slaves and the survivors of state-sanctioned segregation." He muses that for future generations of Black Americans, the Black experience in America will marked by the initials B.B.O. and A.B.O. – "Before Barack Obama" and "After Barack Obama."[2]

However, Harris makes clear that Obama's election was anything but the post-racial miracle that many proclaimed it at the time to be. Rather, race was a consistent factor in the 2008 election, ever since Obama emerged as a Black candidate with a real shot at the presidency, and the candidate walked a fine line by embracing a kind of "race neutral" politics, which barred his staunch advocacy of issues perceived to be uniquely African American.

In the presidential campaign, Obama's markedly nonracial messages had some in the Black community doubting his authenticity. This was further complicated by being the son of a White mother and a Kenyan father, having grown up outside of the continental United States, and being born a generation after the Civil Rights Movement. Jesse Jackson reportedly described him as "acting white" for not attending a march in Jena, Louisiana, to protest the suspect imprisonment of six Black teenagers. When asked if he was "authentically Black enough" in a July 2007 debate, Obama responded, "You know, when I'm catching a cab in Manhattan … I think I've given my credentials."[3]

Yet the issue of Obama not being "Black enough" would not go away. When his presidential campaign got started, African-American media giant Tavis Smiley remarked that "Obama has not had the quintessential Black experience in America;" questioning whether Obama had paid sufficient dues, Smiley quipped that "most Black folk got to know Barack the same way White folk got to know him – two years ago when he gave that speech at the Democratic Convention." On Obama's fitness as a figure around which Blacks should rally, Smiley declared that he "is no Jesse Jackson. For that matter, Barack Obama is no Shirley Chisholm. When Shirley Chisholm ran in '72, when Jesse ran in '84 and '88, they had long-standing relationships with the Black community. So there's some courting here that Barack is going to have to do. I don't know whether or not, after the courtship, if Black America is going to decide that we're going to date, much less be wed to him."[4]

Around the same time, Princeton Professor Cornel West criticized Obama for beginning his campaign in Springfield, Illinois, a predominantly White community, instead of at Tavis Smiley's annual State of Black America conference. Author Debra Dickerson commented that Obama is not "Black" from an American political and cultural viewpoint because that term refers to those descended from West African slaves. The Reverend Al Sharpton, now a staunch Obama supporter, announced at the time of Obama's presidential run, "Just because you are our color doesn't make you our kind."[5] Months later, Obama himself noted the salience of race in the primaries, declaring, "This is not to say that race has not been an issue in this campaign. At various stages in the campaign, some commentators have deemed me either 'too Black' or 'not Black enough' … The press has scoured every exit poll for the latest evidence of racial polarization, not just in terms of White and Black, but Black and brown as well."[6] Even Michelle Obama had initial doubts about Mr. Obama's blackness. Describing her feelings about her first encounter with her future husband eighteen years earlier, she declared: "I've got nothing in common with this guy. He grew up in Hawaii! Who grows up in Hawaii? He was biracial. I was like, okay, what's that about? And then it's a funny name, Barack Obama. Who names their child Barack Obama?"⁷

Perhaps legal scholar Paul Butler put it best: "Blackness has always been a social construct, not a genetic one. That is how a person like Barack Obama, whose mother was white, can call himself Black." He continues:

> Here are some of the ways that Barack Obama is Black. He says that he is. He went home to Africa. He is married to a Black woman. He plays basketball and walks with a swag, especially in front of other Black people. He has benefited from affirmative action. He is very cool. Here are some of the ways that Barack Obama is post-Black. He does not like talking about race. Race discrimination does not appear to have limited his opportunities. He went home to Ireland. His mother was White and his sister is Indonesian. He is not angry. White folks sometimes temporarily forget about race around him.⁸

While many Blacks were excited about Obama's candidacy, it was often accompanied by a degree of ambivalence and apprehension. Following a July 2007 debate between Hillary Clinton and Obama at Howard University, Amina Luqman wrote in the *Washington Post*:

> The average Black American onlooker can't help feeling proud but also just a little hurt watching Obama. Proud of his ability to traverse minefields on a national political landscape and hurt by what America demands of Black candidates seeking public acceptance and trust. During the debate, Black Americans in the audience sat, hands poised, yearning to applaud a Black candidate able to articulate our passions and sense of injustice. We wanted to hear that he understood and loved us – not in the general, "we the people" sense but in the specific. Yet we know that with each utterance about injustice, each puff of anger or frustration about racism, we lose the very thing we seek: a viable Black candidate. The closer Obama comes to us, the further he would be from winning the nomination and the presidency.⁹

In the New Hampshire primary in January 2008, race was blamed when Obama, after sporting a 10- to 12-point lead over Hillary Clinton in polls, lost the vote by three points. For weeks the pundits debated whether the polling error was due to the so-called "Bradley Effect," named for former Los Angeles mayor Tom Bradley, an African-American politician whose lead in polls dried up at the ballot box, and the "Wilder Effect," whose namesake was another African American man who saw his ten-point advantage vanish as Virginians cast their ballots for governor in 1989. Had Americans lied to pollsters about their willingness to vote for an African American candidate? Did deep-seated, perhaps barely conscious, racism take hold of them behind closed doors and convince them to vote for a White candidate over a Black one? Or were there other explanations?[10]

Following New Hampshire, the issue of race took front and center, as the nation's attention turned to the South Carolina primary. There was the comment from Hillary Clinton in which she declared that "Dr. King's dream began to be realized when President Johnson passed the Civil Rights Act," adding "It took a president to get it done."[11] Critics interpreted her statement as playing down King's importance in the Civil Rights Movement. Later, an unnamed Clinton advisor was quoted as saying, "If you have a social need, you're with Hillary. If you want Obama to be your imaginary hip Black friend and you're young and you have no social needs, then he's cool." Then there was Andrew Cuomo, New York's attorney general and another Clinton supporter, who used the phrase "shuck and jive" in a way that seemed pointed at Obama. When Obama went on to beat Clinton by 28 points in South Carolina and performed better than expected among the state's White voters, Bill Clinton was asked why it took two Clintons to try to beat Obama in South Carolina. "Jesse Jackson won South Carolina twice, in '84 and '88," he said, though the reporter had not mentioned Jackson. "[Jackson] ran a good campaign. And Senator Obama ran a good campaign here. He's run a good campaign everywhere." Clinton's comment seemed a clear attempt to dismiss both Obama's victory and his candidacy as nothing more than a repetition of the former Black presidential candidate's loss a decade earlier.[12]

According to journalists Dan Balz and Haynes Johnson, Senator Edward Kennedy's decision to endorse Obama after that primary occurred in large part because he "worried that the Clintons were trying to turn Obama into the Black candidate – the Jesse Jackson of 2008." With Kennedy's endorsement, as well as that of his niece, Caroline Kennedy, any chances of that happening were effectively neutralized.[13]

The Kennedy's were not the only ones concerned by the racist tenor of Bill Clinton's remarks. Many African Americans, who had once referred to him as the first

9 | THE BEGINNING AND END OF "POST-RACIAL AMERICA"

Black president" began to express a "seething, barely-contained rage" and "revulsion" at the Clintons.[14] Wrote Terence Samuel:

> The Clintons do not seem to understand that the kind of revulsion they are generating in what was once the heart of their base is not your garden-variety political frustration. It is born out of a historical anger that requires 25 minutes in the supermarket aisle or 900 words on the op-ed page of *The New York Times* to explain. The idea that Obama, having played by all the rules and won by all the traditional measures, could lose the nomination because of Clinton's argument that he is unelectable because he is Black, is profoundly revolting to many Black people.[15]

By mid-February, the idea of Obama being post-racial was beginning to pick up steam. *U.S. News and World Report* printed a story titled, "Does Obama's Winning Streak Prove that Race Does Not Matter?"[16] Yet the theme of Obama's Blackness emerged in a big way in March when ABC News began to air incendiary videos of Obama's longtime pastor, Jeremiah Wright, which had appeared on YouTube and soon were seen non-stop on cable news. In one sermon, delivered shortly after September 11, Wright argued that terrorist acts against the U.S. were payback for American atrocities: genocide against Native Americans, the bombing of Hiroshima and Nagasaki, and support for apartheid in South Africa. Wright then denounced the United States for its treatment of African Americans:

> When it came to treating her citizens of African descent fairly, America failed. She put them in chains ... in slave quarters ... on auction blocks, in cotton fields ... in inferior schools ... substandard housing ... in scientific experiments ... in the lowest paying jobs ... outside the equal protection of the law, kept them out of their racist bastions of higher education and locked them into positions of hopelessness and helplessness ... gives them the drugs, builds bigger prisons, passes a three-strike law and then wants us to sing "God Bless America." No, no, no! Not God Bless America. God damn America – that's in the Bible – for killing innocent people. God damn America for treating our citizens as less than human.[17]

At first, Obama tried to distance himself from Wright, calling his statements "inflammatory and appalling." However, he soon realized that his relationship with the pastor, if not confronted directly, would consume his entire campaign. The result, a speech delivered by Obama on March 18, 2008, in Philadelphia's National Constitution Center, was 37 minutes long. Titled "A More Perfect Union," it became known as Obama's "Race Speech" and was the most closely watched of all of the addresses he had yet made. In the estimation of Obama's chief campaign strategist, David Axelrod, it was "probably the most important moment of the whole campaign."[18]

In the speech, Obama made it clear that he was not willing to abandon Wright:

> I can no more disown him than I can disown the Black community. I can no more disown him than I can my White grandmother – a woman who helped raise me, a woman who sacrificed again and again for me, a woman who loves me as much as she loves anything in this world, but a woman who once confessed her fear of Black men who passed by her on the street, and who on more than one occasion has uttered racial or ethnic stereotypes that made me cringe. These people are a part of me. And they are a part of America, this country that I love.

He went on to turn his speech into what *The Washington Post* deemed "a teachable moment," in which he "addressed the pain, anger, and frustration of generations of Blacks and Whites head on – and offered a vision of how these experiences could be surmounted, if not forgotten."[19] Reminding his audience that Wright came from a time of Jim Crow segregation, Obama continued:

> For the men and women of Reverend Wright's generation, the memories of humiliation and doubt and fear have not gone away, nor has the anger and bitterness of those years. That anger may not get expressed in public, in front of White coworkers or White friends. But it does find voice in the barbershop or the beauty shop or around the kitchen table. At times, that anger is exploited by politicians, to gin up votes along racial lines or to make up for a politician's own failings.
>
> And occasionally it finds voice in the church on Sunday morning, in the pulpit and in the pews. The fact that so many people are surprised to hear that anger in some of Reverend Wright's sermons simply reminds us of the old truism that the most segregated hour of American life occurs on Sunday morning.[20]

9 | THE BEGINNING AND END OF "POST-RACIAL AMERICA"

Another theme to emerge during the 2008 election was that Obama was "playing the race card" and milking the race issue. During the primaries, in March, former vice presidential candidate Geraldine Ferraro, who was working for the Clinton Campaign, stated that "If Obama was a White Man, he would not be in this position. And if he was a woman of any color, he would not be in this position. He happens to be very lucky to be who he is." When the Obama campaign complained, she claimed her words were being twisted: "Every time that campaign is upset about something, they call it racist," she said. "I will not be discriminated against because I'm white. If they think they're going to shut up Geraldine Ferraro with that kind of stuff, they don't know me."[21]

During the general-election campaign, Obama was subjected to charges that he was milking the race issue. At a Missouri rally on July 30, Obama alluded to race as being a potential factor in the election: "Nobody really thinks that Bush or McCain have a real answer for the challenges we face. So what they're going to try to do is make you scared of me. You know, he's not patriotic enough. He's got a funny name. You know, he doesn't look like all those other presidents on those dollar bills.... He's risky." On a previous occasion, he was more explicit: "We know what kind of campaign they're going to run. They're going to try to make you afraid of me. He's young and inexperienced, and he's got a funny name. And did I mention he's Black?"[22]

Perhaps Randall Kennedy summed up the 2008 campaign best, noting that "it was not the presence but the paucity of racial misconduct" that was the most striking feature of the election. He writes:

> In a nation as large, heterogeneous, and rambunctious as the United States, in a contest for the presidency involving the first Black standard-bearer of a major party, there were bound to be outbreaks of social ugliness, including racist affronts. It should have come as no surprise that there were people who likened Obama to an ape, who called him "nigger," who scorned the Obamas for being "uppity," who warned of chicken bones and watermelon rinds festooning the White House, and who vowed never to vote for a Black man for the presidency whatever the circumstances. Surprising to me is that there wasn't more of an anti-Black reaction.[23]

With Obama's historic election, America basked in the glow of having elected an African-American president. Obama had won the popular vote by six points,

52 percent to 46 percent, and according to exit poll data, Obama won 43 percent of the White vote, a slight improvement on John Kerry's 41 percent, as well as garnering 95 percent of the Black vote, 67 percent of the Hispanic vote, and 62 percent of the Asian vote. Not surprisingly, for many, the question as to whether America had become post-racial had been answered. Political commentator Chris Matthews's remarked, "I forgot he was Black tonight for an hour," following President Obama's first State of the Union address. Author Shelby Steele asked, "Does victory mean that America is now officially beyond racism?"; columnist Matt Bai asked, "Is Obama the End of Black Politics?"; the cultural critic Touré questioned, "Who's Afraid of Post-Blackness?"

A Rasmussen poll taken two days after the election found that the percentage of African-American voters who viewed American society as "fair and decent" jumped from 24 percent to 42 percent in just a month.[24] Rasmussen also found that 70 percent of African American voters thought relations between Blacks and Whites were getting better, up from 37 percent that September.[25]

Writing of Obama's success in the 2008 election, sociologist Enid Logan notes, "While Blackness worked in Obama's favor in many respects, it was his specific deployment of Blackness that was key." In other words, Obama "did race right." Logan writes:

> Obama positioned himself as a "next-generation" or "post-racial" Black candidate, carefully avoiding the appearance of anger, protest, victimhood, or "grievance." At a number of key moments in the election, he crucially differentiated himself from the styles and tactics of other Black public figures that many Whites (and non-Whites) had come to strongly dislike. Thus he was able to neutralize the "problematic" aspects of Blackness while highlighting the redemptive ones.[26]

Still, in the wake of the election, there was strong evidence that predictions of post-racialism were premature at best. For instance, in some states and counties in the Deep South, Obama fared significantly worse among White voters than did Kerry in 2004. A robust body of research concluded that anti-Black sentiments were predictive of greater opposition to Obama. Additionally, electoral forecasting models predicted that racial prejudice cost Obama between 3 and 5 percent of the vote.[27] A day after the election, *The New York Times* stated that Obama's race appears to have been the critical deciding factor in pushing a large number of White Southerners away from the Democrats:

Here in Alabama, where Mr. McCain won 60.4 percent of the vote in his best Southern showing, he had the support of nearly 9 in 10 Whites, according to exit polls, a figure comparable to other Southern states. Alabama analysts pointed to the persistence of traditional White Southern attitudes on race as the deciding factor in Mr. McCain's strong margin. Mr. Obama won in Jefferson County, which includes the city of Birmingham, and in the Black Belt, but he made few inroads elsewhere. "Race continues to play a major role in the state," said Glenn Feldman, a historian at the University of Alabama, Birmingham. "Alabama, unfortunately, continues to remain shackled to the bonds of yesterday.... There's no other explanation than race."[28]

One incident during Obama's first term stands out as a telling example of the role that race played in terms of perceptions of the president. On July 16, 2009, Sergeant James Crowley, responding to the report of a possible break-in at a Harvard-owned home, arrested renowned Harvard Professor Henry Louis Gates, Jr. at his home. When Crowley arrived, he questioned Gates about his presence in the home. Gates, showed Crowley his Harvard identification card and driver's license but responded to Crowley's questions with his concerns about being targeted because he was Black. Gates was booked, handcuffed, and brought to jail for "exhibiting loud and tumultuous behavior." With the nation divided as to who was at fault, Obama offered these comments:

> Now, I don't know, not having been there and not seeing all the facts, what role race played in that. But I think it's fair to say, number one, any of us would be pretty angry; number two, that the Cambridge Police Department acted stupidly in arresting somebody when there was already proof that they were in their own home; and number three, what I think we know separate and apart from this incident is that there is a long history in this country of African-Americans and Latinos being stopped by law enforcement disproportionately. That's just a fact ... And even when there are honest misunderstandings, the fact that Blacks and Hispanics are picked up more frequently and often time for no cause casts suspicion even when there is good cause. And that's why I think the more that we're working with local law enforcement to improve policing techniques ... the safer everybody is going to be.[29]

Though in the end, Obama scheduled a private outing at the White House dubbed as BeerGate where he, Gates, Vice President Joseph Biden, and Crowley bonded over beers, Obama's comments sparked a public outrage. A Pew Research Center poll found that 45 percent of Whites disapproved of Obama's handling of the situation.[30] On the other end of the spectrum, Deval Patrick, governor of Massachusetts, who is Black, commented, "In some ways, this is every Black man's nightmare and a reality for Black men" and "You ought to be able to raise your voice in your own house without risk of arrest." Said Professor Michael Eric Dyson:

> Had Gates been a White professor trying to get inside his home, and called on his driver to help him jar his door open, he probably wouldn't have as readily aroused the suspicion of neighbors. And when police arrived to check out the premises, they probably wouldn't have been nearly as ready to believe the worst about the occupant of a home who clearly wasn't engaged in a criminal act. Whatever one believes about what happened, Gates clearly wasn't the beneficiary of the benefit of the doubt, a reasonable expectation since he posed no visible threat.[31]

Writes legal scholar Angela Onwuachi-Willig:

> For Obama, his comments about the arrest marked him first as a Black man, then as the president. Unlike his predecessors, Obama, because he is Black, simply could not condemn Crowley's actions in arresting Gates without being identified as racially biased. The public reaction to Obama's comment revealed that our society has not moved beyond race, even in how it sees its president.[32]

WHOSE LIVES MATTER?

If the issue of race was subdued, if not coded, during Obama's first term, during his second term it exploded to take center stage, in the form of high-profile killings of Black men (and boys) recorded on video. For many White Americans, who for decades demanded to see what they wanted to see – that it's just law enforcement doing their job to protect us –, it was becoming harder to cling to that position.

As Obama's second term continued and video evidence of shootings of unarmed Black men circulated on social media, Obama began speaking up more and more. One could say that "fourth quarter Obama" finally felt free to talk directly

9 | THE BEGINNING AND END OF "POST-RACIAL AMERICA"

and honestly with the American public about race, something that many African Americans wished he had done from the beginning.

On February 26, 2012, George Zimmerman, a neighborhood watch captain in Sanford, Florida, called 911 to report "a suspicious person" in the neighborhood. Moments later, neighbors reported hearing gunfire, and 17-year-old African American Trayvon Martin was found dead. Zimmerman, who admitted to the shooting, was injured in the altercation but not charged at the time by the Sanford Police Department, who said that there was no evidence to refute his claim of self-defense and that Florida's stand your ground law prohibited law-enforcement officials from charging him. Zimmerman was eventually charged and tried in Martin's death, but he was acquitted of second-degree murder and of manslaughter on July 13, 2013. Six days later, President Obama gave a 17-minute speech, in which he spoke about racial profiling and the state of race relations in the country:

> You know, when Trayvon Martin was first shot I said that this could have been my son. Another way of saying that is Trayvon Martin could have been me 35 years ago. And when you think about why, in the African American community at least, there's a lot of pain around what happened here, I think it's important to recognize that the African American community is looking at this issue through a set of experiences and a history that doesn't go away.
>
> There are very few African American men in this country who haven't had the experience of being followed when they were shopping in a department store. That includes me. There are very few African American men who haven't had the experience of walking across the street and hearing the locks click on the doors of cars. That happens to me – at least before I was a senator. There are very few African Americans who haven't had the experience of getting on an elevator and a woman clutching her purse nervously and holding her breath until she had a chance to get off. That happens often.[33]

A year later, on July 17, 2014, Eric Garner, an African-American man, was put in a chokehold by police in Staten Island, New York City and held down on the sidewalk, pleading, "I can't breathe." An hour later, he was pronounced dead. The New York City Medical Examiner's Office attributed Garner's death to a combination of a chokehold, compression of his chest, and poor health.

Three weeks later, on August 9, Officer Darren Wilson shot and killed Michael Brown, another African America man, after a scuffle in Ferguson, Missouri. For four hours, Brown's dead body remained in the summer sun, face down, blood flowing. Neighbors, shocked at the violence and the police's disrespect for Brown's corpse, took photos and shared video. "They killed him for no reason … they just killed this nigger for no reason," said one man in a video recorded just after shooting.

Garner's death had sparked outrage. However, the protests and demonstrations paled in comparison to what unfolded in Ferguson. After accounts that Brown had his hands up when he was shot, protesters chanted, "Hands up, don't shoot." Protests, peaceful and violent, including vandalism and looting, continued for more than a week in Ferguson and across the country, and they dominated cable networks and social media. Americans watched armored vehicles move down small-town streets as military-clad police officers shot tear gas into crowds of peaceful demonstrators. Violence committed against African Americans continued, with one event following another in what seemed to be rapid-fire succession.

In September 2014, Americans watched video from the dashboard camera of South Carolina State Trooper Sean Groubert, who shot a Black motorist, Levar Jones, as he reached down to get his wallet and driver's license. "I just got my license! You said get my license!" yelled Jones, who was shot several times but remarkably survived. Groubert was fired and charged with felony assault and battery.

In November, several weeks after a St. Louis grand jury declined to indict Officer Wilson in the death of Brown, which sparked riots and protests in Ferguson and surrounding areas, Cleveland police officers Frank Garmback and Tim Loehmann killed Tamir Rice, 12, who was holding a toy gun. On April 4, 2015, Rice's death was followed by the killing of Walter Scott in Charleston, South Carolina. According to the official report, Officer Michael Slager stopped Scott for a broken taillight, and Scott resisted arrest, taking control of Slager's taser. However, a bystander stated that Scott had struggled with Officer Slager but then ran away; Slager fired eight times, killing Scott.[34]

The year 2015 brought with it more police violence directed at African-American men, keeping the issue front and center. On April 12, Baltimore police arrested Freddie Gray, and video footage captured police dragging Gray to the police van. Gray, who sustained injuries to his neck and spine while being transported by the police, fell into a coma and died a week later. Protests were organized, resulting in riots with at least 19 police officers injured, approximately 200 people arrested, 154 vehicle fires, 15 structural fires, hundreds of police and Maryland Army National Guard troops deployed, and a state of emergency declared in the city.[35] Weeks later, a New York Times/CBS poll found "profound" racial divisions in views of how the

9 | THE BEGINNING AND END OF "POST-RACIAL AMERICA"

police use deadly force. Blacks were more than twice as likely as Whites to say police in most communities are more apt to use deadly force against a Black person – 79 percent of Blacks compared with 37 percent of Whites.[36]

Though not related to police violence, on June 17, in Charleston, South Carolina, White supremacist Dylann Roof opened fire at the historic Black African Methodist Episcopal Church, killing nine people, including the pastor, State Senator Clementa Pinckney. Roof left behind a collection of racist selfies and a racist manifesto explaining his actions, and the incident provoked a push to remove the Confederate flag from public buildings.[37]

After the massacre in Charleston, Obama seemed to be much more unequivocal in haters of confronting head-on issues of race, racial hatred, and America's seeming determination to lock away Black men. Days later, in an interview for the podcast "WTF with Mark Maron," the president used the N-Word, declaring "Racism, we are not cured of it. And it's not just a matter of it not being polite to say nigger in public. That's not the measure of whether racism still exists or not. It's not just a matter of overt discrimination. Societies don't, overnight, completely erase everything that happened 200 to 300 years prior."[38]

He followed that up in a powerful, moving eulogy for Rev. Pinckney. President Obama addressed American racism head-on, noting how much more likely Black and Hispanic men are to be incarcerated. The eulogy helped put the issue of racial violence and hate before the national public in a way no president has ever done. "None of us can or should expect a transformation in race relations overnight," said President Obama. "Every time something like this happens, somebody says we have to have a conversation about race. We talk a lot about race. There's no shortcut. And we don't need more talk."[39]

After a couple days of hedging, South Carolina Governor Nikki Haley led the entire South Carolina political establishment in declaring that it was time to end the war of symbolism over the Confederate flag and retire it to a museum. Just two weeks later, Obama addressed the 106th national NAACP convention. Here he proposed a criminal justice reform plan, which included a reconsideration of who we send to jail and why, arguing that the justice agenda needed to resolve the huge disparities in school quality and discipline that begins as soon as kids set foot in their first classrooms. He pointed out other racial disparities that determine who gets hired, who graduates from college, who gets a police force that protects them, and who gets police that think of themselves as an occupying force. Said the president:

> Here's the thing: Over the last few decades, we've also locked up more and more nonviolent drug offenders than ever before, for

longer than ever before. And that is the real reason our prison population is so high. In far too many cases, the punishment simply does not fit the crime. If you're a low-level drug dealer or you violate your parole, you owe some debt to society. You have to be held accountable and make amends. But you don't owe 20 years. You don't owe a life sentence. That's disproportionate to the price that should be paid.[40]

Two days later, during a visit to a federal prison in El Reno, Oklahoma, Obama delivered a speech in which he noted how much more likely Black and Hispanic men are to be incarcerated, declaring: "When they describe their youth, these are young people who made mistakes that aren't that different from the mistakes I made and the mistakes that a lot of you guys made. The difference is that they did not have the kind of support structures, the second chances, the resources that would allow them to survive those mistakes."[41]

A major movement that emerged during Obama's last quarter was Black Lives Matter, which took form following the acquittal of George Zimmerman in the murder of Trayvon Martin. Prior to that it was just a hashtag on Twitter and only burst into the public's awareness during the demonstrations in Ferguson. While one of hundreds of organizations protesting in Ferguson, Black Lives Matter emerged as one of the best-organized and visible organizations, using Twitter and Facebook to organize and online conference calls to plan strategy. Black Lives Matter is a "model for how Black liberation groups in the 21st century can organize an effective freedom rights campaign," and by August 2015, the movement had at least 23 chapters in the United States, Canada, and Ghana, with Black people in London, Paris, and in Africa and Latin America planning additional chapters.[42] In 2014, Alicia Garza, cofounder of the organization, declared:

> When we say Black Lives Matter, we are talking about the ways in which Black people are deprived of our basic human rights and dignity. It is an acknowledgement that Black poverty and genocide is state violence. It is an acknowledgment that one million Black people are locked in cages in this country – one half of all people in prisons or jails – is an act of state violence. It is an acknowledgment that Black women continue to bear the burden of a relentless assault on our children and our families, and that assault is an act of state violence.[43]

9 | THE BEGINNING AND END OF "POST-RACIAL AMERICA"

On August 8, 2015, Black Lives Matter Movement activists disrupted and ultimately shut down a 5,000-person rally in Seattle, Washington, where Democratic presidential candidate Senator Bernie Sanders was slated to speak. Sanders remained silent; however, he has since embraced much of the group's rhetoric. Hillary Clinton, who shied away from open talk about race in her first presidential run, has also chosen to openly criticize racism and bias among Whites, in part a response to the demands of Black Lives Matter. "Our problem is not all kooks and Klansmen. It's also the cruel joke that goes unchallenged. It's the offhand comment about not wanting those people in the neighborhood," she said in a speech after the Charleston shooting. "Let's be honest, for a lot of well meaning, open-minded White people, the sight of a young Black man in a hoodie still evokes a twinge of fear."[44]

The most common response to Black Lives Matter has been "All Lives Matter" or, referring to the police, "Blue Lives Matter," despite that Black Lives Matter has never called for the killing of police. It has never said that Black lives matter more than any other lives. Los Angeles activist Patrisse Cullors, one of the founders of BLM, has been eloquent in explaining why the movement has been necessary and how it's more than about police treatment of African Americans. On the progressive *Democracy Now* radio show in July, 2016 she said:

> We have one million Black people living inside U.S. jails and prisons. We need to be talking about that. What are we going to do to reduce the jail and prison population? And what are we doing to ensure that when those folks come home, they actually have jobs to go back to, they actually have their voting rights restored? I want to talk about what it means to divest from policing and divest from this prison system that has completely destroyed Black families across the nation, and reinvesting into poor communities, reinvesting into allowing us to have access to healthy food, access to jobs, access to shelter. It's really simple, and yet it hasn't – it hasn't been done.[45]

But in nearly every interview, Cullors and her other BLM co-founders, Alicia Garza and Opal Tometi, have to face the question: Shouldn't you have called it Black Lives (also) Matter, you know, to avoid confusion? Perhaps the best response was from Felonious Monk, who tells fellow Black comedian Larry Wilmore: "If I break my leg, I do not want the doctor telling me, 'All legs should be healed,'" Monk explained. "I want the doctor to fix *my* leg."[46]

That it needs to be said clearly that Black lives matter, in fact, that a movement needs to be built around it – and that so many Americans reflexively believe that the name Black Lives Matter itself is racist and exclusionary – shows that the nation has a long way to go in terms of overcoming its racist roots and realizing greatness.

Under the presidency of Donald J. Trump, it is unlikely that any racial progress will be made. A poll in January 2020 found that after three years of Donald Trump, 65 percent of African Americans said it was a bad time to be Black in America and eight in 10 described the president as a "racist."[47] When Ahmaud Arbey was shot to death while jogging, Trump said it was "very disturbing" but added the possibility that there was "something that we didn't see on the tape" that might have provoked the gunmen. His refusal to condemn the murder, not surprisingly, led to outrage from the Black community, who recognized that Trump was giving a nod to his "largely White coalition," according to the *Washington Post*. "This killing is just the most egregious example right now of how sick people are and how racist they are in this country at the moment," said Representative Bonnie Watson Coleman, of New Jersey. "I don't care if you're Black walking down the street with a Bible in your hand – if a White person sees you, there's a good chance that you're going to be confronted." "When you have hate emanating from the Oval Office," said Karen Bass, the head of the Congressional Black Caucus, "why are you surprised?"[48]

The year 2020 will always be marked by the Covid-19 virus. Yet even as we face an unprecedented disease pandemic, Black America once again is disadvantaged as a group. According to a study by APM Research Lab in late May 2020, the overall mortality rate for African Americans was 2.4 times as high as the rate for Whites and 2.2 times as high as the rate for Asians and Latinos.[49] For example, in Michigan, African-Americans make up 14 percent of the state's population, but they have accounted for 33 percent of its reported infections and 40 percent of its deaths. Twenty-six percent of the state's infections and 25 percent of deaths were in Detroit, a city that is 79 percent African-American. In Chicago, Blacks made up 52 percent of the city's confirmed cases and 72 percent of deaths, much higher than their population percentage in the city. While part of the problem is caused by pre-existing health conditions, such as diabetes, asthma, heart disease, and obesity, clearly the one-sided death toll reflects a long history of institutional racism, as Black people are more likely to be poorer, underemployed, condemned to substandard housing, and given inferior healthcare because of their race.[50]

The racism, systematic and otherwise, that has afflicted Blacks in the United States from 1619 to the present has few parallels in world history. Still, in 2020, there is evidence that perhaps for the first time since America's founding, Whites, at least younger Whites, are having their eyes opened to what African-Americans have experienced, and continue to experience. While there is hope, especially with an upcoming presidential election, there is also the recognition that there have been centuries of false starts and broken promises. Perhaps, for the first time in American history, the ugly stain of racism against Blacks will, at least begin to be relegated to the annals of earlier generations who have been so tainted by its legacy.

NOTES

1. Winant, Howard. "Just Do It: Notes of Politics and Race at the Dawn of the Obama Presidency." *Du Bois Review* 6, No. 1 (2009), 49.
2. Harris, Fredrick. *The Price of the Ticket: Barack Obama and the Rise and Decline of Black Politics*. (Oxford: Oxford University Press, 2014), 188.
3. Tesler, Michael, and David O. Sears, *Obama's Race: The 2008 Election and the Dream of a Post-Racial America*. (Chicago: University of Chicago Press, 2010), 4.
4. Kennedy, Randall. *The Persistence of the Color Line: Racial Politics and the Obama Presidency*. (New York: Pantheon, 2011), 90.
5. Carbado, Devon W. and Mitu Gulati. *Acting White?: Rethinking Race in "Post-Racial" America*. (Oxford: Oxford University Press, 2015), 9.
6. Alim, H. Samy and Geneva Smitherman. *Articulate While Black: Barack Obama, Language, and Race in the U.S.* (Oxford: Oxford University Press, 2012), 64.
7. Alexander, Elizabeth. eds. Kenneth W. Mack and Guy-Uriel Charles. "Free Black Men," *The New Black: What Has Changed – and What Has Not – with Race in America Paperback*. (New York: The New Press, 2013), 192.
8. Butler, Paul. "The President and the Justice: Two Ways of Looking at a Post-Black Man," in *The New Black: What Has Changed – and What Has Not – with Race in America*, 65.
9. "Obama's Tightrope," *The Washington Post*, July 6, 2007. http://www.washingtonpost.com/wp-dyn/content/article/2007/07/05/AR2007070501828.html.
10. "The Bradley Effect," *The New York Times Magazine*, September 26, 2008.
11. "Clinton's King Comment 'Ill-Advised,' Obama Says," *Washington Post*, January 14, 2008. http://www.washingtonpost.com/wp-dyn/content/article/2008/01/13/AR2008011303624.html.
12. "Desperate Husband," *The New York Times*, January 28, 2008. http://www.nytimes.com/2008/01/28/opinion/28kristol.html?pagewanted=print.
13. Balz, Don and Haynes Johnson. *The Battle for America: 2008*. (New York: Viking, 2009), 173.
14. Logan, Enid. *"At This Defining Moment": Barack Obama's Presidential Candidacy and the New Politics of Race*. (New York: New York University Press, 2011), 63.

15. "On the 2008 Primary and Black Anger," *The American Prospect*, April 25, 2008. http://prospect.org/article/2008-primary-and-Black-anger.
16. "Does Obama's Winning Streak Prove that Race Does Not Matter?" *U.S. News & World Report*, February 15, 2008. http://www.usnews.com/news/campaign-2008/articles/2008/02/15/-does-obamas-winning-streak-prove-that-race-doesnt-matter.
17. Alim, H. Samy and Geneva Smitherman, *Articulate While Black*, 68.
18. Kinder, Donald R. and Allison Dale-Riddle. *The End of Race?: Obama, 2008, and Racial Politics in America*. (New Haven: Yale University Press, 2012), 41.
19. Kennedy, Randall. *The Persistence of the Color Line*, 123.
20. "Barack Obama's Speech on Race," *The New York Times*, March 18, 2008. http://www.nytimes.com/2008/03/18/us/politics/18text-obama.html.
21. "Ferraro's Obama Remarks Become Talk of Campaign," *The New York Times*, March 12, 2008. http://www.nytimes.com/2008/03/12/us/politics/12campaign.html?_r=0.
22. Kennedy, Randall. *The Persistence of the Color Line*, 158.
23. Ibid., 159.
24. Rasmussen Reports, November 10, 2008. http://www.rasmussenreports.com/public_content/politics/obama_administration/november_2008/number_of_Black_voters_who_view_society_fair_and_decent_nearly_doubles_after_election.
25. *U.S. News & World Report*, November 12, 2008. http://www.usnews.com/opinion/articles/2008/11/12/data-points-barack-obamas-impact-on-Black-voters.
26. Logan, 59.
27. Lee, Taeku. "Déjà Vu All Over Again? Racial Contestation in the Obama Era," *The New Black: What Has Changed – and What Has Not – with Race in America Paperback*, 34.
28. "For South, a Waning Hold on National Politics," *The New York Times*, November 10, 2008. http://www.nytimes.com/2008/11/11/us/politics/11south.html?_r=0&pagewanted=all.
29. Onwuachi-Willig, Angela. "An Officer and a Gentleman," *The New Black: What Has Changed – and What Has Not – with Race in America*, 149.
30. Pew Research Center, "Obama's Ratings Slide Across the Board," July 30, 2009. http://www.people-press.org/2009/07/30/obamas-ratings-slide-across-the-board/.
31. Michael Eric Dyson, "Professor Arrested for 'Housing While Black'", CNN, July 22, 2009, http://edition.cnn.com/2009/LIVING/07/22/dyson.police/index.html.
32. Willig, 149.

33. "Remarks by the President on Trayvon Martin," July 19, 2013. https://www.whitehouse.gov/the-press-office/2013/07/19/remarks-president-trayvon-martin.
34. "How Ferguson Changed America," *Slate*, August 2, 2015. http://www.slate.com/articles/news_and_politics/politics/2015/08/the_ferguson_anniversary_michael_brown_s_death_12_months_ago_led_to_america.html.
35. "Baltimore, By the Numbers: 200 Arrests, 15 Fires, 19 Officers Injured," *The Washington Post*, April 28, 2015. https://www.washingtonpost.com/local/baltimore-by-the-numbers-200-arrests-15-fires-19-officers-injured/2015/04/28/60d8b836-edae-11e4-a55f-38924fca94f9_story.html.
36. "Negative View of U.S. Race Relations Grows, Poll Finds," *The New York Times*, May 4, 2015. http://www.nytimes.com/2015/05/05/us/negative-view-of-us-race-relations-grows-poll-finds.html.
37. "Charleston: Governor, Senators Join In Saying Confederate Flag Should Go," *CNN*, June 24, 2015. http://www.cnn.com/2015/06/22/us/charleston-church-shooting-main/.
38. "Obama Uses N-word, Says We Are 'Not Cured' of Racism," *CNN*, June 22, 2015. http://www.cnn.com/2015/06/22/politics/barack-obama-n-word-race-relations-marc-maron-interview/.
39. "Remarks by the President in Eulogy for the Honorable Reverend Clementa Pinckney," June 26, 2015. https://www.whitehouse.gov/the-press-office/2015/06/26/remarks-president-eulogy-honorable-reverend-clementa-pinckney.
40. "Remarks by the President at the NAACP Conference," July 14, 2105. https://www.whitehouse.gov/the-press-office/2015/07/14/remarks-president-naacp-conference.
41. "Remarks by the President after Visit at El Reno Federal Correctional Institution," July 16, 1015. https://www.whitehouse.gov/the-press-office/2015/07/16/remarks-president-after-visit-el-reno-federal-correctional-institution.
42. Ruffin, Herbert. "Black Lives Matter: The Growth of a New Social Justice Movement." http://www.Blackpast.org/perspectives/Black-lives-matter-growth-new-social-justice-movement.
43. "A Herstory of the #BlackLivesMatter Movement by Alicia Garza," *The Feminist Wire*, October 7, 2014. http://www.thefeministwire.com/2014/10/Blacklivesmatter-2/.
44. "Hillary Clinton Calls America's Struggle with Racism Far From Over," *The New York Times*, June 20, 2015. http://www.nytimes.com/2015/06/21/us/politics/hillary-clinton-calls-americas-struggle-with-racism-far-from-over.html?_r=0.
45. http://www.democracynow.org/2015/7/24/part_2_Blacklivesmatter_founders_on_immigration.

46. "In 5 Minutes Larry Wilmore Explains Why Saying "#AllLivesMatter" Is Offensive," July 23, 2015. http://www.alternet.org/media/5-minutes-larry-wilmore-explains-why-saying-alllivesmatter-offensive.
47. Wootson Jr., Cleve R., Vanessa Williams, Dan Balz and Scott Clement. "Black Americans Are Deeply Pessimistic About the Country Under Trump, Whom More Than 8 in 10 Describe as 'a Racist,' Post-Ipsos Poll Finds, *The Washington Post*, January 17, 2020. https://www.washingtonpost.com/politics/Black-americans-deeply-pessimistic-about-country-under-president-who-more-than-8-in-10-describe-as-a-racist-post-ipsos-poll-finds/2020/01/16/134b705c-37de-11ea-bb7b-265f4554af6d_story.html.
48. Linskey, Annie. "Young Jogger's Death Upends Conversation at a Time of Racial Pain," May 10, 2020. https://www.washingtonpost.com/politics/young-joggers-death-upends-conversation-at-a-time-of-racial-pain/2020/05/09/8d02f248-9149-11ea-a9c0-73b93422d691_story.html
49. "The Color of Coronavirus: Covid-19 Deaths by Race and Ethnicity in the U.S.," APM Research Lab, May 27, 2020. https://www.apmresearchlab.org/covid/deaths-by-race.
50. Taylor, Keeanga-Yamahtta. "The Black Plague," *The New Yorker*, April 16, 2020. https://www.newyorker.com/news/our-columnists/the-Blackplague?utm_campaign=falcon&utm_source=linkedin&utm_brand=tny&utm_social-type=owned&utm_medium=social&mbid=social_facebook.

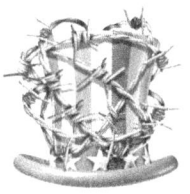

PART 3

HISPANIC AMERICANS

WHEN Republican presidential nominee Donald Trump descended the elevator, swarmed by media, to announce his candidacy in June 2015, his first shot across the bow in his pugilistic campaign was aimed at Mexicans. That day, and nearly every day after, he made immigration the centerpiece of his campaign. But the term Comprehensive Immigration Reform (CIR) did not escape from his lips that June day. Nor did he reach out to U.S. Latinos, as his own Republican party claimed to believe in doing.

Instead, he said this: "When Mexico sends its people, they're not sending their best. They're not sending you. They're not sending you. They're sending people that have lots of problems, and they're bringing those problems with them. They're bringing drugs. They're bringing crime. They're rapists. And some, I assume, are good people." Assuring his audience that his comments were not exclusive to Mexicans, he added, "It's coming from more than Mexico. It's coming from all over South and Latin America, and it's coming probably – probably – from the Middle East. But we don't know. Because we have no protection and we have no competence, we don't know what's happening. And it's got to stop, and it's got to stop fast."[1] A month later, he visited the U.S.–Mexico border in Laredo, Texas and insisted to reporters, "There is great danger with the illegals, tremendous danger with illegals," before boasting that he had a "great relationship" with Latinos.[2]

It was not the first time, nor will it likely be the last, that Hispanics have been vilified as unwanted intruders. Or killed because of it.

In what some have described as the deadliest attack on Latinos in recent American history, on August 3, 2019, Patrick Crusius, a 22-year-old White man from Allen Texas, shot and killed 23 people and injured two dozen others, in a Walmart in El Paso, Texas. Authorities say Crusius drove about 700 miles overnight from North Texas, with the stated objective of killing as many Mexicans as he could. In February 2020, Crusius was indicted by prosecutors on 90 federal charges, including 22 counts of committing a hate crime resulting in death, 22 counts of use of a firearm to commit murder, 23 counts of a hate crime involving an attempt to kill, and 23 counts of use of a firearm during a crime. It will be up to Attorney General William Barr to decide whether to pursue the death penalty.

Minutes before Crusius' shooting spree, someone, undoubtedly Crusius, posted a "manifesto" to 8chan, a dark website notorious for hosting lawless message boards where manifestos have appeared before mass shootings. It begins by praising the manifesto of the gunman who killed 51 Muslims at two mosques in New Zealand earlier that year and cites a White supremacist theory known as "The Great Replacement." The theory postulates that a secret group of elites is working to destroy the White race by replacing them with immigrants and refugees. "This attack is a response to the Hispanic invasion of Texas," the manifesto says. It notes that many migrants return to their home countries to reunite with family, stating that "the Hispanic population is willing to return to their home countries if given the right incentive. An incentive that myself and many other patriotic Americans will provide." The author warns that terrorist attacks will "remove the threat of the Hispanic voting bloc," adding, "This is just the beginning of the fight for America and Europe." El Paso City Council member, Cassandra Hernandez, whose district includes the Walmart store, said "The mass shooting our community endured is clearly a symptom of a much larger problem that the United States has to face fully. Execution or life imprisonment for a White supremacist will not stop ethnic cleansing in other Hispanic communities like El Paso. This heinous hate crime on the US-Mexico border is the definition of domestic terrorism invoked by White nationalism."[3]

In reality, immigration from Mexico is negative, meaning that more Mexicans are leaving than are arriving in the U.S. From 2009 to 2014, 1 million Mexicans and their families left the U.S. for Mexico, while an estimated 870,000 Mexican nationals left Mexico to come to the U.S., a smaller number than the flow of families from the U.S. to Mexico.[4] While the giant share of growth in the Hispanic population will come from those born in the United States, the rhetoric from the White House is more a propos to an invasion. Xenophobia and resistance to immigration are no strangers to America, but it seems for White Americans, the appearance of Mexicans and other Latin Americans, so many of whom are not White, is a source of great concern, one that is only magnified by a president throwing gasoline on the flames.

NOTES

1. "Donald Trump Announces a Presidential Bid," *The Washington Post*, June 16, 2015. https://www.washingtonpost.com/news/post-politics/wp/2015/06/16/full-text-donald-trump-announces-a-presidential-bid/.
2. "At Texas-Mexico Border, Donald Trump Cites 'Great Danger' from Immigrants," *Los Angeles Times*, July 23, 2015. http://www.latimes.com/nation/nationnow/la-na-trump-texas-border-20150723-story.html.
3. "El Paso Walmart Shooting Suspect Charged with Federal Hate Crimes," *Al Jazeera USA*. February 7, 2020, https://www.aljazeera.com/news/2020/02/el-paso-walmart-shooting-suspect-charged-federal-hate-crimes-200207202430822.html.
4. Gonzalez-Barrera, Ana. "More Mexicans Leaving Than Coming to the U.S.," *Pew Research Center*, November 19. 2015. https://www.pewresearch.org/hispanic/2015/11/19/more-mexicans-leaving-than-coming-to-the-u-s/.

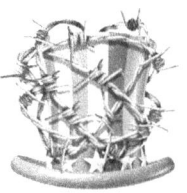

10

CONQUESTS

WRITING of Mexican Americans, historian Robert R. Treviño notes, "Racism has dogged Mexican immigrants (and native-born) far longer and more virulently than it did any European group that at some given time suffered from American anti-immigrant hysteria and nativism."[1] It is ironic, given that unlike European immigrants, Hispanics did not cross an ocean to arrive here. Rather, Puerto Rico and a gargantuan swath of Mexico were acquired through conquest, occupation, and exploitation. As a Mexican saying goes, "The border crossed us; we did not cross the border." In the 20th century, the mass immigration of Mexicans and Puerto Ricans – the two largest Hispanic groups – experienced exploitation and racism, laying the foundation for subsequent patterns of social and economic inequality of Hispanics. To quote the great historian Corey McWilliams, writing, in 1948, of our relationship with Mexico:

> It is important to remember that Mexicans are a conquered people in the Southwest, a people whose culture has been under incessant attack for many years and whose character and achievements, as a people, have been consistently disparaged … Throughout this struggle, the Anglo-Americans have possessed every advantage: in numbers and wealth, arms and machines … More is involved, in situations of this kind, than the defeat of individual ambitions,

for the victims also suffer from the defeat of their culture and of the society of which they are a part.[2]

The history of the United States is generally told in terms of the western expansion of Anglo pioneers. Fundamental to the American narrative is that we are a nation of immigrants, those who fled oppression in Europe in search of life, liberty, and the pursuit of happiness. What this perspective ignores, however, is the exploitative, brutal manner by which we have conducted ourselves in our dealings with our southern neighbors. It also ignores the enormous contribution of Hispanic culture to American history and progress. In order to grasp the role of Hispanics in the building of America, it behooves us, in the words of historian Felipe Fernández-Armesto, to "tilt the map," to get a sense of our history along a "north-south" axis, rather than the "east-west" perspective, which has engulfed itself into the American narrative.[3]

The Hispanic imprint on the United States is unmistakable, particularly in the Southwest and West. There are over 2,000 cities and towns in the United States with Spanish names, including over 400 in California, 250 in Texas and New Mexico, and over 100 in both Colorado and Arizona. In Colorado, the names of 19 counties are in Spanish. Spanish names appear in Nevada, Wyoming, Utah, Oregon, Montana, and Idaho, and often the original Spanish names have been Anglicized, as is the case in Waco, California, (originally Hueco); other times, Spanish and English names have been combined, such as Buena Park, Altaville, and Minaview.[4] The name California comes from a mythical island from the 1510 Spanish novel *Las Sergas de Esplandián* by Garci Rodríguez de Montalvo. Colorado means "red colored;" Florida means "flowery;" Nevada translates to "snowy;" and Montana comes from *montaña*, meaning mountain. In cowboy parlance, the words buckaroo, corral, chaps, desperado, lasso, ranch, rodeo, and stampede are all of Spanish origin.

Indeed, the first European settlement in what is now the United States of America was not in Jamestown, as most of us have been taught, but Puerto Rico, in 1505. Eight years later, Juan Ponce de Leon, set sail for Florida in search of the Fountain of Youth, and in 1557, Santa Elena, in what is now South Carolina, was established as Spain's first Florida colony; the viceroy of New Spain mistakenly thought it was near Zacatecas, Mexico. Florida's first enduring colony was founded in 1565 by Pedro Menéndez de Avilés at St. Augustine, and it was to be the region's most significant city for nearly three centuries.[5]

Florida's historical importance, however, lies more in being a launching pad for subsequent Spanish exploration and settlement. In 1527, a 300-man inland expedition headed by Pánfilo de Narváez, the former governor of Cuba, set out from present-day Tallahassee; after a barrage of Indian attacks, the expedition was reduced to four men, including the second-in-command, Álvar Núñez Cabeza de Vaca, who after spending a year in Indian captivity, trekked 6,000 miles across North America, arriving in northern Mexico in 1534. Five years later, Francisco Vázquez de Coronado marched from central Mexico into present-day Arizona, New Mexico, Texas, Oklahoma, and Kansas; that same year, Hernando de Soto sailed from Cuba and explored Georgia, South Carolina, Alabama, Mississippi, Arkansas, and Louisiana. By the mid-1500s, the "Tierra Nueva" to the north had been well explored, and its fertile lands, unconverted souls, and unexploited labor sources beckoned the Spanish king's representatives in Mexico to send settlers.

Once explored, the Catholic Church dispatched Franciscan, Dominican, and Jesuit monks to convert the Natives.[6] The Franciscans founded nearly forty missions in Florida, Georgia, and Alabama alone. While most were abandoned, missions in the Southeast laid the foundation for such cities as San Antonio, El Paso, Santa Fe, Tucson, San Diego, Los Angeles, Monterey, and San Francisco.[7] Writes Juan Gonzalez:

> The Florida missions and settlements left a greater imprint on frontier American culture than we might believe.... The knowledge the missionaries imparted to the Indians, whether in agriculture, language, customs, or technology, did not disappear when the last monk departed. Rather, it remained part of Indian experience, so that by the time Anglos began settling in the Southeast, they discovered the "civilized tribes," among them the Creeks, the Cherokees, and the Choctaws. Even some of the most nomadic and fierce of the Southwest nations, the Apaches, Comanches, and Kiowas, partially assimilated into Spanish society.[8]

Meanwhile, the frontiers of Mexico crept northward. In 1580, an expedition of Franciscans and laymen, mostly miners, left to settle New Mexico. However, the laymen soon returned to Mexico, and an expedition a few years later found that the monks had been killed by Indians. In 1598, the Spanish army arrived at the Rio Grande, and a city was founded, San Juan de los Caballeros; in 1610, the capital was established in Santa Fe. Though the Spanish crown sponsored the New Mexican venture, spending 2,390,000 pesos during the 17th century to settle the province, it was the Franciscans who received over half the funding, and they controlled the region. In 1613, Fray Isidro Ordoñez effected a coup d'état, arresting the governor and seizing his powers.[9]

During the 16th century, Spain was chiefly occupied with its mission outposts in Florida and New Mexico. However, beginning in the 17th century, encroachments by the English colonies, which spanned from New England to Jamaica, and French traders, pushing southward along the Mississippi River, made it an imperative that the Spanish set their sights northward. Additionally, French and English buccaneers from the West Indies were marauding Spanish settlements in Florida and the coastal towns of Mexico. As European empires and commercial interests clashed, the relative isolation of the Spanish colonies in North America was coming to an end. A buffer was needed, and the region called Texas, which lay between New Mexico and included parts of what is now Louisiana, perfectly fit the bill.[10]

In 1718, a Franciscan, Fray Antonio de Olivares, established a mission, the Alamo, with colonists from the Canary Islands and heavy subsidies from the Spanish crown. It would become Spain's most impressive success. Peace with the Apaches enabled the colonists to farm, and by 1790, the town's population had about 1,500 Spaniards, with 4,000 in the entire province. Despite some successes, however, the Texas colonies were a constant source of consternation for Spain. Tensions between church and state were endless, and disease killed thousands, including a particularly virulent smallpox epidemic in the late 1770s and early 1780s.[11]

The Seven Years War, known in the United States as the French and Indian War, which lasted from 1754 until 1763, marked a turning point in Spanish North America. In 1762, King Charles of Spain acquired the vast expanse of Louisiana in a treaty signed at Fontainebleau with his cousin, Louis XV of France, though it was retroceded to France in 1800. In 1763, following its defeat at the hands of Great Britain, France withdrew from continental North America, and Spain ceded Florida to the British. The disappearance of France provided relief to Texas in its role as a buffer region, and the illusion of security fed Spanish interest in Arizona, which had been founded in 1690. At the same time, the fear of encroachments by Russia and Britain led Spain to move into Alta California and the Pacific Northwest. Headed by Captain Gaspar de Portola, the governor of Baja California, and Fray Junípero Serra, a Franciscan, Spain established a chain of missions, presidios, and pueblos along the California coast between 1769 and 1817, including San Diego in 1769, Monterey in 1770, San Francisco in 1776, Los Angeles in 1781, and Santa Barbara in 1782.[12]

At first, California's coastal Indians greeted the Spaniards amicably. However, conflict ensued as the Spanish soldiers blatantly disregarded Indian territorial rights and customs and began to sexually assault Native women. To discourage these sexual attacks, Father Serra began to promote intermarriage to "establish Catholic family life" and "to foster alliances between the soldiers and the Indians." As a result, by 1794, the majority of non-native people in California were officially classified as being of mixed race, though many were Cataláns, Basques, Irish, and Black. In 1777, only a third of the men and a quarter of the women who founded San Francisco and San Jose identified themselves as White Spaniards.[13] In Los Angeles, over half of the founding families were of African heritage; and Jews from the Iberian Peninsula sought refuge from the Inquisition in the province of New Mexico.[14] Despite this racial potpourri, however, Spanish *peninsulares* (Spaniards born in Spain) overwhelmingly were the *adelantados*, the officials and the priests who governed.[15]

These Spaniards brought with them a complex system of racial and social stratification that had evolved in New Spain. Until 1537, the issue of whether Indians were rational, indeed human, was a subject of debate. However, on June 2, 1537, Pope Paul III issued a papal bull, *Sublimus Deus*, which declared that Native Americans were indeed true men, made "in the image of God," and capable of rational thought. The term *gente de razón*, people of reason, emerged as a designation for all the crown's Christianized subjects, be they of any race.[16] However, as notes Gregory Rodriguez, "widespread miscegenation led those at the top of society … to cling to the concept of racial purity in order to maintain their … position of power and authority in society."[17]

By the 17th century, the peninsular-born Spanish elite and their American-born progeny, *criollos*, formulated a rigid system of racial categorization, the *sistema de castas*, which placed themselves at the top, those of mixed race, *castas*, in the middle, and Blacks, both free and slave, at the bottom. Generally speaking, the darker the *casta*, the lower the ranking. According to one caste list employed in 18th century New Spain:

> Spaniard and Indian beget mestizo
> Mestizo and Spanish woman beget castizo
> Castizo woman and Spaniard beget Spaniard
> Spanish woman and Negro beget mulatto
> Spaniard and mulatto woman beget morisco
> Morisco woman and Spaniard beget albino
> Spaniard and albino woman beget torna atrás
> Indian and torna atrás woman beget lobo
> Lobo and Indian woman beget zambaigo
> Zambaigo and Indian woman beget cambujo
> Cambujo and mulatto woman beget albarazado
> Albarazado and mulatto woman beget barcino
> Barcino and mulatto woman beget coyote
> Coyote woman and Indian beget chamiso
> Chamiso woman and mestizo beget coyote mestizo
> Coyote mestizo and mulatto woman beget ahí te estás.[18]

As interracial marriage became more common, racial lines became increasingly blurred in New Spain, and this was no different in the northern frontier. In Texas, the caste system broke down rapidly, and skilled *castas* were frequently allowed to change their racial designation. One mason who worked on the mission in San Antonio appears in four different documents with three different racial identities – Indian, mestizo, and Spaniard. In 1779, a sculptor was listed as a mulatto in the census, but after amassing wealth, he was labeled as Spanish in 1793. Writes Rodriguez, "In colonial Texas socioeconomic mobility trumped racial exclusivity."[19]

In Alta California, early settlers reflected the existing racial classification practice, albeit with some modifications. There were few Spaniards among the area's first inhabitants, mostly officials of the clergy, crown, and military, and a largely nonwhite, influential and wealthy group of landowners emerged to provide the frontier with an "aristocratic-like" society. These upper class "*Californianos*" came to embrace the term "*gente de razón*" and imbued it with a non-Indian, non-Mexican biological standing. Living in isolation from New Spain allowed the Californianos a certain distance from their indigenous roots, and a "penchant for Spanish affiliation" prevailed, later resulting in the social ostracism of incoming settlers from Mexico.[20]

In his book *Two Years before the Mast*, published in 1840, the traveling New Englander, Richard Henry Dana, describes the aristocratic culture of Alta California:

> They can be distinguished, not only by their complexion, dress, and manners, but also by their speech; for calling themselves, Castilians, they are very ambitious speaking the pure Castilian, while all Spanish is spoken in a somewhat corrupted dialect by the lower classes. From this upper class, they [become] more and more dark and muddy, until you come to the pure Indian, who runs about with nothing upon him but a small piece of cloth.

Yet Dana notes that just a single drop of Spanish blood was enough "to raise one from the position of a serf, and entitle him to wear a suit of clothes – boots, hat, cloak, spurs, long knife … and to call himself Español, and to hold property, if he can get any."[21]

By 1800, the United States had emerged with a prosperous economy, while Mexico lagged behind, plagued by civil anarchy, a large landless class, and capital flight; its per capita income was nearly half that of its northern neighbor, and it produced little more than half the number of goods and services.[22] Border disputes over Florida, the Louisiana Purchase of 1803, and the Pacific Northwest were a source of constant friction between the United States and Spain until the Adams-Onís treaty of

1819, which ceded Florida to the United States, while Arizona, Utah, New Mexico, Texas, a strip of Wyoming, three-quarters of Colorado, and the southwestern corner of Kansas and the Oklahoma panhandle went to Spain. When the Mexican Republic was established in 1821, it occupied the largest territory in the Western Hemisphere and was twice the size of the United States.[23]

ACQUISITION OF TEXAS AND WAR WITH MEXICO

Despite having renounced its claim on Texas, many in the United States continued to have pretensions toward the area and believed that Congress had no right or power to relinquish an "American possession." The Mexican government, desperate for settlers, opened Texas to Anglo settlers. In 1821, Stephen Austin founded the colony of San Felipe de Austin, and by 1830, about 20,000 freemen and 2,000 slaves had settled there. The settlers resented conditions set by the Mexican government that restricted immigration and mandated that settlers become Catholic and take an oath of allegiance to Mexico. In 1826, President John Quincy Adams offered to buy Texas for $1 million, which Mexico refused. In the summer of 1832, American colonists were routed by troops following their attack on a Mexican garrison, and in October, 55 delegates, headed by Austin, met in San Felipe de Austin and drafted a resolution calling for more autonomy. The next year, Austin was imprisoned after writing the San Antonio *ayuntamiento*, the municipal government, asking it to declare Texas a separate state. A year later, he concluded, "War is our only recourse. There is no other remedy."[24]

In 1836, Santa Anna led an army of 6,000 conscripted soldiers across the desert to Texas, many of whom were Mayan and spoke no Spanish. About 1,800 marched to San Antonio where Texan and non-Texan reinforcements took refuge in the Alamo, and after a thirteen-day siege, nearly all defenders were killed. Following the Alamo and the defeat of another garrison at Goliad, southeast of San Antonio, "Remember the Alamo! Remember Goliad!" became a rallying cry to arms for Anglo-Americans, and volunteers, weapons, and money poured into Texas. That same year, Sam Houston and an army of about 1,100 men captured Santa Anna in a surprise attack at San Jacinto, and the Lone Star Republic was born, paving the way for nine years of hostilities with Mexico, which refused to accept the defeat as final, and, ultimately, the Mexican-American War.[25]

The issue of whether to annex Texas aroused bitter controversy in the United States between the North and the South. In the North, abolitionists, determined to prevent the further spread of slavery, argued that annexation would cause the dissolution of the Union and be a bone of contention between the United States and Mexico, as well as Great Britain, which was strongly abolitionist and also had financial interests at stake. Southern states, on the other hand, declared that refusal by Washington to annex would justify secession; the legislatures of Alabama, Mississippi, Tennessee, and other southern states adopted resolutions arguing for annexation and declaring it necessary in order to prevent England from gaining control and using Texas as a base to oppose slavery in the United States.

In 1844, James K. Polk, a strong advocate of annexation and U.S. expansion, won the presidency, and in March 1845, the Congress of the United States passed an annexation resolution, which was approved by outgoing president John Tyler. The Texas Congress accepted the terms offered by the United States, and on December 29, Texas became a state.[26] There ensued a dispute with Mexico, which claimed the border to be not at the Rio Grande River but 150 miles to the north at the Nueces River, and Mexico broke off diplomatic relations with the United States. Polk, now president, ordered General Zachary Taylor and an army of 4,000 men into the disputed area, and he sent a minister plenipotentiary, John Slidell, on a mission to Mexico to negotiate. When Mexico refused to accept Slidell's credentials and Taylor's troops were met with arms, Polk drafted a declaration of war, claiming that Mexico had "shed American blood upon the American soil." In May 1846, Congress declared war.[27]

Although many Americans at the time believed that the United States had provoked the war in a flagrant land grab, those clamoring for territorial expansion overwhelmed them. The poet Walt Whitman declared: "Yes: Mexico must be thoroughly chastised! We have reached a point in our intercourse with that country, when prompt and effectual demonstrations of force are enjoined upon us by every dictate of right and policy."[28]

Others opposed the war and the acquisition of Mexican territory and its "colored mongrels" on racial grounds. Senator John C. Calhoun, a defender of slavery, told the Senate, "We have never dreamt of incorporating into our Union any but the Caucasian race – the free White race." Andrew Donelson, the nephew of Andrew Jackson, warned President Polk, "We can no more amalgamate with her people than with negroes."[29]

Once war was declared, the Americans executed a brutal and bloody campaign, and atrocities committed against Mexicans were the norm. Wrote Captain Ulysses S. Grant, "Some of the volunteers and about all the Texans seem to think it perfectly right to impose on the people of a conquered city to any extent, and even to murder them where the act can be covered by the dark. And how much they seem to enjoy acts of violence too!" General Winfield Scott acknowledged that American soldiers had "committed atrocities to make Heaven weep and every American of Christian morals blush for his country. Murder, robbery, and rape of mothers and daughters in the presence of tied-up males of the families have been common all along the Rio Grande." In early 1848, a few months after Scott's army occupied Mexico City, the two countries signed the Treaty of Guadalupe Hidalgo, and Mexico accepted the Rio Grande as the Texas border and ceded California, New Mexico, Nevada, and parts of Colorado, Arizona, and Utah, a total of over one million square miles, to the United States for a mere $15 million.[30]

Thousands of Mexicans now found themselves living within the United States, though the treaty did permit them to either remain in the U.S. or move across the new border into Mexico; those that stayed were guaranteed "the enjoyment of all the rights of citizens of the United States according to the principles of the Constitution." Most stayed, if only because their homes were north of the Rio Grande, and they became second-class citizens, "foreigners in their own land." The war had been premised on the doctrine of "*manifest destiny*" and a "belief in American Anglo-Saxon superiority." As one Mexican diplomat predicted, "Descendants of the Indians that we are, the North Americans hate us, their spokesmen depreciate us … they clearly manifest that their future expansion begins with the territory that they take from us and pushing aside our citizens who inhabit the land."

Mexicans found themselves powerless as Anglos enacted laws, such as the "Greaser Act," an anti-vagrancy act that defined vagrants as "all persons … of Spanish or Indian blood."[31] Additionally, the widespread confiscation of Mexican property prompted many owners to sell their land at bargain prices.[32]

The disparaging way Anglos viewed Mexicans is aptly depicted in the account of Lieutenant J.H. Simpson, who, traveling to New Mexico in 1849, described the first man he saw as "a swarthy, copper-colored young Mexican, of eighteen or twenty years, most miserably clad, driving the sheep before him.… With brimless hat on, a forlorn blanket about his shoulders, and pantaloons which were only an apology for such, hugged his only wrapper, his steps slow and measured, I thought he looked the very personification of patience and resignation." Mexicans, according to historian Corey McWilliams, "came to be synonymous, to most Anglo-Americans, with the lowest possible status."[33]

In the 1850's, Anglo-Americans, who distinguished themselves as "White folks," expelled entire communities of Mexicans, including Austin in 1853 and 1855. Architect Frederick Olmstead, in his book *A Journey through Texas*, an account of his saddleback trip through the state in 1856 and 1857, cites a newspaper article he encountered describing the uprooting of Mexicans in Matagorda County:

> The people of Matagorda County have held a meeting and ordered every Mexican to leave the county. To strangers this may seem wrong, but we hold it to be perfectly right and highly necessary; but a word of explanation should be given. In the first place, then, there are none but the lower class or "Peon" Mexicans in the county; secondly, they have no fixed domicile, but hang around the plantations, taking the likeliest negro girls for wives; and thirdly, they often steal horses, and these girls, too, and endeavor to run them to Mexico. We should rather have anticipated an appeal to lynch law, than the mild course which has been adopted.[34]

Fueled by bitter memories of the Alamo and the Mexican American War, there was resentment and antipathy on both sides. According to historian David Montejano, the basic rules "called for a separation of Mexican and Anglo cowboys and a general authority structure in which Anglo stood over Mexican."[35] Violence against Mexicans was commonplace. Mexicans, like Juan "Cheno" Cortina, who challenged the authority structure, were labeled as "*bandits*" and "outlaws." In 1859, Cortina, the son of a wealthy landowner, shot a Brownsville marshal after he brutally beat a drunken Mexican ranchero, and then rode into town with fifty followers, raised the Mexican flag, and shot to death the local jailers and four other Whites. Within months, Cortina organized an army of five to six hundred men and defeated the local Texas Rangers. He eluded capture, even when pursued by federal troops headed by Colonel Robert E. Lee, and became the "most feared Mexican American in Texas." He launched guerrilla raids into Texas from the safe haven he was granted in Mexico and called for the liberation of Mexicans and the extermination of the Anglo "*tyrants*," whom he called "flocks of vampires, in guise of men."[36]

When, following the Treaty of Guadalupe Hidalgo, the United States acquired Alta California, the first concern that Americans had was to make the area safe for its citizens. Because of their numbers, the native Californians were considered a threat. In the words of one contemporary observer: "The authorities made it an aim everywhere, and particularly … in San Francisco, to build up a community that would overawe the Mexican population of the entire territory and create such an interest on the other side that the country could never go back to Mexico. The tendency of all their acts was in that direction – throwing out great inducements for people to come here who would be anything else but Mexican."[37]

With the discovery of gold in California in 1848, prospectors flooded into the territory, which became a state in 1850. Questions soon emerged regarding the role of Mexicans living in the new state. First, the majority of Mexicans living there were native Californians, who would automatically become citizens unless they turned down the offer. Second, the only significant group of Latin Americans to come to California once the Gold Rush began were Chileans, Peruvians, and Sonorans of northern Mexico, people of considerable value who knew mining and could serve by example and instruction in the mines.

When the Gold Rush began, things went smoothly. However, by 1849, as more Anglos poured into the mines, prejudice against foreigners mounted, particularly in the southern mines where many Mexicans were congregated. Foreign miners were notified that "none but Americans [are] allowed" on the North and Middle Forks of the Stanislaus River, and some Mexican miners were ousted from Sherlock's Diggings in Mariposa. In Calaveras Diggings, when a group of Chileans resisted, first by legal appeals and then by force, three of their leaders were shot, and the rest were flogged and then banished from the mines.[38]

American rhetoric about the "rights" of Americans and the need to suppress "foreign trespassers" mounted. In April 1850, a miner's tax of $20, an "excessive" amount, was imposed on all foreigners. The result was an exodus of Mexicans, aggravated by an extremely dry winter that ruined some of the southern mining camps. Though the law was repealed the following year, by September 1850, half to three-quarters of the estimated 15,000 to 25,000 Mexican miners – about 10,000 of whom were from Sonora alone – had left the mines, leaving some to wonder if the anti-immigrant legislation had the result of "keeping out not the gambler, the cut-throat and the thief, but the industrious sober foreigner – the ordinary worker who had the same ups and downs as his American counterpart."[39]

During the last half of the 19th century, as cotton production increased in Texas, in large part driven by the building of new railroad lines across the region, there was a convergence of Blacks from the east and Mexicans from the south, as both worked together on plantations, and Anglo cotton farmers relied on both to plant and pick cotton, often using vagrancy laws to compel them to work. A common perception of the time was that Mexicans were "specially fitted for the burdensome task of bending his back to picking the cotton and … grubbing the fields." The arrival of Mexican laborers and the "gradual but sure Latinizing of central Texas" was characterized by one Texan researcher at the time as an invasion of "voracious insects"; he reported that "Mexicans did not hit the interior cotton lands with the impact of a hurricane, but seeped in silently and undermined the rural social structure like termites eating out the sills of a wooden house." According to historian Neil Foley, "The presence of Mexicans and Blacks in their midst as sharecroppers and day laborers became a visible reminder to White tenants that they were but one rung removed from the social, economic, and racial stigma of sharecropping."[40]

NOTES

1. Treviño, Robert R. "Teaching Mexican American History," *OAH Magazine of History*, Vol. 19, No. 6, Nov., 2005, 19.
2. McWilliams, Corey. *North from Mexico: The Spanish-Speaking People of the United States*. (New York, NY: Greenwood Press, 1968), 132.
3. Fernández-Armesto, Felipe. *Our America: A Hispanic History of the United States*. (New York, NY: W.W. Norton & Company, 2014), xx.
4. Ibid., 294.
5. Ibid., 4.
6. Gonzalez, Juan. *Harvest of Empire: A History of Latinos in America*. (New York, NY: Penguin Books, 2011), 9.
7. Ibid., 16.
8. Ibid.
9. Fernández-Armesto, 51.
10. Bolton, Herbert E. *The Spanish Borderlands*. (New Haven, CT: Yale University Press, 1921), 207.
11. Fernández-Armesto, 72.
12. Fontana, Bernard L. *Entrada: The Legacy of Spain and Mexico in the United States*. (Albuquerque, NM: The University of New Mexico Press, 1994), 188.
13. Rodriguez, 66.
14. Ruiz, Vicki L. "Nuestra América: Latino History as United States History," *The Journal of American History*, Vol. 93, No. 3 (Dec., 2006), 657.
15. Fontana, 168.
16. Miranda, Gloria E. "Racial and Cultural Dimensions of 'Gente de Razón' Status in Spanish and Mexican California," *Southern California Quarterly*, Vol. 70, No. 3 (Fall 1988), 267.
17. Rodriguez, Gergory. *Mongrels, Bastards, Orphans, and Vagabonds: Mexican Immigration and the Future of Race in America*. (New York, NY: Pantheon Books, 2007), 47.
18. Ibid.
19. Ibid., 63.
20. Miranda, 271.
21. Dana, Richard Henry *Two Years Before The Mast*. (New York, NY: Cosimo Inc., 1965), 83.
22. Raat, W. Dirk and Michael M. Brescia. *Mexico and the United States: Ambivalent Vistas*. (Athens, GA: The University of Georgia Press, 2010), 62.
23. Fontana, 188.

24. Acuña, Rodolfo. *Occupied America: A History of Chicanos.* (New York, NY: Pearson Longman, 2002), 46.
25. Raat and Bescia, 76.
26. Barker, Eugene C. "The Annexation of Texas," The *Southwestern Historical Quarterly*, Vol. 50, No. 1 (Jul., 1946), 50.
27. Acuña, 50.
28. Whitman, Walt. "On the Mexican War and Annexation of Territory," 1846. http://nationalhumanitiescenter.org/ows/seminarsflvs/Whitman.pdf.
29. Foley, Neil. *The White Scourge: Mexicans, Blacks, and Poor Whites in Texas Cotton Culture.* (Berkeley, CA: University of California Press, 1997), 22.
30. Takaki, Ronald. *A Different Mirror: A History of Multicultural America.* (New York, NY: Back Bay Books, 1993), 176.
31. Ibid., 177.
32. Montejano, David. *Anglos and Mexicans in the Making of Texas, 1836–1986.* (Austin, TX: The University of Texas Press, 1987), 30.
33. McWilliams, 149.
34. Olmstead, Frederick Law. "A Journey through Texas; or, a Saddle-Trip on the Southwestern Frontier," 1857; in Montejano, 28.
35. Ibid., 83.
36. Montejano, 72; Acuña, 71.
37. Morefield, Richard Henry. "Mexicans in the California Mines, 1848-5," *California Historical Society Quarterly*. Vol. 35, No. 1 (Mar., 1956), 37.
38. Ibid., 38.
39. Carrigan, William D. and Clive Webb. "The Lynching of Persons of Mexican Origin or Descent in the United States, 1848 to 1928," *Journal of Social History*. Vol. 37, No. 2 (Winter 2003), 422; Morefield, 40.
40. Foley, 36.

11

CHEAP LABOR AND MOB VIOLENCE

WITH THE arrival of larger numbers of Anglo-Americans to Texas in the 1870s and 1880s, violence committed against Mexicans increased as many Anglos perceived that Mexicans, by working for lower wages, were stealing their jobs and lowering the standard of living in their neighborhoods. Additionally, there were frequent conflicts between Blacks and Mexicans as Anglo employers hired "cheap Mexican labor" to displace Blacks. In 1894, a riot broke out between Mexicans and Blacks accompanied by some "wild White boys" in Bee County, just north of Corpus Christi, which culminated in a raid on the Mexican quarter and the "Ku-Kluxing" of the residents. In the late 1890s, a group of Anglo vigilantes rose up in Hays County, south of Austin, to warn planters not to rent to Mexicans and Blacks. In three neighboring counties, White tenant farmers threatened violence on landowners who rented to Mexicans or hired them as laborers.[1] Many Mexicans were forced to seek the protection of the local Anglo powerbrokers, who treated them as "serfs."[2]

Most Anglos ascribed to Mexicans the classification of being non-White Indian mestizos or peons, and Mexicans were treated as racial foreigners. While those Mexicans who ventured out of Texas into the Deep South were bequeathed the status of "white," given the relative absence of "Negro blood" running through their veins, in Texas, becoming White and therefore American was unattainable to all those except Mexicans of the highest socio-economic positions. Many Mexicans, particularly White Mexicans, bought into this. The Mexico of Porfirio Díaz, whose rule lasted from 1876 to 1910, extolled the virtues of Europe, especially French culture, and as a result, refugees from his regime had learned the benefits of whiteness before coming to the United States. Yet these benefits only went so far in Texas, and Anglos were reluctant to accept any Mexican as an equal. Writes Neil Foley, "When Anglo Texans married Mexicans, they often juggled the nomenclature to whiten their spouses by calling them Spanish Americans or simply Spanish. Mexican men, however, were only rarely accorded status as White persons, such as when they were owners of large ranches with marriageable daughters." Once back in Texas, "Mexican Jim" thus reverted to being the Mexican Santiago Tafolla, for in Texas, unlike antebellum Georgia, Mexicans were still Mexicans.[3]

Mexicans were an integral part of the workforce used for railroad construction in the Southwest, as well as mining, particularly in Arizona, New Mexico, and California. During the 1880s, they made up a majority of laborers laying tracks for the Texas and Mexican railroad. By 1900, the Southern Pacific Railroad had 4,500 Mexican workers in California. Even when they did the same work as Anglos, their wages were substantially lower. According to historian Ronald Takaki, in the silver mines of Arizona Mexican workers found themselves in a "caste labor system," earning between $12 and $30 a month and a weekly ration of flour; White workers received between $30 and $70 a month, plus board. Forced to live in towns owned by the mining companies, Mexicans had no other option but to pay high prices for food and clothing at the company stores, frequently on credit, and many found themselves in debt.[4] Said one mine owner, "My own experience has taught me that the lower class of Mexicans ... are docile, faithful, good servants, capable of strong attachments when firmly and kindly treated. They have been '*peons*' for generations. They will always remain so, as it is their natural condition."[5]

In California, Mexican labor was deemed superior to Chinese workers, as fears of the "yellow peril" gripped early twentieth century imaginations. A San Francisco minister wrote in 1926, "The Mexican is the preferred of all the cheap labor available to the Southwest. On Oriental labor, Chinese and Japanese and Hindu, the verdict has already been cast. California has swung our national jury to an almost unanimous vote."[6]

The subordinate racial status of Mexicans, their low wages, and their expertise and skill in performing certain jobs, such as mining, led to enmity from the native Anglos, and violence, usually extralegal, followed. According to historians, William D. Carrigan and Clive Webb, between 1848 and 1928 mobs lynched at least 597 Mexicans. They note that between 1848 and 1879 Mexicans were lynched at a rate of 473 per 100,000 of the population, an astounding figure when considering that the highest lynching rate for African Americans was in Mississippi, between 1880 and

1930, with 52 victims per 100,000. While the rate of Mexican lynchings declined to 27 per 100,000 between 1880 and 1930, due to an increased population and substantial pressure from the Mexican government, the numbers were still staggering; an estimated 282 Mexicans were lynched in Texas and in California, and at least 163 Mexicans were lynched between 1848 and 1860. According to the notes of a miners' meeting in 1850, "Many persons of Spanish origin, against whom there had not been a word of complaint, have been murdered by these ruffians. Others have been robbed of their horses, mules, arms, and even money, by these persons, while acting as they pretended under the authority of the law."[7]

Most lynchings occurred at the hands of vigilantes, who summarily executed victims by mobs, acting "less out of a rational interest in law and order than an irrational prejudice towards racial minorities." Suspected Mexican criminals were snatched from courtrooms or prison cells and then executed. For example, in June 1874, Jesus Romo, arrested for robbery and attempted murder near Puente Creek in California, was grabbed from the arresting officer by a gang of masked men who tied a rope around his neck and hanged him. The *Los Angeles Star* commended the decision to dispense with legal formalities, declaring that Romo was "a hardened and blood-stained desperado, who deserved richly the fate which overtook him."[8]

Such atrocities frequently involved the active collusion of legal officials. In February 1857, a Justice of the Peace assembled an audience of Mexicans outside the San Gabriel mission to watch as he decapitated Miguel Soto and then stabbed repeatedly at the corpse. According to Carrigan and Webb, the most systematic abuse was by the Texas Rangers, whose brutality toward Mexicans was "tantamount to state-sanctioned terrorism;" it is estimated that they murdered thousands of Mexicans. In March 1881, Rangers crossed the border into Mexico and illegally arrested Onofrio Baca on a charge of murder, illegally returned him to the United States, and handed him over to a mob which "strung [him] up to the cross beams of the gate in the court house yard until he was dead." Thomas Wilson, the U.S. Council in Matamoros, testified to Congress that "when an aggression is made upon a Mexican, it is not much minded. For instance, when it is known that a Mexican has been hung or killed … there is seldom any fuss made about it; while, on the contrary, if a White Man happens to be despoiled in any way, there is a great fuss made about it by those not of Mexican origin." As late as 1916, a Wisconsin newspaper observed: "There are still lynchings in the far west, especially along the Mexican border; it would hardly seem to be open to question, although they escape the average collector of statistics. The subject is one that invites searching inquiry."[9]

One consequence of the brutality inflicted on Mexicans was the proliferation of Mexican "*bandits*," who served as a symbol of resistance to Anglo mob rule.

These men were hailed by Mexicans as folk heroes. Juan Cortina was perceived, in the words of one Anglo at the time, as the "champion of his race – as the man who would right the wrongs the Mexicans had received." The lives of these outlaws were hailed in the *corridos* sung throughout the border region. In one *corrido*, the legend of Joaquin Murrieta is immortalized:

> *Now I go out onto roads*
> *To kill Americans*
> *You were the cause*
> *Of my brother's death*
> *You took him defenseless*
> *You disgraceful American.*

Additionally, Spanish-language newspapers, such as *El Clamor Público* and *El Fronterizo*, published countless editorials protesting the lynchings, and in the first decades of the 20th century, Mexican civil rights organizations, such as La Gran Liga Mexicanista de Beneficiencia y Protección and the League of United Latin American Citizens (LULAC), were formed "to strike back at the hatred of some bad sons of Uncle Sam who believe themselves better than the Mexicans because of the magic that surrounds the word white." Still, the fear of mob violence kept many from participating. In the words of one organizer, "The Mexican people were afraid of coming into town for a meeting because they thought they were going to be shot at or lynched if we had our meeting at the courthouse."[10]

AN "ENLIGHTENED CIVILIZATION" ACQUIRES PUERTO RICO AND EXPLOITS MEXICO

On February 15, 1898, the United States Battleship Maine, anchored at the port of Havana, was suddenly blown up, in an explosion which tore out her bottom and sank her, killing 260 officers and men on board. Claiming that the explosion was an act of sabotage, the American press blamed the Spanish government, and a "Remember the Maine" mentality gripped the country, reminiscent of the "Remember the Alamo" frenzy that had led to the annexation of Mexican territory. Responding to public pressure and its own expansionist ambitions, the U.S. Congress declared war against Spain and invaded Cuba and Puerto Rico. In the end, under the terms of the peace treaty entered into at Paris with Spain, sovereignty over the Island of Puerto Rico and its peoples was transferred to the United States. Thus marked the end of the last

Spanish settlement in the New World, as Puerto Rico, Cuba, the Philippines, and Guam entered the sphere of American life.[11]

Americans considered the acquisition of Puerto Rico as a saving grace to the people of the island. Upon seizing it, General Nelson Al Miles declared that its people would now have "the advantages and blessings of enlightened civilization."[12] The goal of the U.S. government was to Americanize Puerto Rico and garner the approval of its people to justify American control. English was established as Puerto Rico's official language, schools were used to inculcate American values and accelerate the adoption of English, and the new colonial government changed the name of the island to "Porto Rico."

According to Edna Acosta-Belén and Carlos E. Santiago, both Puerto Rico and Cuba became "pawns in a larger plan to consolidate U.S. military and geopolitical interests and its hegemonic power" in the Caribbean and the rest of the hemisphere. While Cuba was allowed to become an independent republic in 1902, its sovereignty was limited by the Platt Amendment, which gave the United States free rein to intervene in Cuban affairs whenever it deemed it necessary. Independence was not offered to Puerto Rico, however, and it was designated as "an unincorporated territory," essentially a powerless colonial status under the jurisdiction of the U.S. Congress.[13] While few Puerto Ricans migrated to the United States during these early years of domination – in 1910, the total U.S. Puerto Rican population was only 1,513 – the economic dependency and political subordination of Puerto Rico put in place would set the stage for much larger migrations, the first of which began after the Second World War.[14]

At the time, for its labor needs, the United States turned to Mexico, and the transportation revolution of the early 20th century created the demand for Mexican labor and led to the proliferation of automobiles and trains, which transported Mexicans to the U.S. border and points beyond. By 1900, an estimated 100,000 Mexican immigrants lived in the United States, up from 42,000 in 1870. The number increased to 1,400,000 by the 1930 census.[15] Though at the turn of the century, 69 percent of Mexicans resided in Texas, the population in California soared over the next 30 years, particularly in Los Angeles, where many were recruited to work on the railroads. In a 1908 report to the U.S. Department of Labor, economist Victor S. Clark noted an increasing number of Mexicans outside of the Southwest. By the 1920s, Mexicans were used to harvest sugar beets in Minnesota, pack meat in Chicago, assemble cars in Detroit, and can fish in Alaska.[16]

Until World War I, the labor flow from Mexico to the United States was essentially free, and during the second decade of the century, events on both sides of the border precipitated a relative explosion in the Mexican population within the United States. The Mexican Revolution, which lasted roughly from 1910 to 1920, shook Mexico to its core, led to economic and socio-political upheaval and sparked an exodus from Mexico. In the United States, the irrigation of arid land, the invention of the refrigerator car, and the emergence of a nationwide distribution system led to the growth of agribusiness and a shift from small farm local production to large-scale production for the world market and the demand for Mexican laborers to do the harvesting.

In 1917, the U.S. Congress passed an immigration act that placed restrictions on both Europeans and Mexicans, including a literacy test, a medical examination, a head tax, and an investigation to determine that the potential immigrant would not become a public charge.[17] However, railroad, agricultural, and mining companies launched an aggressive campaign to provide exemptions for Mexicans, whom they needed as cheap laborers. The *Los Angeles Times*, whose owner employed hundreds of Mexicans, carried an article warning of serious consequences due to the "exodus" of Mexicans from Texas. A member of the California Fruit Growers' Exchange claimed that a serious shortage of workers would hamper the harvest of crops in Southern California. The Los Angeles Chamber of Commerce sent a telegram to the U.S. immigration commissioner requesting that Mexican laborers be excluded from the provision of the immigration act, which denied admission to aliens who could not read the English language. Despite the strong, often violent, resistance of labor unions, within six months, Congress yielded, allowing the Secretary of Labor to suspend the literacy test and head tax of the law.[18]

Additionally, the entry of the United States into World War I led to an acute labor shortage, and in May 1917, the United States established a program authorizing the INS Commissioner to "control and regulate the admission and return of otherwise inadmissible aliens for temporary admission," which led to the arrival of about 500,000 Mexican workers before 1921. After the war, with the continued growth of agribusiness and the implementation of laws restricting European immigration in the 1920s, Mexican workers, beset by mass dislocation due to urban industrialization and the mechanization of agriculture in Mexico, continued to arrive in large numbers.[19]

In 1924, Congress established the U.S. Border Patrol, whose 450 agents were responsible for patrolling the Mexican and Canadian borders. According to historians Francisco E. Balderrama and Raymond Rodríguez, the agents used their extensive powers selectively in order to serve the needs of growers and industrialists. When Mexican workers were needed to harvest crops or labor in the mines, regulations were loosely enforced; however, when the supply of Mexican labor exceeded demand, the "strict letter of the law" was enforced. They write:

11 | CHEAP LABOR AND MOB VIOLENCE

> Although the United State government did not consider the Mexicans a serious immigration threat during the early twentieth century, neither were they greeted or welcomed with open arms. Mexicans were often accorded rude treatment, even when following official procedures and seeking legal entry. Immigration officials consistently displayed disdain and obnoxious behavior ... All immigrants, men, women, and children, were herded into crowded, examination pens. As many as five hundred to six hundred persons were detained there for endless hours without benefit of drinking fountains or toilet facilities.[20]

During the 1920s, large numbers of Mexican Americans formed enclaves in farm-producing areas or moved to cities; by 1930, 51 percent of the Mexican population in the U.S. lived in urban areas, which spawned racist nativism among Anglos. In Santa Paula, located in Ventura County, California, immigration ignited fears in the Anglo community, and White supremacists expressed their displeasure through a campaign of Ku Klux Klan (KKK) intimidation. KKK meetings were held in public, often at the top of a hill overlooking the Mexican zone, and were used to repress and intimidate the Mexican community. An article in The *Ventura Daily Press* in July 31, 1923 reported: "The Klan is an organization for all native born White Americans. It believes in the tenets of the Christian religion, White supremacy, protection of our White womanhood, preventing unwarranted strikes by foreign agitators, limitation on immigration, and that much needed local reform, law and order." The Klan organized a membership drive in Ventura and Santa Barbara Counties, and over 400 new members were initiated. Klan activity took place throughout Ventura County, with membership ceremonies held in the Ojai Hills in 1923 and in the Santa Paula Hills in 1924.[21]

Mexican American children were often forced to attend segregated schools employing a "No Spanish" rule; this was often justified by the increased application of I.Q. testing, always administered in English, which frequently resulted in Mexican children being relegated to special classes for the mentally inferior or mentally retarded.[22] William Sheldon of the University of Texas at Austin used I.Q tests to measure the mental ability of Mexican Americans in Texas and concluded that Mexican students had only "85 percent of the intelligence" of White students. Thomas Garth of the University of Denver found that the median IQ of those tested was 78.1, and concluded there was a connection between Mexican children's heritage and their low I.Q. According to scholars Martha Menchaca and Richard R. Valencia:

Language was the most common rationale used to segregate Mexican students. Allegedly, Mexican students were not permitted to attend classes with Anglo students because they needed special instruction in English. The pedagogical rationale was that the limited – or non-English-speaking – Mexican children would impede the academic progress of Anglo children. The racial overtones of these practices were blatantly seen when Mexican-American students who did not speak Spanish were also forced to attend Mexican schools. The need to acculturate Mexican students in special Americanization classes was a second major excuse used to justify segregation. Mexican students were characterized as dirty, dull, un-Christian, and lacking any social etiquette. Therefore, the educational belief was that Mexicans needed special classes where they would learn to emulate their Anglo-American peers.[23]

At the same time, attempts were made by churches and community organizations to assimilate the Mexican population. Still, sentiments were strong that Mexicans were unassimilable and undesirable. Said Congressman Albert Johnson in 1929, "The time [has] come again when it [is] necessary for Congress to save California for Californians." Sociologist W. Garnett argued: "Negroes and Mexicans, of course, constitute our main non-assimilable population elements…" and would "bring racial complication to a section which heretofore [has] been blessed with freedom from this vexatious problem." Other opponents of Mexicans warned of health problems, racial miscegenation, and the displacement of Anglo workers. *Saturday Evening Post* writer Kenneth L. Roberts declared: "One can see the endless streets crowded with the shacks of illiterate, diseased, pauperized Mexicans, taking no interest whatever in the community, living constantly on the ragged edge of starvation, bringing countless numbers of American citizens into the world with the reckless prodigality of rabbits."[24]

Yet as historian George L. Sanchez points out, there was another side to Mexican urban life. During the 1920s and 1930s, Mexicans living in Los Angeles had a vibrant cultural life, and Mexican music thrived, given the advent of radio. As commercial interests took hold, advertisers found a booming market for Spanish-language broadcasts, and although many Anglos felt that only English should be heard on American airwaves, they were silenced by Corporate America's goal of reaching Mexican consumers. During the 1920s, the number of hours dedicated to Spanish exploded. Sanchez writes:

11 | CHEAP LABOR AND MOB VIOLENCE

Key to the success of Spanish-language broadcasting was its appeal to the thousands of working-class Mexican immigrants within the reach of a station's radio signal. Radio, unlike *La Opinión* and other periodicals, reached Mexican immigrants whether or not they could read. In addition, the content of radio programming focused … more on [the tastes] of the masses … Programming was dominated by "traditional" music from the Mexican countryside, rather than the orchestral, more "refined" sounds of the Mexican capital and other large urban centers. "The *corrido*, the shouts, and all that stuff was popular with working people," remembered [disk jockey Pedro J.] González. Although some bemoaned the commercialization of the *corrido* tradition and its removal from its "folk tradition," most Mexican immigrants found this transformation to their liking because it fit well with their own adaptations to urban living.[25]

NOTES

1. Ibid., 37.
2. Montejano, 70.
3. Foley, 24.
4. Takaki, Ronald. *A Different Mirror: A History of Multicultural America*. (New York, NY: Little, Brown and Company, 1993), 185.
5. Ibid., 187.
6. Romo, Ricardo. "Responses to Mexican Immigration, 1910–1930," in Michael R. Ornelas, *Beyond 1848: Readings in the Modern Chicano Historical Experience*. (Dubuque, IA: Kendall Hunt Publishing, 1993), 117.
7. Carrigan and Web, 414.
8. Ibid.
9. Ibid., 416.
10. Ibid., 426.
11. Acosta-Belén, Edna and Carlos E. Santiago. *Puerto Ricans in the United States: A Contemporary Portrait*. (Boulder, CO: Lynee Rienner Publishers, 2006), 35.
12. MacDonald, Victoria-María. "Hispanic, Latino, Chicano, or 'Other'?: Deconstructing the Relationship between Historians and Hispanic-American Educational History," *History of Education Quarterly*. Vol. 41, No. 3, Autumn, 2001, 371.
13. Acosta-Belén and Santiago, 41.
14. Ibid., 48.

15. Balderrama, Francisco E. and Raymond Rodríguez. *Decade of Betrayal: Mexican Repatriation in the 1930s.* (Albuquerque, NM: University of New Mexico Press, 2006), 9.
16. Ibid., 8.
17. Sánchez, George J. *Becoming Mexican American: Ethnicity, Culture and Identity in Chicano Los Angeles, 1900–1945.* (New York, NY: Oxford University Press, 1993), 55.
18. Romo, 121.
19. Daniels, Roger. *Guarding the Golden Door*, 89.
20. Balderrama and Rodríguez, 11.
21. Menchaca, Martha and Richard R. Valencia. "Anglo-Saxon Ideologies in the 1920s–1930s: Their Impact on the Segregation of Mexican Students in California," *Anthropology & Education Quarterly*, Vol. 21, No. 3 (Sep., 1990), 236.
22. Acuña, 176.
23. Menchaca and Valencia, 230.
24. Romo, 129.
25. Sánchez, 184.

12

DOUBLE STANDARDS

DURING ECONOMIC hard times, people worried about their livelihood often come to see hard-working others as a very real threat. Nativism rose, not surprisingly, during the Great Depression. During the 1930s, between 500,000 and one million returned to Mexico, many by deportation, and according to one estimate, over half of those deported were actually U.S. citizens.[1]

According to historian Mae M. Ngai, although the Immigration Service did not organize or fund the "repatriation" of Mexicans, it "encouraged [it] by generating an atmosphere of fear of deportation." In 1931, police and immigration officials raided *La Placita*, the center of the Mexican *colonia* in downtown Los Angeles, lining up about four hundred people and demanding to see passports. Such raids were commonplace during the Depression. According to the witness of an immigration raid in San Fernando, "The deputy sheriffs arrived in late afternoon when the men were returning home from working in the lemon groves. They started arresting people.... The deputies rode around the neighborhood with their sirens wailing and advising people to surrender themselves to the authorities. They barricaded all the exits to the *colonia* so that no one could escape." In 1939, at the request of the Mexican government, the Immigration Service transported over 1,200 Mexicans throughout Texas – mostly families and about half being U.S. citizens – to Brownsville, where they were forced to cross the border and settle on small plots of agricultural land, which had been established for them by the Mexican government. Writes Ngai,

"The repatriation of Mexicans was a racial expulsion program exceeded in scale only by the Native American Indian removals of the 19th century."[2]

Notwithstanding the deportations of the '30s, in 1940, the Census estimated over 2 million Hispanics living in the United States, of which about 78 percent were of Mexican origin; according to one estimate, about three-quarters of these were born in the United States.[3] Still, by World War II, most Mexicans were still socially, culturally, and politically removed from the American mainstream. Historian David G. Gutiérrez notes that one source of interethnic tensions may have been the Anglo reaction to the emergence of a "*pachuco gang*" subculture among second generation youth. He writes:

> These groups of pachucos (sometimes called cholos) were characterized by their use of a hybrid English-Spanish slang dialect known as caló, the adornment of their bodies with tattoos, and most conspicuously, by a distinctive style of dress, the zoot suit. Zoot suits were part of a fashion ensemble that included long jackets with exaggerated shoulders, pegged pant legs, thick-soled shoes, long watch chains, and wide-brimmed pancake hats worn over duck-tail haircuts that were then in style not only among many young Mexican Americans but among some urban African American and Filipino youths as well.[4]

Shortly after the outbreak of the war, two incidents intensified the public's awareness of Pachuco gangs and provoked concerns about Mexicans living in the mainstream's midst. One that received widespread press attention was the Sleepy Lagoon murder case in August 1942, which followed when the dead body of José Diaz was found near Sleepy Lagoon, a water-filled gravel pit in south-central Los Angeles used by Mexicans. Diaz may have been a member of a gang, the Downey Boys, and police suspected that members of a rival gang, the 38th Street Club gang had beaten him. In a flagrant miscarriage of justice, over six hundred youths were arrested, and 22 members of the gang were charged with criminal conspiracy. According to the prosecution, "every defendant, even if he had nothing whatsoever to do with the killing of Diaz, was chargeable with the death," and during the trial, the judge, Charles W. Fricke, permitted many irregularities, including not allowing the defendants to cut their hair, change their clothes, or consult with counsel, and the press portrayed them as hoodlums. Captain E. Duran Ayres, the head of the Foreign Relations Bureau in the Los Angeles Sheriff's Department, submitted a report stating that the Mexican's "desire to kill, or at least let blood" was an "inborn characteristic that has come down through the ages," noting that Mexicans were descendants of Aztecs, who sacrificed 30,000 victims a day. Although the verdict was later overturned, twelve of the defendants were convicted of murder and five of assault.[5]

A second well-reported outbreak of violence occurred during the so-called Zoot-Suit Riots, in Los Angeles, which erupted in June 1943 after a group of Mexican-American men allegedly attacked a group of sailors flirting with some Mexican-American women. That night, sailors broke into the Carmen Theater and beat up the Mexican-American men in the audience, tearing off their zoot-suits. Police arrested the victims. The following evening, a group of 200 sailors and their allies rented cabs, cruised down Whittier Boulevard, and beat up Mexican-American youth. The press portrayed the sailors as heroes, with headlines such as "Zoot-Suiters Learn Lesson in Fight with Servicemen." Two days later, thousands of soldiers, sailors, and civilians descended on pachucos in downtown Los Angeles, pulling them from streetcars and movie theaters, beating them, and tearing off their zoot-suits. Over the next few days, hundreds of Hispanics were arrested, and fear gripped the Mexican community of Los Angeles. When First Lady Eleanor Roosevelt wrote in her nationally syndicated column that "longstanding discrimination against the Mexicans in the Southwest" was the cause of the riots, the *Los Angeles Times* responded with the headline "Mrs. Roosevelt Blindly Stirs Race Discord."[6]

World War II may not have put an end to White America's bigotry against those of Mexican descent in their midst, but it did end the perceived economic threat that Mexicans posed. Mexicans were essential to the American war effort, and an estimated 350,000 Mexican Americans fought in the Armed Forces. Unlike African Americans, they did not fight in segregated units, which resulted in not only an intimate interchange with non-Hispanics, but following the war, the demand for equal rights, dignity, and respect. Writes historian Mario T. García:

> The convulsions of the Great Depression combined with new economic and political opportunities during World War II and with the historic discrimination in the Southwest against Mexicans and rising expectations among Mexican Americans to give birth to a new leadership, cognizant of its rights as U.S. citizens and determined to achieve them ... Together this generation forged a spirited and persistent struggle for civil rights, for first-class citizenship, and for a secure identity for Americans of Mexican descent. Mexican Americans identified with the World War II slogan: "Americans All."[7]

As had occurred during World War I, World War II also brought with it acute labor shortages, particularly agricultural labor, and once again, the United States turned to Mexico. Given the past experience of Mexican immigrants to the U.S., the Mexican government, an ally in the war, insisted on having a say, and there were high level negotiations between the two countries that resulted in the promise that workers would receive a minimum wage, decent working and living conditions, and round-trip transportation. Established by an executive agreement between President Roosevelt and Mexican President Manuel Ávila Camacho in July 1942, the *bracero* program (named for the Spanish term meaning "manual laborer," or more literally "one who works using his arms") was legalized by Congress in 1943. Between 1943 and 1949, an estimated 400,000 braceros came to work under the program.

Despite the guarantees extended to workers, braceros were essentially "bound" by the terms of the contract. They were forced to put money into a "savings fund" into which they were required to deposit 10 percent of their wages, with the promise that it would be paid to them upon their return to Mexico. Additionally, wives and children were not allowed into the country, and any "breach" of the contract, such as stopping work, resulted in deportation.[8]

Although the bracero program did grant braceros the formal right to join American unions, when they did speak out or attempt to unionize, growers, with the support of government forces, undermined their efforts. Historians Justin Akers Chacón and Mike Davis write: "By individualizing the contract, collective bargaining was precluded. This secured a way to detach bracero labor from the rest of the working class and legally redefine temporary workers as the virtual property of the owners."[9]

Well aware of this, the government in Mexico City, which moved considerably to the right under Miguel Alemán, had much to lose should there be a rift with the United States, as American capital began to flow into Mexico. Additionally, the Mexican government benefited by having an escape valve for dispossessed farmers, and the Mexican economy was the beneficiary of about $30 million in remittances, making the Bracero Program the third largest "industry" in Mexico.[10] Despite the remittances, with the resulting outflow of labor, Mexican landowners pressured the Mexican government to take action. In December 1943, the Mexican Embassy in Washington, D.C. wrote to the U. S. Secretary of State requesting that the U.S. government "adopt the measures which may be appropriate to prevent the illegal entry of Mexican workers not in possession of bracero contracts." The Embassy warned that if control was not established over the flow of illegal immigration into the U.S., Mexico would "affect a complete revision of the [Bracero] agreements." Within six months, the chief supervisor of the U.S. Border Patrol, W.F. Kelly, launched an "intensive drive on Mexican aliens" by deploying Special Mexican Deportation Parties throughout the country, armed with planes and trucks "to target, apprehend, and deport undocumented Mexican nationals."[11]

When the Bracero Program was first announced, countless Mexicans were rejected by the recruitment center, which had been established in Mexico City, or refused the terms of the six-month long contracts, and many crossed the U.S. border, often through Texas, as undocumented workers, or *mojados*, wetbacks, as they were known. According to historian Kelly Lytle Hernández, total apprehensions doubled from 16,330 in 1943 to 33,681 in 1944, while the number of interrogations reported by the U.S. Border Patrol increased nearly twentyfold, from 473,720 in 1940 to 9,389,551 in 1943. By the early 1950s, Border Patrol officers were apprehending so many Mexicans that INS centers were filled beyond capacity.[12]

Mexicans were not the only Spanish-speaking group to migrate to the United States in large numbers after the Second World War. The war's end coincided with the first large influx of Puerto Ricans, whose population on the mainland increased from 69,967 individuals in the 1940s to 887,662 in the 1960s. Although the Jones Act of 1917 granted citizenship to Puerto Ricans, thereby eliminating any legal barriers to migration, it was not until the 1950s that Puerto Ricans began to arrive in large numbers, due to high unemployment in Puerto Rico and the introduction of low-cost air travel; the six-hour flight from San Juan to New York City cost less than $50. Another contributing factor was the 1951 referendum in which the Puerto Rican population voted overwhelmingly to become a U.S. commonwealth, renouncing its prior status as a colony.

In 1960, 21 percent of Puerto Ricans migrated from the island, and most went to New York City. In 1970, nearly 70 percent of the Puerto Rican born population on the U.S. mainland lived in the New York metropolitan area.[13] During these peak years of Puerto Rican migration, known as the "Great Migration," those arriving were typically young and urban, with little education and limited occupational skills. They came to the U.S. because of limited employment opportunities in Puerto Rico and the lure of plentiful low skilled manufacturing jobs in New York City.

Life in the metropolis was difficult, and most were severely economically disadvantaged. It was during the Great Migration that social scientists began to examine the "*Puerto Rican problem*" in New York City, and they focused on Puerto Ricans struggling with English, dropping out of school, working in in low-paying, dead-end jobs, unemployment, and living in dilapidated housing.[14] Wrote one scholar in 1951:

> A primary evil for the new migrants is the lack of decent housing. High-rent slums are typical of Harlem. Yet to these areas must the Puerto Rican go because he is an out-cast in other areas until he

is properly adjusted or because of his dark skin. It is difficult to get "started" as high rents and food costs continue to keep living standards and savings down. New York officials hope to relieve the conditions by housing projects with rents costing $9.00 per room per month.[15]

Another obstacle facing Puerto Ricans was racial discrimination, and they were frequently stigmatized as "lazy, ignorant, criminally prone, sexually obsessed, physically unfit, culturally unassimilable, and dark-skinned aliens [even though they were U.S. Citizens]."[16] The musical drama *West Side Story* accurately illustrates many of the hardships faced by Puerto Rican immigrants living in New York City in the 1950s. The Puerto Ricans in the story are harassed and assaulted by the Jets, a neighborhood gang composed of White immigrants that occupied the neighborhood before. The police in the musical, Officer Krupke and Detective Schrank, treat the Puerto Ricans with contempt, referring to them as "Spics" and other racial slurs. Detective Schrank confides to Riff, the leader of the Jets, that they are on the same side and that he will "lend a hand" in the fight against the Puerto Ricans. Writes sociologist Clara Rodríguez:

> Puerto Ricans presented an enigma to Americans because, given the European-American perspective, Puerto Ricans were an ethnic group comprising more than one racial group. From such a perspective, Puerto Ricans were racially both Blacks and Whites; ethnically, they were neither. Thus placed, Puerto Ricans early found themselves caught between two polarities yet dialectically at a distance from both. Puerto Ricans were considered neither White nor Black. Yet they considered themselves more than White or Black.[17]

According to historians Leonard Dinnerstein and David M. Reimers, "The Puerto Rican experience in New York and other major cities on the continent is probably closer to that of the European immigrants who landed on the East Coast and settled in urban areas than to that of the Mexicans in the West." In New York, Puerto Ricans replaced the earlier European immigrants, particularly Italians and Jews, in the low-level factory jobs in which they worked and in the urban slums they had inhabited. Like the Europeans, they spoke a different language; unlike them, Puerto Ricans were not white. Although higher status is accorded to lighter skinned people in Puerto Rico, this was hardly preparation for the many Puerto Ricans who learned that, on the mainland, "the darker their skin, the greater the difficultly in gaining acceptance and adjusting to the dominant culture."[18]

Another group to enter the United States in large numbers during this time were Dominicans, many of whom entered the country illegally. It is estimated that from 1960 to 1996, over 700,000 migrated to the United States, and most, like Puerto Ricans, settled in New York City. Lacking documentation, their opportunities for employment were limited; even among the legal immigrants, few spoke English, and many lacked skills and education, particularly among those coming from rural areas.[19] Like Puerto Ricans, racial discrimination exacerbated the difficulties encountered by Dominicans. About 75 percent of the Dominican population is mulatto and 10 percent is Black. However as Latin American scholar Jorge Duany notes, "Racial prejudice and discrimination [against Blacks] have been central features of … Dominican identity," and it is likely that the actual number of Blacks is significantly much higher, especially by the common standard of hypodescent applied in the United States, whereby a "single drop" of Black blood qualifies one as Black. Because of discrimination, many Dominicans in New York settled in areas adjacent to African-American neighborhoods or in Dominican enclaves, such as Washington Heights. Writes Duany, "The racialization of Dominican immigrants has been a prime obstacle to their successful incorporation into the labor and housing markets of the United States."[20]

Meanwhile, tensions were brewing in the American West, spurred on by a marked increase in Mexican immigration. In the late 1940s and early 1950s, a rebellion took place in south Texas between farmers and ranchers, who depended on illegal workers, and the U.S. Border Patrol. Writes historian Kelly Lytle Hernández, the former used "everything in their arsenal. They met officers at their gates with shotguns. They ostracized officers in the community. They charged the Border Patrol with violating American freedoms at home, and they accused officers of fostering communism abroad."[21]

By the early 1950s, there was a "crisis of control" along the U.S.-Mexico border, which culminated in the notorious Operation Wetback in the summer of 1954, during which the INS, headed by Commissioner Joseph Swing, executed a blatantly military operation.[22] According to Swing, the "alarming, ever-increasing, flood tide" of undocumented Mexican workers constituted "an actual invasion of the United States." He responded with a campaign involving approximately 750 immigration officers, 300 jeeps, cars, and buses, and 7 airplanes, in an operation focused on South Texas and southern California, but extending as far as Chicago. At the campaign's outset, about 3,000 undocumented workers were apprehended a day, about 170,000 during the first three months; in all, the INS apprehended 801,069 Mexican migrants from 1953 through 1955.²³ In January of 1955, Swing declared, "The day of the wetback is over."²⁴

Still, under the Bracero Program, the Mexican population continued to grow, reaching a peak in 1956 when 445,000 Mexicans were contracted to work, mostly in agriculture, 75 percent in Texas and California alone. However, because of the increased mechanization of agricultural, the demand for workers began to decline, particularly after 1960. Additionally, the program came under increasing attack by Mexican activists such as César Chavez and Ernesto Galarza, as well as church groups, who were appalled at the conditions that braceros faced. In 1959, Congressman George McGovern introduced a bill to phase out the importation of Mexican contract laborers.²⁵

In November 1960, the CBS documentary *Harvest of Shame*, presented by journalist Edward R. Murrow, exposed the plight of migrant workers and created a public clamor, which convinced the newly elected President Kennedy that braceros were "adversely affecting the wages, working conditions, and employment opportunities of our own agricultural workers."²⁶ In 1962, Congress passed legislation modifying the Bracero Program, limiting contracts to six months, increasing insurance benefits, and raising wages. By that year, fewer than 200,000 braceros were entering the U.S., the smallest number since Operation Wetback, and by 1964, the number of braceros was lower than at any other time since the program was institutionalized.²⁷

The Bracero Program was allowed to expire on December 31, 1964. In 1965, passage of the Hart-Cellars Act ended the immigration quota system that had so dramatically favored northern Europeans and allocated visas on the basis of skills and family ties to U.S. residents, rather than national origins. The legislation initially created numerical quotas of 170,000 people from the Eastern Hemisphere and 120,000 from the Western Hemisphere, but in 1976, the hemispheric caps were abandoned in favor of a total ceiling of 290,000 visas, with each nation capped at 20,000 visas per year.²⁸ Importantly, the new law placed numerical limits on Mexican migration, at the same time the Bracero Program was being shut down.

Hart-Cellars was designed to redress "the wrongs done to those from Southern and East Europe," and it was considered to be a modest proposal at the time. On October 3, 1965, President Lyndon Johnson, upon signing the bill at a ceremony in front of the Statue of Liberty, declared, "This bill we sign today is not a revolutionary bill. It does not affect the lives of millions. It will not shape the structure of our daily lives, or really add importantly to our power."²⁹ Johnson, who was expressing what the experts had told him, could not have been more mistaken. While the bill had a minimal impact on European immigration, what the experts missed was the large number of Latin Americans and Asians who had come to the United States after World War II and would come after 1965. They became naturalized citizens in unprecedented numbers, making their family members eligible immigrants.³⁰

COLD WAR, POLITICS, AND IMMIGRATION DOUBLE-STANDARDS

Cold War politics had a strong influence on immigration, with the U.S. giving Cuban refugees a markedly different reception than other Hispanics. During his immigration speech, President Johnson announced, "I declare this afternoon to the people of Cuba that those who seek refuge here in America will find it … Our tradition as an asylum for the oppressed is going to be upheld."³¹ A month earlier, Fidel Castro had announced that all Cubans with relatives in the United States could leave Cuba. "Now we shall see what the imperialists will do or say," Castro remarked, pledging "guarantees and facilities" to exiles returning to Cuba to bring their families back to the U.S.³²

On January 1, 1959, Fidel Castro had taken control of the government of Cuba, and during the first two years of his rule, over 50,000 Cubans fled to the United States. The first wave of refugees consisted of those fleeing for political reasons, mostly professionals, but by the middle of 1961, skilled and semiskilled workers began to arrive in large numbers. Beginning in late 1960, the Cuban government confiscated all refugee property on the island, and those arriving after that time were impoverished; additionally, professionals were prohibited from bringing diplomas or transcripts from universities to the United States, making it nearly impossible to verify their educational qualifications for professional jobs.³³

Although the United States had closed its consular offices in Cuba in January 1961, Cuban nationals were given visa waivers, which were filed in the U.S. and forwarded to the Swiss Embassy in Havana. When cleared, refugees arranged transportation on one of the commercial airlines still operating between Havana and Miami, and at the peak of the program in 1962, over 1,800 refugees were arriving each week. During his first year in office, President Kennedy sent a bill to Congress that became Public Law 87-510, the Migration and Refugee Assistance Act of 1962, which granted Congress permanent authority to appropriate funds for the assistance of refugees.³⁴

Kennedy's Cold War objectives were unequivocal and were expressed in his letter accompanying the bill:

> The successful re-establishment of refugees is importantly related to free world political objectives. These objectives are: (a) continuation of the provision of asylum and friendly assistance to the

oppressed and persecuted; (b) the extension of hope and encouragement to the victims of communism and other forms of despotism, and the promotion of faith among the captive populations in the purposes and processes of freedom and democracy; (c) the exemplification by free citizens of free countries, through actions and sacrifices, of the fundamental humanitarianism which constitutes the basic difference between free and captive societies.[35]

Yet the inflow of Cuban refugees into the Miami area provoked marked resentment among residents, particularly because of the generosity that was bequeathed on the refugees. In 1959, Florida ranked 47th in the nation in terms of welfare funds per inhabitant, and the Cubans, then classified as "temporary visitors," received more money than Florida residents – 100 dollars per month for a married couple, with or without children, compared with the 81 dollars a month paid to Floridian families with dependent children. Additionally, Miamians complained that their Spanish-speaking neighbors were "boisterous, rude, and disrespectful of American laws, especially traffic regulations," using "horns for brakes." They feared that their property values would fall and signs reading "No Cubans Allowed" became commonplace in apartment building windows.[36] Writes historian María Cristina García:

> Parents worried that their children would receive an inadequate education in the Dade County public schools, since educators readily admitted that in trying to accommodate the non-English-speaking Cubans they neglected their other students. Blacks watched in disbelief as Cuban Black and mulatto children attended "White schools," prompting one local minister to write that "the American Negro could solve the school integration problem by teaching his children to speak only Spanish."[37]

As a result of the financial drain on Miami and the growing resentment of its residents, a campaign was launched to convince Cuban refugees to resettle elsewhere in the country, and by June 1963, about 35 percent had found homes outside of Miami.[38]

When the Cuban Missile Crisis erupted in October 1962 and Kennedy placed a quarantine on the island, Castro, in retaliation, cut off all commercial flights to the United States, effectively halting refugees from directly entering the country for the next three years. The moratorium provided "a breathing spell" for the United States, especially the city of Miami, which had to manage over 200,000 Cuban refugees; despite that, another 56,000 Cubans had been able to leave the island and travel to the United States over the next three years, mostly via Spain and Mexico. However, everything changed on September 28, 1965 when Castro announced that Cubans were free to leave, and Johnson declared they would be welcome in the United States. A "memorandum of understanding" was worked out between the United States and Cuba, whereby two chartered planes would leave Cuba daily, five times a week, transporting three to four thousand Cubans to Miami each month.[39] From 1965 to 1973, 3,049 "freedom flights" brought 260,561 Cubans to the United States, making it the largest airborne refugee operation in American history.[40]

On April 1, 1980, six Cubans drove a bus through a fence at the Peruvian embassy in Havana, and they were granted political asylum by the embassy. The Cuban government demanded the five be returned for trial, but when the Peruvian government refused, Castro withdrew all guards and barricades from the embassy compound, and Cuban radio announced that anyone wishing to leave the country was free to go to the Peruvian embassy. Within three days, more than 10,000 Cubans crowded into the embassy requesting asylum. Two weeks later, Castro declared that the port of Mariel would be opened to anyone wishing to leave. On May Day, in a speech directed at President Jimmy Carter, Castro declared, "Anybody who wishes to go to any other country where he is received, good riddance." Cuban officials packed boat after boat with refugees, and many were unseaworthy. Additionally, an estimated 500 boats arrived in Mariel from south Florida ports during the first week alone, with Cuban exiles rushing to rescue family members, and there were hundreds more in the weeks that followed. On May 6, Carter declared a state of emergency in Florida, and two tent cities were erected in Miami, while tens of thousands of refugees were flown to isolated military bases.[41] In what became the next wave of Cuban immigration, some 125,000 Cubans fled to U.S. shores in about 1,700 boats, overwhelming the U.S. Coast Guard and creating a crisis of confidence regarding President Carter's leadership.[42]

As the boatlift progressed, it became evident that Castro was using it to rid the country of "undesirables," as Cuban police removed people from hospitals and jails and forced them to board boats. An estimated 1,500 had serious mental conditions, and another 1,600 had chronic medical problems; additionally, it was discovered that 26,000 of *los marielitos*, as the refugees came to be called, had criminal records. Although, in actuality, only about 2,000 had committed serious felonies, in the press and in public opinion, the refugees were stigmatized as criminals, troublemakers, social deviants, and homosexuals. Miami mayor Maurice Ferre, a Puerto Rican, moaned that Castro had "flushed these people on to us." Jimmy Carter's mother,

Lillian, told reporters, "I'll tell you the truth. I hope they don't come to Plains [Georgia]."[43] Writes historian María Cristina García:

> Most Americans initially sympathized with the Cubans' plight, and they applauded the refugees' courage at the Peruvian Embassy. Those sentiments changed, however, when it became clear that the United States was to play host again to thousands of Cuban refugees, this time during an economic recession when they could ill afford to do so … The discovery of the criminal element, however, proved the principal factor in turning public opinion against the boatlift. Never before, according to public opinion, had a neighboring country committed such an act of aggression against the United States.[44]

Complicating the reception of the Mariel refugees was their race. An estimated 15 to 40 percent were Black or mulatto, compared to about 3 percent of those Cubans who had arrived in prior migrations.[45] One exile described feeling caught between two communities, one White and Cuban, the other African American, stating "White Cubans welcome us because we're Cuban, but with a big 'but' because we're Black, and Black Americans welcome us because we're Black, but with a big 'but' because we're Cuban." An account of one Afro-Cuban, Joel, and his encounter with a White Cuban policeman, is illustrative:

> The point is driven home to Joel one night when a White Cuban-American policeman stopped and frisked him. Joe had been celebrating Valentine's Day in a popular Cuban restaurant with his uncle and three women friends. The policeman said to him, "I've been keeping an eye on you for a while. Since you were in the restaurant. I saw you leave and I saw so many Blacks in the car, I figured I would check you out." The White Cuban-American police officer disconnected Joel from his national identity and placed him firmly on the Black side of America's principal divide, between whiteness and Blackness.[46]

Cuban immigration was to change the face of Miami, and the 900,000 or so Cubans that arrived revitalized a sleepy southern city and made it into a major international hub, where Spanish is often the language of communication. By 1980, there were about 10,000 businesses in the city owned by Cubans, putting monolingual

Anglos at a stark disadvantage.[47] Despite the success of so many Cubans, or perhaps because of it, the result has been progressive Anglo flight from Miami. In the 1990s alone, about 95,000 Whites left Miami-Dade County. Migration of Whites to Miami is at a virtual standstill, while in neighboring Broward County, the White non-Hispanic population increased by about 82,000 between 1990 and 1997. For many Whites, Miami now felt like a "foreign country," and they felt overwhelmed by the presence of so many Spanish-speakers. In the words of one Miami executive who moved from Miami to Broward County:

> You order a Coke without ice and you get ice. You say no starch and you get starch. You call government offices, and they can't take a decent message in English. You spell your name letter by letter and they get it wrong. They keep saying 'Que? Que? Que?' (Spanish for "What?") You go to the mall, and you watch as the clerks wait on the Spanish speakers before you. It's like reverse racism. You realize, my God, this is what it is like to be the minority.[48]

NOTES

1. Sánchez, 106; Justin Akers Chacón and Mike Davis, *No One is Illegal: Fighting Racism and State Violence on the U.S. – Mexico Border*. (Chicago, IL: Haymarket Books, 2006), 193.
2. Ngai, Mae M. *Impossible Subjects: Illegal Aliens and the Making of Modern America*. (Princeton: Princeton University Press, 2005), 73.
3. Gratton, Brian and Myron P. Guttmann. "Hispanics in the United States, 1850–1900: Estimates of Population Size and National Origin," *Historical Methods*. Summer 2000, Vol. 33, No. 3, 142.
4. Gutiérrez, David G. *Walls and Mirrors: Mexican Americans, Mexican Immigrants, and the Politics of Ethnicity*. (Berkeley, CA: University of California Press, 1995), 123.
5. Acuña, 247; Neil Foley, *Mexicans in the Making of America*, (Cambridge, MA: Belknap Press, 2014), 91.
6. Ibid., 251.
7. García, Mario T. *Mexican Americans: Leadership, Ideology, and Identity, 1930–1960*. (New Haven, CT: Yale University Press, 1991), 2.
8. Daniels, *Guarding the Golden Door*, 90.
9. Chacón and Davis, 140.
10. Ibid., 145.

11. Hernández, Kelly Lytle. *Migra!: A History of the U.S. Border Patrol.* (Oakland, CA: University of California Press, 2010), 116.
12. Ibid., 119.
13. Borjas, George J. "Labor Outflows and Labor Inflows in Puerto Rico," *Journal of Human Capital*, Vol. 2, No. 1, Spring 2008, 35.
14. Perez y González, María E. *Puerto Ricans in the United States.* (Westport, CT: Greenwood Press, 2000), 36.
15. Hunker, Henry L. "The Problem of Puerto Rican Migrations to the United States," *The Ohio Journal of Science.* Vol. 51, No. 6, November 1951, 344.
16. Duany, Jorge. eds. Maura I. Toro-Morn and Marisa Alicea. "Puerto Rico: Between the Nation and the Diaspora – Migration to and from Puerto Rico," in *Migration and Immigration: A Global View.* (Westport, CT: Greenwood, 2004), 187.
17. Rodríguez, Clara E. "Puerto Rican Studies," *American Quarterly*, Vol. 42, No. 3, September 1990, 444.
18. Dinnestein, Leonardo and David M. Reimers. *Ethnic Americans: A History of Immigration.* (New York, NY: Columbia University Press, 1999), 143.
19. Dinnerstein and Reimers, 144.
20. Duany, Jorge. "Reconstructing Racial Identity: Ethnicity, Color, and Class among Dominicans in the United States and Puerto Rico," *Latin American Perspectives.* Vol. 25, No. 3, May 1998, 161.
21. Hernández, 165k.
22. Rodríguez, 166.
23. Ngai, 155.
24. Hernández, 196.
25. McWilliams, Corey. *North from Mexico: The Spanish-Speaking People of the United States.* (New York, NY: Praeger, 1990), 316.
26. University of California, Davis, "Braceros: History, Compensation," *Rural Migration News*, April 2006, Volume 12, Number 2. https://migration.ucdavis.edu/rmn/more.php?id=1112.
27. Calavita, Kitty. *Inside the State: The Bracero Program, Immigration, and the I.N.S.* (New York: Routledge, 2010), 155.
28. Daniels, *Guarding the Golden Door*, 134.
29. Johnson, Lyndon B. "Remarks at the Signing of the Immigration Bill, Liberty Island, New York," October 3, 1965. http://www.lbjlib.utexas.edu/johnson/archives.hom/speeches.hom/651003.asp.
30. Daniels, 137.
31. Johnson, "Remarks at the Signing of the Immigration Bill," http://www.lbjlib.utexas.edu/johnson/archives.hom/speeches.hom/651003.asp.

32. Daniels, 138.
33. García, María Cristina. *Havana USA: Cuban Exiles and Cuban Americans in South Florida, 1959–1994.* (Berkeley, CA: University of California Press, 1996), 26.
34. Thomas, John F. "Cuban Refugees in the United States," *International Migration Review*, Vol. 1, No. 2, Spring 1967, 47.
35. Carlin, James A. *The Refugee Connection: Lifetime of Running a Lifeline.* (Basingstoke, UK: Palgrave Macmillan, 1989), 79.
36. García, 29.
37. Ibid.
38. Ibid., 35.
39. Ibid., 38.
40. Masud-Piloto, Felix. *From Welcomed Exiles to Illegal Immigrants: Cuban Migration to the U.S., 1959–1995.* (Lanham, MD: Rowman & Littlefield Publishers, 1995), 68.
41. Masud-Piloto, 85.
42. García, *Havana USA*, 46.
43. Ibid., 70.
44. García, María Cristina. ed. by David G. Gutiérrez. "Exiles, Immigrants, and Transnationals: The Cuban Communities of the United States," in *The Columbia History of Latinos in the United States Since 1969*. (New York: Columbia University Press, 2004), 164.
45. García, *Havana USA*, 68.
46. Sawyer, Mark Q. *Racial Politics in Post-Revolutionary Cuba*, (Cambridge, UK: Cambridge University Press, 2005), 163.
47. Dinnerstein and Reimers, 146.
48. "A White Migration North from Miami," *The Washington Post*, November 11, 1998. http://www.washingtonpost.com/wp-srv/national/longterm/meltingpot/melt1109.htm.

13

THE BIRTH OF THE ILLEGAL IMMIGRANT

WHEN THE Hart-Cellars Act was passed in 1965, neither the dependence on Mexican labor nor the need of Mexican nationals to find jobs disappeared. As sociologist Donald S. Massey notes, the 4.5 million Mexican migrants admitted under the Bracero Program had led to the development of closely connected social networks linking communities in Mexico to jobs and employers in the United States. When the program ended and opportunities for legal entry disappeared, the "massive inflow from Mexico simply reestablished itself under undocumented auspices."[1] In essence, the Act transformed legal migrant workers into "illegal immigrants." Writes historian Aviva Chomsky:

> Suddenly, legal migration for Mexicans, after so many years of being encouraged, was closed off. But the demand for Mexican labor, and Mexican workers' need for jobs, continued.... The abolition of the Bracero Program was supposed to create better, more equal treatment for Mexicans in the United States, in keeping with the civil rights movements of the era, including a growing farm-worker movement. It failed miserably.[2]

According to Chomsky, the number of Mexican migrants in the country without a green card rose from 88,823 in 1961 to over a million a year by the mid-1970s, abetted by the "leniency" of U.S. authorities at the time, who made it "rather easy to cross the border." It was at this time, writes Massey, that magazine articles began to proliferate with a Mexican "threat narrative," characterized by two distinct themes:

> On the one hand, migrants from the south were portrayed as a brown "flood" that would "inundate" American culture and "drown" its society. On the other hand, undocumented migrants were portrayed as "invaders" who "swarmed" across the border in "banzai charges" to overrun "outgunned" Border Patrol agents who fought vainly to "hold the line" against the "alien invasion." As the Cold War climaxed, the war on drugs accelerated, and the war on terror came to dominate public rhetoric, martial metaphors overtook marine metaphors.[3]

A decade after Hart-Cellars passed, the rise in undocumented workers, while largely unseen in the day-to-day lives of average Americans, was sensationalized in the mainstream media, leading to calls for the government to "do something" about these foreign invaders.

In December 1974, the cover of *American Legion Magazine* depicted the United States as being overrun by "illegal aliens," replete with images of Mexicans storming across the U.S.–Mexico border, breaking down a sign that reads "USA Border" and another one reading "Keep Out."[4] The Commissioner of the I.N.S, General Leonard Chapman, in 1976, published an article in *Reader's Digest*, "Illegal Aliens: Time to Call a Halt!", alleging that the agency was "out-manned, under-budgeted, and confronted by a growing, silent invasion of illegal aliens" that threatened to become a "national disaster."[5] In 1977, *U.S. News and World Report* featured the cover headline: "Border Crisis: Illegal Aliens Out of Control?", which asserted that Mexicans were abusing welfare, displacing citizens from jobs, and taking to crime, referring to Mexican immigrants as "invaders" and stating that the "U.S. has lost control of its borders." Two years later, the same magazine estimated that by the year 2025, undocumented immigrants might account for 10 percent of the population.[6] A 1977 *Time* magazine article, described the alleged crisis in ominous, military terms:

> The U.S. is being invaded so silently and surreptitiously that most Americans are not even aware of it. The invaders come by land, sea and air. They fly commercial and private aircraft; they jump ship or sail their own boats; they scale mountains and swim rivers. Some have crawled through a mile-long tunnel; others have

13 | THE BIRTH OF THE ILLEGAL IMMIGRANT

squeezed through the San Antonio sewerage system. No commandos or assault troops have shown more ingenuity and determination in storming a country that tries to keep them out.[7]

In the late 1970s, widespread dissatisfaction with President Carter, in no small way attributable to his handling of the Mariel refugee crisis, and outrage over the perceived inability of the INS to control the borders reached a crescendo during the Iranian hostage crisis, when the nation learned that the agency did not even know how many Iranian students were living in the U.S. Additionally, Carter was under strong pressure from labor unions, as well as the NAACP, which viewed illegal aliens as taking jobs from Americans, particularly Black Americans.[8] Looking for solutions, in the late 1970s, Carter asked the National Commission for Manpower Policy for a study as to whether the H-2 temporary-worker program, created in 1953, should be expanded in order to offer employers an alternative to hiring illegal workers. In May 1979, the commission's chairman advised Ray Marshall, Carter's Secretary of Labor, that he was "strongly against" it, stating that cheap foreign labor was "addictive," it would not slow unauthorized immigration, and that a program bearing any resemblance to the Bracero Program would be "vehemently opposed" by Mexican Americans.[9]

Carter ended his term without taking any decisive action, although he did have a role in establishing a joint presidential-congressional commission, the Select Commission on Immigration and Refugee Policy (SCIRP). However, SCIRP's report, which recommended closing the "back door" to undocumented immigration while "slightly" opening the front door to accommodate more legal immigration, was completed after Carter's term of office and was handed over to the new president, Ronald Reagan, in March 1981.[10] Just five days after SCIRP released its report, Reagan established the President's Task Force on Immigration and Refugee Policy, appointing Attorney General William French Smith as chairman. In his memos, Reagan stated that the Task Force's work should include consideration of "the adequacy of the U.S. legal framework and improved methods for the control of illegal immigration and the handling of mass asylum or immigration crises."[11]

Exacerbating the problem was that beginning in the late 1970s, and continuing through the 1980s, there was a mass exodus from Central America to the United States, due to guerrilla wars in Nicaragua and El Salvador and political strife in Honduras and Guatemala. A well-traveled route began to develop from Central America to the U.S.-Mexican border, particularly in California and Texas, and ultimately, many applied for political asylum. The Reagan administration, as part of its Cold War driven foreign policy, actively discouraged Salvadorans and Guatemalans from applying for political asylum: their approval rates were less than 3 percent in 1984, compared with 12 percent for Nicaraguans, most of whom were opponents of the socialist Sandinista government, and far below the 32 percent of Poles and 60 percent of Iranians who were given sanctuary. The INS used detention centers and built tent cities to house the applicants, based on the theory that detention would deter others from coming. Although migration from Central America declined with the end of the conflicts in the early 1990s, the Central American immigrant population continued to grow, as did the social networks developed to assist political refugees facilitated economic migration for many individuals entering the United States illegally.[12]

For Reagan, taking control of the illegal immigration issue was a priority, and he framed border control as an issue of national security. In June 1983, speaking at a Republican fundraiser about Communist insurgencies in Central America, Reagan predicted "a tidal wave of refugees – and this time they'll be 'feet people' and not 'boat people' – swarming into our country seeking a safe haven from communist repression to our south."[13] By 1986, Reagan was linking border control to the threat of foreign terrorism, declaring in a televised speech that "terrorists and subversives are just two days' driving time from [the border crossing at] Harlingen, Texas." A year later, the president's cabinet-level Task Force on Terrorism warned that extremist groups would likely "feed on the anger and frustration of recent Central and South American immigrants who will not realize their own version of the American dream." According to Massey, Durand, and Malone, by the end of the decade, the "metaphor of a 'flood' had given way to martial images of a threatened 'invasion.' The border was 'under siege,' border patrol officers were 'outgunned,' and they constituted a 'thin green wall' trying to 'hold the line.'"[14]

As early as 1982, the Reagan Administration had proposed legislation to give the president new authority to declare "immigration emergencies," during which the border could be sealed by the military and aliens considered threats to national security could be rounded up and detained without warrant. Although the proposed immigration emergency bill failed to pass, in 1986, the Immigration Reform and Control Act (IRCA), spearheaded by Senator Alan Simpson (R-Wyo.) and Representative Peter Rodino (D-N.J.), was signed into law by President Reagan and took effect on January 1, 1987, which ushered in a new era of immigration.[15]

The new law allocated additional resources to expand the Border Patrol, offered amnesty for undocumented migrants who could prove continuous residence in the U.S. after January 1, 1982, and gave Reagan the authority he wanted to declare an "immigration emergency" if large numbers of unauthorized migrants were to come across the border. Additionally, it required employers to verify that workers carried

13 | THE BIRTH OF THE ILLEGAL IMMIGRANT

documentation establishing their right to work in the country and established stiff fines and possible criminal prosecution for repeated offenses. Ultimately, the IRCA provided residence documents to more than three million people, three-quarters of whom were Mexican.

While IRCA served to placate those clamoring for something to be done about an immigration crisis seemingly out of control, the law, according to political scientist Peter Andreas, exacerbated, rather than remedied, the situation. Instead of discouraging illegal immigration, the law reinforced and expanded well-established migration networks, as Mexican migrants who had returned to Mexico came back to the U.S. to claim their legalization papers, and those legalized provided a secure base for new immigrants.[16] Additionally, an unintended consequence of the minimally enforced employee sanctions was to create a booming business in falsified documents. In an article in *The New York Times*, Roberto Suro claimed there had been "fraud on a huge scale." The result was to create a potent backlash against illegal immigrants in the 1990s, especially in California.[17]

Media images of migrants as drug traffickers proliferated in the early and mid-1980s, as U.S. anti-drug trafficking efforts attempted to curtail the success of Colombian smugglers in southern Florida. Cartels began cooperating with associates in Mexico and shifted their routes to San Diego, where drug seizures skyrocketed; on September 16, 1986, *The Tribune*, one of San Diego's two major newspapers at the time, declared the border a "war zone." At the same time, local officials complained of a drastic decline in opportunities for U.S. citizens as a result of unauthorized migrants. The Sheriff of San Diego County proposed stationing U.S. Marines every 15 or 20 feet along the border, declaring:

> Illegal aliens are gradually affecting the quality of life as we know it. For example, now we have to admit illegal aliens into our colleges, which means my grandchildren may not be granted entry because of an illegal alien and they'll probably require her to be bilingual.[18]

Other states jumped onto the anti-immigrant bandwagon, with a series of referenda to make English the state official language – particularly between 1984 and 1988. In 1987 alone, five states made English their official language.[19] However, during the 1992 presidential campaign, Democrats largely maintained silence on the issue of illegal immigration. In Bill Clinton's first budget proposal, the new president called for a reduction of 93 Border Patrol agents, and the Office of Management and Budget soon announced that the agency would have to "do more with less" in terms of resources.[20]

TERRORISM, SAFETY, AND NEW LINES IN THE SAND

By the early 1990s, fear of illegal immigration was not just about losing jobs or the nebulous "American way of life;" it was about safety, and this sentiment widened beyond anti-immigration hard-liners. In 1993, the assassination of two CIA agents by an unauthorized immigrant outside of the organization's Virginia headquarters and the bombing of the World Trade Center by suspected unauthorized immigrants led to public outrage over the perceived loss of control of the borders. Significantly, the discovery of the ship *Golden Venture*, off the coast of New York City in June 1993, with a cargo of 286 Chinese immigrants, brought the issue of unauthorized immigration to a boil.[21] In a July press conference, Clinton, concerned about the political fallout, declared:

> The simple fact is that we must not, and we will not, surrender our borders to those who wish to exploit our history of compassion and justice. We cannot tolerate the traffic in human cargo, nor can we allow our people to be endangered by those who would enter our country to terrorize Americans.... Today we send a strong and clear message. We will make it tougher for illegal aliens to get into our country.[22]

By this time, politicians tried to outdo each other in taking a tough stance on boundary enforcement and unauthorized migration, and Clinton was not to be outdone. On September 19, Silvestre Reyes, Border Patrol Chief of the El Paso sector, launched Operation Blockade, later renamed Operation Hold-the-Line due to protests from the Mexican government, by deploying 400 agents and their vehicles in a visible show of force along a 20-mile section of the El Paso–Ciudad Juarez border. It was a "radical departure" from the prior Border Patrol strategy of apprehending unauthorized immigrants only after they had crossed the border. In the words of scholar Joseph Nevins, Operation Blockade was "a political sideshow designed for public consumption to demonstrate the Clinton Administration's seriousness about cracking down on unauthorized immigration."[23]

In October 1994, the INS launched a similar operation along the busiest stretch of border in San Diego, replete with high-intensity floodlights to illuminate the border and an eight-foot steel fence along fourteen miles of border. Border Patrol officers were stationed every few hundred yards behind the fence, which came to be known as the "*tortilla curtain*," and sophisticated hardware, such as motion detectors, infrared scopes, and trip wires, were deployed in the "no-man's-land." Write Massey, Durand,

13 | THE BIRTH OF THE ILLEGAL IMMIGRANT

and Malone, "Operation Gatekeeper put an end to the chaotic images of migrants running through traffic that had so troubled California's voters. Once again, the border appeared to be 'under control.'" However, putting up blockades in El Paso and San Diego did not stop undocumented migrants from entering the United States; it simply channeled them to other, less visible locations along the two-thousand-mile border. As a result, the agency was compelled to launch new operations in other areas, such as "Operation Safeguard" in Nogales, Arizona and "Operation Rio Grande" in southeast Texas, as well as expanding existing operations along longer expanses of the Mexican border.[24]

California Governor Pete Wilson took immigrant bashing to new levels in his 1994 bid for reelection. His campaign featured televised video footage of illegal immigrants dashing across the border from Mexico into crowded highway traffic, against which a narrator said, "They keep coming. Two million illegal immigrants in California. The federal government won't stop them at the border, yet requires us to pay billions to take care of them. Governor Wilson sent the National Guard to help the Border Patrol. But that's not all." Wilson then pledged to do more: "For Californians who work hard, pay taxes, and obey the laws, I am suing to force the federal government to control the border, and I'm working to deny state services to illegal immigrants. Enough is enough." The image of men, women, and children in so-called Banzai runs was broadcast across the nation and galvanized public attention, reinforcing the image of a nation overrun. Writes Andreas:

> The scenes ... were not only exploited for political gain by Governor Wilson but projected the message that lax border controls were the root of the illegal immigration problem. Left out of this message was the anemic condition of workplace controls, the economic reliance of key sectors of the California economy (particularly agriculture) on illegal foreign workers, and the fact that 40–50 percent of the unauthorized immigrants in the country had not entered illegally but simply overstayed their visas.[25]

Also on the California ballot in 1994 was Proposition 187, named the Save Our State (SOS) initiative, which proposed barring undocumented immigrant children from attending public schools, requiring school administrators to request documentation from "suspect" children, and withholding all non-emergency medical care from undocumented persons. The referendum passed by a vote of 59 percent to 41 percent, not surprising, given that a 1993 survey of 1,031 southern Californians found that 87 percent believed illegal immigration to be a very serious or somewhat serious problem, and one of the most frequently cited concerns was that undocumented immigrants were a burden on taxpayers.[26]

Though the law was subsequently declared unconstitutional by a federal judge, it was not without its consequences. There were reports of a McDonald's worker who insisted on seeing immigration documents before serving a customer, a pharmacist who refused to fill a prescription for a "suspected" undocumented person, and a customer at a restaurant who asked the cook for his green card, adding "It's a citizen's duty to kick out illegals." A hotel owner called the police when a U.S. citizen would not show immigration documents when registering for a room. Pregnant women were reportedly afraid to seek prenatal care for fear of deportation, and in at least one case, a child died when the parents postponed seeing a doctor.[27] According to the *Christian Science Monitor*:

> Already a fifth grade teacher in one California school district has assigned her students to report their own immigration status and that of their parents. And a school security guard in Atherton, California, the day after the election, told two American-born Latinas, "We don't have to let Mexicans in here anymore."[28]

In 1996, more than 500 anti-immigrant state-level bills were introduced across the United States, 37 in Arizona alone. That year, Congress passed and President Clinton signed the Anti-Terrorism and Effective Death Penalty Act (AEDPA) and the Illegal Immigration Reform and Immigrant Responsibility Act (IIRIRA), which cumulatively empowered the INS to arrest, detain, and deport unauthorized immigrants while significantly curtailing immigrant rights to appeal. AEDPA declared that an order of deportation against an alien committing an array of crimes "shall not be subject to review by any court," and it expanded the definition of criminal grounds for deportation to include crimes classified as misdemeanors in state courts. Additionally, the law considered offenses retroactively, such that past convictions could be used as a basis for deportation. The IIRIRA authorized the construction of a fourteen-mile fence along the U.S.–Mexico border, doubled the force of border patrol agents, allowed for immigration officials to summarily deport individuals apprehended within one hundred miles of the border, and barred legal immigrants from federal welfare provisions for the first five years of their U.S. residency. Note sociologists Karen Manges Douglas and Rogelio Sáenz, the new legislation "would become a boon to private prison companies" as the law began to require "the detention of all immigrants, including permanent residents, facing deportation for most criminal violations until the final resolution of the case."[29]

13 | THE BIRTH OF THE ILLEGAL IMMIGRANT

By 1999, the Border Patrol had grown to nearly 8,000 agents, and inspectors and had a goal of hiring 80 new officers per month, for which it offered a signing bonus. A 1997 article in the *Federal Times* reported that "Border Patrol agent" and "immigration inspector" were among the top 10 categories for job growth in the federal workforce, as the number of officers between 1986 and 1999 more than doubled. At the same time, the INS budget had reached $4.2 billion, nearly eight times its 1986 level, with over $900 million going to the Border Patrol alone, which had acquired a vast array of new hardware, including 58 helicopters, 43 airplanes, 355 night-vision scopes, and high-tech devices, such as electronic intrusion-detection sensors, closed-circuit TV systems, infrared radar, electronic fingerprinting systems, and microwave communications.[30]

However, such measures have been far from effective. Rather, as notes migration scholar Wayne A. Cornelius, they have only served to redistribute the geography of illegal entries. He writes:

> Migrants and the people-smugglers who assist them have just detoured around the heavily fortified segments of the border. A rapid decline in apprehensions in the first-fortified El Paso and San Diego areas was accompanied by increases in apprehensions along unfortified segments of the border in Arizona, New Mexico, and Texas. By 2006, the crackdown on illegal entries through Arizona that began in the late 1990s had pushed the migrant traffic back toward San Diego and El Paso, sectors that had been declared "operationally controlled" by the Border Patrol.[31]

Under President George W. Bush, enforcement of immigration law broadened its focus to the country's interior, and tactics included home and workplace raids, neighborhood sweeps, tracking down fugitives who ignored orders to leave the United States, and implementing the 287(g) program that deputized designated state and local police officials to perform federal immigration enforcement functions.[32] Significantly, on October 26, 2001, six weeks after the attacks on September 11, Bush signed into the law the USA Patriot ACT, which granted authorities even greater powers to deport, without hearings or any presentation of evidence all noncitizens, regardless of legal status, whom the Attorney General had "reason to believe" might commit acts of terrorism. "For the first time since the Alien and Sedition Act of 1798," write Douglas S. Massey and Karen A. Prem, "Congress authorized the arrest, imprisonment, and deportation of noncitizens upon the orders of the Attorney General without judicial review."[33]

In 2003, as part of the "War on Terror," the government created the Department of Homeland Security (DHS) and its arm, the U.S. Immigration and Customs Enforcement (ICE), which subsumed the INS, and began to pour "unprecedented amounts of money ... into interior enforcement."[34] ICE launched a series of programs in collaboration with state and local authorities, including the Criminal Alien Program (CAP), which placed ICE officials at state prisons to conduct immigrant screening, and the Secure Communities program, which mandated that police enter the prints of those arrested into a joint FBI and ICE database.[35] Since that time, there has been a drastic escalation in the number of deportations. According to Massey and Pren, prior to the mid-1990s, no more than 50,000 persons had been deported for decades; by the turn of the century, deportations were about 200,000 annually. With the passage of the Patriot Act, the number of deportations increased again, reaching nearly 400,000 in 2009. They write: "None of the terrorist attacks involved Mexicans, and none of the terrorists entered through Mexico. Indeed, all came to the United States on legal visas. Yet ... Mexicans nonetheless bore the brunt of the deportation campaign launched in the name of the war on terrorism, comprising 72 percent of those removed in 2009."[36]

The years after the 9/11 attacks, brought, in the words of author Peter Schrag, "a near orgy of national security measures" aimed not only at terrorists but unauthorized immigrants as well.[37] In 2005, Congress passed the REAL ID ACT, which prohibited states from issuing driver's licenses or other forms of identification to people who could not prove that they were in the country legally. In December of that year, the House passed the Sensenbrenner Bill, which included sections on ways to stop immigration and visa fraud; a mandate for developing a training manual for local police on how to catch illegal immigrants; a requirement that all Border Patrol uniforms be made in the United States; and a provision that anyone who "harbors, conceals, or shields from detection a person in the United States knowing or in reckless disregard of the fact that such person is an alien who lacks lawful authority to be in the United States" was committing a crime.[38]

Although the Sensenbrenner never got Senate approval, the congressional immigration battles, coupled with the growing number of federal raids on workplaces with undocumented workers, sparked demonstrations, and an estimated 3.5 to 5.1 million took to the streets in more than 160 cities throughout the country; demonstrators boycotted workplaces, waved the Mexican flag, and chanted "*Hoy marchamos, mañana votamos*" (Today we march, tomorrow we vote) and "I am not illegal, I am human." Univisión and Telemundo, the two main Spanish-language networks, promoted the demonstrations through public service announcements broadcast during evening newscasts, reporting on the preparations for the marches, interviews with organizers, and even incorporating the subject into the plotlines of telenovelas.[39]

13 | THE BIRTH OF THE ILLEGAL IMMIGRANT

In April 2005, in Arizona, a group calling itself the Minuteman Project stationed scores of men and women along the Mexican border in an effort to track down undocumented immigrants. Described as a vigilante organization by the Bush Administration, the Minuteman Project described itself as "a citizens' Neighborhood Watch on our border," and staked out a 23-mile stretch of border northeast of Nogales, equipped with night-vision goggles, guns, and over 20 plans to survey the area. While the Minutemen have publicly tried to distance themselves from White supremacist groups – a Minuteman Project rally in Rancho Cucamonga, California was called off when members of the Ku Kux Klan showed up to show their support –, the organization, says political scientist Roxanne Lynn Doty, has "provided fertile ground for individuals and groups that promote racist, White supremacist ideologies." In June 2006, the Klan held an anti-immigrant rally in Midland Texas, whose organizer, Steven Edwards, declared: "This country was made by White Europeans for White Europeans." That month, two White supremacy groups organized anti-immigrant rallies in Nashua, New Hampshire, and in July, the San Angelo chapter *of* the Ku Klux Klan planned a rally against undocumented immigration in Amarillo, Texas.[40]

At the same time, conservative commentators, such as *Fox News*' Bill O'Reilly, spoke of the Reconquista, attributing to Mexicans the lines: "You stole our land, and now we're going to take it back by massive, massive migration into the Southwest," "We're going to control those places, because you stole it from us," and "That's the agenda underneath." CNN commentator Jack Cafferty chimed:

> Once again, the streets of our country were taken over today by people who don't belong here.… Taxpayers who have surrendered highways, parks, sidewalks, and a lot of television news time on all these cable news networks to mobs of illegal aliens are not happy about it … March through our streets and demand your rights. Excuse me? You have no rights here, and that includes the right to tie up our towns and cities and block our streets. At some point this could all turn very violent as Americans become fed up with the failure of their government to address the most pressing domestic issue of our time.[41]

NOTES

1. Massey, Douglas S. "America's Immigration Policy Fiasco," *Dædalus*. Volume 142, Issue 3 (Summer 2013), 5.

2. Chomsky, Aviva. *Undocumented: How Immigration Became Illegal.* (Boston, MA: Beacon Press, 2014), 59.
3. Massey, "America's Immigration Policy Fiasco," 9.
4. Chavez, Leo. *The Latino Threat: Constructing Immigrants, Citizens, and the Nation.* (Stanford, CT: Stanford University Press, 2013), 32.
5. Massey, *Dædalus*, 5.
6. Chavez, 33.
7. *Time*, "Immigration: Getting Their Slice of Paradise," May 2, 1977.
8. LeMay, Michael C. *Illegal Immigration: A Reference Handbook.* (Santa Barbara, CA: ABC-CLIO, 2015), 11.
9. Ginsberg, Eli. Chairman of the National Commission for Manpower Policy, Letter transmitted to Secretary of Labor Ray Marshall, May 1, 1979. http://babel.hathitrust.org/cgi/pt?id=umn.31951p009093394;view=1up;seq=108.
10. LeMay, 11.
11. Laham, Nicholas. *Ronald Reagan and the Politics of Immigration Reform.* (Santa Barbara, CA: Praeger, 2000), 6.
12. Zong, Jie and Jeanne Batalova. "Central American Immigrants in the United States," Migration Policy Institute. http://www.migrationpolicy.org/article/central-american-immigrants-united-states.
13. *Washington Post*, June 21, 1983.
14. Massey, Douglas S. Jorge Durand, and Nolan J. Malone, *Beyond Smoke and Mirrors: Mexican Immigration in an Era of Economic Integration.* (New York, NY: Russell Sage Foundation Publications, 2003), 93.
15. Ibid., 97.
16. Andreas, Peter. *Border Games: Policing the U.S.–Mexico Divide.* (Princeton, NJ: Cornell University Press, 2009), 98.
17. *The New York Times*, "Migrants' False Claims: Fraud on a Huge Scale," November 12, 1989.
18. Nevins, Joseph. *Operation Gatekeeper and Beyond: The War On "Illegals" and the Remaking of the U.S.–Mexico Boundary.* (London, England: Routledge, 2010), 96.
19. Massey, Durand, and Nolan, 99.
20. Nevins, 110.
21. Ibid., 109.
22. Ibid., 110.
23. *The New York Times*, November 12, 1989, "Migrants' False Claims: Fraud on a Huge Scale."
24. Massey, Durand, and Malone, 94.
25. Andreas, 98.

26. Calavita, Kitty. "The New Politics of Immigration: 'Balanced-Budget Conservatism' and the Symbolism of Proposition 187," *Social Problems*. Vol. 43, No. 3 (Aug., 1996), 290.
27. Ibid., 291.
28. *The Christian Science Monitor*, December 27, 1994, "Harassment in the Wake of Proposition 187."
29. Douglas, Karen Manges and Rogelio Saenz. "The Criminalization of Immigrants & the Immigration-Industrial Complex," *Dædalus*. Volume 142, Issue 3, (Summer 2013), 199.
30. Massey, Durand, and Malone, 96.
31. Cornelius, Wayne A. "Does Border Enforcement Deter Unauthorized Immigration?" *Impacts of Border Enforcement on Mexican Migration: The View From Sending Communities*. (La Jolla, CA: Center for Comparative Immigration Studies, UCSD, 2007), 3.
32. Jones-Correa, Michael and Els de Graauw. "The Illegality Trap: The Politics of Immigration & the Lens of Illegality," *Dædalus*. Vol. 142, No. 3 (Summer, 2013), 185.
33. Massey, Douglas S. and Karen A. Pren. "Unintended Consequences of US Immigration Policy: Explaining the Post-1965 Surge from Latin America," *Population and Development Review*, Vol. 38, No. 1, March 2012, 15.
34. Golash-Boza, Tanya Maria. *Immigrant Nation: Raids, Detentions, and Deportations in Post-9/11 America*. (Boulder: Paradigm Publishers, 2012), 47.
35. Kibria, Nazli, Cara Bowman, and Megan O'Leary. *Race and Immigration*. (Cambridge, UK: Polity Press, 2014), 47.
36. Massey and Pren, 15.
37. Schrag, Peter. *Not Fit For Our Society: Immigration and Nativism in America*. (Berkeley, CA: University of California Press, 2010), 175.
38. Ibid.
39. Chomsky, 197.
40. Doty, Roxanne Lynn. *The Law Into Their Own Hands: Immigration and the Politics of Exceptionalism*. (Tucson, AZ: University of Arizona Press, 2009), 60.
41. Ibid., 177.

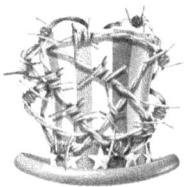

14

IMMIGRATION REFORM IN THEORY, DEPORTATIONS IN PRACTICE

AS A PRESIDENTIAL candidate, Senator Barack Obama expressed a cautious solidarity with migrants, tempered by toughness, advocating a vision of Comprehensive Immigration Reform (CIR). In a May 2008 interview with Univisión anchor Jorge Ramos, he stated, "I cannot guarantee that it is going to be in the first 100 days. But what I can guarantee is that we will have in the first year an immigration bill that I strongly support and that I'm promoting. And I want to move that forward as quickly as possible."[1] In June, he told the National Association of Latino Elected Officials, "We need immigration reform that will secure our borders, and punish employers who exploit immigrant labor; reform that finally brings the 12 million people who are here illegally out of the shadows by requiring them to take steps to become legal citizens." Speaking to the League of United Latin American Citizens that July, Obama declared:

> The system is not working when a young person at the top of her class, a young person with so much to offer this country, cannot attend a public college or university … The system isn't working when … communities are terrorized by ICE immigration raids … When all of that is happening, the system isn't working, and we need to change it!"[2]

Obama's promise of immigration reform paid off in the election. He garnered 67 percent of the record-setting 10 million Latinos who voted, more than any presidential candidate since Bill Clinton was elected in 1996, and Hispanics represented the biggest shift toward the Democrats by any voter group.[3] Additionally, Democrats took control of both houses of Congress. Yet Obama's first term produced little in terms of immigration reform, other than a proposal in 2010, the Development, Relief, and Education for Alien Minors (DREAM) ACT, a measure to grant legal status to certain unauthorized immigrants who entered the United States as children and had completed higher education or military service.[4] The DREAM Act passed the Democratic House, but all but three Republican senators joined five Democrats in opposition, and the bill failed to reach the sixty votes needed to bring it to the floor for debate. The next congressional term brought a Republican majority into the House and ended any hope for CIR legislation in Obama's first term.[5]

According to political scientist Alfonso Gonzales, throughout Obama's first term, the Administration employed a policy of "little carrots and big sticks." The carrots were minor reforms, such as moving away from aggressive work-site raids, and a policy of ostensibly deporting only those migrants dubbed a "high priority" or a threat to public safety or national security. The sticks were a more aggressive implementation of E-Verify, an online worker identification verification system begun under the Bush Administration to check the legal status of workers, and a move toward using increasingly sophisticated technology and surveillance equipment at the border, coupled with the deployment in 2010 of 1,500 National Guard troops along the border, called Operation Phalanx.[6]

Despite the carrots, deportations reached record levels under Obama, rising to an annual average of nearly 400,000 after 2009, totaling 1.5 million during his first term, and ultimately earning him the epithet "Deporter In Chief," by 2011, about 60 percent of Latinos disapproved of the president's deportation policy.[7] Summarizing Obama's first four years, Gonzales writes:

> Rather than being a "revolution" or great transformation, the election of President Obama ... resulted in the strengthening of the very structures that Latino migrant activist and the migrant rights movement were fighting. Obama the candidate and later president pacified immigration reformers by making promises to push through a CIR bill and to curtail state violence against Latino communities. Immigration reformers and their allies across the country sacrificed radical challenges to lethal migration control

polices for the sake of short-term gains and access to powerful administration figures.[8]

However, as sociologists John D. Skrentny and Jane Lilly López argue, Obama used his discretionary powers in order to offer signals to distrusting restrictionist members of Congress that the government was up to the task of securing the borders and preventing future flows of undocumented immigrants.[9] An indication is remarks made by DHS Secretary Janet Napolitano in 2009:

> In 2007, many members of Congress said that they could support immigration reform in the future, but only if we first made significant progress securing the border. This reflected the real concern of many Americans that the government was not serious about enforcing the law. Fast-forward to today, and many of the benchmarks these members of Congress set in 2007 have been met. For example, the Border Patrol has increased its forces to more than 20,000 officers, and DHS has built more than 600 miles of border fencing. Both of these milestones demonstrate that we have gotten Congress' message.[10]

On June 15, 2012, Secretary Napolitano announced the Administration's new policy of Deferred Action for Childhood Arrivals (DACA), which permitted an estimated 1.8 million undocumented immigrants, who were brought to the United States as children and raised here, to obtain temporary relief from removal and, in many cases, employment authorization. While DACA only made a dent in providing a path to citizenship for the estimated 11 million living in the U.S. without documents at the time, it was a powerful demonstration of executive authority, which effectively ended protests from immigration activists.[11]

Yet DACA was a far cry from comprehensive reform, and Obama's lack of tangible results continued to be a thorn in the president's side throughout his reelection campaign. For instance, during a September Univisión town hall meeting, the president was confronted by Jorge Ramos on the lack of action seen in his first term. Said Ramos:

> Mr. President, I want to ask you something that is known as the "Obama promise" … I'm going to quote you: "But I can guarantee that we will have, in the first year, an immigration bill that

I strongly support." ... You promised that. And a promise is a promise. And with all due respect, you didn't keep that promise.

Obama responded by indicating that Congress had blocked his efforts and his limits in terms of executive authority:

> There's the thinking that the President is somebody who is all-powerful and can get everything done. In our branch of – in our system of government, I am the head of the executive branch. I'm not the head of the legislature; I'm not the head of the judiciary. We have to have cooperation from all these sources in order to get something done. And so I am happy to take responsibility for the fact that we didn't get it done, but I did not make a promise that I would get everything done, 100 percent, when I was elected as President.
>
> What I promised was that I would work every single day as hard as I can to make sure that everybody in this country, regardless of who they are, what they look like, where they come from, that they would have a fair shot at the American Dream. And I have – that promise I've kept.[12]

Obama's goodwill proved to be good enough for Latino voters, especially in contrast to Republican challenger Mitt Romney, who promised to veto the DREAM Act and advocated a policy of "self-deportation," which was to be actively encouraged by tough government sanctions against employers. Nearly 72 percent of Latinos voted to reelect the president, and according to the polling group Latino Decisions, Latinos were "nationally decisive" in a U.S. presidential election for the first time in history.[13] Political scientist Gary Segura called the election a "watershed" moment:

> The results of the 2012 election have awakened the Republican Party to their impending demographic disaster. Substantial growth in the size and power of the Latino vote – and an overwhelming tilt in that vote against their nominee – paints a bleak future for Republican electability. Coupled with startling Democratic vote share among Asian Americans (73%), and an ever more resolute and motivated African American vote, demography may be destiny for the GOP.[14]

14 | IMMIGRATION REFORM IN THEORY, DEPORTATIONS IN PRACTICE

Meanwhile, at the state level, hard line stances and even harsher rhetoric against immigrants emerged. In April 2010, Arizona Governor Jan Brewer signed the Support Our Law Enforcement and Safe Neighborhoods Act (SB 1070) into law, the most draconian immigration law enacted in decades. Its key provisions included requirements that police officers investigate the immigration status of all individuals they stop if they suspected the detainees are in the country unlawfully; mandatory detention of individuals who are arrested, even for minor offenses, if they cannot prove they are authorized to be in the United States; and stipulations that allow law enforcement officers to arrest a person without a warrant if the officer has probable cause to believe that the person has committed an offense subject to removal from the country. Said State Senator Russell Pearce the act's chief sponsor:

> We have a responsibility to protect our citizens and to protect the integrity of our country and the government which we live under … It will do no good to forgive them because millions more will come behind them, and we will be overrun to the point that there will no longer be a United States of America but, a North American Union of open borders. I ask you, "What form of government will we live under?" How long will it be before we will be just like Mexico? We have already lost our language; everything must be printed in Spanish. We have already lost our history since it is no longer taught in our schools. And we have lost our borders.[15]

The law was challenged by the Justice Department, and it reached the Supreme Court, which delivered a split decision in June 2012, upholding its "show me your papers" provision but blocking others on the grounds that they interfered with the federal government's role in setting immigration policy. Writing for the majority, Justice Anthony M. Kennedy stated, "Arizona may have understandable frustrations with the problems caused by illegal immigration while that process continues, but the state may not pursue policies that undermine federal law." In his dissent, Justice Antonin Scalia argued that states should have the right to make immigration policy if the federal government is not enforcing its own policies.[16]

It wasn't just happening in Arizona, and the legislative push for anti-immigrant laws wasn't restricted to Republican-controlled states either. With the Democratic wipeout in the 2010 elections, Republicans now controlled the majority of state houses. In the following year copycat laws to Arizona's SB 1070 were proposed in more than 35 states, and passed in five.[17]

From the White House, rhetoric about the need for CIR, not a crackdown on "illegals," continued. In November 2014, President Obama delivered a televised address that asserted the powers of the Oval Office to reshape the nation's immigration system and challenged members of the incoming Republican-controlled Congress to reverse his actions, declaring that deporting millions is "not who we are," and citing scripture saying, "We shall not oppress a stranger for we know the heart of a stranger – we were strangers once, too."

The centerpiece of the president's announcement was a new program for unauthorized immigrants who are the parents of United States citizens, making about four million people eligible for legal status, deferring their deportation, and allowing them to work legally. The president's plan would also ease requirements for the DACA program by extending eligibility to people who entered the United States as children before January 2010, increasing the deferral period to three years from two years and eliminating the requirement that applicants be under 31 years old; it also included actions to direct law enforcement priorities toward criminals, allow high-skilled workers to move or change jobs more easily, and streamline visa and court procedures.[18] Defending his presidential authority, Obama declared:

> The actions I'm taking are not only lawful, they're the kinds of actions taken by every single Republican president and every Democratic president for the past half-century ... To those members of Congress who question my authority to make our immigration system work better, or question the wisdom of me acting where Congress has failed, I have one answer: Pass a bill.

Later in the speech, the president asked rhetorically:

> Are we a nation that tolerates the hypocrisy of a system where workers who pick our fruit and make our beds never have a chance to get right with the law? ... And whether our forebears were strangers who crossed the Atlantic, or the Pacific, or the Rio Grande, we are here only because this country welcomed them in.[19]

But now that Republicans controlled both houses of Congress, Obama knew that there was little chance that CIR would pass. The "power of the pen" was limited in this arena, and Republicans challenged any directive proposed by Obama. House Speaker John A. Boehner (R-Ohio) called Obama's legacy one of "lawlessness." On February 16, 2015, a federal judge in Texas temporarily blocked the executive action.

14 | IMMIGRATION REFORM IN THEORY, DEPORTATIONS IN PRACTICE

The judge, responding to a suit filed by 26 Republican-run states, did not rule on the legality of immigration orders but said there was sufficient merit to the challenge to warrant a suspension while the case goes forward. "No law gave the administration the power … to give 4.3 million removable aliens what the Department of Homeland Security itself labels as 'legal presence,'" stated the judge. "In fact the law *mandates* that these illegally-present individuals be removed."[20]

DISCRIMINATION, TRUMPISM, AND MULTICULTURALISM

In the first two decades of the 21st century, White America's attitude toward Hispanics and Hispanic immigrants has been a mixed bag. That ambivalence is reflected in the responses of lawmakers. Take the case of California. In 2004, Governor Arnold Schwarzenegger praised the Minutemen for doing "a terrific job," while vetoing bills that would have made undocumented residents eligible to receive a driver's license. Yet in 2007, he signed a bill prohibiting cities from requiring landlords to check whether tenants are in the country legally. Two years later, in the midst of a $24 billion deficit, he renounced those blaming the problem on illegal immigrants. "I'm glad they can get the [state's] services," he said, adding, "Everything we eat today is picked and created by undocumented immigrants, to a large extent. Every time we go and move into a building, a lot of those buildings are built by undocumented immigrants' hands."[21]

In no small part due to media sensationalism fueling the perception that undocumented immigrants are flooding the nation, regardless of immigration status, Latinos continue to experience racism. According to a 2010 survey by Pew, about six-in-ten Latinos say discrimination against Hispanics is a "major problem," preventing them from succeeding in America, and about a third say they, a member of their family, or a close friend have experienced discrimination in the past five years because of their race or ethnic group.[22] As one example, anti-illegal immigration ordinances have been placed in some communities, which include penalties for landlords who rent property to undocumented individuals; this results in landlords being more likely "to resort to shortcuts, such as discriminating based on accent, surname, appearance, or other ethnic markers" and, ultimately, discrimination in the housing sector for all Latinos, regardless of their documentation status.[23]

Additionally, Latinos are 1.5 times more likely to obtain high cost loans than Whites when applying for housing finance. According to Madeline Troche-Rodriguez, "Beginning with the home buying process, Latino families are restricted in the kinds of homes they can purchase by the real estate and banking industries, and more recently, many have fallen victim to predatory mortgage brokers."[24] In education, many young Latinos are put at a disadvantage by English-only classrooms that discourage bilingualism. Additionally, research has shown that the differential treatment from teachers toward Latino students has a negative influence on performance in school.[25]

Sometimes discrimination can be of a more subtle variety, and there are indications that post-Donald Trump's rhetoric, things are getting worse. Writes journalist Tina Vasquez, "I've lived in Los Angeles for 29 of my 30 years. As a light-skinned, biracial Latina in one of the most diverse and Mexican-centric cities in the nation, I have never been asked the type of questions I'm now fielding from White people." She continues:

> A couple of weeks ago, while I was running errands in my neighborhood, a stranger asked me if I was "illegal." Around 10 minutes earlier another stranger asked me if I spoke English. Both were White and one of them even called me "señorita." Then, late last week, I was standing in line to use the ATM when a White Man approached me cautiously, asking if I spoke English. He was lost and said he didn't want to be in a "bad area" longer than he needed to. He was holding a King Taco cup in his hand. I've seen White guys like him at the neighborhood taco spot. Stay for the tacos, leave before you have to interact with Mexicans who are serving you … This is the world Trump wants when he says he's going to "make America great again." It's the America of 1950s TV shows, where people of color don't exist in the lives of White Americans unless they're being served or entertained by them.[26]

Although Mr. Trump did not invent "White supremacy" or "White resentment" toward people of color, he did, as expressed by Nicholas Confessore in *The New York Times*, "open the door to assertions of White identity and resentment not seen so broadly in American culture in over half a century, according to those who track patterns of racial tension and antagonism in American life."[27]

There is a divide, to be sure, and American attitudes about Hispanic Americans, Hispanic immigrants, and undocumented workers – still often viewed by many as the same group – remain contradictory as ever, and a deepening, though small, backlash against the browning of America is quite vocal about its displeasure.

Today, how one views immigrants and, in many ways, how one views Hispanics depends on one's political views. A 2019 Pew Research study found that 83 percent of Democrats felt that immigrants strengthen American because of their hard work

14 | IMMIGRATION REFORM IN THEORY, DEPORTATIONS IN PRACTICE

and talents, compared to only 38 percent of Republicans. Pew found that, in aggregate, 62 percent of U.S. adults feel that immigrants strengthen the country, compared with 28 percent who say that they are more of a burden because "they take our jobs, housing and health care."[28] In 1994, the opposite was true: Nearly two-thirds of Americans said immigrants were a burden, while 31 percent said they strengthened the country.[29] Another Pew study in 2015 showed that nearly three-quarters of Americans – including 80 percent of Democrats, 76 percent of independents, and 56 percent of Republicans – say undocumented immigrants currently living in the U.S. should be allowed to stay in this country legally if they meet certain requirements.[30]

Perhaps for the first time, Americans have a net positive reaction toward the undocumented. A Pew survey from August of 2016 found that 76 percent of Americans nationwide say undocumented immigrants are "as honest and hard-working" as U.S. citizens and 67 percent said they are no more likely to commit serious crimes.[31]

One of the darkest chapters in America's immigration story has been the often horrific detention of unauthorized immigrants, most of whom are from Central America and many of whom are children, in detention facilities at the Mexican border. According to *The Guardian*, immigrants, including asylum seekers and legal migrants, wait more than four weeks to be released, though some have been held inside for years or even decades. In September 2019, there were more than 52,000 people confined in jails, tents, and other forms of detention, most of which are for-profit.[32] At the end of 2019, American immigration officials had apprehended over 76,000 minors traveling without their parents – 52 percent more than during the prior year, based on figures from United States Customs and Border Protection.[33] Donald Trump's aggressive policy toward immigrants has coincided with an exodus of children fleeing Central America. According to the Human Rights Watch:

> Almost all of the women and children we spoke with said that they were not allowed to shower, sometimes for days, until just before they were transferred to longer-term detention facilities. Nearly all said that they did not receive hand soap, toothpaste, or toothbrushes in these holding cells, meaning that for the duration of their stay they were not able to wash their hands with soap before and after eating and after using the toilet. Most women said that menstrual hygiene products and diapers were available on request, but several told us they did not have access to these items while in CBP holding cells. If they had these and other toiletries among

their personal property, they were not allowed to retrieve these items while in the holding cells.[34]

What remains to be seen is whether the vilification of Hispanics is a passing phenomenon, one spurred, as has been the case so often in our history, by immigration levels reaching a crescendo, or if their trajectory will more closely resemble that of African Americans, the recipients of an enduring legacy of disdain and discrimination. Given that in 2020, about three-quarters of Hispanics are of the first or second generation in the United States, complete assimilation has yet to occur.

Still, there is power in numbers. As the White share of the population pie continues to dwindle, the Hispanic population is expected to reach about 106 million in 2050, approaching double what it is today. Whatever White America may think, the United States is in the throes of a return to its Hispanic roots. The browning of America, largely driven by Latinos, is a demographic inevitability.

NOTES

1. *The New York Times*, "First-Term Promises Made, Kept and Broken," January 19, 2013.
2. Gonzales, Alfonso. *Reform Without Justice: Latino Migrant Politics and the Homeland Security State*. (Oxford, England: Oxford University Press, 2014), 125.
3. *The New York Times*, "In Big Shift, Latino Vote Was Heavily for Obama," November 6, 2008.
4. Kibria, Bowman, and O'Leary, 55.
5. *The New York Times*, "Immigration Vote Leaves Obama's Policy in Disarray," December 18, 2010.
6. Gonzales, 146.
7. 2011 Pew Research Center, "As Deportations Rise to Record Levels, Most Latinos Oppose Obama's Policy." http://www.pewhispanic.org/2011/12/28/as-deportations-rise-to-record-levels-most-latinos-oppose-obamas-policy/.
8. Gonzales, 151.
9. Skrentny, John D. and Jane Lilly López. "Obama's Immigration Reform: The Triumph of Executive Action," *Indiana Journal of Law and Social Equality*. Vol. 1, No. 2, Fall 2013, 68.
10. "Prepared Remarks by Secretary Napolitano on Immigration Reform at the Center for American Progress," November 13, 2009. http://www.dhs.gov/news/2009/11/13/secretary-napolitanos-speech-immigration-reform.
11. Skrentny and López, 75.

12. Remarks by the President at Univision Town Hall with Jorge Ramos and Maria Elena Salinas, September 20, 2012. https://www.whitehouse.gov/the-press-office/2012/09/20/remarks-president-univision-town-hall-jorge-ramos-and-maria-elena-salina.
13. Gonzales, 154.
14. Segura, Gary. "What Latinos Want – Immigration Reform Bill," November 27, 2012. http://www.latinodecisions.com/blog/2012/11/27/what-latinos-want/.
15. Theodore, Nik. "Policing Borders: Unauthorized Immigration and the Pernicious Politics of Attrition," *Social Justice*. Vol. 38, No. 1/2, 93.
16. "Blocking Parts of Arizona Law, Justices Allow Its Centerpiece," *The New York Times*, June 25, 2012.
17. "164 Anti-Immigration Laws Passed Since 2010? A MoJo Analysis," *Mother Jones*, March/April 2012. http://www.motherjones.com/politics/2012/03/anti-immigration-law-database
18. "What Is President Obama's Immigration Plan?" *The New York Times*, November 20, 2014.
19. "Obama, Daring Congress, Acts to Overhaul Immigration," *The New York Times*, November 20, 2014.
20. "Federal Judge in Texas Blocks Obama Immigration Orders," *The Washington Post*, February 17, 2015.
21. Schrag, 186.
22. "Illegal Immigration Backlash Worries, Divides Latinos," Pew Research Center, October 28, 2010. http://www.pewhispanic.org/2010/10/28/iii-discrimination-deportation-detainment-and-satisfaction/.
23. Oliveri, Rigel C. "Between a Rock and a Hard Place: Landlords, Latinos, Anti-Illegal Immigrant Ordinances, and Housing Discrimination," *Vanderbilt Law Review*. Vol. 62, No. 1, 2009, 55.
24. Troche-Rodriguez, Madeline. "Latinos and Their Housing Experiences in Metropolitan Chicago: Challenges and Recommendations," *Harvard Journal of Hispanic Policy*. Vol. 21, 2009, 17.
25. Torres, Héctor L., Anita O'Conor, Claudia Mejía, Yvette Camacho, and Alyse Long. "The American Dream: Racism towards Latino/as in the U.S. and the Experience of Trauma Symptoms," *Interamerican Journal of Psychology*. Vol. 45, No. 3, 363.
26. Vasquez, Tina. "I've Experienced a New Level of Racism since Donald Trump Went after Latinos," *The Guardian*, September 9, 2015. https://www.theguardian.com/commentisfree/2015/sep/09/donald-trump-racism-increase-latinos.

27. "For Whites Sensing Decline, Donald Trump Unleashes Words of Resistance," *The New York Times*, July 13, 2016. http://www.nytimes.com/2016/07/14/us/politics/donald-trump-white-identity.html?emc=edit_ta_20160713&nlid=67105089&ref=cta&_r=0.
28. Jones, Bradley. "Majority of Americans Continue to Say Immigrants Strengthen the U.S.," Pew Research Center, January 31, 2019. https://www.pewresearch.org/fact-tank/2019/01/31/majority-of-americans-continue-to-say-immigrants-strengthen-the-u-s/.
29. "Modern Immigration Wave Brings 59 Million to U.S., Driving Population Growth and Change Through 2065," Pew Research Center, September 28, 2015. http://www.pewhispanic.org/2015/09/28/chapter-4-u-s-public-has-mixed-views-of-immigrants-and-immigration/.
30. "Broad Public Support for Legal Status for Undocumented Immigrants" Pew Research Center, June 4, 2015. http://www.people-press.org/2015/06/04/broad-public-support-for-legal-status-for-undocumented-immigrants/.
31. "Trump Supporters Differ from Other GOP Voters on Foreign Policy, Immigration Issues," Pew Research Center, May 11, 2016. http://www.pewresearch.org/fact-tank/2016/05/11/trump-supporters-differ-from-other-gop-voters-on-foreign-policy-immigration-issues/.
32. Kassie, Emily. "Detained: How the U.S. Built the World's Largest Immigrant Detention System," *The Guardian*, September 24, 2019. https://www.theguardian.com/us-news/2019/sep/24/detained-us-largest-immigrant-detention-trump.
33. Villegas, Paulina. "Detentions of Child Migrants at the U.S. Border Surges to Record Levels," *The New York Times*, October 29, 2019. https://www.nytimes.com/2019/10/29/world/americas/unaccompanied-minors-border-crossing.html.
34. "In the Freezer: Abusive Conditions for Women and Children in US Immigration Holding Cells," *Human Rights Watch*, February 28, 2018. https://www.hrw.org/report/2018/02/28/freezer/abusive-conditions-women-and-children-us-immigration-holding-cells.

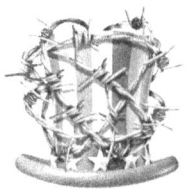

PART 4

ASIAN AMERICANS

IN 2012, Pew Research Center published a glowing report on the state of Asians in the United States that was met by widespread criticism by Asian-American activists. Highlights included a median household income of $66,000 for Asian Americans, compared to $49,800 for Americans as a whole, and Asian-American median household wealth at $83,500 versus $68,529 for the U.S. population. Pew reported that nearly half of all Asian-American adults have a college degree, compared with 28 percent of adults in the country, and that Asian Americans are more satisfied with their lives overall (82 percent versus 75 percent), their personal finances (51 percent versus 35 percent) and the general direction of the country (43 percent versus 21 percent).[1]

Yet rather than basking in the light of such favorable statistics, 30 Asian American and Pacific Island groups, "an alphabet soup of organizations," criticized the report. "This study perpetuates false stereotypes," charged the Japanese Citizens League. The Asian & Pacific Islander American Scholarship Fund and the National Commission on Asian American and Pacific Islander Research in Education jointly announced that the study "only reinforces the mischaracterizations of Asian American students."[2]

The Pew study provoked such a strong reaction because it touched a nerve on many fronts. It ignored that Asian Americans have an overall poverty rate of 13 percent, including 38 percent of Hmong, 29 percent of Cambodians, 19 percent of

Laotians, and 17 percent of Vietnamese. It did not mention that the high school dropout rate among Southeast Asian Americans is a staggering 40 percent of Hmong, 38 percent of Laotians, and 35 percent of Cambodians. Additionally, it did not consider the results of a Gallup survey, which showed that 31 percent of Asian Americans reported incidents of employment discrimination, the largest of any group, with African Americans constituting the second largest at 26 percent.[3]

Rather, the Pew study seemed to suggest that all is rosy for Asian Americans, in essence confirming the stereotype of the "model minority," silently achieving the American dream while other minorities, as if by their own choice, are left behind. In the words of historian Vijay Prasad, "It is easier to be seen as a stereotype than as a problem. We don't suffer genocidal poverty and incarceration rates in the United States, nor do we walk in fear and a fog of invincibility."[4] Writes Min Zhou, a sociologist:

> One consequence of the model-minority stereotype is that it reinforces the myth that the United States is devoid of racism and accords equal opportunity to all, fostering the view that those who lag behind do so because of their own poor choices and inferior culture. Celebrating "model minorities" can help impede other racial minorities' demands for social justice by pitting minority groups against each other. It can also pit Asian Americans against Whites.[5]

According to sociologists Rosalind S. Chou and Joe R. Feagin, being viewed as a model minority does not prevent Asian Americans from experiencing racial hostility and discrimination, particularly mocking and caricaturing. In their research, Chou and Feagin found that the Asian Americans whom they interviewed were "excluded and othered," often overtly. They conclude that for Asian Americans, racism is a constantly lived experience, which manifests with "a subtle or covert face, leaving its targets to wonder if an incident was indeed generated by discriminatory intent."[6] One of their respondents described his experience in the workplace working as a cabinetmaker:

> If you are Asian, they always pick on you. It doesn't matter how good you are. I used to have a boss, and he would come to the shop and make fun of me, like talking in [mock] Chinese language … You don't hear them making fun of Whites, do you? If you make fun of them, then they will get angry … Take the

N-word, they banned that word, but they are still calling the Chinese "Chinaman."[7]

Legal scholar Frank H. Wu, in his book *Yellow: Race in America beyond Black and White*, describes the bundle of stereotypes he encountered growing up Asian in America. In the eyes of White Americans, because of his race, he found projected onto him, any one of dozens of images attributed to Asians:

> I could turn around and find myself transformed into Genghis Khan, Tojo, Charlie Chan, Fu Manchu, Hop Sing, Mr. Sulu, Kato, Bruce Lee, Arnold on *Happy Days*, Sam on *Quincy, M.E.* I was the Number One Son, intoning "Ah so," bending at the waist and shuffling backwards out of the room, with opium smoking, incense burning, and ancestor worshipping … My mother and my girl cousins were Madame Butterfly from the mail order bride catalog, dying in their service to the masculinity of the West, and the dragon lady in a kimono, taking vengeance for her sisters. They became the television newscaster, look-alikes, with their flawlessly permed hair.[8]

Being racialized as "perpetual foreigners" is another challenge that Asian Americans face. While stereotypes, such as the "yellow peril," may be fading into the background of history, with immigration rates from Asia at an all-time high, Americans of Asian ancestry find themselves still having to constantly prove that they are "truly America."[9] Historian William Wei writes, "Whether negative or positive, stereotypes are essentially false images that obscure the complexity and diversity that is an inherent feature of Asian Americans as well as other people. Whether it be the Chinese launderer, the Korean grocery store owner, or the South Asian Maharaja, this kind of imagery reinforces the stereotype in the American mind that Asians, American or not, are 'other.' "[10]

NOTES

1. Pew Research Center, "The Rise of Asian Americans," June 19, 2012. http://www.pewsocialtrends.org/2012/06/19/the-rise-of-asian-americans/.
2. "Asian-Americans Reject 'Good' News in Pew Report," *The Daily Beast*, June 26, 2012. http://www.thedailybeast.com/articles/2012/06/26/asian-americans-reject-good-news-in-pew-report.html.

3. The White House Initiative on Asian Americans and Pacific Islanders, "Critical Issues Facing Asian Americans and Pacific Islanders." https://www.whitehouse.gov/administration/eop/aapi/data/critical-issues.
4. Prasad, Vijay. *The Karma of Brown Folk*. (Minneapolis, MN: University of Minnesota Press, 2003), 6.
5. Zhou, Min. "Are Asian Americans Becoming White," *Contexts*. Vol. 3, No. 1, Winter 2004, 33.
6. Chou, Rosalind S. and Joe R. Feagin, *The Myth of the Model Minority: Asian Americans Facing Racism*. (Boulder, CO: Paradigm Publishers, 2010), 221.
7. Ibid., 83.
8. Wu, Frank H. *Yellow: Race in America Beyond Black and White*. (New York, NY: Basic Books, 2003), 5.
9. Zhou, 36.
10. Wei, William. *The Asian American Movement*. (Philadelphia, PA: Temple University Press, 1993), 50.

15

EXOTIC ORIENTALS AND CHINESE IMMIGRANTS

WHEN CHINESE workers began arriving in large numbers to work the gold mines of California in the middle of the 19th century, contact with Asians on American shores had been only sporadic, limited to encounters with the occasional merchants who wound their way to North America or those Chinese or Filipinos that escaped the Asian slave trade in Latin America after having been brought to the Americas on Spanish galleons that frequented the port of Acapulco. However, perceptions of Asia have a long history in Western Civilization, dating at least as far back as Ancient Greece. As the centuries rolled on, these attitudes had a palpable impact on how subsequent generations viewed Asians.

THE EXOTIC ORIENTAL

Perhaps the most influential book about Asia was *The Travels of Sir John Mandeville*, which made a powerful impact on Europeans' views of Asia from about 1366, when the book was first published, into the eighteenth century. "Mandeville" was a pseudonym for the author or group of authors who claimed to have traveled from England as far as Cathay. The book, which made a great impression on Christopher Columbus, constructed Asia as a fanciful place, describing one-eyed and headless beasts, giants, pygmies, and cannibals, not to mention bounties of gold, silver, and other precious gems.[1] About the island of "Calonak" near Java, Mandeville wrote:

> The king of that country hath as many wives as he will. For he maketh search all the country to get him the fairest maidens that may be found, and maketh them to be brought before him. And he taketh one one night, and another another night, and so forth continually suing; so that he hath a thousand wives or more.
>
> And he lieth never but one night with one of them, and another night with another; but if that one happen to be more lusty to his pleasure than another. And therefore the king getteth full many children, some-time an hundred, some-time a two-hundred, and some-time more. And he hath also into a 14,000 elephants or more that he maketh for to be brought up amongst his villains by all his towns.

Describing the great emperor Chan of Cathay, Mandeville writes:

> [He] hath his table alone by himself, that is of gold and of precious stones, or of crystal bordered with gold, and full of precious stones or of amethysts, or of lignum aloes that cometh out of paradise, or of ivory bound or bordered with gold. And every one of his wives hath also her table by herself. And his eldest son and the other lords also, and the ladies, and all that sit with the emperor have tables alone by themselves, full rich. And there is no table but that it is worth an huge treasure of goods.[2]

It was out of these tales, that the vision of the Orient came to be spun, an image soaked in opulence, exoticism, and mystery, in dramatic opposition to the rational and organized West. In his classic book *Orientalism*, Edward Said meticulously traces the development of Western conceptions of the East, encapsulated in fabricated journeys, fables, and stereotypes, to form a "polemical confrontation":

> Consider how the Orient ... became known in the West, as its great complementary opposite since antiquity. There were the Bible and the rise of Christianity; there were travelers like Marco Polo who chartered the trade routes and patterned a regulated system of commercial exchange ... there were fabulists; there were the

redoubtable conquering Eastern movements, principally Islam, of course; there were the militant pilgrims, chiefly the Crusaders … These are the lenses through which the Orient is experienced, and they shape the language, perception, and form of the encounter between East and West.[3]

For Said, the construction of the Orient in Western minds was an exercise in the self-affirmation of European identity, one deeply rooted in the power politics of imperialism and domination. He writes: "The Orient is watched, since its almost (but never quite) offensive behavior issues out of a reservoir of infinite peculiarity; the European, whose sensibility tours the Orient, is a watcher, never involved, always detached … The Orient becomes a living tableau of queerness."[4]

In the early years, Americans, as former colonial subjects had a much different relationship with Asia than did Europe, although they inherited the outlook that Asia was an exotic and otherworldly place. In the dawning years of the new republic, England was the "Other" against which Americans measured themselves, their culture, and their political identity, according to historian Shelley Sang-Hee Lee. China, in particular was "an imagined place of fabulous luxuries, an advanced civilization that the founding fathers and mothers sought to emulate, which held a prominent place for revolutionaries." Americans, like Europeans, were fascinated with Chinese luxury goods. It was Chinese tea that was dumped into the harbor during the Boston Tea Party, a protest against England's excessive tax on tea imported into the colonies, and sipping tea and displaying fine Chinese porcelain was a means for elites to demonstrate their status.[5]

Additionally, Chinese culture played an influential role in the thinking of the founding fathers, particularly Thomas Jefferson and Benjamin Franklin. Franklin wrote, "Could we be so fortunate so as to introduce the industry of the Chinese, their arts of living and improvement in husbandry … America might become in time as populous as China." For many early Americans, China also represented a potential important trade partner. In 1783, John Ledyard, who voyaged with Captain James Cook to Asia, published the first book in the United States dealing with the Pacific, and he gave detailed descriptions of goods made by Chinese artisans and noted what price could be had in China for North American furs.[6]

The diaries, journals, and letters of American traders who arrived in China, beginning in 1785, betray an ethnocentric fascination with the Chinese, laden with a mocking contempt. According to one account, "The first impulse of an American, when he sees for the first time a Chinese, is to laugh at him. His dress, if judged by our standards, is ridiculous, and in a Mandarin, a stately gravity sets it off for a double derision. His trousers are a couple of meal bags ... his shoes are huge machines, turned up at the toe, his cap is fantastic and his head is shaven except on the crown, when there hangs down a tuft of hair as long as a spaniel's tale."[7]

Common themes were the Chinese alleged taste for dogs, cats, and rats, their theater music, which one trader likened to "ten Jackasses braying, five brazier's pounding on the copper boiler of a steamboat, thirty bag-pipers and a sexton pulling a cracked bell." The focus on "strange and curious objects" was complemented by a featuring of gambling, prostitution, and drugs, which demonstrated the "moral debasement" of the people, including polygamy and infanticide.[8]

Beginning in the 1840s and 1850s, Chinese laborers, mostly from the Guangdong province, sojourned to Hawaii and the United States, in hopes of striking it rich and one day returning home, though many were also seeking sanctuary from conflicts at home, including the British Opium Wars of 1839 to 1842 and 1856 to 1860, peasant rebellions, and the clan wars between 1855 and 1877 in Guangdong between the *Punti* and *Hakkas*, in which close to a million died and thousands of villages were destroyed. The Chinese gave names to their destinations – *Tan Heung Shan* ("Fragrant Sandalwood Hill") for the kingdom of Hawaii and *Gam Saan* ("Gold Mountain") for California.

Nearly all the early migrants were men; the majority were married and left their wives in China. They were generally illiterate or with little schooling, and when gold was discovered at John Sutter's Mill in 1848, they went with high hopes of mining gold or seeking other opportunities of employment. One of the labor brokers who frequented Chinese port cities declared, "Americans are very rich people. They want the Chinaman to come and make him very welcome. They will have great pay, large houses, and food and clothing of the finest description.... It is a nice country, without mandarins or soldiers.... Money is in great plenty and to spare in America."[9]

The first Chinese to migrate to Hawaii were skilled at sugar making, including a "sugar master," who arrived in 1802 on a ship engaged in the sandalwood trade. By the 1830s, several sugar companies run by Chinese entrepreneurs were operating on the islands of Maui and Hawaii. However, they were soon supplanted by *haoles* (Caucasians) who, observing their success, began to establish larger, more capital-intensive plantations. At first, sugar plantation managers relied on Hawaiian labor; however, many Hawaiians had subsistence plots of their own, and opted against the harsh working conditions of the plantations. Importantly, Hawaii's indigenous population was in sharp decline – by 1860, it was about a fifth of what it had been when Captain Cook first landed on the island – and many succumbed to the diseases brought by Americans and Europeans.

15 | EXOTIC ORIENTALS AND CHINESE IMMIGRANTS

In 1850, producers organized the Royal Hawaiian Agricultural Society and commissioned a British ship captain to recruit laborers from China. He returned with 200 laborers in 1851. By 1864, sugar demand had skyrocketed in the United States, and the Hawaiian government organized a board of immigration to recruit contracted Chinese in Hong Kong; between 1876 and 1899, an average of a couple thousand a year, mostly men, entered Hawaii.[10] However, because of the unforgiving work and abusive *luna* (overseers), most of these Chinese plantation workers did not sign on for a second term after their contracts expired. They became peddlers and merchants or rice cultivators.[11]

CHINESE IN CALIFORNIA

Far more Chinese landed in California than anywhere else in the United States. California was taken from Mexico during the war in 1848, the same year that gold was discovered, and a year later, at California's first constitutional convention, which began the process of California becoming a state, delegates made it clear that they wanted no competition from slave labor in the mining districts, for "the labor of the White Man brought into competition with the Negro is always degraded." By the end of the first week, the California delegates unanimously resolved the issue: "Neither slavery nor involuntary servitude, unless for punishment of crimes, shall ever be tolerated in this state." Although Chinese men who came to the United States were not enslaved, Chinese immigrants were quickly labeled "coolies," a designation that indicated they were in the country against their will.[12]

The coolie trade refers specifically to Chinese and East Indians bound under contract to provide service for a specified period of time, usually between five to eight years. It was "a forced international labor migration of immense proportions," notes historian Evelyn Hu-Dehart, totaling well over half a million people between 1842 and 1870.[13] Between 1838 and 1917, more than 419,000 South Asians went to British West Indian plantations in British Guiana, Trinidad, and Jamaica as coolies; an estimated 140,000 Chinese men were taken to Cuba from 1847 to 1874, and 90,000 more arrived in Peru between 1849 and 1874. By the end of the 19th century, Asian indentured laborers were settled in Cuba, Peru, British Guiana, Trinidad, Jamaica, Panama, Mexico, Brazil, and Costa Rica.[14]

Writes Gary Okihiro, a scholar of Asian American studies:

> Chinese and Asian Indian "coolies" were sold and indentured to European and American ship captains in a barter called by the Chinese "the buying and selling of pigs." The Chinese coolies,

or "pigs," were restrained in "pigpens" ... Once on board the ship, they were placed below deck in the hold, where they were usually confined for the duration of the transpacific passage.

Overcrowding and a short supply of food and water led to revolts, suicides, and murders ... As many as a third of the coolies died during the journey across the Pacific on board ships bound for the Americas. Coolies were sold in the open market, following advertisements that appeared in the local newspapers. Prospective buyers inspected the human merchandise, lined up on a platform, before the bargaining began, and the Asians were "virtually sold to the planters."[15]

According to historian Ronald Takaki, the Chinese migrants to the United States and Hawaii were not coolies per se. Some paid their own way. However, most of them borrowed the necessary funding under the credit-ticket system, whereby a broker would loan the money for the voyage, which would be paid back with exorbitant interest.[16] However, because Chinese arrived in the United States in the middle of the slavery controversy and due to the fact that American ships often carried Chinese coolies to South America and the Caribbean, the association between Chinese immigrants and slavery took hold.

Abolitionists were concerned that Chinese immigration amounted to a kind of "quasi-slavery." Congressman Robert McLane of Maryland, who had been commissioner to China between 1853 and 1855, testified that Chinese bound for California were held in jails prior to their departures. C.E. De Long, the former minister to Japan, declared "These coolies are more absolute slaves than ever the negroes of the South were."[17]

According to historian Elliott Young, although there were differences between the contract labor systems in Cuba, Peru, and the British West Indies and the credit-ticket system employed in the United States, "these were distinctions of degree and not kind." Both bound Chinese labor to multiyear contracts, and though the practice was banned by the 1862 Anti-Coolie Bill and the 1865 Alien Contract Labor Law, the practice continued well into the twentieth century. The primary difference was that while in Cuba and Peru, the coolie trade was regulated and overseen by the government, the credit-ticket system was "largely invisible to state authorities." As a result, the U.S. government could "wash its hands" of the matter and "maintain the illusion that Chinese migrants were all voluntary free laborers." Young writes:

> The distinction between a coolie and a free laborer was ideological. Coolie was not a legal term but rather a vague notion of cheap and easily exploitable labor that was almost inextricably linked to Asians ... In the popular imagination, all Chinese in California were seen as "coolies," whether or not they were contract laborers.[18]

The United States did play an active role in the recruiting and transportation of Chinese laborers. In 1848, an American policymaker, Aaron H. Palmer, submitted a plan to Congress recommending the development of steam transportation in the Pacific whereby Chinese laborers could be imported to build the transcontinental railroad and cultivate land in California. "No people in all the East are so well adapted for clearing wild lands and raising every species of agricultural product ... as the Chinese," he declared.[19]

Yet nothing was more alluring than gold. Despite the arrival in 1849 of about 100,000 Whites in California, the boom created a remarkable labor shortage, and according to Roger Daniels, mining paid the highest wages in the world.[20] By the early 1850s, many local newspapers claimed the Chinese had overrun California. In July 1852, the *Daily Alta California* wrote that "every gulch and ravine" is now filled with Chinese miners, and "an American emigrant can hardly find room to pitch his tent." One miner complained to his parents: "This country is fast getting filled up with Chinamen. They are coming by thousands all the time. The miners in a great many places will not let them work. The miners hear [sic] drove off about 200 Chinamen about two weeks ago but they have com [sic] back about as thick as ever." That year, the state reenacted The Foreign Miners' Tax which forced foreign miners to pay exorbitant amounts for the right to mine. During these years, in which miner's removed a billion dollars' worth of untaxed gold, Chinese miners paid $58 million to the state, amounting to one-fourth to one-half of California's revenue. Writes Jean Pfaelzer, a professor of American Studies, by 1852, "In the eyes of the American legal system, the Chinese were becoming Black."[21]

The worst, however, was yet to come. In the spring of 1853, Governor John Bigler predicted that the number of Chinese living in California would swell to millions and called for "novel if not extraordinary legislation" to halt Asian immigration. City codes and town ordinances emerged that outlawed intermarriage and denied non-Whites the vote, the right to sit on a jury, and access to homesteads. In 1855, the California state legislature assessed a fifty-dollar fee on immigrants ineligible to become citizens of California – by U.S. law, only Whites could be naturalized. The state forced Chinese immigrants to pay medical indemnity bonds and required shipmasters to post five hundred dollars for each Chinese passenger to "relieve the government of the expenses of sick immigrants." In 1858, the legislature announced that it had the constitutional right "to exclude any class of foreigners she may deem obnoxious to her interest, either socially or politically." In 1862, it levied a "police tax" of $2.50 per month on all Chinese over the age of eighteen who did not mine or produce rice, sugar, tea, or coffee, all items that were not produced in California at the time. The logs of collectors are replete with tales of extortion, harassment, torture, and murder. Said one "I was sorry to have to stab the poor fellow; but the law makes it necessary to collect the tax; and that's where I get my profit." Said another: "He was running away, and I shot to stop him."[22]

The Civil War and, with it, the building of a transcontinental railroad, opened a new chapter in the lives of Chinese immigrants, one of backbreaking work under treacherous conditions. In 1862, the Central Pacific Railroad Corporation was awarded the contract to lay tracks eastward from Sacramento, and the Union Pacific obtained the contract westward from Omaha. It was the Central Pacific Railroad, which had to traverse several mountain ranges, that recruited Chinese workers away from the mines, and they became the backbone of the company's construction crew for both skilled and unskilled tasks.

The railroad printed handbills, sent recruiters to China, particularly Guangdong province, and negotiated lower rates with the steamship companies for the ocean voyage. Additionally, in 1868, China and the United States signed the Burlingame Treaty, whereby China, in exchange for "most favored nation" status, agreed to recognize the "inherent and inalienable right of man to change his home and allegiance and also the mutual advantage of free migration and emigration of their citizens … for purposes of … trade or as permanent residents.…"[23] Historian Sucheng Chang describes the ghastly working conditions on the railroad:

> Thousands of Chinese worked underground in snow tunnels around the clock through the winter of 1866. It took all summer and fall to grade the route thus created, but before tracks could be laid, winter descended again with even heavier snowfalls. As one of the Central Pacific's engineers admitted years later, "a good many men" (i.e., Chinese) were lost during the terrible winter of 1867. The bodies of those buried by avalanches could not even be dug out until the following spring. Once the tracks descended the eastern slopes of the Sierras, the Chinese crews sped across the hot, dry plateaus of Nevada and Utah until the two ends of the railroad joined at Promontory Point, Utah in 1869.[24]

15 | EXOTIC ORIENTALS AND CHINESE IMMIGRANTS

When railroad construction jobs dried up, after 1869, thousands of Chinese laborers drifted into San Francisco, where they helped to expand the city's emerging industries in shoes, textiles, and cigars, marking the transition of an increasing number to urban dwellers. By the 1870s, the city's Chinatown was home to almost a quarter of all Chinese in California; they comprised nearly half of the men working in the city's factories, and there were an estimated 5,000 Chinese entrepreneurs. At the pinnacle of power were six powerful district associations, known as the Chinese Six Companies, with the purported mission of brokering passage, resolving disputes, protecting members, and advocating on behalf of the entire community.[25]

However, the Six Companies also had a dark side, often torturing Chinese immigrants who defied them. According to one officer's account, he inflicted "severe corporal punishment upon many of his more humble countrymen … cutting off their ears, flogging them or keeping them chained." Additionally, the Six Companies brokered a deal with the shipping companies, which enabled them to issue exit permits that verified that a miner had paid his debts before he could sail back to China, giving them an absolute grip over any Chinese hoping to return.[26]

By the 1870s, Chinese began to venture beyond San Francisco, within California and beyond, and they were frequently recruited as cheap sources of labor. In the Sacramento–San Joaquin River deltas, they were hired to construct levees, dikes, and ditches; they also constructed roads, cleared land, planted, pruned, and harvested grapes for the Napa and Sonoma Valleys' wine industry. By the turn of the century, 95 percent of the Chinese population in the Sacramento and San Joaquin delta region worked as farmhands and fruit packers, as well as in other agriculture-related jobs, though they were paid considerably less than Whites doing the same work. Chinese were recruited to work in shoe factories in North Adams, Massachusetts and on plantations in the South. By 1880, there were Chinese communities in New Orleans and in Mississippi, where they occupied an "in-between" space between Blacks and Whites. There were emerging Chinatowns in Chicago, Boston, St. Louis, Philadelphia, and New York, as well as towns, like Butte, Montana. In New York, the number of Chinese was over 2,000, with most settling in the Five Points neighborhood on the Lower East Side of Manhattan, and many Chinese immigrants married Irish immigrant women.[27]

As the number of Chinese grew, not surprisingly, there was a backlash, with California being the focal point, but by no means was it the only locus of anti-Chinese sentiment. By 1870, there were a number of mass demonstrations in San Francisco calling for an end to Chinese immigration, the halting of federal subsidies to the steamship companies that profited from the influx of Chinese, and the repeal of the Burlingame Treaty. One of the slogans was: "We want no slaves or aristocrats.

The coolie labor system leaves us no alternative – starvation or disgrace. Mark the man who would crush us to the level of the Mongolian slave."[28] Laws were passed, such as The Cubic Air Ordinance, which called for tenements to have at least 500 cubic feet of air for each inhabitant; it was enforced only in Chinatown, with the intent, as stated by the Board of Supervisors, to "drive [the Chinese] to other states...."[29] In 1870, during proceedings to ratify the Fourteenth Amendment, Congress debated whether Asians should be included in the naturalization statute which made "persons of African descent," in addition to "White persons," eligible for citizenship. Despite arguments by Massachusetts Senator Charles Sumner to make naturalization color blind, he was defeated, and Asian immigrants, as a group, would be ineligible for citizenship until 1952.[30]

Responding to what was becoming a growing clamor for immigration restrictions against the Chinese, in 1874, President Ulysses S. Grant declared:

> I call the attention of Congress to a generally conceded fact – that the great proportion of the Chinese immigrants who come to our shores do not come voluntarily, to make their homes with us and their labor productive of general prosperity, but come under contracts with headmen, who own them almost absolutely. In a worse form does this apply to Chinese women. Hardly a perceptible percentage of them perform any honorable labor, but they are brought for shameful purposes, to the disgrace of the communities where settled and to the great demoralization of the youth of those localities. If this evil practice can be legislated against, it will be my pleasure as well as duty to enforce any regulation to secure so desirable an end.[31]

Chinese immigration at that time was a political hot potato, and many, especially those who were anti-union – the labor syndicates had coalesced on an anti-coolie platform –, were pro-immigration. In 1867, California Republicans passed a resolution "in favor of voluntary immigration ... from whatever nationality it may come." However, as Daniels notes, "This was a hedge, as Republican politicians could claim the Chinese were not 'voluntary' immigrants." But their opponents, and probably many voters, interpreted it as simply "pro-Chinese."[32]

The issue of prostitution by Chinese women was a cornerstone of the arguments employed by those against Chinese immigration during the 1870s and 1880s, as was that of opium use and gambling. In 1876, a congressional committee conducted an intensive investigation of Chinese immigration in San Francisco, and prostitutes were a central concern. According to the testimony of a San Francisco policeman: "As far as the Chinese women are concerned in San Francisco, with very few exceptions, I look upon them as prostitutes. The exceptions are very rare where they are not prostitutes ... I look upon them as slaves, sold for such and such, an amount of money to be worked out at prostitution." According to another account, out of 2,000 Chinese women in San Francisco, "there are not a half-dozen who possess any virtue." The 1880 U.S. Census, which recognized prostitution as an occupation, reported that there were 101 Chinese brothels that year. However, as historian Yong Chen notes, the census likely overstated the number of prostitutes, as census takers "had a very strong inclination to register females, including even very young girls, as prostitutes." In reality, many Chinese women worked as shoe binders, servants, tailors, launderers and gardeners.[33]

References to Chinese opium use were ubiquitous in the 1870s and 1880s, though it was seen as being less threatening than prostitution, and according to the medical consensus at the time, it was considered less harmful to society than alcohol. In 1881, one doctor stated that "the effect of opium is peculiarly soothing and tranquilizing. ... The effects of liquor or wine, as compared with those of opium, are coarse and brutalizing." Said a missionary at the end of the century: "The Chinaman may yell over his drinking game, and curse and swear at the gaming table, [but] he quiets down in the opium den." According to historian Yong Chen, even those who were anti-Chinese did not believe that opium consumption made them a social threat. A doctor declared in 1876: "It is rather better for us that they should smoke opium, for if they drink liquor to some excess, I do not know what would become of us.... When they smoke opium they are inoffensive, so far as we are concerned, because when they get under its influence they drop off and go to sleep."[34]

Chinese opium dens, or "hop joints," were "put on display" for White tourists, presented as an indicator of Chinese "inferiority and degradation." In 1876, Dr. John L. Mears commented: "The higher civilizations prefer liquor-alcohol." Writing of an opium den in the 1870s, another observed, "The opium smokers [are] each clinging to his pipe endeavoring to get one more full whiff, with the tenacity of a drowning man hanging to a floating wreck." Still, for those opposed to Chinese immigration, the use of opium provided a strong argument that they were "physically and mentally self-destructive," evidence of their "racial degeneration."[35]

Writes historian K. Scott Wong:

> In the eyes of the press and the critics of the Chinese, "Chinatown" was a site of cultural pollution. In this sense, "Chinatown" was a "borderland" where cultures collided and were often transformed,

though usually for the worse ... The theme of White women being lured into laundries or "opium dens" appears frequently in anti-Chinese literature. In each of the stories concerning raids on opium dens, soon after the raid, it was reported that White women or girls, in various stages of undress, were found at each site.[36]

By 1876, anti-Chinese fervor had grown to a fever pitch throughout the country, and according to Daniels, "principled political opposition to the anti-Chinese movement" was "all but nonexistent." In 1878, following a congressional investigation of the Chinese "problem," Congress sent President Rutherford B. Hayes the so-called Fifteen Passenger Bill, which stipulated that only fifteen Chinese per ship could enter the United States and called for the abrogation of certain parts of the Burlingame Treaty pertaining to immigration. In the main address in support of the bill, Representative Horace F. Page of California excoriated the Chinese as "filthy ... aliens [who] are unfitted by education, habits, religious superstition, and by their inborn prejudices to assume any of the duties of American citizenship;" he continued, saying Chinese "inspire a profound irritation and discontent among all citizens of all classes" and "retard desirable immigration from Europe."[37]

President Hayes vetoed the anti-Chinese bill, and his veto stood, but by this time, the exclusion of Chinese immigrants was just a matter of time. In 1880, a new treaty was signed with China, which gave the United States the unilateral right to "regulate, limit or suspend" the arrival of Chinese laborers. On May 6, 1882, President Chester A. Arthur signed the notorious "Chinese Exclusion Act," which suspended Chinese immigration for a period of 10 years. It was renewed in 1892, under the Geary Act, which extended Chinese exclusion for another ten years and imposed other restrictions, including requiring all Chinese in the United States to obtain a certificate of residence, for which each was required to demonstrate that his stay in the country was legal.[38]

Violence committed against Chinese became a fact of life in the West, and in the estimation of Daniels, "with the exception of American Indians, no group there suffered as much from violence as did the Chinese."[39] Political scientist Sucheng Chang writes that violence against Chinese and other Asian immigrants can be divided into three types: "the maiming and wanton murder of individuals, spontaneous attacks against and the destruction (usually by fire) of Chinatowns, and organized efforts to drive Asians out of certain towns and cities."[40]

In Los Angeles, in 1871, 21 Chinese were murdered by White mobs, representing a sizeable percentage of the population. It is estimated that over 100 Chinese were killed in Idaho in 1866 and 1867, and there were major anti-Chinese riots in Denver, in 1880; in Rock Springs, Wyoming in 1885; and in Seattle, Tacoma, and Portland in 1885 and 1886. In the Snake River Massacre of 1887, 31 Chinese were mutilated and murdered by a White gang in Hells Canyon Gorge in Oregon. Daniels, writing of the escalation of violence in the 1880s, explains:

> The national climate of opinion, pervaded by racism and a burgeoning feeling of ethnic superiority … certainly contributed not just to the violence but also to the virtual unanimity with which the White majority put its seal of approval on anti-Chinese ends if not means … Another factor was probably psychological. The national anti-Chinese campaign was not just a crusade for the halting of immigration. In terms of rhetoric, at least, it was a campaign to get rid of Chinese.[41]

Arguing in 1901 in favor of Chinese exclusion, California Senator James D. Phelan, who campaigned on a slogan of "Keep California White," wrote:

> The Chinese, by putting a vastly inferior civilization in competition with our own, tend to destroy the population on whom the perpetuity of free government depends. Without homes and families; patronizing neither school, library, church nor theatre; lawbreakers, addicted to vicious habits; indifferent to sanitary regulations and breeding disease; taking no holidays, respecting no traditional anniversaries, but laboring incessantly, and subsisting on practically nothing for food and clothes, a condition to which they have been inured for centuries, they enter the lists against men who have been brought up by our civilization to family life and civic duty. Our civilization having been itself rescued from barbarism by the patriots, martyrs and benefactors of mankind, the question now is: Shall it be imperiled? Is not Chinese immigration a harm?[42]

NOTES

1. Okihiro, Gary. *Margins and Mainstreams: Asians in American History and Culture.* (Seattle, WA: University of Washington Press, 2014), 13.
2. Mandeville, Sir John. *The Travels of Sir John Mandeville: The Fantastic 14th-Century Account of a Journey to the East.* (Mineola, NY: Dover Publications, 2006), 127.

3. Said, Edward W. *Orientalism*. (New York, NY: Vintage Books, 1979), 142.
4. Ibid., 103.
5. Lee, Shelley Sang-Hee. *A New History of Asian America*. (New York, NY: Routledge, 2014), 12.
6. Ibid.
7. Miller, Stuart Creighton. *The Unwelcome Immigrant, The American Image of the Chinese, 1785–1882*. (Berkeley, CA: University of California Press, 1969), 29.
8. Ibid., 35.
9. Takaki, Ronald. *Strangers from a Different Shore: A History of Asian Americans*. (New York, NY: Back Bay Books, 1998), 31.
10. Leong, Yau Sing. ed. by Arlene Lum. "From Kwangtung to the Plantations, Farms, Stores and Beyond," in *Sailing for the Sun: The Chinese in Hawaii, 1789–1989*. (Honolulu, HI: University of Hawaii Press, 1990), 75.
11. Chang Sucheng. *Asian Americans: An Interpretive History*. (New York, NY: Twayne Publishers, 1991), 27.
12. Pfaelzer, Jean. *Driven Out: The Forgotten War Against Chinese Americans*. (New York, NY: Random House, 2008), 38.
13. Hu-Dehart, Evelyn. "Chinese Coolie Labor in Cuba in the Nineteenth Century: Free Labor of Neoslavery," *Contributions in Black Studies*, 1994. Vol. 12, No. 5, 38.
14. Lee, Erika. *The Making of Asian America: A History*. (New York, NY: Simon and Schuster, 2015), 28.
15. Okihiro, 38.
16. Ibid., 35.
17. Miller, 152.
18. Young, Elliot. *Alien Nation: Chinese Migration in the Americas from the Coolie Era through World War II*. (Chapel Hill, NC: University of North Carolina Press, 2014), 46.
19. Takaki, Ronald. *Strangers from a Different Shore: A History of Asian Americans*. (New York, NY: Back Bay Books, 1998), 22.
20. Daniels, Roger. *Asian America: Chinese and Japanese in the United States since 1850*. (Seattle, WA: University of Washington Press, 1988), 12.
21. Pfaelzer, 53.
22. Ibid., 54.
23. Chang, Iris. *The Chinese in America: A Narrative History*, (New York, NY: Viking, 2003), 57.
24. Chang (Sucheng), 31.
25. Chang (Iris), 77.
26. Pfaelzer, 39.

27. Lee, *The Making of Asian America*, 60.
28. Daniels, *Asian America*, 38.
29. Ibid., 39.
30. Ibid., 43.
31. Grant, Ulysses S. Sixth Annual Message to the Senate and House of Representatives, December 7, 1874. http://genius.com/Ulysses-s-grant-presidential-speeches-1874-written-annotated.
32. Daniels, 44.
33. Chen, Yong. *Chinese San Francisco, 1850–1943: A Trans-Pacific Community.* (Stanford, CT: Stanford University Press, 2000), 81.
34. Ibid.
35. Ibid., 88.
36. Wong, K. Scott. ed. by Jean Yu-Wen Shen Wu and Min Song. "The Eagle Seeks a Helpless Quarry: Chinatown, The Police, and The Press, The 1903 Boston Chinatown Raid Revisited," in *Asian American Studies: A Reader.* (New Brunswick, NJ: Rutgers University Press, 2009), 73.
37. Gyory, Andrew. *Closing the Gate: Race, Politics, and the Chinese Exclusion Act.* (Chapel Hill, NC: University of North Caroline Press, 1998, 138.
38. Daniels, 55.
39. Ibid., 58.
40. Chang (Sucheng), *Asian Americans: An Interpretive History*, 48.
41. Ibid., 65.
42. Phelan, James D. "Why the Chinese Should Be Excluded," *The North American Review*. Vol. 173, No. 540, Nov., 1901, 674.

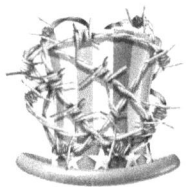

16

THE GENTLEMAN'S AGREEMENT WITH JAPAN

IT WAS within a decade of Chinese exclusion that immigration from Japan began to take hold. For two centuries, between 1623 and 1841, under the Tokugawa Shogunate, Japan was essentially closed to foreigners, and Japanese were prevented from leaving. However, with the Meiji Restoration of 1868, which marked Japan's entry into modernity, Japan borrowed the concepts of "emigration" and "colonization" from the West, which the Japanese political and intellectual elites began to use interchangeably in the context of nation building and expansion.

A leader in the move toward Meiji modernization was Fukuzawa Yukichi, who saw emigration as a means of promoting commerce with the United States, and he viewed Japanese immigrants in American trading ports as a "commercial linkage between their homeland and their new country of residence." In a commentary entitled "Leave Your Homeland at Once," Yukichi appealed to Japanese patriotism, stating that Japanese traders living abroad would add significantly to Japan's national assets. He wrote:

> [A Japanese emigrant] shall be regarded as a loyal subject. For while sacrificing himself at the time of national crisis is a direct way of showing loyalty, engaging in various enterprises abroad is

an indirect way of discharging patriotism.... When examining the example of Englishmen, no one would fail to see [that emigration] shall lead to the enrichment of Japan as well.[1]

Following Fukuzawa's directive, some Japanese went to New York City to enter the silk trade as early as 1876, and others ventured to West Coast cities; after the establishment of San Francisco's first *Issei* (first generation) import businesses, a number of individuals followed in the ensuing decades and formed a small but central merchant class in early Japanese America. One of the earliest guides on "going to America," written by *Issei* already living on the continent, stated: "The United States is a land for new development, which awaits the coming of ambitious youth. Come, our brethren of 3,700,000! ... When you come to the United States, you must have the determination to create the second, new Japan there, which also helps enhance the interest and prestige of the imperial government and our nation."[2]

However, what they found in America was a rigid racialized hierarchy with Whites at the top and cheap Asian labor at the bottom, a pecking order that became especially harsh after Chinese exclusion. "With no possibility of Japanese ascendancy in the game of mastering the Western frontier," historian Eiichiro Azuma writes, "the Issei's Americanized rendition of peaceful expansionism primarily sought ... the building of a collective economic base, the control of farmlands, and the construction of Japanese settlement 'colonies,' under the established order of the White racial regime."[3]

While the early Japanese immigrants were largely entrepreneurs, beginning in the mid-1880s, most were either students evading conscription or, importantly, *dekasegi*, emigrants of rural origin, who were inspired by a "success boom," which swept Japanese popular culture and exalted self-made men such as Andrew Carnegie, Theodore Roosevelt, Cornelius Vanderbilt, and John D. Rockefeller, who became symbols for the boundless opportunities that America allegedly offered workers. The *dekasegi* laborers were largely immune to the valorization of emigration extolled by the elite, and most came to either Hawaii or the United States between 1885 and 1908, based on, as one worker put it, the "rumor that [it] would pay off handsomely." One large contributing factor to the exodus of *dekasegi*, as in the case of many Mexicans, was the commercialization of agriculture, which left many farmers in Japan landless and sent them in search of wage labor. At the same time, the entry of free market forces into villages opened the minds of many to opportunities of which they had never dreamed.

Though most arriving on Hawaiian or American shores were entrepreneurial laborers, many were so-called "private-contract emigrants" whose initial expenses were paid for by employers; prior to 1894, the Japanese government had sponsored worker emigration. In 1898, nine emigration companies were in operation. By 1906, there were 30, plus nine individual brokers, who transported Japanese workers to Australia, Peru, Mexico, the Fiji Islands, and Brazil, as well the United States and Hawaii.[4] Between 1895 and 1908, 130,000 Japanese left for the continental United States and Hawaii, though many of the latter went to California at the termination of their contracts, where they could expect to earn twice as much as did field hands in Hawaii and four to six times what they would have earned as common laborers in Japan.[5]

Complicating the issue of Japanese workers arriving to the United States was the issue of contract labor. In 1885, the United States, in response to anti-slavery and anti-coolie concerns, had outlawed the importation of contract laborers. Many would-be immigrants were denied entry to the U.S. because officials mistook agreements with emigration companies as labor contracts. As historian Shelley Sang-Hee Lee notes, "The lines between 'free' and 'unfree' … were always blurrier than officials portrayed, for it was rare that any immigrant traveled completely on their own resources." Despite this, beginning in the late 1890s, American steamships were the primary mode of passage from Japan to Hawaii and the U.S. mainland, and Japanese continued to arrive in large numbers.[6]

By 1905, Japanese immigration exploded into a national and international issue, as fears of the "Yellow Peril," which built on a well-worn narrative that had been applied to the Chinese but took on greater urgency given Japan's rise as an economic and military power. As historian John Dower observed, "The vision of the menace from the East was always more racial rather than national. It derived not from concern with any one country or people in particular, but from a vague and ominous sense of the vast, faceless, nameless yellow horde: the rising tide, indeed, of color."[7] On February 23, a full-page article in the *San Francisco Chronicle* exclaimed: "The Japanese Invasion, The Problem of the Hour," and warned that "once the [Japanese] war with Russia is over, the brown stream of Japanese immigration" would grow to a "raging torrent." Scare headlines proliferated at the time, including: "Japanese: A Menace to American Women," "The Yellow Peril – How Japanese Crowd Out the White Race," and "Crime and Poverty Go Hand in Hand with Asiatic Labor."[8]

As had been the case with the Chinese, Japanese were declared to be "unassimilable," and the press was replete with exaggerated examples of how Japanese were unlike Americans, indeed worse than the Chinese who had come before them. Chester H. Rowell, editor of the *Fresno Republican*, a so-called racial moderate, declared in 1909:

The Chinese will keep a contract; the Japanese will not. Chinese business, like American business, is based on the assumption of the inviolability of contracts. Therefore the American and the Chinese can understand each other, on this point. But the Japanese seems to have no comprehension of the contract as a fundamental obligation, while the American cannot understand how a man can have any virtue who lacks this one ... The Japanese does not recognize a contract as a moral obligation, and the American therefore assumes that he has no sense of any moral obligation. In an industrial system based on contract the Japanese must acquire a new sort of conscience, or he will remain an industrial misfit.[9]

In an influential 1904 essay entitled "The Yellow Peril," author Jack London bemoaned the differences between the Japanese and American soul, Americans being, says London, "a religious race, which is another way of saying that we are a right seeking race." London continues:

"What do you think of the Japanese?" was asked an American woman after she had lived some time in Japan. "It seems to me that they have no soul," was her answer. This must not be taken to mean that the Japanese is without soul. But it serves to illustrate the enormous difference between their souls and this woman's soul ... This Western soul did not dream that the Eastern soul existed, it was so different, so totally different....[10]

In 1900, with the rise of anti-Japanese sentiment on the West Coast, the Japanese foreign ministry ended the departure of Japanese laborers to the U.S., relaxing it in 1902 only for those who had previously worked abroad. However, this law was widely defied, as many *dekasegi* workers posed as businessmen, and others entered the U.S. by way of Canada or Mexico.[11] White nativism grew without check, driven by the rapid increase in the Japanese population, particularly following the arrival of more than 40,000 after the 1898 annexation of Hawaii, and White forces coalesced around the government, demanding an exclusion act similar to what had been done in the case of the Chinese. In Seattle, in 1906, a cartoonist, Arthur E. Fowler, launched a magazine called "The Yellow Peril" and organized a Seattle branch of the Japanese-Korean exclusion league, which generated 10,000 signatures on an "anti-Japanese coolie" petition.[12]

16 | THE GENTLEMAN'S AGREEMENT WITH JAPAN

However, officials in Washington were aware that Japan, which had demonstrated its military prowess in the Russo-Japanese War of 1904–05, would not submit to a humiliating exclusion law. In May 1905, delegates from 67 labor and political organizations formed the Japanese-Korean Exclusion League with the slogan "Absolute Exclusion of the Asiatic." In October 1906, they succeeded in convincing the San Francisco School Board to force Japanese and Korean students to attend the city's segregated Oriental School, which was already being attended by Chinese. In February 1907, President Theodore Roosevelt, though privately sympathizing with the exclusionists but fearing a reaction from Japan, ordered that the order be revoked. However, the segregationists held firm, and the next month, an agreement was reached. On March 14, Roosevelt issued an executive order that excluded from the continental United States any aliens arriving from Hawaii, Canada, or Mexico. Additionally, the President began diplomatic negotiations with Japan to restrict any further immigration of workers from Japan.

Japanese ascendency in Asia in the early twentieth century also led to the departure of thousands of Koreans from Korea to the United States, many fleeing Japanese rule. In 1905, Japan had defeated Russia in the Russo-Japanese War, and it declared Korea a protectorate, formally annexing the country in 1910. The Japanese-controlled government banned emigration of Koreans in order to prevent them from competing with Japanese laborers in Hawaii and to keep them at home to support Japanese initiatives.[13] However many did manage to leave Korea, some to be free of the "Japanese enemy," others to improve their economic condition, particularly in 1901 and 1902, which brought a cholera epidemic, drought, floods, and a locust plague. Between 1903 and 1920, about 8,000 Korean sailed to the United States, especially between 1903 and 1905, and many landed in Hawaii to work on plantations.[14]

In California, where most Korean immigrants settled on the mainland, they found work as farm laborers, often working in cooperative Korean "gangs" or alongside California's diverse agricultural labor force. The agricultural towns of Dinuba, Reedley, Sacramento, and Delano attracted nearly 83 percent of the early Korean population in the United States. Others went inland, working in mines in Utah, Colorado, and Wyoming and on the railroads in Arizona. Like other Asian immigrants they were predominately young and male, but many were also clergymen, former soldiers, and students. About 70 percent were literate and 40 percent were Christian, having been converted by American missionaries.[15]

Koreans retained strong ties to their homeland. However, because of Korea's status as a Japanese colony, these ties took on a passionate nationalism focused on Korean independence. An editorial in the San Francisco Korean language newspaper

Sinhan Minbo declared: "We have no country to return to. We are a conquered people."¹⁶ Because they had no intentions of returning to Korea, given its occupied status, Korean males, who made up the bulk of the population, sent for picture brides. The Korean National Association, whose founding resolution was "All Koreans in America regard Japan as an enemy nation," played a leading role in building the cause of Korean independence and held mass protests to condemn Japan's annexation of Korea. In 1913, in Hemet, California, after a mob of Whites descended on a group of Korean laborers and expelled them, the Japanese consulate in San Francisco offered the victims assistance and began negotiations with Secretary of State Williams Jennings Bryan.¹⁷ Still, Koreans were subjected to much of the same discrimination as were Chinese and Japanese. They were condemned by the Asiatic Exclusion League as undesirable aliens and, like the Japanese, were prohibited in President Roosevelt's 1907 executive order from migrating from Hawaii. Indeed, as Takaki notes, most Whites associated Koreans with Japanese. Like the Japanese, they were often barred from renting housing by White landlords, and refused service in public recreational facilities and restaurants.¹⁸

In San Francisco, violent attacks on Japanese residents became the norm; in the summer and fall of 1906, there were nearly 300 attacks on Japanese in the city. In the spring of 1907, tensions erupted. On the night of May 20, a mob of about 20 Whites destroyed the Horseshoe Restaurant, a Japanese establishment, and then attacked a Japanese bathhouse across the street. The following night, a mob attacked Japanese homes and businesses across the city. Police were called, but none came, and the violence lasted for several nights. The Japanese Association of San Francisco protested: "Hardly a day goes by ... that some threatening demonstration is not made by roughs and hoodlums against the Japanese," and it reached such proportions that President Roosevelt stationed troops nearby with orders to quell future riots.

Roosevelt's order barring Japanese migration from Hawaii provoked a large influx of Japanese workers into Canada. In Vancouver, newspapers reported that Japanese were "swarming in by shiploads from Japan and Honolulu," and that "feeling[s] of panic" were strong in the cities. "White Canada Forever" became a popular song: "For White Man's land we fight. To Oriental grasp and greed we'll surrender, no never. Our watchword be 'God save the King.'" Violence directed at Japanese in cities in both Canada and the United States continued unabated, and as a result, both countries began to negotiate with Japan to restrict Japanese immigration.

On January 25, 1908, the United States signed the Gentleman's Agreement with Japan, so named because Japan agreed to the terms voluntarily rather than be subject to a humiliating Japanese exclusion bill. It was an informal agreement, whereby the United States would not impose restriction on Japanese immigration, and Japan

16 | THE GENTLEMAN'S AGREEMENT WITH JAPAN

would not allow further emigration to the U.S. Three days later, Canada and Japan signed a nearly identical agreement.[19]

As Japanese in the U.S. began to make the transition from sojourners to permanent residents, *Issei* made extensive efforts to adapt themselves to American society. Immigrant leaders undertook moral reform campaigns to help contradict negative perceptions of Japanese among Whites, attacking Japanese patronage of Chinese gambling houses, Japanese prostitution, and other elements that might cast Japanese in a negative light. For instance, in 1918, after it was revealed in a survey that Japanese were losing an estimated $3 million annually, largely in Chinese gambling establishments, the Japanese Association of America ordered newly formed anti-gambling committees to encourage Japanese immigrants to report the names of gamblers to their home towns in Japan, and publish their names and photos in the *Issei* press. Additionally, Japanese community leaders, in order to counter arguments that Japanese were not able to adapt to American customs, began to make strong arguments in favor of what was called *gaimenteki dōka*, or outward assimilation. According to historian Yuji Ichioka, these leaders advocated that:

> All Japanese immigrants, regardless of sex, had to adopt American clothing. They had to refrain from wearing Japanese garments in order to avoid being perceived as foreign interlopers … It also involved adapting one's physical living environment to conform to American ways. Living quarters and furnishings had to meet specific American standards as much as possible. Conversely, things visibly and conspicuously Japanese, such as large signs written in Japanese, had to be eschewed as much as possible … Wives were advised to walk alongside their husbands, not behind them, so as to avoid reinforcing the negative stereotype of Japanese women as being enslaved by Japanese men … Instead of celebrating Japanese national holidays, they had to commemorate American ones like Independence Day and Thanksgiving day.[20]

One notable feature of the Japanese experience in the United States, which provoked the contempt of Whites, was the "picture bride" system. To Japanese, the system was analogous to the traditional custom of arranged marriage, whereby parents worked with go-betweens to help in the selection of suitable partners for their sons and daughters. Additionally, compared to Chinese women, Japanese women were more receptive to the idea of traveling overseas; they were more educated. The Meiji government required the education of girls, which included instruction in English, and Japanese custom stipulated that women should enter their husband's family. As a result of picture brides, by 1920, women represented 46 percent of the Japanese population in Hawaii and 35 percent in California.[21]

Yet Whites were outraged by the arrival of picture brides, and major West Coast newspapers published flurries of articles calling it a "barbaric practice" in which women were coerced into marriage without regard to love or morality. "Japanese Picture Brides Are Swarming Here" was a typical headline directed at the boatloads of "strange-looking" and "simple-minded" women arriving on American shores.[22] In the words of a Japanese woman interpreter at Angel Island, San Francisco's port of entry for most immigrants from Asia:

> People have a great many wrong ideas about Japanese picture brides and Japanese women coming to America. I know that Japanese do not send women to be prostitutes. They are married and usually they are happy. Sometimes when the age is very different they are not so happy, but with us Japanese, love comes after marriage.[23]

In addition to the cries of immorality, which the picture bride system reputedly fostered, Californians, led by State Senator James D. Phelan, labeled the practice as a Japanese ploy to secure land. The Alien Land Law, passed by the California legislature in 1913, prohibited immigrants from owning or leasing land; to circumvent the law, many *Issei* obtained picture brides and subsequently purchased land in the name of their American born *Nisei* children. Phelan charged: "These women are not only wives but laborers; they go to work with their children strapped upon their backs and accomplish the dual purpose of defeating the [immigration] law by getting in actual laborers and of defeating the land law by getting [through] the birth route persons eligible to hold land." Write Lee and Yung, "Phelan raised the alarm that California was rapidly becoming a Japanese colony and he vowed to change the laws and "exterminate this menace as a matter of self-defense."[24]

Despite their attempts to assimilate, Japanese experienced constant discrimination from White Americans. Writes Ronald Takaki:

> The newcomers were usually viewed and treated as a distinct group. Racist curses repeatedly stung their ears: "Jap Go Home," "God Damn Jap!" "Yellow Jap!" "Dirty Jeff!" Ugly graffiti assaulted their eyes at railroad stations and toilets: "Japs Go Away!" "Fire the Japs!" On the street corners of Santa Monica Boulevard and

Sunset Boulevard in Los Angeles, scribblings on the sidewalks threatened: "Japs, we do not want you." Outside of a small town in the San Joaquin Valley, a sign on the highway warned: "No More Japs Wanted Here." The term "Jap" was so commonplace it was even used unwittingly ... "Hello, Jap," or "Hello, Mr. Jap," in a friendly way whenever he saw us ... He didn't know that "Jap" was not the correct word ...

But discrimination went beyond words ... When the newcomers tried to rent or buy houses, they were turned down by realtors who explained: "If Japanese live around here, then the price of the land will go down." At theaters, Japanese were often refused admittance or seated in the segregated section ... In the cities they were pelted with stones and snowballs, and the businesses were vandalized – the store window smashed and the sidewalks in front smeared with horse manure.[25]

In the definitive example of Japanese assimilation, Takao Ozawa, born in Japan, filed for naturalization in Alameda County, California on October 16, 1914. In his brief, Ozawa declared his unswerving allegiance to the United States: "In name, General Benedict Arnold was an American, but at heart he was a traitor. In name, I am not an American, but at heart I am a true American." Ozawa then stated the circumstances of his life. He had not registered his marriage or the birth of his children with the Japanese Consulate, but rather to the American government; he had no connections with any Japanese churches or schools; he sent his children to an American church; he spoke English at home and his children could not speak Japanese; he and his wife were both educated in American schools, and he had lived continuously in the United States for 28 years. Additionally, Ozawa argued that his skin was White in tone. Ozawa concluded that he had "steadily prepared to return the kindness which our Uncle Sam has extended to me ... so it is my honest hope to do something good to the United States before I bid farewell to this world."[26]

Ichioka observes:

> Ozawa fulfilled all the nonracial requirements for naturalization set by the [Immigration] Act of 1906. According to this statute, an applicant had to file a petition of intent to naturalize at least two years prior to formal application ... he had filed his petition of intent on August 1, 1902 ... He satisfied the five-year continuous resident requirement. He had lived in the United States and

Hawaii for more than twenty years. His personal character and English fluency ... met the requirements related to moral fitness and knowledge of the English language. Fully qualified ... his case was impeccable from a legal point of view.

What stood in the way of citizenship was his race. He was unsuccessful in the lower court and was subsequently turned down by the District Court for the Territory of Hawaii. The Supreme Court took up the Ozawa case in 1922. In its ruling, handed down by Justice George Sutherland, the Court rejected Ozawa's claim that his skin was white, since "even among Anglo-Saxons ... [there are] swarthy brunette[s] who are ... darker than many of the lighter hued persons of the brown or yellow races." Rather, Sutherland argued that the intent of the constitution was to convey citizenship only on Caucasians:

> On behalf of the appellant it is urged that we should give to this phrase ["free White person"] the meaning which it had in the minds of its original framers in 1790 and that it was employed by them for the sole purpose of excluding the Black or African race and the Indians then inhabiting this country. It may be true that those two races were alone thought of as being excluded, but to say that they were the only ones within the intent of the statute would be to ignore the affirmative form of the legislation.
>
> The provision is not that Negroes and Indians shall be excluded, but it is, in effect, that only free White persons shall be included. The intention was to confer the privilege of citizenship upon that class of persons whom the fathers knew as white, and to deny it to all who could not be so classified. It is not enough to say that the framers did not have in mind the brown or yellow races of Asia. It is necessary to go farther and be able to say that had these particular races been suggested, the language of the act would have been so varied as to include them within its privileges.[27]

NOTES

1. Azuma, Eiichiro. *Between Two Empires: Race, History, and Transnationalism in Japanese America.* (Oxford, England: Oxford University Press, 2005), 23.
2. Ibid.
3. Ibid., 24.

4. Lee (Shelley Sang-Hee), 42.
5. Azuma., 31.
6. Lee, (Shelley Sang-Hee), 44.
7. Dower, John W. *War Without Mercy: Race and Power in the Pacific War.* (New York, NY: Pantheon, 1987), 156.
8. Ibid.
9. Rowell, Chester H. Chinese and Japanese Immigrants – A Comparison," *Annals of the American Academy of Political and Social Science*, Vol. 34, No. 2, 5.
10. From Jack London, "The Yellow Peril" (1904); reproduced with Lon Kurashige and Alice Yang Murray, eds. *Major Problems in Asian American History.* (Boston, MA: Houghton Mifflin Company, 2003.
11. Lee, (Shelley Sang-Hee), 43.
12. Lee (Erika), *The Making of Asian America*, 126.
13. Ibid., 113.
14. Lee, (Shelley Sang-Hee), 45.
15. Lee (Erika), 115.
16. Ibid, 120.
17. Ibid., 121.
18. Takaki, *Strangers from a Different Shore*, 271.
19. Lee (Erika), *The Making of Asian America*, 102.
20. Ibid., 185.
21. Takaki, *A Different Mirror*, 247.
22. Lee, Erika and Judy Yung. *Angel Island: Immigrant Gateway to America.* (Oxford, England: Oxford University Press, 2010), 130.
23. Ibid., 121.
24. Ibid., 130.
25. Takaki, *Strangers From A Different Shore*, 181.
26. Ichioka, 219.
27. U.S. Supreme Court, Takao Ozawa v. U.S., 260 U.S. 178, 1922. http://caselaw.findlaw.com/us-supreme-court/260/178.html.

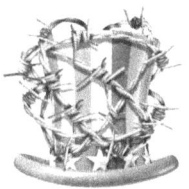

17

EAST INDIANS AND FILIPINOS

IN THE CASE of Indians, beginning in early colonial times, and through the early 1900s, small numbers had passed through North America for academic, business, and religious purposes. India also became a symbol of spirituality for many Americans beginning in the middle to late 1800s. American philosophers, like Henry David Thoreau and Ralph Waldo Emerson, were students of Indian scriptures, and the Theosophical Society, founded by Helena Petrovna Blavatsky, drew heavily on Indian philosophy and became popular in America during the last quarter of the nineteenth century. Indeed, the term "Boston Brahmin" was coined during this time.

The first direct exposure for many Americans to Indians on a large scale was the well-publicized speech of Swami Vivekananda at the First Congress of Religions at the 1893 Chicago World's Fair. In a 1911 article from the publication *Current Literature*, an unnamed author worried that Vivekananda and other "Hindoo," Muslim, and Zoroastrians, represented an "Oriental propagandist" menace that threatened to undermine the "spiritual health" of America. The author cited cases of people, primarily women, who had been cast under a spell and driven mad by Indian mystics. One example was that of Aloise Reuss, "a woman of culture and refinement [who] was taken, screaming and praying, from the Mazdaznan Temple of the Sun, to be incarcerated, a raving maniac, in an Illinois asylum." Indeed, much of the reporting of the early 20th century focused on the dangers of so-called Oriental religion. Newspapers sensationalized the death of a New York writer, Dr. William

R.C. Latson, a man "saturated in the lore of the East," who was found mysteriously dead in his apartment, and a young Jewish girl, who allegedly called Vivekananda "her man-god" or "guru'" and committed suicide. "This new religion seems to me to be of the devil," said her sister.[1]

Compared to other Asian groups, the number of South Asians arriving in the United States was much smaller, totaling 8,055 between 1910 and 1932, a number paling when compared to the numbers that were brought to the British West Indies as coolies between 1838 and 1918. Those early years coincided with British colonial rule in India, the end of the African slave trade in the British Empire, and an aggressive recruitment campaign, all of which colluded to bring 419,000 South Asians as indentured laborers to British Guiana, Trinidad, and Jamaica. By the turn of the twentieth century, decades of economic dislocation, high taxes, and the loss of subsistence farming land caused by British colonial policies led to the devastation of countless South Asian families, particularly in the Punjab region in present-day India and Pakistan, which suffered a population explosion, drought, famine, and deadly epidemics during that same period. Additionally, 4,000 miles of new roads and highways, combined with steamship travel, made the extraordinarily long journey to North America more feasible. When exclusionary laws in the United States and head taxes in Canada were enacted against the Chinese, labor recruiters shifted their efforts away from China and toward India, in particular the Punjab.[2]

The Indians arriving in the United States were mostly young men who had been independent farmers. Those who were married often left their wives and children at home, as the passage to America was costly. Many intended to return home. Additionally, many had been away from their home for years, having migrated throughout the British Empire, sometimes as soldiers, before arriving in the United States. Of the early 20th century Indian immigrants, 85 to 90 percent were Sikhs, a small minority in India, and the vast majority came from only six districts in the Punjab.[3]

Despite being largely Sikh, South Asians were collectively labeled "Hindus" or "Hindoos," in order to distinguish them from American Indians. They arrived at West Coast ports and tended to remain in California, Oregon, and Washington, though there were smaller groups that settled in the Northeast, Midwest, and South, some of whom came by way of Latin America. One of the main attractions of Northern California was the similarity in weather and geographical conditions found there to that of the Punjab. Immigrants discovered that many of the agricultural products that they were familiar with were also produced in California, which in part accounts for their success in the agricultural industry.[4]

Despite their small numbers, the Indians arrived when anti-Asian sensibilities burned, and furor over a "Hindu Invasion" and a "Tide of Turbans" gripped America, particularly in San Francisco, where workers saw yet another ploy to use cheap Asian labor to lower wages.⁵ Indians were categorized as being the least assimilable of all the immigrants from Asia, despite being considered by many anthropologists of the day to be "Aryans" or "Caucasians." According to the *San Francisco Chronicle* in 1928: "Certain races are excluded because their minds and manners of living are different from ours. That applies to Hindus even more than to Chinese and Japanese."⁶ In "The West and the Hindu Invasion," published in the *Overland Monthly* in 1908, Agnes Foster Buchanan wrote:

> Another stranger [seeks] the Western coast – the land of promise. He is tall of stature, straight of feature, swarthy of color. But unlike the other visitors, this last is a brother of our own race – a full-blooded Aryan, men of like progenitors with us ... The Hindus in the Hindu invasion is the latest racial problem with which we of the West have to deal.⁷

Religious Sikh men, who wore the *dastar*, a turban, were especially targeted. One newspaper described them as "dirty and gaunt and with a roll of pagan dry goods wrapped around [their] head[s]."⁸ According to the Dillingham report issued in 1911 by the U.S. Immigration Commission:

> The East Indians on the Pacific coast are almost universally regarded as the least desirable race of immigrants thus far admitted to the United States. In point of desirability they are placed far below the Japanese, Chinese, and other Oriental races found in the United States. The White workingmen regard them as a menace just as the previous unrestricted immigration of Japanese and Chinese was. They accept low wages and threaten to undermine the position of White men in such occupations as they are capable of entering. Experience so far has shown them that at the same wages they cannot compete with White men, for they are generally the least efficient race employed...⁹

A particularly violent episode occurred in 1907, when a mob of 500 White workers in Bellingham, Washington rioted with the objective of driving a community of Indian lumber mill workers out of the city. The rioters broke windows, threw rocks, and indiscriminately beat people, pulling men out of their barracks, all the while chanting "Death to the Hindus." Six Indians were hospitalized, 410 were placed in protective custody in the Bellingham jail, and 750 fled northwards to the Canadian border, hoping to settle there and gain protection under the British flag. There were other incidents. A month later, White workers in eastern Washington met Indians migrating from Canada and forced them back across the border. In November, in Everett, Washington, 500 White men shepherded all "Hindoos living on the waterfront ... [into] the City Hall for protection." Ostensibly, the fault rested with the Indian immigrants. Said one account: "In California, the insolence and presumption of Japanese, and the immodest and filthy habits of the Hindoos are continually involving them in trouble, beatings, and otherwise ... In all cases, we may say the Oriental is at fault."[10]

The most notorious case of anti-Indian discrimination occurred in Canada, when a shipload of Indians arrived at Canadian shores on the Japanese steamship, the *Komagata Maru*. In 1908, Canada had passed the Continuous Journey decree, which excluded immigrants who had not come on a "continuous voyage" directly from their country of birth or citizenship when entering Canada. The order was passed to effectively exclude Indians, given that there was no direct steamship service from India to Canada, without explicitly discriminating against them, a political requisite, given that Indians were British subjects. In 1914, as part of a campaign to defy the law, Gurdit Singh, a Sikh contractor, chartered the *Komagata Maru*, to bring Indians to Canada, advertising that he would "not return back until the real result will be out." The ship sailed on April 6 from Hong Kong with a Japanese crew and 165 Sikhs. In Shanghai, it picked up 111 additional passengers, and by the time it left Kobe and Yokohama, there were 376 people en route to Vancouver. Arriving on Canadian shores, the *Komagata Maru* was allowed to proceed to Vancouver, but it was not permitted to dock. No passengers were allowed to leave the ship, and immigration agents in Vancouver established a special patrol to prevent any passengers from escaping. The passengers mutinied and refused to release control of the ship, while Vancouver police and immigration officials prepared a large tugboat to forcibly remove the passengers and put them on another steamship bound for Hong Kong.[11] On the morning of July 21, the *Rainbow*, a 3,600-ton Canadian naval cruiser armed with 12 heavy caliber guns and machine guns, approached the ship as a crowd of thousands gathered. Writing of the confrontation years later, Singh recalled, "The warships were preparing for action and ... we were preparing for death." Ultimately, the ship and its passengers were returned to Calcutta.[12]

Prior to 1909, most Indians came to the United States by way of British Columbia; however, when the Continuous Voyage law closed Canadian doors to Indian immigration, the majority entered the United States through San Francisco.[13] By the fall of 1910, a number of federal officials began to express concern about the growing number of immigrants from India. On August 11, 1910, William R. Wheeler, a member of the Immigration Commission, wrote to Charles P. Neil, the United States Commissioner of Labor, that the "influx of Hindus" at the port of San Francisco was "alarming" and asserted that "the administration is justified in adopting any policy which will keep these undesirables out." In September 1910, Daniel J. Keefe, Commissioner General of Immigration and Naturalization, warned his commissioners in El Paso, Honolulu, Montreal, San Francisco, and Seattle that that steamship line agents were recruiting "Indian coolies to migrate to the United States." Keefe conceded to a fellow immigration officer that there was no law directed at the exclusion of Hindus as a race. However, he added, if the immigrants were "not found to belong to some of the definitely excluded classes such as paupers, criminals, or contagiously diseased," they should be excluded by other means, including being "persons of poor physique" or persons "likely to become public charges."[14] The arbitrary denial of admissions to Indians combined with a 1917 U.S. law creating an "Asiatic barred zone," which employed degrees of latitude and longitude to deny entry to South and Southeast Asians, effectively excluded all Indians except for students, visitors, and diplomatic envoys.[15]

Although Indians in the United States tended to settle in California and the Pacific Northwest, they sprang up in unexpected places, such as New York City and Louisiana. The 1900 federal census recorded 12 men from "Hindoostan" living in New Orleans, all of whom were likely members of a Bengali "peddler network," men who initially peddled goods on the New Jersey seashore selling Asian goods to American consumers, but soon spread out to other areas. On May 25, 1900 the *Daily Heard* of Biloxi, Mississippi published a story about a group of these peddlers in New Orleans, which began with the author's musings about a growing population of Indians there:

> You know we have quite a colony of East Indians here who wear Black skullcaps and long-tailed frock coats and prowl about town peddling rugs and such like. I must confess there [has] always been something strangely fascinating to me in the appearance of these fellows. They look so preternaturally solemn, and have such an air of Oriental mysticism … that I can't help believing they are as wise as Solomon and are laughing in their sleeves at us poor barbarians while incidentally they are loading us up with their ridiculous rugs.[16]

Indians in the early 20th century, like other Asians as well as Mexicans, occupied a kind of in-between racial status, between Blacks and Whites. In New Orleans, most Bengalis integrated into the city's African American community, and many married African American or Creole women. In New York, Bengalis generally settled in Harlem, often marrying African American or Puerto Rican women, and by the 1930s, they could be seen working in a wide range of jobs.[17] In Imperial Valley, California, east of San Diego and along the Mexican border, a substantial community of Punjabi farmers settled, and most married Mexican women. Although California's anti-miscegenation laws prohibited the marriage between people of different races, these marriages were generally accepted because Punjabis were considered non-white, and marriage licenses were routinely issued.[18] Among these mixed families, a dual Punjabi-Mexican identity emerged in the area, and children of the second generation often socialized together, sharing not only a common ethnic and cultural identity, but also the strict upbringing exercised by their parents, particularly their fathers.[19]

The in-between status of Indians became a salient topic in the early decades of the 20th century, given that U.S. naturalization laws limited citizenship to Whites. Beginning in 1907, Indians began to apply for naturalization, armed with the argument that they belonged to the "Aryan" or "Caucasian" race, the prevalent view among anthropologists at the time. Between 1912 and 1914, five Indians were granted citizenship, while 60 more obtained it between 1916 and 1923.[20] One such applicant was Bhagat Singh Thind, who had been granted citizenship by an Oregon court in 1920 on the grounds that he was Caucasian, but the federal government appealed to the Ninth Circuit Court of Appeals, which requested instruction from the Supreme Court on the question: "Is a high caste Hindu of full Indian blood, born at Amrit Sar, Punjab, India, a White person?" In addressing the question, the Court conceded that Thind was a "Caucasian," yet it voted to revoke his citizenship, arguing: "It may be true that the blond Scandinavian and the brown Hindu have a common ancestor in the dim reaches of antiquity, but the average man knows perfectly well that there are unmistakable and profound differences between them today." The Court continued:

> What we now hold is that the words "free White person" are words of common speech, to be interpreted in accordance with the understanding of the common man, synonymous with the word "Caucasian" only as that word is popularly understood.[21]

FILIPINOS: A COLONIZED PEOPLE

The Philippines became a colony of the United States in 1898 with the signing of The Treaty of Paris, which formally ended the Spanish-American War and resulted in the cession of the Philippines, Puerto Rico, Guam, and Cuba to the United States.

Filipino revolutionaries, led by Emilio Aguinaldo, who had fought for independence for Spain, turned their attention to the United States and refused to recognize American sovereignty. They battled American soldiers in the Philippine-American war which lasted from 1899 to 1902, in which 4,500 Americans and as many as a million Filipinos lost their lives.

Following the war, the issue became what to do with Filipinos, who were described as savages, rapists, dogs, and monkeys. President William McKinley opted for the path of "benevolent assimilation," whereby the United States would educate, civilize, and elevate Filipinos. In the words of William Howard Taft, then the chairman of the U.S. commission to establish the colonial government, Filipinos were "little brown brothers" who would need "fifty or one hundred years" supervision "to develop anything resembling Anglo-Saxon political principles and skills."[22]

On January 20, 1899, President McKinley appointed the First Philippine Commission, a five-person group headed by Dr. Jacob Schurman, president of Cornell University, which conducted extensive ethnological studies to investigate conditions in the islands and make recommendations. The resulting report, "The Native People of the Philippines," deeply tinged by turn of the century racial thinking, divided Filipinos into "three sharply distinct races – the Negrito race, the Indonesian race, and the Malayan race." Negritos, the report stated:

> ... are the disappearing remnants of a people which once populated the entire archipelago. They are, physically, weaklings of low stature, with Black skin, closely-curling hair, flat noses, thick lips and large clumsy feet. In the matter of intelligence they stand at or near the bottom of the human series, and they are believed to be incapable of any considerable degree of civilization or advancement.[23]

Of the Indonesian race, which was said to be confined to the large island of Mindanao, the report classified its members as being "physically superior" to Negritos and Malayans:

> They are tall and well developed, with high foreheads, aquiline noses, wavy hair, and often with abundant beards. The color of their skins is quite light. Many of them are very clever and intelligent. None of the tribes have been Christianized. Some of them have grown extremely fierce and warlike as a result of their long struggle with hostile Malayan people. Others, more happy in their surroundings, are pacific and industrious.[24]

Members of the Malayan race, which constituted the majority of Filipinos, were said to be the result of "intermarriage with Chinese, Indonesians, Negritos, Arabs, and to a limited extent, Spaniards and other Europeans." They were described as having brown skin that is "distinctly darker than that of the Indonesians, although very much lighter than that of the Negritos. The nose is short and frequently considerably flattened."[25] Additionally, the report identified a fourth group, Mestizos, of which there were two classes: those of European-Filipino extraction and the offspring of Chinese-Filipino parentage. According to the report, those of mixed European descent were "usually the most important and noble," having "in its very blood the nature and the culture of a superior race."[26]

The report found deficiencies in the "moral makeup" of Filipinos to be evidence of their unfitness for self-government, particularly their purported inability to control their savage instincts. The commissioners linked this to the tropical climate of the Philippines and other environmental factors, which produced a "relative enervation of the cerebral mass" that manifested in alternating displays of rage and docility, characterized by laziness and frivolity, resulting in "lazy habits" and a "worthless character." As sociologist Rick Baldoz notes, such claims were used as claims of legitimacy of the American colonial project, as such people were reputedly incapable of self-rule and transforming the islands into a modern capitalist economy.[27]

In 1904, William Howard Taft, now the Civil Governor of the Philippines, instructed the Philippine Commission to organize a Filipino exhibit at the Louisiana Purchase Exposition, held in St. Louis. The federal government spent one million dollars on the exhibit, which featured over 1,100 Filipinos, over 100 structures, and 75,000 artifacts, in order to "bring together the personnel and the material that make up those ... troublous isles of the East which are now Uncle Sam's particular share of the White Man's burden." Included in the exhibit was a Philippine "reservation" featuring a range of "tribes," the most popular being the Igorotte and Negrito villages, which featured "outright savages" in "G-string breechclouts." That summer, a delegation of "chiefs" from the exposition traveled to Washington, D.C. to meet with President Theodore Roosevelt at the White House, part of a public relations display to highlight the civilizing role of the U.S. government in the Philippines. A brief national controversy erupted when American officials voiced their concern that the chiefs would arrive at the White House without pants, an embarrassment that was averted when the "little naked savages" arrived fully clothed and the chiefs displayed an appropriate "childlike reverence" for "the Great White Father." When the chiefs arrived in Portland for another exhibition, *The Washington Post* announced: "The dog-eaters have come, and Portland is glad." *The Portland Oregonian* gave detailed accounts of Igorotte villagers slaughtering a "fat juicy puppy" as part of the performance.[28]

17 | EAST INDIANS AND FILIPINOS

The first group of Filipinos to migrate to the United States were students sponsored under the *Pensionado* Act, begun in August 1903 as part of Taft's plan to inculcate young Filipino students into American democracy and send them back to the Philippines to become pro-American leaders. The first group of 100 was screened from a group of 20,000 applicants, and by 1907, there were 183 students enrolled in 47 colleges and universities. The majority of Filipinos, however, would arrive as laborers, first in Hawaii, where the need for unskilled plantation workers was exacerbated by Chinese exclusion and the Gentleman's Agreement with Japan; by 1909, Koreans were barred from immigrating as well.

Hawaiian sugar planters preferred to import Filipino labor for several reasons. First, they fell to the bottom of the hierarchy among plantation workers and were paid the lowest wages. Second, since the Philippines was a U.S. colony, Filipinos were technically U.S. nationals due to their colonial status. Third, Filipinos were viewed as leverage, an alternative labor source to use against Japanese workers who were staging strikes. Filipinos were perceived to be docile and subservient and, thereby, not prone to striking. In 1909, the Hawaiian Sugar Planters Association (HSPA) sent agents, known as "drummers," to Manila to begin large-scale recruiting, and they sent recruits to Hong Kong to draw up labor contracts, supply provisions, and arrange transportation. By the end of the year, they brought 803 Filipinos to Hawaii, and the following year 4,173 arrived on the islands.[29]

As other Asian groups either returned to their home countries or migrated to the mainland – by necessity, a clandestine undertaking – Filipinos began to represent an increasingly large percentage of the Hawaiian sugar plantation working population. By 1912, 9.7 percent of laborers were Filipino, and their numbers increased to 29.4 percent in 1920.[30] Filipinos performed the most labor-intensive types of fieldwork, such as planting, cane cutting, hoeing, fertilizing, and hauling. Laborers in the field worked a grueling ten-hour day while those in the mills worked twelve hours. Complaints from Filipino workers about exploitative conditions in the 1910s attracted the attention of officials in the Philippines, who threatened to halt immigration to Hawaii unless protections were implemented. The government of the Philippines eventually passed a bill that mandated basic rights and protections for Filipino workers brought to Hawaii, including a guarantee of return passage back to the Philippines at the end of their contract.[31]

During the first decade of the twentieth century, few Filipinos lived on the mainland. In 1910, only 406 of the 2,767 Filipino immigrants residing in the United States lived outside of Hawaii, the largest group being a community of 109 near New Orleans, dating back to a group of Filipino mariners who had jumped ship from a Spanish schooner as early as 1763. By 1920, 5,603 lived on the mainland, mostly on the West Coast, working in agriculture or as servants or restaurant and hotel workers. The population increased dramatically during the 1920s, when about 45,000 Filipinos arrived on the Pacific coast, about 16,000 of these coming from Hawaii.

Like the other Asian groups arriving before them, most were young, single men – the ratio was 14 males to one female – with little formal education, and few spoke either English or Spanish.[32] As U.S. nationals, Filipinos were not subject to immigration laws, and they were the only foreign nationals allowed to enlist in the U.S. armed forces, though they were restricted to joining only the Navy during World War I, and they were mostly relegated to the role of stewards who took care of officers. Most Filipinos, however, were migrant laborers, following the seasons, cutting asparagus, picking fruit, thinning lettuce, and working in lumber mills and canneries in northern California and the Pacific Northwest.[33] An important stop in the migrant circuit was in Alaska, where Filipino "Alaskeros" worked in the canned salmon industry. Recruitment had begun in the 1910s, when canners sent labor agents to Hawaii to enlist workers from the sugar plantations, and by 1928, 3,916 Filipinos worked in the canneries, more than the combined total of Japanese and Chinese workers.[34]

By the time that Filipinos began settling on the West Coast, anti-Asian nativism was entrenched, and Filipinos faced a similar brand of legal and extralegal discrimination that earlier arrivals from Asia had encountered. Like other Asians, they were barred from living in most White neighborhoods, and as a result, "Little Manilas" sprung up in Los Angeles, San Francisco, and Seattle. Stockton, California's Little Manila was the largest in the country.

However, there were differences, too, in their treatment, stemming from Filipinos' colonized status and the prevailing perceptions that the Philippines were backwards. Filipinos were frequently portrayed as uncivilized tribal people and "jungle folk," as the president of California's Immigration Study Commission labeled them, possessing a "primitive moral code." According to Judge D.W. Rohrback of Monterey County, they were "little brown men about ten years removed from a bolo and breechcloth." Congressman Richard J. Welch called Filipino immigration "one of the gravest problems that has ever faced the people of the Pacific Coast."[35]

Filipino author Carlos Bulosan, in his autobiographical account of life in the United States, *America Is in the Heart*, written in 1943, describes a discussion among Filipino men at a political gathering in Los Angeles:

> "How come we Filipinos in California can't buy or lease real estate?" a man asked.
> "Why are we denied civil service jobs?" asked another.

17 | EAST INDIANS AND FILIPINOS

"Why can't we marry women of the Caucasian race? And why are we not allowed to marry in this state?"

"Why can't we practice law?"

"Why are we denied the right of becoming naturalized American citizens?"

"Why are we discriminated against in relief agencies?"

"Why are we denied better housing conditions?"

"Why can't we stop the police from handling us like criminals?"

"Why are we denied recreational facilities in public parks and other such places?"[36]

A significant obstacle that Filipinos faced were constant allegations of a tendency to flout the color line in terms of sexual relations, and they were persistently depicted as over-sexualized predators with a particular affinity for White women. In his memoir, *I Have Lived With The American People*, Philippine-born poet and novelist Manuel Buaken quotes an American lawyer asking a White man in a trial involving a Filipino-White couple, "How many of you fellows have ever seen a Filipino woman?" The man responded, "Not one of us apparently had ever seen a Filipino woman. It was as if we had all somehow thought of the Filipinos as an entirely male race, sprung directly from the earth."[37] Said one man testifying before the House Committee on Immigration and Naturalization in 1930, "The Filipinos are ... a social menace as they will not leave our White girls alone and frequently intermarry." Typical statements about Filipinos included:

"The lovemaking of the Filipino is primitive, even heathenish."

"The Filipinos are hot little rabbits, and many of these White women like them for this reason."

"Filipino boys, with perfect candor, have told me bluntly and boastfully that they practice the art of love with more perfection than White boys, and occasionally one of the [white] girls has supplied me with information to the same effect."[38]

According to a contemporary article by C.M. Goethe, "Filipino Immigration Viewed as a Peril":

The Filipino tends to interbreed with near-moron White girls. The resulting hybrid is almost invariably undesirable.

> The ever-increasing brood of children of Filipino coolie fathers and low-grade White mothers may in time constitute a serious social burden ... [and] immediate exclusion is tragically necessary to protect our American seed stock.[39]

The issue of intermarriage between Filipino men and White women became a hotly contested one, and there were several cases whereby Filipino men challenged Sections 60 and 69 of the California civil code, which specifically outlawed marriages between "White persons" and members of the "negro" and "Mongolian" races. Filipinos argued that according to the accepted racial doctrine, they were "Malays" and, therefore, exempted from the state's anti-miscegenation code. In 1920, Edward Bishop, Assistant County Counsel in Los Angeles, issued a ruling in a case involving Leonardo Antony, a Filipino war veteran, and his Mexican American fiancée, Luciana Brovencio, who was legally classified as white, when they were denied a license to wed by the Los Angeles County marriage bureau. Bishop concluded that though there were scientists who would classify the Malayans as an offshoot of the Mongolian race, "Mongolians" are yellow and not brown people, and therefore, Filipinos were not subject to the matrimonial restrictions of Section 69.[40]

The California State Court of Appeals took up the issue, in 1933, in the case *Roldan v. Los Angeles County and the State of California*. Salvador Roldan, a Filipino, had his application for marriage to his British fiancée, Marjorie Rogers, rejected by the county court in 1931. The California State Court of Appeals handed down a precedent-setting decision for the lower courts to follow. The court concluded that the legal category "Mongolian" had been used "to designate the class of residents whose presence caused the problem at which all the [exclusionist] legislation was directed, ... the Chinese, and possibly contiguous people of like characteristics," adding that "there was no thought of applying the name Mongolian to a Malay." Despite the ruling, which exempted Filipinos from California's anti-miscegenation law, county clerks across the state refused to issue marriage licenses, and Idaho, South Dakota, and Arizona amended their anti-miscegenation laws to include "Malays."[41]

Whereas relations between Chinese and Japanese men and White women appeared in headlines only occasionally, they were common in the case of Filipinos, and White wrath often focused on what were known as "taxi dance halls," where Filipino men paid for dances with young White female dancers after purchasing tickets at 10 cents each. As the Filipino population grew, fears of miscegenation and labor competition grew, and violence directed at them escalated, particularly as White migrants from the Dust Bowl entered California from Texas, Oklahoma, and Arkansas, where membership in the Ku Klux Klan and anti-Black lynching were commonplace. On New Year's Eve in 1926, White men raided hotels and pool halls in Stockton, stabbing and beating eight Filipino men. Filipinos were expelled from the Yakima Valley in Washington; Filipino laborers were attacked in Dinuba, California for socializing with White women, and mobs attacked Filipino men in Exeter, Modesto, Turlock, and Reedley, California.[42] Most famously, in January 1930, in the farming community of Watsonville, mobs of Whites, provoked by a photograph in the local newspaper, the *Evening Pajaronian*, of a Filipino man with a White teenage girl, attacked Filipinos in the dance hall, on the streets, and in nearby labor camps. Smaller bands raided Filipino residences, beating several occupants until police arrived. According to the *San Jose Mercury Herald*, between 60 and 70 carloads of Filipinos arrived from neighboring areas, armed with knives and guns. On January 22, a mob of men fired on a Filipino bunkhouse, killing 22-year-old Fermin Tobera. A day later, anti-Filipino violence spread to San Jose, where several Filipino men were beaten and stabbed.[43]

Calls for Filipino exclusion grew, particularly with the dawn of the Depression. However, the status of Filipinos as U.S. nationals created a significant legal and political obstacle for those who would exclude them. Oddly enough, as historian Erika Lee observes, Filipino nationalists, who seeing an opportunity, argued that excluding Filipinos from the United States without granting independence to the Philippines would be "unjust" and "un-American," thereby tarnishing America's international reputation. Pedro Gil, a leader in the Philippine House of Representatives, testified to the U.S. Congress that if the United States wanted to restrict Filipinos, it would need to offer a quid pro quo and liberate the Philippines.

The result was a compromise, the Tydings-McDuffie Act, signed into law by President Franklin D. Roosevelt on March 24, 1934, which granted the Philippines commonwealth status and promised independence within 10 years. It also changed the status of Filipinos living in the U.S. to "aliens."[44] A year later, Congress approved the Filipino Repatriation Act, which established a "voluntary" repatriation program to organize the return of Filipinos living in the U.S. to the Philippines. The program lasted until July 1941, but despite efforts by INS officials to rid the country of Filipinos, only 2,064 were repatriated.[45]

NOTES

1. South Asian American Digital Archive, "The Heathen Invasion of America," November 1911. https://www.saada.org/item/20111101-442.
2. Lee (Erika), *The Making of Asian America*, 125.
3. Lee (Erika) and Yung, 148.

4. Gonzales Jr., Juan L. "Asian Indian Immigration Patterns: The Origins of the Sikh Community in California," *International Migration Review*. Vol. 20, No. 1 (Spring, 1986), 40.
5. Lee (Erika), *The Making of Asian America*, 136.
6. Lee and Yung, 149.
7. Buchanan, Agnes Foster. "The West and the Hindu Invasion," *Overland Monthly*, April 1908. https://www.lib.washington.edu/specialcollections/collections/exhibits/southasianstudents/docs/the-west-and-the-hindu-invasion-buchanan
8. Jensen, Joan M. *Passage from India: Asian Indian Immigrants in North America*. (New Haven, CT: Yale University Press, 1988), 51.
9. Dillingham, William P. and the United States Immigration Commission. "Reports of the Immigration Commission (1907–1910)," 1911. (San Bernadino, CA: Ulan Press, 2012), 349.
10. Melendy, H. Brett. *Asians in America: Filipinos, Koreans, and East Indians*. (Boston, MA: Twayne Publishers, 1977), 192.
11. Lee (Erika), *The Making of America*, 138.
12. Sohi, Seema. *Echoes of Mutiny: Race, Surveillance, and Indian Anticolonialism in North America*. (Oxford, England: Oxford University Press, 2014), 135.
13. Dillingham and the United States Immigration Commission, 676.
14. Lee (Erika), *The Making of Asian America*, 137.
15. Daniels, *Guarding the Golden Door*, 46.
16. Bald, Vivek. *Bengali Harlem and the Lost Histories of South Asian America*. (Cambridge, MA: Harvard University Press, 2013), 27.
17. Ibid., 172.
18. Leonard, Karen Isaksen. *Making Ethnic Choices: California's Punjabi Mexican Americans*. (Philadelphia, PA: Temple University Press, 1992), 63.
19. Ibid., 144.
20. Melendy, 216.
21. *United States Supreme Court, U.S. v. Bhagat Singh Thind*, (1923), No. 202. http://caselaw.findlaw.com/us-supreme-court/261/204.html.
22. Lee (Erika), *The Making of Asian America*, 144.
23. United States Commission to the Philippines, "Report of the Philippine Commission to the President." Part Two, January 31, 1900 – December 20, 1900, 11.
24. Ibid.
25. Ibid.
26. Ibid., 343.
27. Baldoz, Rick. *The Third Asiatic Invasion: Migration and Empire in Filipino America, 1898–1946*. (New York, NY: NYU Press, 2011), 37.

28. Ibid., 40.
29. Melendy, 31.
30. Takaki, Ronald. *Pau Hana: Plantation Life and Labor in Hawaii, 1835–1920.* (Honolulu, HI: University of Hawaii Press, 1983), 28.
31. Baldoz, 52.
32. Melendy, 42.
33. Ngai, Mae M. *Impossible Subjects: Illegal Aliens and the Making of Modern America.* (Princeton, NJ: Princeton University Press, 2004), 103.
34. Baldoz, 61.
35. Lee (Erika), *The Making of Asian America*, 185.
36. Bulosan, Carlos. *America Is in the Heart: A Personal History.* (Seattle, WA: University of Washington Press, 2014), 266.
37. Buaken, Manuel. *I Have Lived with the American People.* (Caldwell, ID: Caxton, 1948), 132.
38. Rudy P. Guevarra, Jr., *Becoming Mexipino: Multiethnic Identities and Communities in San Diego*, (New Brunswick, NJ: Rutgers University Press, 2012), 135.
39. Ibid., 136.
40. Baldoz, 91.
41. Ibid., 98.
42. Lee (Erika), *The Making of Asian America*, 186.
43. Tsu, Cecilia M. *Garden of the World: Asian Immigrants and the Making of Agriculture in California's Santa Clara Valley.* (Oxford, England: Oxford University Press, 2013), 179.
44. Lee (Erika), *The Making of Asian America*, 188.
45. Zhao, Xiaojian and Edward Park (editors), *Asian Americans: An Encyclopedia of Social, Cultural, Economic, and Political History.* (Santa Barbara, CA: Greenwood, 2013), 418.

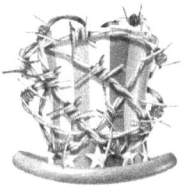

18

FROM ALLIES AND ALIENS TO MODEL MINORITY

WORLD WAR II impacted different Asian communities in the United States in different ways. For Japanese Americans, lives were shattered when immigrants and those born in the United States were systematically rounded up and placed in internment centers, following the signing of Executive Order 90966 on February 19, 1942, just 74 days after the Japanese attack on Pearl Harbor. There was no dissenting vote in Congress. Koreans, classified by the Alien Registration Act of 1940 as subjects of Japan, though not incarcerated, were identified as "enemy aliens."[1]

On the other hand, Chinese, Indians, and Filipinos fared much differently as a result of the war. China was an important ally, and in 1943, after decades of exclusion, immigration quotas, albeit small ones, were allotted to Chinese nationals, and Chinese immigrants were granted the right to become citizens. With the War Brides Act of 1946, Chinese wives of American citizens were allowed to immigrate on a nonquota basis. Additionally, in 1946, Congress passed a bill granting naturalization to Indians and Filipinos living in the U.S. and allowing a small but symbolic number to immigrate to the United States. At the same time, the "aliens ineligible to citizenship" category was retained for Korean and Japanese women, as well as all non-Chinese Southeast Asians.

There are few events in American history more shameful than the incarceration of Japanese-Americans during the Second World War, an incident that evoked a formal apology from President Ronald Reagan in 1988, as well as a restitution payment of $20,000 to each survivor. At the time of the Pearl Harbor attack, there were about 300,000 people of Japanese origin living in the United States, though more than half resided in Hawaii, which had yet to become a state, and few from the islands were incarcerated. However, 120,000 people, most of whom lived in California, Washington, and Oregon, were forcibly relocated to what were formally called assembly centers, though Roosevelt himself called them "concentration camps."[2]

As Takaki observes, evacuees were allowed to take to the assembly centers only what they could carry and had to sell most of their personal possessions. On arrival, each family was given a number and housed in stockyards, fairgrounds, and racetracks. Said one internee, "The assembly center was filthy, smelly, and dirty. There were roughly 2,000 people packed in one large building. No beds were provided, so they gave us gunny sacks to fill with straw; that was our bed." Most of the camps were located in remote desert areas. Said actor George Takei years later, "I was too young to understand, but I remember soldiers carrying rifles, and I remember being afraid."[3]

In 1943, the government required all internees to answer loyalty questionnaires, which asked if they would be willing to "swear unqualified allegiance to the United States," and if they were Nisei, if they were "willing to serve in the armed forces of the United States on combat duty, wherever ordered." Ten thousand Nisei answered in the affirmative, of which 1,208 served. Those who answered in the negative were sentenced to prisons, such as Leavenworth Federal Penitentiary, where they served with hardened criminals. When the evacuation order was rescinded and the War Relocation Authority began to close the camps, Roosevelt ordered internees to be "scattered" throughout the country, though most boarded trains for Los Angeles, Seattle, and San Francisco, where they were met with signs reading "No Japs Allowed" and "No Japs Welcome."[4]

While the malice directed toward Japanese-Americans seems beyond the pale of understanding today, it is important to keep in mind the national narrative which developed at the time, one which was encouraged by the Roosevelt Administration. Historian Emily S. Rosenberg argues that throughout the war, the cry of "Remember Pearl Harbor" instilled in Americans a sense of the "treacherous character of the enemy" and was used to "underscore the morality of the cause." The war, she states, was justified "in terms of national character rather than national interest," rooted in a "highly personalized and religiously tinged language of retribution."[5]

Japanese-Americans, hardly responsible for the Pearl Harbor attack, faced the brunt of American hostility. As historian Scott Kurashige observes:

Whites – not just the longtime agitators but almost universally – developed a new level of repulsion toward Japanese-Americans. People who had for a generation shopped at Japanese-American markets and taken in stride the mark that Issei gardeners had left on the ... landscape now feared that every yellow face was a potential enemy saboteur ... Political leaders created a lethal combination by encouraging anti-Japanese racism as an expression of wartime patriotism.[6]

In stark contrast, when the U.S. declared war on Japan, the status of Chinese in the U.S. changed from vilified "heathens" and "mice eaters," to friends and allies fighting a war against the dreaded Japanese. Two weeks after Pearl Harbor, on December 22, 1941, *Time* magazine explained "How to tell your friends [the Chinese] from the Japs":

Virtually all Japanese are short. Japanese are likely to be stockier and broader-hipped than short Chinese. Japanese are seldom fat; they often dry up and grown lean as they age. Although both have the typical epicanthic fold of the upper eyelid, Japanese eyes are usually set closer together. The Chinese expression is likely to be more placid, kindly, open; the Japanese more positive, dogmatic, arrogant. Japanese are hesitant, nervous in conversation, laugh loudly at the wrong time. Japanese walk stiffly erect, hard heeled. Chinese, more relaxed, have an easy gait, sometimes shuffle.[7]

As early as 1937, *Time* named Chinese Nationalist leader Chiang Kai-shek and his wife, May-Ling Soong, as "Man and Wife of the Year." During congressional hearings on repealing Chinese exclusion in 1943, a congressman from Missouri said, "All at once we discovered the saintly qualities of the Chinese people. If it had not been for December 7, I do not know if we would have ever found out how good they were."[8]

Between 12,000 and 15,000 Chinese Americans, about 20 percent of the U.S. adult Chinese male population, enlisted in the armed forces during World War II, serving in both integrated and all-Chinese units, the most visible being the 14th Air Service Group (ASG), which consisted of nine units and accounted for about 10 percent of Chinese Americans in the military. Along the West Coast, shipyards and airplane factories hired Chinese at impressive rates; by 1943, about 5,000 Chinese were employed throughout Bay Area defense industries, making up about 15 percent of shipyard workers. Momentum grew for the elimination of Chinese exclusion, particularly because the Japanese were using it as propaganda in an effort to generate hostility of Chinese toward the United States, and in November 1943, the Magnuson Act was passed, which repealed all or part of 15 anti-Chinese statutes passed between 1882 and 1915.[9] President Roosevelt threw the weight of his office behind the measure, writing in a letter to Congress that passing the bill was vital to correcting the "historic mistake" of Chinese exclusion, and he emphasized that the legislation was "important in the cause of winning the war and of establishing a secure peace."[10]

The United States faced an analogous situation in India. Thousands of American troops were stationed there during the war, and Indians worried about American designs as they established air bases, supply depots, and outposts. Additionally, Indian demands for independence from Great Britain grew, and in 1942, President Roosevelt suggested dominion status as a means of garnering Indian support, but he reversed his position when he realized how deeply Winston Churchill opposed an independent India. On February 1, 1944, President Roosevelt assured Indians that the sole American objective in India was to defeat Japan, but Indian hostility toward Americans only increased.

To Roosevelt, a show of goodwill by restoring citizenship and establishing a token quota of immigrants seemed like a logical step. When Congress lifted immigration and naturalization barriers for the Chinese in 1943, Indian activists began to demand similar rights for Indians, and Sirdar Jagjit Singh, president of the India League of America, convinced representatives Clare Booth Luce, a Republican, and Emanuel Celler, a Democrat, to introduce an identical bill for Indians in the House. Opposition was stiff in the House committee, however, and in March, 1945, Roosevelt sent William Phillips, who had visited India as the president's personal representative, to testify secretly in favor of the bill. Roosevelt wrote the chairman of the committee that statutory discrimination against Indians "now serves no useful purposes, and [is] incongruous and inconsistent with the dignity of both our peoples." The bill was soon moved onto the House floor, where it passed in October 1945. After resistance in the Senate, in July 1946, the Luce-Celler Act was passed and signed by President Harry Truman, which allowed both Indians and Filipinos to become naturalized citizens and a token quota of 100 from each country to immigrate to the United States each year.[11]

Filipino-American morale was bolstered by what had become widespread praise of the Filipino war effort. Filipinos were caught up in the patriotic fervor that engulfed the nation, and their zeal became even more pronounced as reports of high civilian casualties in the Philippines made the headlines. Filipinos arrived in multitudes to U.S. recruiting offices, but found, much to their dismay, that they were ineligible to serve, due to their status as noncitizen nationals, though many had previously served in World War I. As the war progressed, the status of Filipino-Americans vacillated, depending on the exigencies of the U.S. government. When it came to their responsibility under the Alien Registration Act, enacted in June 1940, which required all non-citizen adult residents to register with the government, they were classified as "aliens," which meant that the government retained the right to detain or expel them for any subversive activity. However, they were deemed as "citizens" with regard to the Selective Service Act, which required them to register for military service and enabled them to be drafted. As Rick Baldoz explains, there was an underlying logic to this seeming contradiction. "When it came to exacting maximal loyalty and martial sacrifice from Filipinos," he writes, "U.S. authorities considered them to be citizens, with the requisite obligation to defend the nation and provide military service to the state during the war. When it came to the state's reciprocal obligation to extend the full spectrum of rights and protections accorded to citizens, then Filipinos were classed as aliens or nationals, with a limited claim to civic benefits and privileges."[12]

In January 1942, the First Filipino Infantry Battalion, a special unit of the U.S. Army, was formed, which Secretary of War Henry Stimson announced was in recognition of the "intense loyalty and patriotism of those Filipinos who are now residing in the United States." Their conscription, according to Stimson, would provide them with the "eventual opportunity of fighting on the soil of their homeland," which by the spring of 1942, was fully under Japanese control. Although Filipinos were allowed to serve in "White" combat units, they were strongly encouraged to join up with Filipino outfits. The number of enlistees swelled and reached regiment strength by the summer of 1942; a second regiment was formed a few months later.[13]

Those Filipinos who did not serve in the military were employed in wartime production, in manufacturing plants that produced planes, ships, and armaments. The Filipino Federation of America pledged the undivided loyalty of its members to the U.S. government and promised to "crush the enemies of democracy," adding that it was the "duty of every Filipino" to do his part to preserve the "high ideals and principles of American democracy." In early 1942, Filipino soldiers garnered a path to citizenship when Congress passed the Second War Powers Act, which expedited naturalization for aliens or nationals serving in the U.S. military and established procedures for the naturalization of soldiers serving overseas.[14]

On July 4, 1946, two days after Truman signed the Luce-Celler Act into law, making citizenship a possibility for all Filipino-Americans, the U.S. and Philippines signed a treaty that provided for the recognition of the independence of the Republic of the Philippines and the relinquishment of American sovereignty. But citizenship for first generation Korean- and Japanese-Americans would have to wait six more years, until the passage of the Immigration and Nationality Act (INA) of 1952, also known as the McCarran-Walter Act, which repealed the laws excluding the immigration and naturalization of Asians. The Act left a mixed legacy. On the one hand, it removed blatantly racist laws, such as the Chinese Exclusion Act of 1882 and the 1917 Asiatic Barred Zone. On the other hand, 70 percent of all immigrant slots were, as in 1924, allotted to natives of the United Kingdom, Ireland, and Germany. Additionally, it instituted a concept called the Asia-Pacific Triangle, whereby immigration of people from Asia was capped annually at 2,000, while each Asian country within the Triangle was permitted 100 immigrants.[15] Such restrictions would remain in place until 1965.

POSTWAR AMERICA: DIVERGENT VIEWS OF ASIAN GROUPS

The advent of the Cold War brought with it, like World War II, divergent attitudes toward different Asian groups, reflecting as much America's geopolitical concerns as events occurring in the United States. After China "fell" to Communism in 1949, Americans now distinguished between the hostile Chinese on the Communist mainland and the "loyal" Chinese nationalist forces, the Kuomintang, in Taiwan, and many Chinese living in the United States found themselves under suspicion of being part of a dangerous communist threat. These fears were exacerbated in 1950 when Chinese Communists joined North Koreans in battle against South Korean and American troops, and the media resurrected images of "yellow hordes" bent on world conquest. The situation of Chinese Americans was all the more tenuous because during the years of Chinese exclusion, the practice of illegal Chinese immigration had become pervasive, and at least a quarter of the Chinese population living in the United States in 1950 was unlawfully present; tens of thousands of Chinese were so-called paper sons, those who entered the U.S. during the first half of the twentieth century by posing as the sons of Chinese who had American citizenship due to native birth.[16]

The government's solution to the problem was the Chinese Confession Program, whereby Chinese Americans were subjected to the humiliating process of confessing their hitherto fraudulent claim to citizenship, list the names of their true and "paper" family members, and assure authorities that they were not communists. At the same time, the State Department, concerned about the effect of Communist propaganda on perceptions of the United States, developed campaigns showcasing the achievements and "Americanness" of Chinese in the United States.[17]

Japan, once a dreaded foe, was now America's ally, and as the U.S. established military bases throughout Japan in order to "contain" Communist aggression in Asia, tens of thousands of soldiers became romantically involved with Japanese women, many of whom returned to the United States under the War Brides Act, passed in December 1945.[18] Between 1947 and 1964, about 72,700 Asian women entered the United States, of which 45,853 were Japanese, 14,435 Filipina, 7,000 Chinese, and 6,500 Korean, and women's migration helped balance the heavily male-skewed gender ratios of Asia-American communities. Japanese military brides, for example, made up 80 percent of Japanese immigrants in the 1950s and entered at an annual rate between 2,000 and 5,000 in the 1950s and 1960s.[19] Following the Korean War, Americans also took a strong interest in adopting Korean children, as the conflict had resulted in the separation of ten million families, the widowing of half a million wives, and the abandonment of tens of thousands of children, many of whom were the offspring of American GIs and Korean women. National publications ran articles about the children and the humanitarian work being done on their behalf and encouraged American families to adopt Korean orphans.[20]

The Immigration Act of 1965 totally changed the rules of the game for Asian Americans as well as Hispanics, though the law was not expected to make an appreciable change in the nature of future immigrants. It scrapped the national origins quota system and the Asia-Pacific Triangle in favor of overall hemispheric limits, allowing for twenty thousand immigrants per country from the Eastern Hemisphere, while spouses, minor children, and parents of U.S. citizens were exempted. Immigrants from the Eastern Hemisphere were to be admitted based on a preference system favoring family members, professionals, and artists, needed skilled and unskilled laborers, and refugees.

The *Wall Street Journal* made the erroneous prediction that the family-preference system "insured that the new immigration pattern would not stray radically from the old one." Representative Emanuel Celler of New York assured Congress: "Since the people of … Asia have very few relatives here, comparatively few could immigrate from those countries because they have no family ties in the U.S." At that time, the Asian population in the United States was so small, just one half of one percent, that the Japanese American Citizens League observed: "Although the immigration bill eliminated race as a matter of principle, in actual operation immigration will still be controlled by the now discredited national origins system, and the general pattern of immigration which exists today will continue for many years to come."[21]

However, designating employment desirability and family reunification as criteria for admittance led to a sharp increase in the number of Asians, not only from established populations, namely Chinese and Filipinos, but also those from other Asian countries with a small or nonexistent population, and the composition of the U.S. Asian population changed rapidly.[22]

In 1960, over half of Asian Americans were Japanese, a quarter were Chinese, and 20 percent were Filipinos. By 1985, while the proportion of Chinese and Filipinos remained relatively the same, Japanese Americans accounted for only 15 percent of the Asian American population. During those 25 years, Korean and Indian immigrants took advantage of amendments to immigration law that led to a shift toward highly skilled immigrants, and U.S. military involvement in Southeast Asia and the end of the Vietnam War in the early 1970s led to waves of Vietnamese, Laotian, and Cambodian refugees. In 1985, Southeast Asians accounted for nearly 20 percent of Asian Americans while Koreans and Asian Indians each accounted for about 10 percent.[23]

The growth of the Southeast Asian population was indeed precipitous. From a population of about 15,000 in 1975, by the late 1990s, the number of Southeast Asians in the U.S. increased to about one million.[24] Of the first refugees arriving in 1975, most were political evacuees who fled during the Communist takeover, fearing reprisals because of their employment positions, economic status, or religious beliefs. In 1976–77, the U.S. Attorney General, under the Indochinese Parole Program, authorized the admission of refugees, and beginning in 1978, there was a mass exodus of Southeast Asians, many of whom had been "reeducated" by the Communist government. Nearly all had spent time in refugee camps in Indonesia, Malaysia, Thailand, and Hong Kong. The United States accepted 44,500 Vietnamese refugees in 1979, 95,000 in 1980, 86,000 in 1981, and 44,000 in 1982. While there was a great sense of sympathy for the refugees, a Gallup Poll and a Harris Survey reported that more than half of Americans did not favor their resettlement in the United States; they were a reminder of an unpopular war, one with huge casualties for the U.S.[25]

Refugee policy was inexorably linked to Cold War politics, and the United States introduced the 1975 Indochina Migration and Refugee Assistance Act, the 1980 Refugee Act, and the 1987 Amerasian Homecoming Act, which facilitated the arrival of Vietnamese and other Southeast Asians, as well as mixed race people who were the product of unions between Asian women and American men serving in the military.[26] Although government officials attempted to scatter the refugee families around the country, in order to facilitate their blending in to American societies, refugees reorganized themselves and established their own distinct Southeast Asian communities.[27]

As demographer William H. Frey notes, Asian immigration waves continue to bring gains to Asian populations. In the 20-year period from 1990 to 2010, the Chinese population more than doubled to 3.3 million, and the Asian Indian population more than tripled to 2.8 million, becoming the second-largest Asian population in the United States; Filipinos, Vietnamese, and Koreans also increased by large numbers. The only decline was that of the Japanese-American population. These six groups make up 85 percent of the Asian population, with the remaining 15 percent consisting primarily of Pakistanis, Hmong, Cambodians, Laotians, Thais, Bangladeshis, Indonesians, Burmese, and Nepalese.[28]

BUILDING THE MODEL MINORITY MYTH IN POSTWAR AMERICA

Before World War II, White Americans, for the most part, considered Asian Americans, who were more often called Oriental or just Chinese or Japanese – the two major Asian-American groups at the time – regardless of their ancestry, as unable to or unfit to assimilate into greater society. "Aliens ineligible for citizenship" was the legal phrase used to discriminate against Asians in the early 20th century in the exclusionary state and federal laws passed in the 1910s and 1920s. Immigrants and even their U.S.–born children were steered into occupations such as farming, gardening, restaurants, and laundry, and lived in Little Tokyo and Chinatown ghettoes. The underlying premise was not only that they were considered unassimilable; they were not white.

With the demise of Exclusion in the 40s and 50s, restrictions on employment and neighborhoods were relaxed. By the 1960s, Asian Americans enjoyed a radical transformation in social standing as the model minority stereotype emerged. The idea was that Asians were highly intelligent, technically skilled, hard-working, disciplined, serious, upwardly mobile, and thrifty, all solid American values. Asian students were expected to exceed their allotment of spaces at top universities, fill the upper economic brackets, and not make any waves politically. They embodied many of the attributes that Americans saw in themselves, a symbol of American exceptionalism, the Horatio Alger story with an immigrant twist. However, in many ways the standing of Asian Americans shifted, at mid-century, from *not White* to *not Black*.

The Immigration Act of 1965 was a game changer for Asian Americans, opening up opportunities for new immigrants and their children to live and work and associate as they wished. But in minimizing considerations of race and national origins and prioritizing family reunification, employability, and refugee status, the U.S. government was not only ending the quota system of immigration. It was also, unwittingly, setting up Asian American immigrants to be perceived as the "better" immigrants.

In the post-World War II era, and particularly after the mid-60s, Asian-American cultural values, usurped and promoted as American cultural values, were praised at the expense of African American cultural values. In fact, one could see the rise of the Model Minority stereotype in the 1960s and 70s as a direct response to urban riots that happened after Civil Rights legislation was passed. The thinking, though not always stated, was, if Asian Americans could work hard and play by the rules and succeed at doing so, other racial minorities should be able to do the same.

The term model minority appears to have been coined in 1966 in a *New York Times* article entitled "Success Story, Japanese American Style." In the article, sociologist William Petersen attributed the success of Japanese Americans after World War II to cultural values, a strong work ethic, family structure, and genetics.[29] In 1971, *Newsweek* added other Asian nationalities to Petersen's thesis on Japanese advancement with an article entitled "Success Story: Outwhiting the Whites." In the late 1980s, as American automakers were being killed by Japanese competition, *Time* profiled "Those Asian-American Whiz Kids" on its cover.[30]

Political activist Scott Nakagawa says that the model minority image, first promoted by Asian-American civil rights leaders to lessen the otherness of Asians, particularly the Japanese in the wake of World War II, was soon used as a lever of White supremacy. He writes:

> To promote the myth, many unflattering facts of life in the Asian ghettos of the period were suppressed. Meanwhile, Asian American accomplishments in the arts, business, and, most of all, World War II were touted as indicators of Asians' suitability for citizenship and ability to vertically integrate themselves into the White middle class. In other words, the Asian American model minority myth was a shield against the persecution of the Chinese and Japanese in the U.S. Sadly, that shield was quickly picked up by opponents of the Black Civil Rights and Black Power movements and used as a weapon against Black Americans who were stereotyped as a "problem minority," mired in crime, unemployment, and inter-generational poverty because of cultural deficits they would do well to overcome by making like Asians and pulling themselves up by their bootstraps.[31]

As historian Madeline Hsu points out, students, particularly Chinese students, had an outsized impact on the image of Asians in the U.S., relative to their numbers. She writes, "Students … demonstrated the possibilities of cultural convergences between Chinese and Americans and presented living examples that Americans could welcome and economically benefit from the presence of the right kind of Chinese: educated, Westernized, well-mannered, and possessed of practical skills and talents." According to historian Ellen Wu, Asian Americans "strategically typecast themselves," as both natural ambassadors to Asia, an area of tremendous strategic importance to the U.S. following World War II, and as culturally aligned to America's post-war social conservatism. Writes Wu:

> Japanese and Chinese Americans harbored a profound interest in characterizing anew their racial image and conditions of citizenship, and they often took the lead in this regard ... [Their] self-stereotyping convinced others ... because it corroborated the nation's cultural conservatism at midcentury. Ethnic Japanese and Chinese emissaries consistently touted their putatively "Oriental" attributes, such as the predisposition to harmony and accommodation, the reverence for family and education, and unflagging industriousness to enhance their demands for equality ... Self representations of Japanese and Chinese American masculinity, femininity, and sexuality, purposely conforming to the norms of the White middle class, were crucial to the reconstruction of aliens ineligible to citizenship into admirable – albeit colored – Americans.[32]

THE END OF THE MODEL MINORITY

Critics of the model minority say the term is overly broad and damaging to Asian communities that are in need of assistance, such as refugees. Others push back against the persistent expectation that "all Asians are smart," which sets the bar far too high for most. Yet numerous Asian Americans, at least those who do not come from countries with a high refugee exodus, tend to hold up that stereotype. Asian Americans have the lowest rates of being arrested.[33] Nationally, Asian Americans tend to get higher grades and have lower rates of drug use and premarital sex. On the other hand, communities with a high number of refugees, Cambodians, Vietnamese, Laotians, and Hmong, have much lower levels of education and a much higher unemployment rate.

Additionally, as sociologists Rosalind S. Chou and Joe R. Feagin note, "Subtle and blatant stereotyping of Asians and Asian Americans still predominates in many areas of U.S. society."[34] In 2006, Adidas launched a new, limited-edition shoe, decorated with the face of an Asian character with bucktseeth, a bowl haircut, and slanted eyes as a logo, provoking a heated debate about racism.[35] That same year, Rosie O'Donnell used the expression "ching chong" to describe Chinese people talking about Danny DeVito's drunken appearance on *The View*: "The fact is that it's news all over the world. That you know, you can imagine in China it's like, 'Ching chong ... ching chong. Danny DeVito, ching chong, chong, chong, chong. Drunk.

The View. Ching chong.'"[36] In March 1997, the *National Review* released a cover titled "Manchurian Candidates," with then President Bill Clinton and First Lady Hillary Clinton as slant-eyed, bucktoothed caricatures in Mao suits and turn-of-the-twentieth-century Chinese hats."[37]

On a daily basis, Asian Americans are continually seen as outsiders, despite that many have been in the United States for generations. Notes Erika Lee, "'Where are you from?' they are continually asked. And when the answers 'Oakland,' 'New York,' or 'Chicago' do not satisfy the questioner, they are asked, 'No, where are you *really* from?' The underlying assumption behind these questions is that Asians cannot possibly be real Americans and do not belong in the United States. Instead, they are perpetual foreigners at worst, or probationary Americans at best."[38]

In her book *Forever Foreigners or Honorary Whites*, sociologist Mia Tuan relates the experience of one fourth-generation Chinese American, in her 20s, of being ridiculed because of her race, one that was compounded by being a newcomer:

> I think I was pretty conscious [of being Chinese] because of being called names and prejudice, and I used to think it's unfair, like, "Why am I this color? How come people used to make fun of you, and you didn't do anything wrong?" I mean, I think it was really sad to have to go through that adjustment, 'cause moving is just a hard enough thing, to move to a new area, when you're settled there. But then to also experience people calling you names and things. You feel very left out. I felt very left out when I was in school. I used to kinda like to hang out by myself and try to avoid certain people that I thought would make fun of me.[39]

For younger Asian Americans, the term model minority is increasingly cringe-worthy, and there has been a vocal pushback against it in recent years. In addition, there has been a growing understanding among younger Asian Americans that their perceived status in society has come at the expense of other groups. In his May 2014 commencement speech to Yale's Asian American alumni, jazz musician and Harvard professor Vijay Iyer said that to succeed in America is, "somehow, to be complicit with the idea of America, which means that at some level you've made peace with its rather ugly past."[40] That same year, this sentiment was underscored by the online forum ChangeLab, which announced a new social media campaign, #ModelMinorityMutiny, which rejected the notion of Asian Americans as the "good" minority because it perpetuates racism against Blacks.

To be viewed as Asian in America, comes with its own baggage, its own limitations. In his commencement address, Iyer describes his challenges of being accepted as a serious jazz musician:

> I've seen my work described repeatedly (mostly by White men, who tend to do most of the talking in jazz) as "mathematical," "technical," "inauthentic," "too conceptual," "jazz for nerds," "dissonant," "academic," and just last month, a "failure." Over the years a racialized component emerges in such language – basically a kind of model minority discourse that presumes that Asians have no soul and have no business trying to be artists, especially in proximity to Blackness, which is, in the White imagination, a realm of pure intuition, apparently devoid of intellect. No such critique, I should add, is typically leveled at White jazz musicians, of which there are many.[41]

In the spring of 2020, with the Covid-19 pandemic, another harmful stereotype, has emerged – one linking Chinese and other Asian Americans to the coronavirus. A May 2020 incident at a Rose Garden press briefing is illustrative. During the briefing, CBS News correspondent Weijia Jiang asked President Donald Trump why he sees coronavirus testing as a global competition when more than 80,000 Americans had died. Trump had been aggressively pushing a debunked conspiracy theory that the coronavirus originated in a Chinese lab, despite a scientific consensus that the virus was not man-made or genetically modified. "Maybe that's a question you should ask China," Trump told Jiang, who was born in China and immigrated to the United States when she was 2 years old. "Don't ask me. Ask China that question, OK?"

Trump tried to move on by calling on Kaitlan Collins, a CNN White House correspondent, but Jiang interjected. "Sir, why are you saying that to me specifically?" asked Jiang. "I'm telling you," Trump replied. "I'm not saying it specifically to anybody. I'm saying it to anybody that asks a nasty question."

"That's not a nasty question," Jiang responded. Trump then looked again to take a question from another reporter. Collins, who had let Jiang ask Trump her follow-up questions, approached the microphone. "I have two questions," Collins said. After responding that she had lost her chance, an angry Trump ended the press conference.

Trump's remarks were met with outrage by many in the Asian American community and beyond. "Asian Americans are Americans. Some of us served on active duty in the U.S. military. Some are on the frontlines fighting this pandemic as paramedics and health care workers," Ted Lieu, a congressman from California, tweeted. Representative Grace Meng of New York replied to Trump: "We are very angry at you. You use racism to disguise your lack of responsiveness and responsibility. American lives of all backgrounds have been lost. Your words have led to increased discrimination against Asian Americans which will outlast the coronavirus." In March, Representative Judy Chu of California said in a statement. "We are now watching in real time as the Republicans change the way they talk about coronavirus, intentionally stoking xenophobia in order to shift attention away from President Trump's truncated response … Trump has repeatedly labeled this pandemic as the 'Chinese virus,' and his loyal Republican followers have come to his defense in increasingly hateful terms. Their words are inciting racism and violence against Asian Americans in the United States."[42]

The coronavirus, fueled by hate speech from the White House, has indeed led to an outbreak of hate incidents directed at Asian Americans. The group STOP AAPI Hate announced that it had received over 1,700 reports of coronavirus related discrimination from Asian Americans in at least 45 states since it launched in March. About 70 percent of those incidents had a clear link to the pandemic, and about 40 percent of cases were reported to police. In California, for example, an elderly man was attacked with an iron bar, and a teenager was taken to hospital after being physically assaulted.

Other Asian Americans have reported being refused service from hotel rooms or Uber rides because of their ethnicity. One Chinese American emergency room doctor in Connecticut noted that several patients asked to be admitted to hospital because they said an Asian person had coughed near them. The same doctor also reported an incident that he experienced personally. "I had my protective equipment on, walked in and introduced myself. Once they heard my surname, they were like 'don't touch me, can I see someone else – can you just not come close to me.'"[43]

While the association of Asian Americans with the coronavirus may fade with time, the image of Asian Americans as hardworking, success-oriented, but not successful enough to usurp White men at the top of the corporate hierarchy, is the most firmly established. Still, there is hope. With an increasing share of Asian Americans being born in the United States, the model minority stereotype is beginning to unravel. It is true, as the Pew Research Center shows, that Asian Americans are the best educated and best paid racial group in the U.S. But the apparent achievement of this highly diverse group only tells part of the story. Nevertheless, the U.S. has come a long way in its representation of Asian Americans from the earlier contacts with this group more than 150 years ago.

NOTES

1. Takaki, *Strangers from a Different Shore*, 365.
2. Daniels, Roger. "Incarcerating Japanese Americans," *OAH Magazine of History*. Vol. 16, No. 3, (Spring, 2002), 19.
3. Takaki, *Strangers from a Different Shore*, 393.
4. Ibid., 397.
5. Rosenberg, Emily S. *A Date Which Will Live: Pearl Harbor in American Memory*. (Durham, North Carolina: Duke University Press Books, 2003), 32.
6. Scott Kurashige, *The Shifting Grounds of Race: Black and Japanese Americans in the Making of Multiethnic Los Angeles*. (Princeton, New Jersey: Princeton University Press, 2008), 117.
7. Takaki, *Strangers from a Different Shore*, 370.
8. Ibid.
9. Lee (Shelley Sang-Hee), 226.
10. U.S. Department of State, "Repeal of the Chinese Exclusion Act, 1943." http://2001-2009.state.gov/r/pa/ho/time/wwii/86552.htm.
11. Jensen, 278.
12. Baldoz, 199.
13. Ibid., 211.
14. Ibid.
15. Campi, Alicia J. "The McCarran-Walter Act: A Contradictory Legacy on Race, Quotas, and Ideology," Immigration Policy Center, June 2004. http://www.immigrationpolicy.org/sites/default/files/docs/Brief21%20-%20McCarran-Walter.pdf.
16. Ngai, *Impossible Subjects*, 204.
17. Wu, Ellen D. "'America's Chinese': Anti-Communism, Citizenship, and Cultural Diplomacy during the Cold War," *Pacific Historical Review*. Vol. 77, No. 3 (August 2008), 391.
18. Spickard, Paul R. ed. Lon Kurashige and Alice Yang Murray. "Marriages Between American Men and Japanese Women After World War II," in *Major Problems in Asian American History*. (Boston, MA: Houghton Mifflin Company, 2016), 341.
19. Lee (Shelley Sang-Hee), *A New History of Asian America*, 248.
20. Ibid., 251.
21. Takaki, *Strangers from a Distant Shore*, 419.
22. Frey, William H. *Diversity Explosion: How New Racial Demographics are Remaking America*. (Washington, D.C.: Brookings Institution Press, 2014), 55.

23. Takaki, *Strangers from a Distant Shore*, 420.
24. Trinh Võ, Linda. eds. Jean Yu-Wen Shen Wu and Min Song. "The Vietnamese American Experience: From Dispersion to the Development of Post-Refugee Communities," *Asian American Studies: A Reader*. (New Brunswick, NJ: Rutgers University Press, 2009), 290.
25. Ibid., 292.
26. Dhingra, Pawan and Robyn Magalit Rodriguez, *Asian America: Sociological and Interdisciplinary Perspectives*. (Cambridge, UK: Polity Press, 2014), 54.
27. Trinh Võ, 293.
28. Frey, 56.
29. "Success Story, Japanese-American Style," *The New York Times*, January 9, 1966. http://inside.sfuhs.org/dept/history/US_History_reader/Chapter14/model minority.pdf).
30. http://time.com/3475962/asian-american-diversity/.
31. "The Model Minority is a Lever of White Supremacy," March 25, 2014. http://www.racefiles.com/2014/03/25/the-model-minority-is-a-lever-of-white-supremacy/.
32. Wu, Ellen D. *The Color of Success: Asian Americans and the Origins of the Model Minority*. (Princeton, NJ: Princeton University Press, 2013), 5.
33. "The Color of Crime: Race, Crime, and Justice in America," New Century Foundation, 2005. http://2kpcwh2r7phz1nq4jj237m22.wpengine.netdna-cdn.com/wp-content/uploads/2011/12/2005-Color-of-Crime-Report.pdf.
34. Chou, Rosalind S. and Joe R. Feagin. *The Myth of the Model Minority: Asian Americans Facing Racism*. (Boulder, CO: Paradigm Publishers, 2010), 9.
35. "Asians Decry Adidas Shoe as a Misstep," *The Washington Post*, April 14, 2006. http://www.washingtonpost.com/wp-dyn/content/article/2006/04/13/AR2006 041301886.html.
36. "How 'Ching Chong' Became The Go-To Slur For Mocking East Asians," *NPR*. http://www.npr.org/sections/codeswitch/2014/07/14/330769890/how-ching-chong-became-the-go-to-slur-for-mocking-east-asians.
37. "Parsing the Politics of Caricature." https://thesocietypages.org/socimages/2009/06/19/guest-post-parsing-the-politics-of-caricature/.
38. Lee (Erika), *The Making of Asian America*, 9.
39. Tuan, Mia. *Forever Foreigners or Honorary Whites? The Asian Ethnic Experience Today*. (New Brunswick, NJ: Rutgers University Press, 1999), 82.
40. Iyer, Vijay. "Our Complicity With Excess." http://aaww.org/complicity-with-excess-vijay-iyer/.
41. Ibid.

42. Choi, David. Trump Broadly Claims Chinese-Americans Are 'VERY Angry' with China, But Some Asian-American Lawmakers Say 'We Are Very Angry at You." *Business Insider*, May 12, 2020. https://www.businessinsider.com/trump-claims-asian-americans-very-angry-with-china-2020-5.
43. "In Six Weeks, STOP AAPI HATE Receives Over 1700 Incident Reports of Verbal Harassment, Shunning and Physical Assaults," *Chinese for Affirmative Action*, May 20, 2020. https://caasf.org/press-release/in-six-weeks-stop-aapi-hate-receives-over-1700-incident-reports-of-verbal-harassment-shunning-and-physical-assaults/.

PART 5

RACE, SCIENCE, AND CLASSIFICATION

Journalist and human rights activist Emma Daly tells the story of Samuel M. Richards, who offers a class in race and ethnic relations at Pennsylvania State University and asks his students to take a DNA test. According to Richards, the tests are very popular. "Everyone wants to take the test, even students who think they are 100 percent one race or another, and almost every one of them wants to discover something, that they're one percent Asian or something. It's a badge in this multicultural world," he said, adding that every one of his White students hopes that the test tells them they are part black. "People want to identify with this pop multiracial culture. They don't want to live next to it, but they want to be part of it. It's cool." An African-American student in Richards' class was surprised to learn that he was 48 percent European. "I had no clue about [it]," he told Daly, "considering both my parents are black. So I'm half white."[1]

Genetic ancestry testing is the use of DNA information to make inferences about someone's ancestry, hundreds or thousands of years into the past. Companies offering the kits like 23andMe and Ancestry.com are growing rapidly, with millions of tests sold worldwide. The popularity of these tests is not surprising, given their widespread availability, relatively low cost, and the well-publicized results from celebrities who have been tested. Oprah Winfrey found that her profile revealed a predominance of sub-Saharan African DNA, placing her origins amongst the Kpelle people, a West African group that resides in the highlands of what is now Liberia and Guinea.[2]

Despite the high demand for DNA testing for genealogy, as well as potential uses in medicine and forensics, mixing genetics and race is tricky business. It's a business that makes some geneticists cringe, because of the questionable science – the industry has been criticized for "selling the imprimatur of science" and accused of invoking "science's power without accepting its limits."[3] According to the organization Sense About Science, "Companies use techniques from this field and sell their findings to people who want to find out about their personal history. The techniques were not designed for this. The information they give is not unique to any individual. While there are other, more specific flaws with these testing services, that fundamental point alone means that the very concept of individual genetic ancestry tests is unsound."[4]

The popularity of genetic tests is particularly ironic, given the shady history of science when it comes to racial matters. Throughout the 19th and 20th centuries, science, particularly anthropology, was used to justify White domination, and the history books are chockfull of examples of scientists using scientific inquiry to "demonstrate" the superiority of Caucasians. In the United States, eugenics – the science that deals with the improvement of hereditary qualities of a race or breed – was popularized in the 1890s, and high school and college textbooks from the 1920s through the 1940s often had chapters touting the social progress to be made from applying eugenics toward undesirable racial populations.[5]

Following the abuses of eugenics by the Nazi regime during World War II, the union of science with race caused many, within the scientific community and beyond, to shudder. Indeed, beginning in the 1950s, the general consensus among scientists was that the concept of race was nothing more than a social construct, with little if any basis in science. However, with advances in genetics and the increasing accuracy of DNA testing, the pendulum has been swinging back, and many scientists are now willing to state with certainty that race does indeed have a biological basis.

However, few scientists doubt that the way we classify people by race is a human creation at best, and an arbitrary exercise at worst. Possibly the best indication that races are constructed, rather than being a natural phenomenon with clearly delineated boundaries, are the continuous changes which the U.S. government has made, working in tandem with scientists, to develop categories used in the U.S. Census. Over the decades, the census has created racial categories, changed them, and, in some cases, eliminated them, nearly always in response to the political exigencies of the times. Sometimes, especially in recent years, census categories have been created to benefit non-Whites; however, when taking the long view, this has been the exception.

Importantly, while there is hardly consensus on what constitutes a race, there is little doubt that scientists and the federal government have a huge impact on how we classify races and, indeed, how we think about ourselves. At times there is consistency between the two. In other instances, the disconnect is gargantuan.

NOTES

1. "DNA Tells Students They Aren't Who They Thought," *The New York Times*, April 13, 2005. http://www.nytimes.com/2005/04/13/nyregion/dna-tells-students-they-arent-who-they-thought.html?_r=0.
2. "African, Asian, Native American: The Amazing Facts About Oprah Winfrey's DNA Test Result & Ethnicity," February 22, 2016. http://www.arogundade.com/oprah-winfrey-ancestral-mitochondrial-dna-testing-result-ethnicity.html.
3. Wagner, Jennifer K., Jill D. Cooper, Rene Sterling and Charmaine D. Royal. "Tilting at Windmills No Longer: A Data-driven Discussion of DTC DNA Ancestry Tests," *Genetics in Medicine*. 14, 2012, 591.
4. http://www.senseaboutscience.org/data/files/resources/119/Sense-About-Genetic-Ancestry-Testing.pdf.
5. Singleton, Marilyn M. "The 'Science' of Eugenics: America's Moral Detour," *Journal of American Physicians and Surgeons*, Vol. 19, No. 4, Winter 2014. http://www.jpands.org/vol19no4/singleton.pdf.

19

EARLY RACIAL THINKING, SOCIAL DARWINISM, AND EUGENICS

THE FIRST attempts to develop an understanding of race, as we understand the term today, were 18th century scientists, spurred on by the "discovery" of unfamiliar lands, as they sought to name, catalog, and describe the races of the world.[1] Prior to that time, knowledge of other peoples was limited to accounts by travelers and explorers who had noted the different physical characteristics of the people they encountered, and normally, what "struck their fancy" was skin color and hair texture."[2]

Among the earliest to develop a human classification system was the French physician, traveler, and philosopher, François Bernier, who in 1684 anonymously published a seven page long pamphlet that distinguished "four or five species or races": the inhabitants of Europe, North Africa, and parts of Asia (including India); Africans; Asiatic; and Lapps – he hesitated on whether to classify the indigenous people of America and the inhabitants of South Africa, into a fifth class.

Bernier wrote:

> Although in the exterior form of their bodies, and especially in their faces, men are almost all different one from the other, according to the different districts of the earth which they inhabit so that those who have been great travelers are often never mistaken in

distinguishing each nation in that way; still I have remarked that there are four or five species or races of men in particular whose difference is so remarkable that it may be properly made use of as the foundation for a new division of the earth.[3]

It was Carl Linnaeus, however, the Swedish botanist, zoologist, and physician famous for the binomial classificatory system, which identified creatures by genus and species – Linneaeus coined the term *Homo sapien* – who made a significantly more lasting impact. In the first edition of his *Systema Naturae*, published in 1735, he classified people, along with apes and sloths, as belonging to the order *Antropomorpha*, which consisted of four human varieties: *Europaeus albesc*, *Americanus rubesc*, *Asiaticus fuscus*, and *Africanus niger*.[4] In the book's tenth edition, published in 1758, he ascribed to each various physical and personality traits: *Europeaeus* was white, ruddy, and muscular; *Americanus* was red, choleric, and erect; *Asiaticus was* yellow, melancholic, and inflexible, *Africanus* was black, phlegmatic, and indulgent.[5]

In 1749, Linnaeus' contemporary, George-Louis Leclerc, the Comte de Buffon, introduced the term "race" into the lexicon of the natural sciences. Buffon believed that humans belonged to the same species and deemed the European as the original race, which "degenerated" into the other identifiable races: Laplanders or the "Polar Race," Tartars or Mongolians, southern Asiatics, Ethiopians, and Malays, the newly discovered people of the South Pacific.[6] He reasoned that climate was the "chief cause of the different colours of men," as well as culture and customs, which he speculated as having affected physical features.[7]

The most enduring of all racial accounts was that of the German physician, Johann Friedrich Blumenbach, often called the father of anthropology. In his 1775 work *On the Varieties of Mankind*, he divided humanity into five races – Europeans, Mongolians, Africans, Americans, and Malays. Blumenbach coined the term "Caucasian" because he believed the women of the Caucasus Mountains to be the most beautiful, and he considered Caucasians to be the most beautiful race and, like Buffon, the original race which degenerated because of climactic influences.

Yet unlike many thinkers of his time, Blumenbach maintained that even the African race, widely believed to be the most degenerate, could produce members that were equal to Caucasians, and he had a library of books written by Africans to prove his point.[8] He is quoted as saying, "There is no so-called savage nation known under the sun which has so much distinguished itself by such examples of perfectibility and original capacity for scientific culture, and thereby attached itself so closely to the most civilized nations of the earth, as the Negro."[9]

19 | EARLY RACIAL THINKING, SOCIAL DARWINISM, AND EUGENICS

In the 19th century, the scientific debate focused on whether human races represented an entirely different species. In the United States, discord around the issue of slavery pressed scientists to offer explanations for the causes of perceived White racial superiority. At the dawn of the Civil War, the so-called American School of Anthropology was born, at the core of which was the theory of polygenism, the belief that separate creations had resulted in a hierarchy of human races. Though it was religious heterodoxy – it conflicted with the biblical view that humans had begun from a single origin, namely Adam and Eve –, by the 1850s, polygenism, and the racism that it engendered, was firmly established as orthodox theory.[10]

The leading advocate of this type of mid-19th century race thinking was Samuel Morton, a physician and professor of anatomy at Pennsylvania Medical College, who advocated that different races were created separately in different geographic areas. In the course of his research, Morton collected hundreds of skulls from around the world and concluded that the Caucasian had the largest cranial capacity, followed by the Mongolian, the Malay, the American, and lastly, the Ethiopian. He supplemented his physical measurements with a description of the mental and moral characteristics of each race; according to Morton, Caucasians had "the highest intellectual endowments," Mongolians were "ingenious" and "imitative," Malays "active" and "predaceous," Native Americans "slow in acquiring knowledge, restless, and revengeful," and Ethiopians "joyous, flexible, and indolent."[11] Morton's work was highly recognized, and according to science historian Stephen Jay Gould, his findings were "reprinted repeatedly during the 19th century as irrefutable data on the mental worth of human beings." Gould writes, "Needless to say, they matched every good Yankee's prejudice – Whites on top, Indians in the middle, and Blacks on the bottom; and, among Whites, Teutons and Anglo-Saxons on top, Jews in the middle, and Hindus on the bottom."[12]

Josiah Nott, a disciple of Morton who owned nine slaves, believed that Blacks and Whites were separate species, and at the height of the Abolitionist movement, he spoke and published prolifically about the natural inferiority of Blacks. In 1843, Nott published an article on miscegenation entitled, "The Mulatto a Hybrid – Probable Extermination of the Two Races If the Whites and Blacks Are Allowed to Intermarry."[13] That same year, writing in the *American Journal of the Medical Sciences*, Nott, in a comparison of a Black and a White woman, observes, "Look first, upon the Caucasian female with her rose and lily skin, silky hair, Venus form, and well chiseled features – and then upon the African wench, with her black and odorous skin, wooly head and animal features – next compare their intellectual and moral qualities, and their whole anatomical structure, and say whether they do not differ as much as the swan from the goose, the horse and the ass, and the apple and pear trees."[14]

Nott's influence was profound in terms of bolstering pro-slavery forces. Three years after he co-published the book *Types of Mankind* with George Robins Giddon, the U.S. Supreme Court decided *Dred Scott v. Sandford* (1857), in which Chief Justice Roger B. Taney detailed how "far below" Negroes were from Whites "in the scale of created beings," in essence giving constitutional legitimacy to Nott's claims.[15]

Also influential was Harvard naturalist Louis Agassiz, who, during the Civil War, measured the skulls of Civil War soldiers and concluded that the significant differences he found between Blacks and Whites implied that God had created distinct human "races." Agassiz, who trained virtually all of the prominent U.S. professors of natural history during the second half of the 19th century, had his first encounter with African Americans in a hotel in Philadelphia, and their features disturbed him. When a Black waiter approached his table, he wanted to flee. Of the experience, he wrote his mother in 1846 that:

> I experienced pity at the sight of this degraded and degenerate race, and their lot inspired compassion in me in thinking that they are really men. Nonetheless, it is impossible for me to repress the feeling that they are not of the same blood as us. In seeing their Black faces with their thick lips and grimacing teeth, the wool on their head, their bent knees, their elongated hands, their large curved nails, and especially the livid color of the palm of their hands. I could not take my eyes off their face in order to tell them to stay far away. And when they advanced that hideous hand towards my plate in order to serve me, I wished I were able to depart in order to eat a piece of bread elsewhere, rather than dine with such service ... God preserve us from such a contact![16]

Medical journals from the mid-19th century are replete with references to alleged Black disabilities as a justification for slavery. According to historians Paul K. Longmore and Lauri Umansky, the most common argument of this variety was that Blacks lacked the intelligence to participate on an equal basis with Whites in society, a deficit that was often attributed to physical causes. An article on the "diseases and physical peculiarities of the negro race" in the *New Orleans Medical and Surgical Journal* explained, "It is this defective hematosis, or atmospherization of the blood, conjoined with a deficiency of cerebral matter in the cranium, and an excess of nervous matter distributed to the organs of sensation and assimilation, that is the true cause of that debasement of mind, which has rendered the people of Africa unable to take care of themselves." In 1851, Dr. Samuel Cartwright described two types of mental illness to which Blacks were especially prone. The first, *Drapetomania*, a condition that caused slaves to run away, was said to be common among slaves whose masters had "made themselves too familiar with them, treating them as equals." The second, a mental disease unique to African Americans was *Dysaesthesia Aethiopis*, commonly known as "rascality," which resulted in a desire to avoid work and cause mischief.[17]

Racial theories in the 19th century were widely circulated in the popular press, accompanied by photographs and etchings. Lectures were a common form of delivery, but they were only part of the performance. Body parts were "dissected in hospital theaters; live specimens, skeletons, and preserved organs were displayed at fairs, museums, and zoos."[18] Racial scientists traveled with ethnological charts, human skulls, and specimens, often as part of minstrel and freak shows, contributing to the representation of Black and other non-Whites as "evolutionarily degenerate and inferior beings."[19]

SOCIAL DARWINISM AND EUGENICS

The year 1859 marked a turning point in the history of scientific ideas of race, when Charles Darwin published *On the Origin of Species*, though his *Descent of Man*, published in 1871, was undeniably more impactful and would ultimately doom polygenism to the archives of science. Darwin's body of work established that races were not separate species and that there was a common ancestor for humanity, which suggested that races emerged through environmental adaptation and evolution. In other words, social and cultural differences could not be reduced to biology. "The most weighty of all the arguments against treating the races of man as distinct species," he wrote in *Descent of Man*, "is that they graduate into each other, independently in many cases … of their having intercrossed."[20] A confirmed abolitionist, Darwin believed that the gap in intelligence and moral sensibilities between civilized people and animals was great; yet, he also believed that the less civilized races fell in the middle. He wrote:

> At some future period not very distant as measured by centuries, the civilized races of man will almost certainly exterminate and replace the savage races throughout the world. At the same time the anthropomorphous apes … will no doubt be exterminated. The break between man and his nearest Allies will then be wider, for it will intervene between man in a more civilized state, as we may hope, even than the Caucasian, and some ape as low as the baboon, instead of as now between the Negro or Australian and the gorilla.[21]

Darwin saw an immense difference between Europeans and savages. When his ship, the *Beagle*, first arrived in Tierra del Fuego, Darwin reacted in disbelief at the sight of the natives who ran to meet it. He wrote in his diary, "It was without exception the most curious and interesting spectacle I had ever beheld. I could not have believed how wide was the difference, between savage and civilized man. It is wider than between a wild and domesticated animal." When a party of natives from Tierra del Fuego, Christianized and civilized in England, returned to the *Beagle*, Darwin noted that they returned to their savage ways, convincing him that primitive behavior was biologically entrenched.[22]

It was Herbert Spencer, not Darwin, who first used the term "survival of the fittest," and it was he who first applied Darwin's tenets of evolution to human society and, ultimately, racist thinking. Spencer believed strongly that races and cultures could be ranked on a scale from inferior to superior, and he emerged as the principal spokesman for Social Darwinism, a social theory based on a brutal struggle for existence that had a profound impact on anthropology, psychology, and the social sciences.[23] According to its proponents, when government and charity organizations provide public education, public health, or a minimum wage, the impact was to contribute to the artificial preservation of the weak. This logic was used to explain and perpetuate societal inequalities, which Social Darwinists believed to be the natural order of society. Writes historian Richard Hofstadter:

> Although Darwinism was not the primary source of the belligerent ideology and dogmatic racism of the late nineteenth century, it did become a new instrument in the hands of the theorists of race and struggle … The Darwinist mood sustained the belief in Anglo-Saxon racial superiority which obsessed many American thinkers in the latter half of the nineteenth century. The measure of world domination already achieved by the "race" seemed to prove it the fittest.[24]

Another leading Social Darwinist was Dr. Benjamin K. Hays, a practicing medical doctor in Oxford, North Carolina and Chairman of the Medical Society of the State of North Carolina. Hays envisioned that as the "beneficent hand" of the Southern White master and Northern liberal receded into history, the downfall and end of the Black race would be an inevitability, as "the weak has ever been dominated by the strong, and where the strong cannot control it will destroy." In a 1906 article, "Natural Selection and the Race Problem," Hays argued that "so long as [the Black] remains subservient his position is secure, and just as soon as he becomes a competitor his fate is sealed."

In Hays' view:

> The superiority of the American negro to his African brother, who is a savage and a cannibal, is due to slavery, and could have been acquired in no other way. Men who ascribe debased characteristics of the negro to slavery show a short-sightedness that is pitiable. The present attainment of the American negro has been solely the result of his close personal contact with the White Man … The negro has been domesticated, but the question is, will he ever become an integral part of Anglo-American civilization … Left to itself, a negro population lapses into barbarism.[25]

Although Spencer favored a laissez-faire approach, many of his followers in the United States preferred more active methods to ensure that the so-called lower races were kept down, thus marking the beginning in the early twentieth century of the eugenics movement, which in the words of its founder, Francis Galton, a cousin of Darwin, advocated "improving the race of a nation" by "increasing the productivity of its best stock."[26] Galton encouraged childbearing among the "fitter stock" of Western society, namely its wealthy Anglo-Saxon upper classes, and discouraged it among those considered "unfit," specifically those of the lower classes and non-Whites.[27] According to Hofstedter, early eugenicists aspired to preserve the "racial stock" as a means of "national salvation," thereby sustaining the belief that the poor are held down by biological deficiency instead of environmental conditions.[28]

During the first three decades of the 20th century, eugenicists harped on Black and White differences, as well as the deleterious influence of Southern and Eastern Europeans on American society. In his work on race and intelligence, *Race Crossing in Jamaica*, Charles Davenport, a Harvard trained biologist and the head of the American eugenics movement from the beginning of the twentieth century until the 1930s, wrote, "We have to conclude that there are racial differences in mental capacity."[29] In their text *Applied Eugenics*, Paul Popenoe and Roswell Hill Johnson wrote that "the Negro race differs greatly from the White race, mentally as well as physically, and that in many respects it may be said to be inferior when tested by the requirements of modern civilization and progress."[30] These eugenicists, according to science historian Michael Yudell, gave race an "unalterable permanence" that, as time would tell, would have a lasting legacy.[31]

In 1923, Joseph Peterson, a psychologist, published a book *The Comparative Abilities of White and Negro Children* that studied over 3,000 White and Black children from the South and concluded that White children performed better on intelligence tests. Peterson was tentative to conclude that the test was conclusive of Black inferiority and posed the question, "Is the great retardation of the Negroes due entirely to lack of opportunity or is it partly at least due to innate deficiencies?" Nonetheless, he believed that testing could lead to the "voluntary regulation of birth rate and elimination by eugenic methods within each race (or national) group of undesirable physical or mental traits, stronger in certain individuals than in others."[32] Writes sociologist Rutledge M. Dennis:

> For many White Americans, the vast coverage given test results only confirmed what they believed only ideologically: that there was a White ethnic hierarchy, and that this hierarchy, despite differences, stood atop all other races, especially the African American. Indeed, the need to believe that African Americans were inferior was a view deeply held by many of their White counterparts during the early years of the current century … Thus, the tests accomplished two purposes: first, they confirmed White superiority; and second, they strengthened the idea that Blacks should be excluded from the core culture of American society.[33]

NOTES

1. Morning, Ann. *The Nature of Race: How Scientists Think and Teach about Human Difference*. (Berkeley, CA: University of California Press, 2011), 25.
2. Lieberman, Leonard. "The Debate over Race: A Study in the Sociology of Knowledge," *Phylon*. Vol. 29, No. 2, 1968, 129.
3. Bernier, François from *Journal des Scavans*, April 24, 1684, in *The Idea of Race*, edited by Robert Bernasconi and Tommy Lee Lot (Indianapolis, IN: Hackett Publishing Co., 200), 1.
4. Eriksen, Thomas Hylland and Finn Sivert Nielsen, *A History of Anthropology*. (London, England: Pluto Press, 2013), 108.
5. Banton, Michael. *Racial Theories*. (Cambridge, MA: Cambridge University Press, 1998), 23.
6. Jackson, Jr., John P. and Nadine M. Weidman, *Race, Racism, and Science: Social Impact and Interaction*. (New Brunswick, NJ: Rutgers University Press, 2006), 18.

7. Smedley, Audrey and Brian D. Smedley, *Race in North America: Origin and Evolution of a Worldview*. (Boulder, CO: Westview Press, 2011), 219.
8. Jackson and Weidman, 20.
9. Bendyshe, Thomas and Johann Friedrich Blumenbach, *The Anthropological Treatises of Johann Friedrich Blumenbach*. (San Bernadino, CA: Ulan Press, 2012), 312.
10. Baker, Lee D. "Columbia University's Franz Boas: He Led the Undoing of Scientific Racism," *The Journal of Blacks in Higher Education*. No. 55 (Spring, 2007), 77.
11. Jackson and Weidman, 49.
12. Gould, Stephen Jay. *The Mismeasure of Man*, (New York, NY: W.W. Norton & Company, 1981), 53.
13. Nott, J.C. "The Mulatto a Hybrid – Probable Extermination of the Two Races If the Whites and Blacks Are Allowed to Intermarry," *The New England Journal of Medicine*. 29, 29–32, 1843.
14. Dewbury, Adam. eds. Regna Darnell and Frederic W. Gleach. "The American School and Scientific Racism in Early American Anthropology," *Histories of Anthropology Annual*, Vol. 3. (Lincoln, NE: University of Nebraska Press, 2007), 139.
15. Baker, Lee D. *From Savage to Negro: Anthropology and the Construction of Race, 1896–1954*. (Berkeley, CA: University of California Press, 1998), 15.
16. Gould, 45.
17. Longmore, Paul K. and Lauri Umansky, *The New Disability History: American Perspectives*. (New York, NY: New York University Press, 2001), 38.
18. Brown, Jayna. *Babylon Girls: Black Women Performers and the Shaping of the Modern*. (Durham, NC: Duke University Press Books, 2008), 77.
19. Rusert, Britt. "The Science of Freedom: Counterarchives of Racial Science on the Antebellum Stage," *African American Review*. Volume 45, No. 3 (Fall, 2012), 291.
20. Darwin, Charles. *The Descent of Man*. (New York, NY: Penguin Books, 2004). 270.
21. Ibid., 183.
22. In Jackson and Weidman, 71.
23. Mayr, Ernst. *The Growth of Biological Thought: Diversity, Evolution, and Inheritance*. (Cambridge, MA: Harvard University Press, 1982), 386.
24. Hofstadter, Richard. *Social Darwinism in American Thought*, (Boston, MA: Beacon Press, 1992), 172.
25. Hays, Benjamin K. "Natural Selection and the Race Problem," Reprinted from *The Charlotte Medical Journal*, May 1905, 8. http://docsouth.unc.edu/nc/hays/hays.html.

26. Baker, *From Savage to Negro*, 91.
27. Dennis, Rutledge M. "Social Darwinism, Scientific Racism, and the Metaphysics of Race," *The Journal of Negro Education*. Vol. 64, No. 3, 1995, 246.
28. Hofstadter, 164.
29. Yudell, Michael. eds Sheldon Krimsky and Kathleen Sloan. "How Science Embraced the Racialization of Human Populations," in *Race and the Genetic Revolution: Science, Myth, and Culture*. (New York, NY: Columbia University Press, 2011), 15.
30. Ibid., 16.
31. Ibid.
32. Yudell, Michael. *Race Unmasked: Biology and Race in the Twentieth Century*. (New York, NY: Columbia University Press, 2014), 84.
33. Dennis, 246.

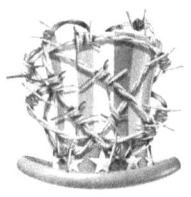

20

MODERN GENETICS AND ANTHROPOLOGY TAKE HOLD

AMONG the first to criticize the linkage of biology to race was W.E.B. Du Bois, who would later recall that he "had too often seen science made the slave of caste and race hate;" he argued that race was a concept not rooted in genetics, but rather, a social construct.[1] According to Du Bois, it was the artificial color line, forged in racism, which prevented Blacks from gaining political, economic, or social equality, ultimately denying them the "cultural and spiritual desire to be one's self without interference from others; to enjoy that anarchy of the spirit which is inevitably the goal of all consciousness." Du Bois was of the conviction that racism was a "passionate, deep-seated heritage, and as such can be moved by neither argument nor fact. Only faith in humanity will lead the world to rise above its present color prejudice." In Du Bois' view, race was a political and social conception, rooted in capitalism, and a paradox of modern democracy.[2] Writing in 1906, Du Bois declared, "The human species so shade and mingle with each other that not only indeed is it impossible to draw a color line between Black and other races, but in all physical characteristics the Negro cannot be set off by itself as absolutely different."[3]

In 1912, Franz Boas, often considered the father of American anthropology, published the paper "Changes in Bodily Form," whereby he found that in just one generation the head shapes of children of long-skulled Nordic immigrants and those of round-headed Slavic and Jewish immigrants were quickly becoming more like each other. In other words, once in an American environment, the children were physically becoming more similar, thereby casting doubt on the idea that race was something permanent and unalterable.[4] He pioneered the idea that classifying human beings by race was difficult, if not arbitrary, writing in 1928, "We have seen that from a purely biological point of view the concept of race unity breaks down. The multitude of genealogical lines, the diversity of individual and family types contained in each race is so great that no race can be considered as a unit. Furthermore, similarities between neighboring races ... are so great that individuals cannot be assigned with certainty to one group or another."[5] In 1934, Ruth Benedict, a student of Boas, published *Patterns of Culture* to combat the ideology of eugenicists and the pervasive influence of biological determinism. She wrote of human beings: "Not one item of his tribal social organization, of his language, of his local religion, is carried in his germ-cell ... Culture is not a biologically transmitted complex."[6]

Yet it was not until the 1930s and 1940s that a substantial number of geneticists, physical anthropologists, and social scientists, on both sides of the Atlantic, began to espouse that the concept of race had no biological validity. In 1935, Sir Julian Huxley, a British evolutionary biologist, joined with the Cambridge anthropologist A. C. Haddon to publish *We Europeans. A Survey of 'Racial' Problems*, which contended, "It is very desirable that the term race as applied to human groups should be dropped from the vocabulary of science."[7]

By the late 1930s, a number of natural scientists were developing what was to be called the "modern synthesis" theory of evolution, which combined Darwinism with information gained from genetics and stipulated that "population," as opposed to physical typology, was the proper unit of study for studying human differences. According to the population perspective, topologists mistakenly homogenize biological differences within human groups and exaggerate the differences between them, as opposed to recognizing that biological variability cannot be so discretely packaged.[8] In the words of Ernst Mayr, one of the 20th century's leading evolutionary biologists:

> The typologist stresses that every representative of a race has the typical characteristics of that race and differs from all representatives of all other races by the characteristics "typical" for the given race. Essentially, it asserts that every representative of a race conforms to the type and is separated from the representatives of any other race by a distinct gap. The populationist also recognizes races but in totally different terms. Race for him is based on the simple fact that no two individuals are the same in sexually reproducing

organisms and that consequently no two aggregates of individuals can be the same. If the average difference between two groups of individuals is sufficiently great to be recognizable on sight, we refer to such groups of individuals as different races.[9]

Notable among populationists was geneticist Theodosius Dobzhansky, who in 1937 published the landmark book, *Genetics and the Origin of Species*, in which he concluded that the number of human races was variable, depending upon what traits were being examined. Dobzhansky, while conceding that human differences are real, concluded that the way we choose to organize these differences is an arbitrary decision and not one that reflects an underlying evolutionary hierarchy.[10] According to George W. Stocking, Jr., an eminent historian of anthropology, "In the long run, it was Boasian anthropology – rather than the racialist writers associated with the eugenics movements – which was able to speak to Americans as the voice of science on all matters of race culture and evolution."[11]

With the rise of Nazism in Germany, pseudoscientific works on race theory proliferated, and there was a concerted attempt among scientists to counter Nazi dogma. In 1937, Boas organized a faculty group at Columbia University and founded the University Federation for Democracy and Intellectual Freedom, which argued that the Nazi regime was propagating a misuse of the term "race" and that science should be freed from this type of political distortion. Also influential during the war was anthropologist Ashley Montagu, who, during the 1940s, published a series of works that further questioned the validity of race as a biological concept, including *Man's Most Dangerous Myth: The Fallacy of Race*, written in 1945, which concluded that a proper understanding of population genetics actually proved the concept of race had no validity. Wrote Montagu:

> The idea of "race" represents one of the greatest errors, if not the greatest error, of our time, and the most tragic. What "race" is everyone seems to know, and is only too eager to tell. All but a very few individuals take it completely for granted that scientists have established the "facts" about "race" and that they have long ago recognized and classified the "races" of mankind. Scientists do little to discourage this view, and, indeed, many of them are quite as deluded as most laymen are about the subject.[12]

In a later passage, he compares the lumping of people into races to the making of an omelet, which he argued is scientifically without meaning:

> The process of averaging the characters of a given group, of knocking the individuals together, giving them a good stirring, and then serving the resulting omelette as a "race" is essentially the anthropological process of race-making. It may be good cooking, but it is not science, since it serves to confuse rather than to clarify. It is this omelette conception of "race" which is so meaningless – meaningless because it is inapplicable to anything real.[13]

With the end of World War II, the revelation of Nazi atrocities conducted in the name of racial purity combined with growing concern about the horrendous treatment of African Americans in the United States instilled a sense of urgency to divorce science from any semblance of racism. Additionally, with the advent of the Cold War, Soviet accusations that the economic success of the United States depended upon the exploitation of colonized people, created the political need to reshape discussions of race.[14]

It was in this context that a 1948 resolution by the United Nations Social and Economic Council called upon the United Nations Educational, Scientific and Cultural Organization (UNESCO) to consider "proposing and recommending the general adoption of a program of dissemination of scientific facts designed to bring about the disappearance of that which is commonly called race prejudice." UNESCO issued a series of statements about race, signed by an impressive collection of the leading sociologists, psychologists, biologists, and anthropologists, beginning in 1950, in an attempt to clarify what was scientifically known and to morally condemn racism. The motivations of UNESCO are clearly articulated in the introduction to its 1952 document, "The Race Concept":

> The long-standing confusion between race and culture has produced fertile soil for the development of racism, at once a creed and an emotional attitude. The virulence with which this ideology has made its appearance during the present century is one of the strangest and most disturbing phenomena of the great revolution of our time. Racial doctrine is the outcome of a fundamentally anti-rational system of thought and is in glaring conflict with the whole humanist tradition of our civilization. It sets at naught everything that UNESCO stands for and endeavors to defend.[15]

The significance of the UNESCO statements was more than a condemnation of racism. Its impact lay in the consensus of a wide array of respected scientists who denied the scientific basis of race, affirming its status as a mere social construct. The 1950 statement, officially authored by Montagu, declared:

> Scientists have reached general agreement in recognizing that mankind is one: that all men belong to the same species, *Homo sapiens*. It is further generally agreed among scientists that all men are probably derived from the same common stock; and that such differences as exist between different groups of mankind are due to the operation of evolutionary factors of differentiation. Historical and sociological studies support the view that genetic differences are not of importance in determining the social and cultural differences between different groups of *Homo sapiens*, and that the social and cultural changes in different groups have, in the main, been independent of changes in inborn constitution.[16]

However, the 1950 statement went beyond what many scientists, particularly the more biologically oriented, were willing to concede – they remained disinclined to go so far as to declare that biological differences between races were purely environmental. A second committee was formed, which issued a revised statement in 1951, one that was a significant retreat from the absolutism of the prior year, and it allowed that traits related to intellect and emotion could indeed vary based on genetic differences between races. The report stated:

> It is possible, though not proved, that some types of innate capacity for intellectual and emotional responses are commoner in one human group than another, but it is certain that, within a single group, innate capacities vary as much as, if not more than, they do between different groups.[17]

The revised statement was a significant accommodation between those who wanted to de-emphasize the importance of racial differences and those who wanted to hold onto the belief that racial differences did exist. For instance, Kenneth Mather, a geneticist at the University of Birmingham, declared that the case against Nazi race theory was not strengthened by "playing down the possibility of statistical differences in … the mental capacities of different human groups." Sir Ronald Fisher, a founding father of modern statistics, argued that "human groups differ profoundly in their innate capacity for intellectual development," presenting the world with the problem of "learning to share the resources of this planet amicably with persons of materially different nature."[18] Yet during the 1950s, "race science" had fallen irrevocably into disrepute, and mainstream anthropology embraced the evolutionary synthesis. Writes historian Nancy Stepan: "The old, classificatory biology of race, with its roots in anatomy and morphology, was replaced by a new evolutionary biology of man, with its roots in genetics, ecology and evolution."[19]

THE PENDULUM SWINGS BACK AND FORTH

Old ideas die hard, and the belief in racial hierarchies, even in scientific circles, was no exemption.[20] A noteworthy example is Carleton S. Coon, a Harvard-trained anthropologist who held a professorship at the university until 1948, when he moved to the University of Pennsylvania. Coon spent much of his career fighting what he viewed as a battle with Boas and the emerging field of cultural anthropology, and he was a staunch advocate of classifying humans into races according to their morphological characteristics. In 1962, he published his most famous work, *The Origin of Races*, in which he argued that *Homo sapiens* evolved from *Homo erectus* by making five evolutionary jumps, corresponding to what he viewed as the five modern races. In the book, which the man who revitalized the Ku Klux Klan in the 1970s, David Duke, described as the "book that would change my life," Coon wrote, "My thesis is, in essence, that at the beginning of our record, over half a million years ago, man was a single species, *Homo erectus*, perhaps already divided into five geographic races or subspecies. *Homo erectus* then evolved into *Homo sapiens* not once but five times, as each subspecies, living in its own territory, passed a critical threshold from a more brutal to a more sapient state."[21] Significantly, Coon contended that "Caucasoids" and "Mongoloids" crossed this threshold much earlier than Africans ("Negroids" and "Capoids") and Australian aborigines ("Australoids"), and his argument was used by segregationists as proof that African Americans were "junior" to White Americans and thereby unfit for full participation in American society.[22]

When the *Origin of Races* was released, Coon had already been waging a public battle concerning the authority of science to "make pronouncements" about race, and in particular, civil rights, a battle that intensified in September 1957 when Arkansas Governor Orval Faubus ordered the National Guard to prevent the Federal Court ordered integration of Central High School in Little Rock. At the forefront of the battle was Coon's purported cousin, Carleton Putnam, an ardent segregationist and White supremacist, with whom Coon was in constant communication.

Putnam, who made a fortune when the airline he founded merged to form Delta Airlines, wrote a well-circulated letter to President Eisenhower, which eventually made it into numerous publications, including *The New York Times*, which argued,

"Any man with two eyes in his head can observe a Negro settlement in the Congo, can study the pure-blooded African in his native habitat as he exists when left on his own resources, can compare this settlement with London or Paris, and can draw his own conclusions, regarding relative levels of character and intelligence – or that combination of character and intelligence which is civilization." In March 1959, Putnam wrote an open letter to Attorney General William Rogers to protest the Supreme Court's *Brown v. The Board of Education* decision, which he argued reflected "a point of view rooted in what I may call modern equalitarian anthropology – a school which holds that all races are currently equal in their capacity for culture, and that existing inequalities of status are due solely to inequalities of opportunity." Putnam went on to claim, "Two generations of Americans have been victimized by a pseudo-scientific hoax in this field [of anthropology and] that this hoax is part of an equalitarian propaganda typical of the left-wing overdrift of our times."[23]

The relationship between Putnam and Coon was no secret in 1962, and the social implications of Coon's *The Origin of Races* were not lost among the new breed of anthropologists who rejected essentialist approaches to race as outdated and dangerous. The American Anthropological Association (AAA) took decisive action to discredit the book, and the organization's president, Sherry Washburn, delivered a scathing denunciation at the AAA Annual Meeting in November 1962; both the AAA and the American Association of Physical Anthropologists (AAPA) issued statements on race to counter Coon's arguments. In 1966, Margaret Mead, a student of both Boas and Benedict, and Dobzhansky organized an American Association for the Advancement of Science symposium, representing an alliance between Boasian cultural anthropologists, evolutionary biologists, geneticists, psychologists, and sociologists, with the objective of delivering a scientific response against a popular racism based on "misinformation" and "evil myths" about race. With the Civil Rights Movement in full force and scientists rising to the occasion, a science of race was becoming as "irrelevant as alchemy or the geocentric solar system."[24]

Spurred on by Coon, by the mid-1960s, with few exceptions, the scientific community had become vocally opposed to any claims linking race and intelligence to genetics, with many "skeptical of the race concept itself."[25] In 1968, George W. Stocking, Jr. began his book *Race, Culture and Evolution* by writing, "I am inclined to view 'race' as a characteristically 19th-century phenomenon."[26]

This happened at a time when Black intellectuals were, following the legacy handed down by W.E.B. Dubois, articulating race as a political construct that had served to rationalize White domination of Blacks. In 1952, the Martinique-born, French educated psychiatrist, philosopher, and revolutionary, Frantz Fanon, published *Black Skins, White Masks*, which presented race as historically constructed by Whites, rather than being biologically innate. In the eyes of Fanon, the Black feels himself "sealed into a crushing objecthood" beneath the White gaze, and as a consequence, "I did not create meaning for myself; the meaning was already there, waiting."[27] A decade later, in *The Fire Next Time*, James Baldwin wrote, "Color is not a human or a personal reality; it is a political reality. But this is a distinction so extremely hard to make that the West has not been able to make it yet ... For the sake of one's children, in order to minimize the bill that they must pay, one must be careful not to take refuge in any delusion – and the value placed on the color of the skin is always and everywhere and forever a delusion."[28]

Still, the voice of racism in the 1960s could hardly be quelled. In November 1965, *U.S. News & World Report* ran an interview with Stanford professor and Nobel Prize–winning physicist William Shockley under the headline: "Is Quality of U.S. Population Declining?" In the interview, Shockley stated:

> If you look at the median Negro IQ, it almost always turns out not to be as good as that of the median White IQ. At least, this is so in the U.S. How much of this is genetic in origin? How much is environmental? ... Actually, what I worry about with Whites and Negroes alike is this: Is there an imbalance in the reproduction of inferior and superior strains? Does the reproduction tend to be most heavy among those we would least like to employ – the ones who would do least well in school? There are eminent Negroes whom we are proud of in every way, but are they the ones who have large families? What is happening to the total numbers? This we do not know.[29]

The following year, Shockley called upon the National Academy of Sciences to "foster research on the effects of heredity, including race, on human behavior." In his letter, Shockley wrote: "I evaluate the marrow of the city's slum problem to be our uncertainty about its genetic aspects and our fear to admit ignorance and to search openly for relevant facts." In 1967, during a speech at Michigan State University, he warned that "unrealistic hope for speeding the Negro's struggle for equality before the real causes of his disadvantages are known may unwittingly inflict untold human suffering on the Negroes themselves."[30]

In 1969, Arthur R. Jensen, a psychologist from the University of California, Berkeley, sparked a media firestorm when he published an article, "How Much Can We Boost IQ and Scholastic Achievement?" in the *Harvard Educational Review*. In the first line, Jensen declared, "Compensatory education has been tried and it apparently has failed," referring to the programs of President Johnson's War on Poverty that offered special educational benefits to poor schools. He continued, "The idea that the lower average intelligence and scholastic performance of Negroes, could involve not only environmental but also genetic factors, has indeed been strongly denounced. But it has been neither contradicted nor discredited by evidence." Jensen went on to argue that children with low IQ scores are both genetically and environmentally challenged, so efforts to raise their IQ through just education are doomed.[31] Advocates of segregation used Jensen's data to fight the desegregation suits filed against many school districts in the South.[32]

According to sociologists Michael Omi and Howard Winant, in the social upheavals of the 1960s, a "great transformation" occurred in terms of "racial awareness" and "racial meaning," in no small part due to the Civil Rights and Black Power Movements.[33] During that time, academics began to take a long hard look at their respective disciplines and call for changes in the way that they were addressing race. In the early 1970s, sociologist Joyce A. Ladner declared the "death of White sociology" and was critical of sociological research done in the name of objectivity and value-neutrality that confirmed and perpetuated racist assumptions about African Americans. "Mainstream sociology, in this regard, reflects the ideology of the larger society, which has always excluded Black lifestyles, values, behavior, attitudes, and so forth from the body of data that is used to define, describe, conceptualize, and theorize about the structure and functions of American society," Ladner wrote.[34] Ladner and other social scientists argued that sociology and other social sciences are not value-free or objective, and they attempted to lay the groundwork for a new Black sociology, one created from the lived experiences and perspectives of Black people, using theories and concepts organic to the Black experience.[35]

A significant breakthrough occurred in the field of genetics in 1972 when Richard Lewontin, an evolutionary biologist at the University of Chicago, published a paper, "The Apportionment of Human Diversity," which confirmed and quantified what the second UNESCO statement had posited 20 years earlier, namely that the genetic variation within populations is significantly greater than the variation between populations. Specifically, after studying variation in 17 genes, Lewontin found that only 6.3 percent of the variation could be attributed to racial membership; conversely, 85.4 percent of the variation occurred within local populations. In other words, Lewontin confirmed that there are more genetic differences between French and Vietnamese than between French and Germans, but both differences are dwarfed by the variation among the French alone.[36] As Lewontin put it, "If the holocaust comes and a small tribe deep in the New Guinea forests are the only survivors, almost all the genetic variation now expressed among the innumerable groups of our five billion people will be preserved."[37]

Based on his results, Lewontin concluded that the perception that there are large differences between human races is "biased" and that "human racial classification is of no social value and is positively destructive of social and human relations ... [No] justification can be offered for its continuance."[38] His findings were later corroborated and extended in 2002, in a major study published in the periodical *Science*, which found that 93 to 95 percent of genetic diversity was found within populations and that half of the 4,199 of the alleles, or different gene forms, that they studied were found in all major regions of the world – only 7.4 percent were exclusive to one region.[39]

Despite that Lewontin had provided a genetic basis for discrediting the concept of race, or perhaps as a result of it, during the 1970s, there was a precipitous rise in genetic explanations for human behavior.[40] For instance, sociologist Troy Duster found that in the mid- to late-1970s, both the popular media and scientific journals published an explosion of articles that staked a renewed claim to the genetic explanation of matters that the prior decade had "laid to rest" as social and environmental. Duster reviewed the *Readers Guide to Periodical Literature* and found that between 1976 and 1982, there was an increase of 231 percent in articles that attempted to use genetics to explain crime, mental illness, intelligence, and alcoholism. Between 1983 and 1988, articles that attributed crime to genetics appeared more than four times as frequently as they had a decade earlier. In 1995, sociologists Dorothy Nelkin and M. Susan Lindee argued that since the 1970s, DNA in popular culture had begun to function as the "secular equivalent of the Christian soul."[41]

The argument over genetics again erupted in 1975, when Edward O. Wilson published the book *Sociobiology: The New Synthesis*. Wilson defined Sociobiology as "the systematic study of the biological basis of all forms of social behavior ... in all kinds of organisms, including humans."[42] While most of the book focused on animals – Wilson was an entomologist –, it attempted to explain human behavior, as well as the behavior of all social animals, in terms of propagating the genes of kin groups, and Wilson believed that human traits, such as male dominance, ethnocentrism and xenophobia, were inherited from our hunter-gatherer ancestors and are programmed into our DNA. According to what Wilson called the "xenophobic principle," a "newcomer is a threat to the status of every animal in the group, and he is treated accordingly. Cooperative behavior reaches a peak among the insiders when repelling such an intruder." He argued that for humans:

> Outsiders are almost always a source of tension. If they pose a physical threat, especially to territorial integrity, they loom in our vision

as an evil, monolithic force, whom we reduce to subhuman status, so that they can be treated without conscience. They are the gooks, the wogs, the krauts, the commies – not like us, another subspecies surely, a force remorselessly dedicated to our destruction, who must be met with equal ruthlessness if we are to survive.[43]

Wilson's book was greeted with an avalanche of criticism. Lewontin, a colleague of Wilson at Harvard, issued a 5,000-word position paper in which he stated, "It is not surprising that the model of society that turns out to be natural, just, and unchangeable bears a remarkable resemblance to the institutions of modern industrial society, since the ideologues who produced these models are themselves privileged members of just such societies."[44] Members of the Sociobiology Study Group (SSG) of Science for the People, published a letter in *The New York Review of Books* and a longer article in the academic journal *BioScience*, describing Sociobiology as "the latest attempt to reinvigorate" theories which in the past have "provided an important basis for the enactment of sterilization laws and restrictive immigration laws by the United States between 1910 and 1930 and also for the eugenics policies which led to the establishment of gas chambers in Nazi Germany."[45] Three years later, Wilson was assaulted during a speech at the annual meeting of the American Association for the Advancement of Science when demonstrators affiliated with the International Committee Against Racism carried anti-Sociobiology placards (at least one displaying a swastika), dumped a pitcher of ice water on Wilson's head, and chanted "Wilson, you're all wet!" The episode "may be the only occasion in recent American history," Wilson wrote, "on which a scientist was physically attacked, however mildly, simply for the expression of an idea."[46]

By the 1980s, however, the sands were again shifting toward a consensus, at least among intellectuals, that race was to be confined to the realm of culture, not biology. As Henry Louis Gates wrote in 1986, "Race, as a meaningful criterion within the biological sciences, has long been recognized to be a fiction. When we speak of 'the White race,' 'the Jewish race' or the 'Aryan race,' we speak in biological misnomers, and more generally, in metaphors."[47] A study of college textbooks written for introductory biological anthropology courses found that among the 22 textbooks published between 1975 and 1979, only five continued to present the view that races exist and ten rejected the concept outright. In a 1985 survey of anthropologists, when asked to indicate agreement or disagreement with the statement "There are biological races within the species *Homo sapiens*," 50 percent of biological anthropologists agreed, and 42 percent disagreed; however, among cultural anthropologists, only 31 percent agreed and 52 percent disagreed.[48]

Highly influential was work emanating from the field of sociology, such as the book *The Declining Significance of Race*, published by sociologist William Julius Wilson in 1978. Wilson argued that "structure trumps culture," that factors holding Blacks back – unemployment, lower levels of education, and the social consequences of living in racially segregated neighborhoods – are less rooted in White racism or any kind of cultural deficiency on the part of Blacks. as many conservatives claimed, and more due to structural factors, such as the imposed segregation of Blacks into urban ghettos, the loss of manufacturing jobs in cities, the suburbanization of the middle class, the detrimental effects of globalization, and political neglect. The consequence, he wrote in his 2009 book with a decidedly less edgy title, *More Than Just Race*, was that "the least upwardly mobile individuals in society – mainly low income people of color – are left behind in neighborhoods with high concentrations of poverty and deteriorating physical conditions."[49]

In part due to its controversial title, *The Declining Significance of Race* evoked a flood of popular criticism, though it was originally intended for a strictly academic audience, prompting psychologist and civil rights activist Kenneth Clark to write, "The belief that class has now supplanted race in the life chances of American Blacks remains a pitiful delusion. This is a dangerous delusion because it drains energy and diverts attention from the stark fact that racial injustices perpetrated against all Blacks – middle-class and under-classed Blacks – remains the unfinished business of American democracy."[50]

In another landmark book, *American Apartheid: Segregation and the Making of the Underclass*, written in 1993, sociologists Douglas S. Massey and Nancy A. Denton argued that racial residential segregation into urban ghettos was the chief culprit behind racial inequality in the United States. They write, "Residential segregation is not a neutral fact; it systematically undermines the social and economic well-being of Blacks in the United States. Because of racial segregation, a significant share of Black America is condemned to experience a social environment where poverty and joblessness are the norm, where a majority of children are born out of wedlock, where most families are on welfare, where educational failure prevails, and where social and physical deterioration abound."[51] Massey and Denton argued that as Blacks adapt to this unforgiving environment of geographic isolation, they evolve attitudes and behaviors leading to their further marginalization, undermining their chances of success in mainstream American society.

The shift in intellectual thinking about race is perhaps best illustrated by the extremely influential book, *Racial Formation in the United States*, first published in 1986 and written by sociologists Michael Omi and Howard Winant, in which they observed that as a result of the work of intellectuals and social activists, "we have now reached the point of fairly general agreement that race is not a biological given but rather a socially constructed way of differentiating human beings." Omi and Winant defined racial formation as the process by which social, economic, and political forces determine racial categories, which, in turn, are shaped by racial meaning; in a subsequent edition, published in 1994, they famously defined it as "the sociohistorical process by which racial categories are created, inhabited, transformed, and destroyed."[52] Arguing that the seemingly "obvious," "natural," and "commonsense" qualities of race, which we all experience, provide evidence of the effectiveness of constructed racial meanings, Omi and Winant write:

> One of the first things we notice about people when we meet them (along with their sex) is their race. We utilize race to provide clues about who a person is. This fact is made painfully obvious when we encounter someone whom we cannot conveniently racially categorize – someone who is, for example, racially "mixed" or of an ethnic/racial group with which we are not familiar. Such an encounter becomes a source of discomfort and momentarily a crisis of racial meaning.
>
> Comments such as, "Funny, you don't look Black," betray an underlying image of what Black should be. We expect people to act out their apparent racial identities; indeed we become disoriented when they do not. The Black banker harassed by police while walking in casual clothes through his own well-off neighborhood, the Latino or White kid rapping in perfect Afro patois, the unending faux pas committed by Whites who assume that non-Whites they encounter are servants or tradespeople, the belief that non-White colleagues are less qualified persons hired to fulfill affirmative action guidelines, indeed the whole gamut of racial stereotypes – that "White men can't jump," that Asians can't dance, etc., etc. – all testify to the way a racialized social structure shapes racial experience and conditions meaning.[53]

Bolstered by sociologists, the idea that race was something intrinsic to one's DNA was becoming to seem archaic at best, but more frequently, blatantly racist. However, there remained doggedness in the determination by some in the scientific community to impose a racial hierarchy on human beings that was preordained by biology. In October 1994, Richard Herrnstein, a psychologist, and Charles Murray, a political scientist, released *The Bell Curve: Intelligence and Class Structure in American Life*, which argued that low IQ, not racism, was responsible for the lower social status of minorities, particularly African Americans, and they urged scholars to avoid focusing on discrimination when discussing social problems. According to the authors:

> The evidence presented here should give everyone who writes and talks about ethnic inequalities reason to avoid flamboyant rhetoric about ethnic oppression. Racial and ethnic differences in this country are seen in a new light when cognitive ability is added to the picture. Awareness of these relationships is an essential first step to construct an equitable America.[54]

According to Herrnstein and Murray, the United States was witnessing the rise of a cognitive elite of people intermarrying and passing on their higher IQs to their children, while an underclass of unemployed men and welfare mothers passed on genetic disadvantages. The result, they predicted, would be a widening gap and, ultimately, the rise of a new conservatism, which would be "along Latin American lines, where to be conservative has often meant doing whatever is necessary to preserve the mansions on the hills from the menace of the slums below."[55] Finally, they postulated, "racism will reemerge in a new and virulent form," ultimately resulting in a "custodial state":

> We have in mind a high-tech and more lavish version of the Indian reservation for some substantial minority of the nation's population, while the rest of America tries to go about its business. In its less benign forms, the solutions will become more and more totalitarian. Benign or otherwise, "going about its business" in the old sense will not be possible. It is difficult to imagine the United States preserving its heritage of individualism, equal rights before the law, free people running their own lives, once it is accepted that a significant part of the population must be made permanent wards of the state.[56]

A remarkable success at the time, *The Bell Curve* debuted as number five on the *Publishers Weekly* bestseller list, where it spent 12 weeks; it spent 15 weeks on *The New York Times* bestseller list. Despite receiving a critical pummeling, the book sold more than 400,000 copies in less than six months.[57]

Co-author Charles Murray denies *The Bell Curve* is primarily about race – Herrnstein died shortly before the book was released – since only two of its

22 chapters center on the issue. Interestingly, he wrote in his proposal for an earlier book, *Losing Ground,* a book which argues that social programs tend to increase poverty by creating incentives to stay on welfare, that "a huge number of well-meaning Whites fear that they are closet racists, and this book tells them they are not. It's going to make them feel better about things they already think but do not know how to say."[58]

In response to the frenzy in the media and popular culture set off by *The Bell Curve*, the Board of Scientific Affairs of the American Psychological Association (APA) concluded that "there was urgent need for an authoritative report" and established a task force, which released its report in August 1995. Specifically citing Jensen's article, the report concluded, "It is sometimes suggested that the Black/White differential in psychometric intelligence is partly due to genetic differences. There is not much direct evidence on this point, but what there is fails to support the genetic hypothesis."[59] Rather, going much further, the report argued that economics was equally inadequate in accounting for achievement gaps:

> To imagine that any simple income and education based index can adequately describe the situation of African Americans is to ignore important categories of experience. The sense of belonging to a group with a distinctive culture, one that has long been the target of oppression, and the awareness or anticipation of racial discrimination are profound personal experiences, not just aspects of socio-economic status. Some of these more deeply rooted differences are addressed by other hypotheses based on caste and culture.[60]

The report discussed other compelling explanations for disparities in results observed in IQ tests. It referenced the work of Nigerian anthropologist John Ogbu, who in his 1978 book *Minority Education and Caste: The American System in Cross-Cultural Perspective*, argued that the children of "caste-like minorities" lack "effort optimism," the conviction that hard work and commitment will be rewarded. As a result, they reject certain behaviors, such as academic achievement or other forms of "acting white," that are seen as characteristic of the dominant group. The APA's report also discussed the work of A. Wade Boykin, one of its authors, which posited that the combination of "constriction and competition" that American schools demand of their pupils conflicts with themes deeply embedded in African American culture. These themes, among them spirituality, harmony, affect, expressive individualism, communalism, and orality, combined with American pedagogical values, lead to many African American children becoming alienated from the educational system. According to Boykin:

> When children are ordered to do their own work, arrive at their own individual answers, work only with their own materials, they are being sent cultural messages. When children come to believe that getting up and moving about the classroom is inappropriate, they are being sent powerful cultural messages. When children come to confine their "learning" to consistently bracketed time periods, when they are consistently prompted to tell what they know and not how they feel, when they are led to believe that they are completely responsible for their own success and failure, when they are required to consistently put forth considerable effort for effort's sake on tedious and personally irrelevant tasks ... then they are pervasively having cultural values imposed on them.[61]

Three years after the APA's report, in 1998, the American Anthropological Association issued a statement that the concept of race is merely "a worldview, a body of prejudgments that distorts our ideas about human differences and group behavior. Essentially, the position taken was that racial beliefs constitute myths about the diversity in the human species and about the abilities and behavior of people homogenized into 'racial' categories." Noting in its first paragraph that about 94 percent of all physical variation lies within, and not between, so-called racial groups, the report stated:

> How people have been accepted and treated within the context of a given society or culture has a direct impact on how they perform in that society. The "racial" worldview was invented to assign some groups to perpetual low status, while others were permitted access to privilege, power, and wealth. The tragedy in the United States has been that the policies and practices stemming from this worldview succeeded all too well in constructing unequal populations among Europeans, Native Americans, and peoples of African descent.[62]

NOTES

1. Du Bois, W.E.B. *Dusk of Dawn: An Essay Toward An Autobiography of a Race Concept*. (Oxford, England: Oxford University Press, 2014), 50.

2. Baker, *From Savage to Negro*, 111.
3. Du bois, W.E.B. *Health and Physique of the Negro American.* (Atlanta, GA: The Atlanta University Press, 1906), 16.
4. Boas, Franz. "Changes in the Bodily Form of Descendants of Immigrants," *American Anthropologist*. Vol. 14, No. 3 (Jul. – Sep., 1912).
5. Boas, Franz. *Anthropology in Modern Life.* (New York, NY: Routledge Revivals, 2013), 62.
6. Benedict, Ruth. *Patterns of Culture.* (Boston, MA: Houghton Mifflin Harcourt, 1973), 12.
7. Michael Banton, *Racial Theories.* (Cambridge, MA: Cambridge University Press, 1998), 102.
8. Gannett, Lisa. "Racism and Human Genome Diversity Research: The Ethical Limits of 'Population Thinking,'" *Philosophy of Science*. Vol. 68, No. 3, 2001, 480.
9. Mayr, Ernst. *Evolution and the Diversity of Life: Selected Essays.* (Cambridge, MA: Belknap Press, 1997), 28.
10. Yudell, "How Science Embraced the Racialization of Human Populations," 18.
11. Stocking, Jr., George W. *Race, Culture, and Evolution: Essays in the History of Anthropology.* (Chicago, IL: University of Chicago Press, 1982). 307.
12. Montague, M.F. Ashley. *Man's Most Dangerous Myth: The Fallacy of Race.* (New York, NY: Columbian University, 1945), 1.
13. Ibid., 34.
14. Reardon, Jenny. *Race to the Finish: Identity and Governance in an Age of Genomics.* (Princeton, NJ: Princeton University Press, 2004), 24.
15. UNESCO, "The Race Concept," 1952. http://docslide.us/documents/unesco-the-race-concept-1952.html.
16. UNESCO, "Statement on Race," July 1950. http://unesdoc.unesco.org/images/0012/001229/122962eo.pdf.
17. UNESCO, "Statement on Race," November 1951. http://unesdoc.unesco.org/images/0017/001789/178908eb.pdf.
18. Reardon, 30.
19. Stepan, Nancy. *The Idea of Race in Science: Great Britain, 1800–1960.* (North Haven, CT: Archon, 1982), 173.
20. Jackson, John P. and Nadine M. Weidman, *Race, Racism, and Science: Social Impact and Interaction.* (New Brunswick, NJ: Rutgers University Press, 2005), 200.
21. Coon, Carleton S. *Origin of the Races.* (New York, NY: Alfred A. Knopf, Inc., 1962), 657.
22. Jackson Jr., John P. "In Ways Unacademical": The Reception of Carleton S. Coon's *The Origin of Races*," *Journal of the History of Biology*. Vol. 34, 2001, 247.

23. Cited in John P. Jackson Jr., *Science for Segregation: Race, Law, and the Case against Brown v. Board of Education.* (New York, NY: NYU Press, 2005), 96.
24. Marks, Jonathan M. *Human Biodiversity: Genes, Race, and History.* (New Brunswick, NJ: Transaction Publishers, 1995), 58.
25. Caspari, Rachel. "From Types to Populations: A Century of Race, Physical Anthropology, and the American Anthropological Association," *American Anthropologist.* Vol. 105, No. 1, Mar. 2003, 66.
26. Reardon, Jenny. *Race to the Finish: Identity and Governance in an Age of Genomics.* (Princeton, NJ: Princeton University Press, 2009), 20.
27. Fanon, Frantz. *Black Skin, White Masks.* (New York, NY: Grove Press, 2008), 90, 113.
28. Baldwin, James. *The Fire Next Time.* (New York, NY: Vintage, 1992), 113.
29. "Is Quality of U.S. Population Declining?" *U.S. News & World Report*, November 22, 1965. https://profiles.nlm.nih.gov/ps/access/BBAOIK.pdf.
30. Yudell, *Race Unmasked*, 176.
31. Shurkin, Joel N. *Broken Genius: The Rise and Fall of William Shockley, Creator of the Electronic Age.* (Basingstoke, UK: Palgrave Macmillan, 2006), 217.
32. Dennis, 247.
33. Omi, Michael and Howard Winant. *Racial Formation in the United States: From the 1960s to the 1990s.* (New York, NY: Routledge, 1994), 100.
34. Ladner, Joyce A. *The Death of White Sociology: Essays on Race and Culture.* (Baltimore, MD: Black Classic Press, 1998), xxiii.
35. Hunter, Margaret. "Rethinking Epistemology, Methodology, and Racism: Or, Is White Sociology Really Dead," *Race & Society.* Vol. 5, 2002, 121.
36. Shiao, Jiannbin Lee, Thomas Bode, Amber Beyer, and Daniel Selvig, "The Genomic Challenge to the Social Construction of Race," *Sociological Theory.* Vol. 30, No. 2, June 2012, 569.
37. Gould, 303.
38. Tattersall, Ian and Rob DeSalle. *Race? Debunking a Scientific Myth.* (College Station, TX: Texas A&M University Press, 2011), 46.
39. Baum, Bruce. *The Rise and Fall of the Caucasian Race: A Political History of Racial Identity.* (New York, NY: New York University Press, 2006), 2010.
40. Yudell, *Race Unmasked*, 184.
41. Nelkin, Dorothy and M. Susan Lindee. *The DNA Mystique: The Gene As a Cultural Icon.* (New York, NY: W. H. Freeman & Company, 1995), 2.
42. Wilson, Edward O. *Sociobiology: The New Synthesis.* (Cambridge, MA: Belknap Press, 1975), 4.

43. Ibid., 286.
44. Hull, David L. *Science as a Process: An Evolutionary Account of the Social and Conceptual Development of Science.* (Chicago, IL: University of Chicago Press, 1988), 227.
45. Albury, W.R. "Politics and Rhetoric in the Sociobiology Debate," *Social Studies of Science.* Vol. 10, No. 4 (Nov., 1980), 522.
46. "'Wilson,' They Said, 'You're All Wet!,'" *The New York Times,* October 16, 1994.
47. Gates, Henry Loius and Abby Wolf. *The Henry Louis Gates, Jr. Reader.* (New York, NY: Basic Civitas Books, 2012), 215.
48. Lieberman, Leonard, Blaine W. Stevenson, and Larry T. Reynolds. "Race and Anthropology: A Core Concept without Consensus," *Anthropology & Education Quarterly.* Vol. 20, No. 2 (Jun., 1989), 69.
49. Wilson, William Julius. *More Than Just Race: Being Black and Poor in the Inner City.* (New York, NY: W. W. Norton & Company, 2009), 46.
50. Steinberg, Stephen. *Race Relations: A Critique.* (Stanford, CT: Stanford University Press, 2007), 97.
51. Massey, Douglas S. and Nancy A. Denton. *American Apartheid: Segregation and the Making of the Underclass.* (Cambridge, MA: Harvard University Press, 1998), 2.
52. Omi and Winant, *Racial Formation in the United States,* (New York, NY: Routledge, 1996), 55.
53. Ibid., 59.
54. Herrnstein, Richard J. and Charles Murray. *The Bell Curve: Intelligence and Class Structure in American Life.* (New York, NY: Simon & Schuster, 1994), 340.
55. Ibid., 518.
56. Ibid., 526.
57. "The Bell Curve Goes Belly Up," *The Journal of Blacks in Higher Education*, No. 30, Winter 2000–2001, 32.
58. "Daring Research or 'Social Science Pornography'?: Charles Murray," *The New York Times Magazine*, October 9, 1994.
59. "Intelligence: Knowns and Unknowns," Report of Task Force established by the Board of Scientific Affairs of the American Psychological Association, August 7, 1995. https://www.mun.ca/biology/scarr/APA%201985%20Intelligence%20-%20Knowns%20and%20Unknowns.pdf.
60. Ibid.
61. Boykin, Wade. "Reformulating Educational Reform: Toward the Proactive Schooling of African American Children," Paper commissioned for "Evaluation and

Education Reform: Students At-Risk Study," American Institutes for Research, 1992. https://archive.org/stream/ERIC_ED367725/ERIC_ED367725_djvu.txt.
62. "American Anthropological Association Statement on 'Race,'" May 17, 1998. http://new.aaanet.org/stmts/racepp.htm.

21

THE RISE OF THE HUMAN GENOME

IN 1990, The Human Genome Project (HGP) was launched, a 13-year-long, publicly funded project initiated with the objective of determining the DNA sequence of the entire spectrum of human genetic mapping. Optimistically, many scientists claimed that the project would provide definitive answers to questions regarding the scientific status of "race" as a biological category.[1] A year later, Luigi Luca Cavalli-Sforza, a geneticist at Stanford University, and a group of leading population geneticists and evolutionary biologists, wrote a letter to the scientific journal *Genomics* and proposed a project to sample and archive the world's genetic population, promising "enormous leaps" in the understanding of "who we are as a species and how we came to be." They warned that social changes had facilitated the mixing of populations, thereby threatening the existence of the groups that held the greatest importance for understanding human evolution – isolated indigenous populations. The group wrote:

> The populations that can tell us most about our evolutionary past are those that have been isolated for some time, are likely to be linguistically and culturally distinct and are often surrounded by geographic barriers … Such isolated populations are being rapidly merged with their neighbors, however, destroying irrevocably the information needed to reconstruct our evolutionary history.[2]

Initially, the letter received a highly positive response. The Human Genome Organization (HUGO), an international body responsible for coordinating activities within the HGP, took strong interest, and in 1994, the organization that would become known as the Human Genome Diversity Project (HGDP) took form. Instead of receiving the expected support, however, the HGDP became the target of outrage. In May 1993, a group of physical anthropologists accused the initiative of using 21st century technology to propagate the racism of 19th century biology. In December of that year, the World Congress of Indigenous People dubbed it the "Vampire Project," charging that the project was more interested in collecting the blood of indigenous people than in furthering their wellbeing. In 1996, UNESCO's International Bioethics Committee issued a report on the HGDP that dealt with the project's potential to contribute to racism. The report concluded that "the scientific goals [of the HGDP] are generally valid" but that the genetic information the project generates could be "misappropriated" and "misused" by racists.[3] By 1998, over a hundred groups advocating for the rights of indigenous people in the United States and around the world signed declarations condemning the project.[4]

In June 2000, Frank Collins, leader of the HGP, and Craig Venter, Head and Chief Scientist of the privately funded company, Celera Genomics, met at the White House with President Bill Clinton to publically announce that the human genome had been successfully mapped. Clinton declared: "Today, we are learning the language in which God created life ... I believe one of the great truths to emerge from this triumphant expedition inside the human genome is that in genetic terms, all human beings, regardless of race, are more than 99.9 percent the same." The president described the discovery as "the most important, most wondrous map ever," while Venter emphatically stated that "what we've shown is the concept of race has no scientific basis."[5]

It seemed at the time that the HGP, bolstered by Clinton's support, had put the final nail in the coffin of the idea that race had any scientific reality. However, subsequent advances in DNA sequencing and the increased speed of computer microprocessors has led to ever-increasingly more sophisticated analysis of human genes. Whereas until roughly the turn of the 21st century, geneticists were limited to examining one-dimensional distributions of a limited number of genes, today's scientists can examine multi-dimensional correlations among distributions of genes, including what is known as junk DNA, or microsatellites. These advances have led to the popularization – once again – of the idea that race, and sometimes human behavior, is embedded within our genetic structure.

In a 2003 paper, "Human Genetic Diversity: Lewontin's Fallacy," statistician and geneticist A.W.F. Edwards critiqued Lewontin's conclusion that dividing humans into races was invalid and demonstrated that it is possible to classify individuals into different racial groups with an accuracy that approaches 100 percent when one takes into account that alleles tend to cluster differently in different populations. In Edwards's words, "Most of the information that distinguishes populations is hidden in the correlation structure of the data." He argued that, even if the probability of misclassifying an individual based on the frequency of alleles at a single locus, or location, is as high as 30 percent, as Lewontin reported in 1972, the misclassification probability becomes close to zero if enough loci are studied.[6] As Armand Marie Leroi, an evolutionary biologist, put it on the Op-Ed page of *The New York Times*:

> Certain skin colors tend to go with certain kinds of eyes, noses, skulls and bodies. When we glance at a stranger's face we use those associations to infer what continent, or even what country, he or his ancestors came from – and we usually get it right. To put it more abstractly, human physical variation is correlated; and correlations contain information.
>
> Genetic variants that aren't written on our faces, but that can be detected only in the genome, show similar correlations. It is these correlations that Dr. Lewontin seems to have ignored. In essence, he looked at one gene at a time and failed to see races. But if many – a few hundred – variable genes are considered simultaneously, then it is very easy to do so.[7]

Edward's work was substantiated in a 2005 study. Neil Risch, human geneticist and professor at the University of California, San Francisco, and his colleagues compared the genetic data for 326 microsatellite markers among 3,636 Whites, African Americans, Asians, and Hispanics and found that only five participants showed genetic cluster membership different from their self-identified racial background.[8]

THE DEBATE CONTINUES

Meanwhile, the battle among scientists rages on. While the acceptance of racial differences is, without a doubt, currently in vogue, there are limits beyond which a scientist may not venture without incurring the wrath of peers and the public. Take the example of the 2015 best-selling book, *A Troublesome Inheritance: Genes, Race, and Human History*, the work of science writer Nicholas Wade. Wade argues that not only are races real, but that they can be characterized by distinct, genetically determined social behaviors, many of which emerged over the last 10,000 years, which have helped to determine a society's economic and historical trajectories. For example, a difference in a racial group's genetically acquired tendency to trust outsiders – and therefore to accept central rather than tribal authority – could explain "much of the difference between tribal and modern societies."[9] He writes:

> Trust and aggression are two significant components of human social behavior whose underlying genetics have already been to some extent explored. There are many other aspects of social behavior, such as conformity to rules, the willingness to punish violators of social norms or the expectation of fairness and reciprocity, that most probably have a genetic basis, although one that remains to be discovered. The fact that human social behavior is to some extent shaped by the genes means that it can evolve and that different kinds of society can emerge as the underlying social behaviors shift.[10]

Perhaps more troublesome, Wade postulates that English populations have a "willingness to save and delay gratification," which "seems considerably weaker in tribal societies," the cause of which he ascribes to genetics, though admitting that "the genetic underpinnings of human social behavior are for the most part still unknown."[11] He asserts that the Jewish population, which "includes more individuals of higher cognitive capacity," are adapted for capitalism, in the way that Eskimos are best suited to an arctic climate or Tibetans to higher altitudes.[12]

Not surprisingly, Wade was barraged with critical reviews ranging from academic journals to the popular press. A letter to *The New York Times Book Review*, signed by more than 100 faculty members in population genetics and evolutionary biology, many of whose work was cited in Wade's book, stated that he misinterpreted their findings. The letter criticizes "Wade's misappropriation of research from our field to support arguments about differences among human societies," adding:

> Wade juxtaposes an incomplete and inaccurate account of our research on human genetic differences with speculation that recent natural selection has led to worldwide differences in I.Q. test results, political institutions and economic development. We reject Wade's implication that our findings substantiate his guesswork. They do not … We are in full agreement that there is no support from the field of population genetics for Wade's conjectures.[13]

21 | THE RISE OF THE HUMAN GENOME

Wade went too far. But clearly, since the turn of the millennium, there has been a fundamental shift in how scientists view race, a shift that was in no small way due to the advances delivered by the HGP. Ironically, in recent years, it is becoming politically incorrect and considered bad science NOT to address race in scientific inquiry. According to sociologist Catherine Bliss:

> While it was commonsensical that the proper sensibility to counter racial discrimination was an emphasis on human universality and colorblindness, in the late twentieth century a shift occurred: the proper corrective to racial discrimination became racial consciousness, a disposition which requires the recognition of difference. If paying too much attention to race had once been a mark of racism, now ignoring racial difference was heralded as a dangerous perpetuation of racial inequality.[14]

Journalist John Entine, author of the book *Taboo: Why Black Athletes Dominate Sports and Why We're Afraid to Talk about It* uses genomic research to back his claim that people of African descent are genetically preconditioned to athletic events, like long-distance running. He writes: "Genetically linked, highly heritable characteristics such as skeletal structure, the distribution of muscle-fiber types, reflex capabilities, metabolic efficiency, lung capacity, and the ability to use energy more efficiently are not evenly distributed among populations and cannot be explained by known environmental factors." Entine continues:

> The fact that 99.8 percent of the population shares the same genes does not 'prove' or even necessarily suggest that there are no population or 'racial' differences. The percentage of overall differences is a far less important issue than which genes are different. Even minute differences in DNA can have profound effects on how an animal or human looks and acts.[15]

As support, Entine quotes Joseph Graves Jr, an evolutionary biologist at Arizona State University as saying, "Evolution has shaped body types and in part athletic possibilities. Don't expect an Eskimo to show up on an NBA court or a Watusi to win the world weightlifting championship. Differences don't necessarily correlate with skin color, but rather with geography and climate. For example, endurance runners are more likely to come from East Africa."[16]

GENETICS AND RACE IN MEDICINE AND BEYOND

In recent years, the common use of DNA testing in medicine has been instrumental in putting a new face on genetics. Prenatal testing is used to detect changes in a fetus's genes or chromosomes before birth. Genetic screening is used just after birth to identify genetic disorders that can be treated early in life, and millions of babies are tested each year in the United States. Diagnostic testing is routinely used to identify or rule out a specific genetic or chromosomal condition. Preimplantation testing is a specialized technique that can reduce the risk of having a child with a particular genetic or chromosomal disorder. Predictive testing is used to detect gene mutations associated with disorders that appear after birth, often later in life.[17] According to Neil Risch, race is essential to help determine "differences in treatment response or disease prevalence between racial/ethnic groups," and he aggressively supports the "search for candidate genes that contribute both to disease susceptibility and treatment response, both within and across racial/ethnic groups."[18]

In 2002, psychiatrist Sally Satel shook up readers of *The New York Times* and *The Wall Street Journal* with articles entitled "I Am a Racially Profiling Doctor" and "One Nation Under Racist Doctors? Don't Believe the Media Hype." Satel attacked the science of promoting colorblind care, and she described real-world medicine as being highly cognizant of race, giving concrete examples of diverse medical settings where clinicians carefully used race to determine how to treat patients. Said Satel, "So much of medicine is a guessing game – and race sometimes provides an invaluable clue. As citizens, we can celebrate our genetic similarity as evidence of our spiritual kinship. As doctors and patients, though, we must realize that it is not in patients' best interests to deny the reality of differences."[19]

As Kenan Malik, author of the book *Strange Fruit: Why Both Sides Are Wrong in the Race Debate* points out, "[That] race has once more become important as a scientific category seems incontestable." Malik points to the development of so-called race specific drugs, such as BiDil®, a heart drug designed to be used only by African Americans, and the use of software programs to determine an individual's race from the shape of the skull, which are now routinely used both by police forces and international organizations to identify bodies in places like marked graves.[20] As part of the HapMap project, a multi-country effort to identify and catalog genetic similarities and differences, geneticists have been analyzing DNA from populations with African, Asian, and European ancestry to help provide data for treating diseases.[21] An oft-quoted paper in the *New England Journal of Medicine*, published in 2003, made the case that "ignoring race and ethnic background would be detrimental to the very populations and persons that this approach allegedly seeks to protect. Information about patients' ethnic or racial group is imperative for the identification, tracking, and investigation of the reasons for racial and ethnic differences in the prevalence and severity of disease and in responses to treatment." The article continues:

> Currently, racial and ethnic minorities in the United States are underrepresented in many clinical studies. If investigators ignored race and ethnic background in research studies and persons were sampled randomly, the overwhelming majority of participants in clinical studies in the United States would be white, and minority populations would never be adequately sampled. In cases in which there are important racial and ethnic differences in the causes of disease or other outcomes or in which there are interactions between race or ethnic background and other factors contributing to these outcomes, such patterns would never be discovered, their causes could not be identified, and the appropriate interventions would never be applied in the groups in which they were needed.[22]

The media buzz surrounding the launch of BiDil is especially revealing. The drug made its first public appearance as a race-specific medication on March 8, 2001, when NitroMed, a biotech firm based in Massachusetts, issued a press release triumphantly announcing the receipt of a letter from the FDA describing the "ultimate approvability" of the drug, pending the successful completion of a confirmatory trial among African Americans with heart failure. On June 23, 2005, the FDA approved BiDil to treat heart failure in "self-identified Black patients."[23]

The Times of London ran a cover story in October 2004, with the headline: "We can treat your heart disease ... if you're Black."[24] *The Wall Street Journal* called it "reality-check time" for scientists who believed that race was biologically meaningless.[25]

These articles and others featured interviews with scientists who said the connection between race and genetics was too "blurry" to make it medically useful, and "We find African genes in Scandinavians, and English genes in Chinese. There is no such thing as a genetically 'pure' population." Charles Rotimi, a genomics researcher at Howard University, worried that there was no definitive research showing that BiDil didn't work in "Whites" too. In a front-page op-ed for *USA Today*, cardiovascular epidemiologist Richard Cooper stated, "The last thing we need is greater acceptance of race in the name of 'science' when there is no scientific evidence."[26]

However, as sociologist Catherine Bliss notes, as genomicists began facing the reality of doing genomics in a health disparities framework, many retreated from a staunch position; one former opponent began supporting the use of race as a "last resort," while another approved using it as "an interim measure."[27]

In addition to advances in medicine and medical treatment as a result of improvements in genetic testing, another use is in the field of forensics, and forensic DNA phenotyping (FDP) is becoming increasingly prevalent as a means of zeroing in on the racial background of those suspected of crimes. FDP analyzes DNA left at a crime scene to locate genotypes linked to ancestry and physical appearance, such as eye or skin color, and uses these genotypes to predict race and appearance. While DNA typing is used to convince a court that the defendant was or was not the same person who left DNA at a crime scene, FDP's objective is to predict, rather than confirm, the identity of a suspect.[28]

Forensic phenotyping became publically visible in a 2003 case involving a series of serial rapes and murders in Louisiana. In June, police officers used a racial profile constructed from DNA left at the scene of the crime to catch the perpetrator. Louisiana police had been searching for a White male suspect after tips from witnesses to the crimes. However, the results of a DNA test provided by DNAPrint Genomics indicated that the suspect was a man with "85 percent African ancestry and 15 percent Native American ancestry." The Chief Scientific Officer of DNAPrint told the officers, "You're wasting your time dragneting Caucasians; your killer is African American." Derrick Lee Todd, an African American man, was later convicted of two murders – he was suspected of killing seven women between 1998 and 2003 – and executed by Louisiana authorities in 2016.

Following the public exposure, DNAPrint's marketing of racial technology created a firestorm, and DNAPrint scientists had to explain why they were selling a technology that could give law enforcement a means to target specific races, produce race-based dragnets, and encourage other forms of racial profiling. The developers of the technology embarked upon a campaign to distance it from racial connotations, and the company removed all mention of race from its website and business reports.[29]

One area where DNA has captured the public's imagination is in DNA ancestry tests. These may have particular significance for African Americans, for whom ancestry is mired in the ugly history of slavery, making traditional approaches to genealogy inaccessible. As Henry Louis Gates put it, "People are riveted by the possibility that they can find the tribe they're descended from, but the Middle Passage prevented us from really finding out. Now for the first time in three centuries we can begin to reverse the Middle Passage." In 2006, Gates hosted *African Ancestry in African American Lives*, a PBS documentary on African Americans' looking for their roots.

21 | THE RISE OF THE HUMAN GENOME

Eleven million people watched as celebrities, such as Oprah Winfrey, Quincy Jones, and Chris Tucker, submitted their DNA for testing. Winfrey further popularized genealogy in her own feature, which culminated in the publication of Gates' book *Finding Oprah's Roots, Finding Your Own*. Winfrey said: "I feel empowered to say, 'This is who you are, this is where you've come from. You've come from strength and power and endurance and pain and suffering and triumph. You've come from all of that. And so imagine now how much more you can be.' "[30] According to Rick Kittles, a geneticist and co-founder of African Ancestry, Inc., "Like many African Americans, we knew nothing about where in Africa our ancestors were from." Oral history traced a family from New York and Georgia; however, DNA testing revealed links to the Hausa people of northern Nigeria, the Ibo of eastern Nigeria, and the Mandinka of Senegal.[31]

Additionally, others with disrupted genealogical records, such as Native Americans, Jews, and Hispanics, may also find meaning in DNA testing. Danny Villarreal, a Hispanic who believed he was of pure Spanish blood, found that he was closely related to Jewish populations in Hungary, Belarus, and Poland. "I was kinda surprised," he said. "I'm a good ol' Catholic boy."[32]

Despite their popularity in recent days, the use of DNA testing to determine one's ancestry can be complicated at best. It works well in groups like African-Americans, whose ancestors in Africa and Europe lived far from each other. Much of the ancestry of today's African-Americans can be traced to West or Central Africa, with a minority from other parts of the continent. However, for other groups, results may be more confusing. According to John Hawks, an anthropologist at the University of Wisconsin-Madison who specializes in human evolution and genetics, "All we know for sure is that such genetic similarities can make ancestry testing very confusing." Hawks writes:

> Many amateur genealogists are interested in whether they might have a Cherokee ancestor, for example. And for some people, [DNA] tests can give a relatively accurate answer about Native-American ancestry. But other people, including Greeks and Ashkenazi Jews, may have "Native American affinity," according to the tests, even if they and their ancestors have never been to America. As far as anthropologists know, there were no lost tribes connecting Greeks, Jews, and ancient Americans. So, maybe this "Native American affinity" reflects the scattering of alleles by prehistoric Asian nomads to the ancestors of Greeks and Jews as well as to American Indians ... [33]

According to Ken Chahine, a biochemist at Ancestry.com, DNA tests can't accurately tell a Spaniard from an Italian yet. Rather, they disclose where on the planet their distant ancestors originated, as determined by where their gene markers appear most abundantly in modern populations.[34] However, given that we do not know where, geographically, one race stops and another begins, assigning someone to a race or admixture of races, is a nebulous proposition.

NOTES

1. Chial, Heidi. "DNA Sequencing Technologies Key to the Human Genome Project," *Nature Education.* Vol. 1. No. 1, 2008, 219.
2. Morgan, Rose M. *The Genetics Revolution: History, Fears, and Future of a Life-altering Science.* (Westport, CT: Greenwood Publishing Group, 2005), 95.
3. Lisa Gannett, Racism and Human Genome Diversity Research: The Ethical Limits of 'Population Thinking,'" *Philosophy of Science.* Vol. 68, No. 3, September 2001, S480.
4. Reardon, *Race to the Finish*, 1.
5. Bliss, Catherine. *Race Decoded: The Genomic Fight for Social Justice.* (Palo Alto, CA: Stanford University Press, 2012), 1.
6. Edwards, A.W.F. "Human Genetic Diversity: Lewontin's Fallacy." *BioEssays.* Vol. 25, No. 8, 2003, 798.
7. Leroi, Armand Marie. "A Family Tree in Every Gene," *The New York Times*, March 14, 2005. http://www.nytimes.com/2005/03/14/opinion/a-family-tree-in-every-gene.html.
8. Tang, Hua, Tom Quertermous, Beatriz Rodriguez, Sharon L R Kardia, Xiaofeng Zhu, Andrew Brown, James S. Pankow, Michael A. Province, Steven C. Hunt, Eric Boerwinkle, Nicholas J. Schork, and Neil J. Risch, "Genetic Structure, Self-Identified Race/Ethnicity, and Confounding in Case-Control Association Studies," *American Journal of Human Genetics.* Vol. 76, 2005, 268.
9. Wade, Nicholas. *A Troublesome Inheritance: Genes, Race and Human History.* (London, England: Penguin Books, 2015), 126.
10. Ibid., 57.
11. Ibid., 184.
12. Ibid., 214.
13. "A Troublesome Inheritance," *The New York Times*, August 8, 2014. http://www.nytimes.com/2014/08/10/books/review/letters-a-troublesome-inheritance.html?_r=0.

14. Bliss, 201.
15. "A Troublesome Inheritance," *The New York Times*.
16. McCann-Mortimer, Patricia, Martha Augoustinos, and Amanda LeCouteur, "'Race' and the Human Genome Project: Constructions of Scientific Legitimacy," *Discourse Society*. Vol. 15, No. 4, July 2004, 424.
17. U.S. National Library of Medicine, The National Institutes of Health. https://ghr.nlm.nih.gov/primer/testing/uses.
18. Yudell, *Race Unmasked*, 204.
19. Bliss, 75.
20. http://www.kenanmalik.com/lectures/race_oslo.html.
21. Malik, Kenan. The Trouble with Race: Science and the Problem of Racial Categories." https://kenanmalik.wordpress.com/2011/03/14/problem-of-racial-categories/.
22. Burchard, Esteban González, Elad Ziv, Natasha Coyl, Scarlett Lin Gomez., Hua Tang, Andrew J. Karter, Joanna L. Mountain, Eliseo J. Pérez-Stable, Dean Sheppard and Neil Risch, "The Importance of Race and Ethnic Background in Biomedical Research and Clinical Practice," *The New England Journal of Medicine*. 2003, No. 348, 1170.
23. Kahn, Jonathan D. "From Disparity to Difference: How Race-Specific Medicines May Undermine Policies to Address Inequalities in Health Care," *Southern California Interdisciplinary Law Journal*. Vol. 15, 2005, 105.
24. "We Can Treat Your Heart Disease … If You're Black," *The Times*, October 29, 2004.
25. Bliss, 80.
26. "Beware of Race-Based Cures," *USA Today*, November 14, 2004. http://usatoday30.usatoday.com/news/opinion/editorials/2004-11-14-oppose_x.htm.
27. Bliss, 79.
28. Sankar, Pamela. eds. Ian Whitmarsh and David S. Jones. "Forensic DNA Phenotyping: Reinforcing Race in Law Enforcement," in *What's The Use Of Race?: Modern Governance and the Biology of Difference*. (Cambridge, MA: The MIT Press, 2010), 53.
29. Bliss, 70.
30. Ibid., 33.
31. Gibson, Lydialyle. "Long Way Home," *University of Chicago Magazine*, Vol. 100, Issue 3, 2007. http://magazine.uchicago.edu/0812/features/kittles.shtml.
32. Jennifer Hochschild, Vesla Weaver, and Traci Burch, 98.

33. "How African Are You? What Genealogical Testing Can't Tell You," *Slate*, March 15, 2006. http://www.slate.com/articles/health_and_science/science/2006/03/how_african_are_you.html.
34. "DNA Detectives Seek Origins of You," *USA Today*, June 13, 2013. http://www.usatoday.com/story/news/nation/2013/06/13/dna-detectives-seek-origins-of-you/2420071/.

22

RACIAL CLASSIFICATION AND THE U.S. CENSUS

WHILE scientists have argued over the question of whether or not race is a real or artificial concept, complicating the issue, and perhaps lending credence to the idea that race is a societal construct, the federal government, in the form of the U.S. Census, has continually changed its system of racial categorization. As Kenneth Pruitt, a political scientist and former director of the census, puts it in his book, *What Is Your Race?: The Census and Our Flawed Efforts to Classify Americans*, "America has statistical races ... They have been deliberately constructed and reconstructed by the government. They are tools of government, with political purposes and policy consequences – more so even than the biological races of the 19th century or the socially constructed races from 20th century anthropology or what are termed identity races in our current times."[1]

Despite all scientists have learned in the field of genomics, it is impossible to deny the arbitrariness of racial classifications as they are – and have been used – in the United States. Definitions of race have varied by state and region, changing over time and in response to politics. In Virginia, for example, during the 1800s, a "white" person was anyone who was less than a quarter Black. However, in order to prevent intermarriage, laws became more restrictive, and by 1924, legislators prohibited anyone with "a single drop of Negro blood from marrying a White person."

Complicating the matter is that the Census Bureau has vacillated in terms of how it classifies race, and the terminologies used have changed over time. For example, mulattoes were a racial category in the 1850, 1860, 1870, 1890, 1910, and 1920 censuses. Mexicans were considered a race in 1930, but not before or after that. Additionally, before 1980, a person's race was determined by the census interviewer; since that time, people have chosen their own race from a list of categories. It doesn't take much imagination to see that the way people see themselves and the way they are seen by census takers have not always been the same.[2] Still, throughout our history, Americans have been obsessed with the idea of racial classification.

Our national obsession is evident when one looks at the U.S. Constitution, although it never mentions the terms "race" or "color." According to Article I, Section 2, Clause 3 of the Constitution, the population was to be counted every 10 years, thereby instituting the decennial census. The same paragraph states:

> Representatives and direct Taxes shall be apportioned among the several states which may be included within this Union, according to their respective Numbers, which shall be determined by adding to the whole Number of free Persons, including those bound to Service for a Term of Years, and excluding Indians not taxed, three fifths of all other persons.[3]

Despite the Constitution's haziness, it clearly made its point. It was understood by all that indentured servants, most of whom were white, were to be counted as free persons and "three fifths of all other Persons" referred to African slaves. In other words, Whites counted. Indians counted, assuming they paid their taxes. Slaves were considered to be a mixture of persons and property, most aptly put by James Madison in the *Federalist* papers: "The federal Constitution therefore, decides with great propriety on the case of our slaves, when it views them in the *mixt character of persons and property*. This is in fact their true character."[4]

By the time of the first census in 1790, the Constitution's race-based intent was clarified, and the census categories of "free white" males and females, free colored (including Native Americans who paid taxes and free Blacks), and "slaves" were called out. This system remained in place until 1840, with only the nomenclature of non-White free persons changing over the decades. Writes Clara E. Rodríguez:

> Theoretically, those in political charge could have chosen another definition for the first category, and consequently, themselves. That is, they could have chosen "free English-speaking males

over sixteen" or "free males of Christian descent" or "of European descent. But they chose color. Having named the central category "white" gave a centrality and power to color that has continued throughout the history of the census.[5]

By 1850, scientific racism had taken hold, and most scientists agreed that a racial hierarchy was determined by nature. This hierarchy had political importance at the time because it provided the justification for attacking or defending slavery. With the country approaching the brink of war and the intensity of the slavery conflict building rapidly, Congress created a special census board, consisting of the secretaries of State and Interior and the postmaster general, to which it granted considerable discretionary authority.

At the helm was Joseph C.G. Kennedy, who served as the superintendent of the census for 16 years. For guidance, Kennedy turned to leaders in the American Statistical Association and the American Geographical and Statistical Society, making the 1850 census the first to "benefit" from scientific advice. These scientists helped Kennedy develop a questionnaire and census-taking procedure that was considerably more extensive than any previous census. Like prior censuses, the 1850 enumeration took note of the "color" of respondents and their "civil condition," whether free or slave. Slaves were identified only as a number recorded along with the name of their owner. Additionally, acknowledging the existence of Black-White and Black-Indian relations, the 1850 census questionnaire included a category for Mulatto.[6]

In the decades following the Civil War, the race question evolved in ways that mirrored political concerns of the time, particularly immigration. The 1860 census, reflecting the growing obsession with immigrant railroad workers, counted Chinese in California, adding Japanese to the state's enumeration in 1870 – both were added in 1890 to the national census. By that year, concerns about miscegenation, or race mixing, had reached a crescendo, fueled by the racial science of the day and concerns about the racial purity of the nation.[7] The census that year created the categories of Black (three-quarters or more Black), Mulatto (three-eighths to five-eighths Black), Quadroons (a quarter Black), and Octoroons (one-eighth or any trace of Black "blood). Over the next 50 years, the government added and deleted racial categories. There were 10 in 1920, including Filipinos, Koreans, and "Hindus." The 1930 census institutionalized the one-drop rule for Blacks by instructing census takers that: "A person of mixed White and Negro blood was to be returned as Negro, no matter how small the percentage of Negro blood; someone part Indian and part Negro also was to be listed as Negro, unless the Indian blood predominated."[8]

With the 1960 census, the categories began to resemble those used today: Aleut, American Indian or Eskimo; Chinese; Filipino; Japanese; Negros; Hawaiian or part-Hawaiian; and White.[9] Additionally, it marked the first census that allowed the self-reporting of race. While intended as a methodological change to correct undercounts of minority populations, allowing individuals to self-identify meant that one's own cultural affiliation and identity came to trump ascribed racial identification, since a person's race had previously been determined by census takers as best they could. According to sociologist C. Matthew Snipp:

> One of the less appreciated implications of the procedural change ... to self-identification was a fundamental redefinition of the meaning of race. Under the old regime, enumerator observation meant that racial identification was based mainly on phenotypical appearances and on the enumerator's visual acuity with respect to cues such as skin color, hair texture, and other anatomical features. The number of African Americans, for example, represented the number of persons displaying the physical characteristics associated with some more or less common notion about African-American phenotypical traits.[10]

In 1970, under pressure from Latino groups, President Nixon ordered that the census include a question about Hispanic ethnicity. However, because millions of census forms had already been printed, the Census Bureau only included it on the long form, asking the five percent who received the more detailed questionnaire to choose whether their "origin or descent" was Mexican, Puerto Rican, Cuban, Central American, or "other Spanish."[11]

Still, as late as the early 1970s, there was little or no standardization in the racial classifications used by various government agencies. Some agencies reported data for Whites and non-Whites; others kept records for Whites, Blacks, and others; a few agencies, such as the Census Bureau, used a larger set of categories. To deal with this lack of consistency, in 1974, the White House's Office of Management and Budget (OMB) took on the task of creating a standard set of racial categories for federal administration. In June, an ad hoc committee was established to coordinate the development of a standard taxonomy and set of definitions for racial and ethnic groups of interest to the federal government, namely, those groups which historically were the subjects of racial oppression and who were the objects of special protections under a host of federal policies and programs.

In 1975, the committee recommended that federal agencies collect data for five groups: American Indians and Alaska Natives, Asians and Pacific Islanders, Non-Hispanic Blacks, Non-Hispanic Whites, and Hispanics. In May 1977, the OMB issued OMB Directive No. 15, instituting the five categories recommended by the committee. Despite a disclaimer that "These classifications should not be interpreted as being scientific or anthropological in nature," Directive No. 15 mandated that all federal agencies, contractors, and grantees use these categories any time that data concerning race was collected. In the words of Snipp, "The impact of Directive No. 15 cannot be underestimated. In many respects, this standard established an official racial cosmology for the United States that permeated every level of government, many if not most large corporations, and many other institutions such as schools and nonprofit organizations."[12]

The 1980 census was the first to ask all people whether they were of "Spanish/Hispanic origin or descent;" if they responded affirmatively, they were instructed to check off one of four boxes – "Mexican," "Cuban," "Puerto Rican," or "other Hispanic (specify)." By doing so, the Census Bureau solidified the idea of Hispanics as an "ethnicity" rather than a race, since the race question was treated separately.

Prior to this, the Census Bureau had used other means to count the number of people we now call Latinos. As mentioned, in 1930, the census had included "Mexican" in the race question. From 1940 to 1980, Puerto Ricans, Mexicans, and other Latinos were classified as "white," unless the census interviewer determined that they belonged to some other recognized race category, such as Black or Asian. Interestingly, in the 1980 census, 40 percent of self-identified Hispanics indicated that they belonged to "some other race," a pretty good indicator that in terms of personal identity, the extant racial labels did not apply.[13]

The 2000 census marked another turning point in census history. For the first time, the questions allowed people to check more than one box when asked their race, representing a victory for many multiracial Americans. In 1993, Congress had begun to investigate a category for people of mixed race, but they were met by staunch opposition by the civil rights community, which argued that this would dilute minority numbers, setting back the civil rights movement by years. Arthur Fletcher, chairman of the U.S. Commission on Civil Rights, testified that he could "see a whole host of light-skinned Black Americans running for the door the minute they have another choice."[14] In its testimony, the NAACP argued that the "creation of a multiracial classification might disaggregate the apparent numbers of members of discrete minority groups, diluting benefits to which they are entitled as a protected class under civil rights laws and under the Constitution itself." The crux of their argument was that the basic purpose of the race classification is "the enforcement of civil rights laws" and not "to provide vehicles for self-identification."[15]

However, for many, the issue indeed was identity affirmation, not social justice. Susan Graham, the White mother of a biracial child and co cofounder of Project RACE (Reclassify All Children Equally), testified in Congress: "I'm not a scholar, attorney, or lawmaker. I'm just a mother ... and whether I like it or not, I realize that self-esteem is directly tied to accurate racial identity ... my child has been White on the U.S. census, Black at school, and multiracial at home, all at the same time." The Association of Multiethnic Americans was more explicit, commenting, "We want choice in the matter of who we are, just like any other community. We are not saying that we are a solution to civil rights laws or civil rights injustices of the past. [It is ironic that] our people are being asked to correct by virtue of how we define ourselves all of the past injustices [toward] other groups of people."[16]

Ultimately, the congressional hearings floundered, bogged down by conflicting agendas and opinions, of which there was no shortage. Representative Tom Sawyer, who had requested the hearings, contended that "[racial] categories of convenience ... convey an illusion of specificity that fails to capture the dynamic patterns of our population." Hawaiian Senator Daniel Akaka requested a separate classification for Native Hawaiians (an argument he won with the 2000 Census): "We have literally fallen through the cracks between definition as Native Americans in many Federal laws and classification as Asian or Pacific Islanders in Federal forms." Representative Norman Mineta demanded respect for Asian-Pacific Americans. "Until the Bureau recognizes [us] as a constituency to be served," he stated, "rather than a problem to be dealt with, this estrangement will persist." Representative Barney Frank said he "wouldn't be here ... if we knew exactly what percentage" of the people in New Bedford and southeastern Massachusetts were of Cape Verdean descent. "Are they African Americans? Are they Black? Are they Cape Verdeans?"[17]

However, within a year, the multiracial category movement picked up steam. Ironically, neoconservatives favored the change, believing that a multiracial census category, by diluting minority numbers, would stymie civil rights protection and ultimately lead to the end of race-conscious government policies. As social scientist Jonathan Y. Okamura writes, neoconservatives seek "to establish and maintain a 'color blind' America in which race has no formal significance" in the allocation of government services and other benefits and resources. Okamura concludes that neoconservatives supported multiracial recognition, "not because they were strongly opposed to continuing discrimination against racial minorities including racially mixed people, but because of its potentially adverse consequences for civil rights laws."[18]

In the 2000 Census, 6.8 million Americans, 2.3 percent of the population checked more than one race.[19] Hispanics were more than three times likely as non-Hispanics to claim a mixture of "two or more races," with most specifying "white" plus another race. Importantly, 42 percent of Latinos chose the non-identifier, "some other race" (SOR), a sizeable category of people, outnumbering the total U.S. population of Asians and American-Indians combined.[20] For them, the OMB racial structure simply did not fit. Rather, as the Panel on Hispanics in the United States noted, checking SOR reflected their "lived experience" and a growing consciousness of Hispanics as a race, rather than ethnicity. According to the Panel:

> Hispanicity … is both imagined and real: imagined because it is a social construct invented by the federal government for the purpose of bureaucratic accounting, and real because it has been rendered so by its use. Through their broad popular usage, the ethnoracial labels "Hispanic" and "Latino" are increasingly being accepted by immigrants and their U.S.-born children as referring to their own identities.[21]

That Hispanics are coming to see themselves as a distinct race is supported by a study by the Census Bureau, which found that when "Hispanic" is not included as a race option, between 56 and 68 percent of Hispanics identify as White. However, when "Hispanic" is included as a racial option, the percentage that identifies as White drops to 13.7 percent.[22] Additionally, a 2015 Pew Research Center survey found that, for two-thirds of Hispanics, their Hispanic background is "a part of their racial background – not something separate."[23]

To address concerns about a rising share of census respondents selecting the "some other race" option – 6.2 percent in 2010 – and the irrelevancy of the current system of racial classification to so many, the Census Bureau had been considering a combined race and ethnicity question for 2020, in which the Hispanic/Latino/Spanish question would be offered alongside the extant racial definitions, though this change did not occur. As a result, the Bureau has launched the "most comprehensive effort in history to study race and ethnic categories," according to Census Bureau officials Nicholas Jones and Roberto Ramirez. "Increasingly, Americans are saying they cannot find themselves [on census forms]," Jones stated. Still, a proposed change is not without controversy, and some Latino groups have voiced concern that eliminating the separate question about Hispanic origin would result in a decrease in the number of Hispanics counted by the census.[24]

Evidence of the fluidity of race, or perhaps more correctly stated the irrelevancy of the OMB racial classification for Hispanics, was revealed in May 2014, when the Pew Research Center and the Census Bureau announced that 2.5 million Hispanics changed their race from SOR in 2000 to "white" in 2010. Another 1.3 million people switched in the other direction. "Do Americans change their race? Yes, millions do," said study co-author Carolyn A. Liebler, a University of Minnesota sociologist who worked with Census Bureau researchers.[25]

RACE IN LATIN AMERICA

Important to consider is that views of race and racial classifications vary greatly between Latin American countries and the United States. A general rule is that racial classification in Latin American countries tends to focus on appearance, rather than origin as the primary criterion, often based on a skin color continuum, and unlike the United States, where hypodescent or the "one drop rule" has had a long, historical precedent, Latin Americans frequently use numerous intermediate or mixed-race categories.

However, Latin America is anything but homogenous, and attitudes toward race are no exception. For example, while many Latin American countries adopted nation-building narratives of race mixture, or *mestizaje*, countries like Argentina and Costa Rica did not. Additionally, attitudes towards African ancestry and "blood" are markedly different between countries. According to sociologists Edward Telles and Tianna Paschel, "In Brazil, race mixture narratives held that Blacks and African culture were central to the nation; in Colombia, they ignored or downplayed Blackness while greatly valuing whiteness; and, in the Dominican Republic, they excluded Blacks and African culture by regarding them as backward and foreign." In a study published in 2014, Telles and Paschel found stark differences between racial self-identification and actual skin color in four Latin American countries with sizable Black populations: Panama, the Dominican Republic, Colombia, and Brazil. On one extreme was Panama where there was a high correlation between having Black skin and a Black identity; in the Dominican Republic, less than half of the darkest Dominicans identified as Black, while the majority identified as "mestizo" or "Indio."[26]

Mexico, which has a national ideology built on indigenous identity and mestisaje, serves as another case in point. The primary ethnic distinction recognized in today's Mexico is that between indigenous people and the rest of the population, which is assumed to be of mixed-race origin. The boundary between the two is based on cultural and linguistic differences, rather than on ancestry or skin color, and as a result, is extremely fluid. However, as notes sociologist Andrés Villarreal, "Despite a state-sponsored and popular ideology that explicitly rejects any further racial or phenotypical distinctions within the majority *mestizo* population, many Mexicans today express a preference for whiter skin and European features." In his research, Villarreal found "profound social stratification by skin color" in Mexico, in that people with darker skin had significantly lower levels of educational attainment and occupational status, were more likely to live in poverty, and less likely to be affluent, even when all other differences besides skin color were controlled for.[27]

In Latin America, racial considerations include not just skin color but also hair texture and color, eye color, and facial features, and full siblings often are considered to belong to different "races." One anthropologist identified at least nineteen different racial categories commonly used in Puerto Rico. Also, social considerations greatly influence racial classifications. As sociologist Wendy Roth points out, "Greater socioeconomic status, prestige, or social networks can lead to a lighter classification, giving rise to the common expression that 'money whitens.' "[28] A study of prominent Puerto Ricans families in the 1950s stated that "[a]nyone who is accepted into the upper class is considered non-Negro, despite his physical appearance." In Puerto Rico, there is a common expression, "*Y tu abuela, ¿dónde está?*" ("And your grandmother, where is she?") from a poem by Fortunato Vizcarrondo, which refers to a person who, in trying to pass for White, hides the fact that there is a darker grandmother lurking in the genetic past with African ancestry. In her study of Puerto Ricans and Dominicans, Roth found that:

> Someone who is dark or has African features may refer to a man of medium skin tone as *blanco*. But that same man might be described as *trigueño* by someone of light color who has European features. In both Puerto Rico and the Dominican Republic, it is common for a child to be nicknamed *la blanquita* or *el negrito*, not because she or he is objectively White or Black but because she or he is the lightest or darkest in the family. Similarly, the same person may identify a woman as *trigueña* at one moment and as *morena* at the next, even in a single conversation, based on the context or the implicit comparison.[29]

According to Roth, racial terms can have different meanings when used in different contexts, and the same racial label can be used as a term of endearment, an insult, or a sexual come-on. She continues:

> Racial terms may serve as euphemisms, to avoid negative associations; the terms *indio* and *trigueño*, for example, are often used

to avoid describing someone as *negro*. A darker person might be called trigueño out of deference, but in an argument or brawl he might have the epithet "Dirty negro!" hurled at him. Terms are often selected, perhaps even subconsciously, according to the meaning a person wishes to convey. Much like the semantic distinction between using the informal *tú* or the formal *usted*, racial continuum terms can be used to treat people with respect or disrespect, to create solidarity, to include or exclude.[30]

In many Latin American countries, the concept of race has long been associated with nationality, and since at least the late 19th century, the word *raza* has often been used synonymously with "nation" or "people." *La raza* is commonly used by Mexicans to refer to "our people," and Mexicans often use the phrase "*Viva la Raza*," especially in public speeches; Dominican leaders frequently used the words "race" and "nation" interchangeably, often to distinguish the Dominican people from their Haitian neighbors. Throughout Latin America, Columbus Day is known as el *Día de la Raza* to commemorate the day that marked the creation of a new people forged in the blending of races. In his 1925 book, *La Raza Cósmica* ("The Cosmic Race") Mexican writer José Vasconcelos described Latin Americans as having the blood of all the world's races, thereby transcending the peoples of the "old world."[31]

Hispanics are not the only group being studied by the Census Bureau for possible inclusion as a separate racial category. People of Middle Eastern and North African backgrounds are classified as White according to the 2020 census definition, yet are often unsure of how to identify themselves on census forms. According to recent focus groups conducted by the Bureau, "Many participants ... felt that the inclusion of the examples of Egyptian and Lebanese with the White racial category was "wrong" or "inaccurate." These comments were often connected to the recommendation that there be a separate racial category for those who would identify as Middle Eastern, North African, or Arab."[32]

The census, like DNA testing, is a work in progress. Changes have always been the norm, and the future will be no exception. Just as we Americans are now coming to grips with the enormity of demographic change that has gripped the country in recent decades, the Census Bureau, is struggling to classify us in a manner that better reflects who we have become, while at the same time, balancing advances in science with political demands. We can only hope that, unlike so many prior periods of our history, change will reflect the better nature of our scientists and politicians and not serve the baser elements of fear and self-interest.

NOTES

1. Prewitt, Kenneth. *What Is Your Race?: The Census and Our Flawed Efforts to Classify Americans.* (Princeton, NJ: Princeton University Press, 2013), 3.
2. Rodríguez, Clara E. *Changing Race: Latinos, the Census, and the History of Ethnicity in the United States.* (New York, NY: New York University Press, 2000), 41.
3. Ibid., 66.
4. Hamilton, Alexander, James Madison, and John Jay. *The Federalist; or The New Constitution.* (White Fish, MT: Kessinger Publishing, 2010), 296.
5. Rodríguez, 69.
6. Snipp, C. Matthew. "Racial, Measurement in the American Census: Past Practices and Implications for the Future, *Annual Review of Sociology.* Vol. 29 (2003), 566.
7. Ibid.
8. Ibid. 568.
9. "Measuring Race and Ethnicity across the Decades: 1790–2010," U.S. Census Bureau. http://www.census.gov/population/race/data/MREAD_1790_2010.html.
10. Snipp, 570.
11. López, Ian Haney. "Race on the 2010 Census: Hispanics and the Shrinking White Majority," *Daedalus.* Vol. 134, No. 1, Winter 2005, 44.
12. Snipp, 572.
13. Rodríguez, Clara E. eds. José A. Cobas, Jorge Duany, and Joe R. Feagin. "Counting Latinos in the U.S. Census," in *How the United States Racializes Latinos: White Hegemony and Its Consequences.* (Boulder, CO: Paradigm Publishers, 2009), 42.
14. Williams, Kim M. *Mark One or More: Civil Rights in Multiracial America.* (Ann Arbor, MI: University of Michigan Press, 2008), 42.
15. Prewitt, 133.
16. Ibid.
17. Williams, 45.
18. Okamura, Jonathan Y. eds. Hamilton McCubbin, Krystal Ontai, et al. "Bridges of Barriers: Multiracial Families and Race Relations," in *Multiethnicity and Multiethnic Families: Development, Identity, and Resilience.* (Bloomington, IN: Xlibris, 2010), 52.
19. U.S. Census Bureau, "The Two or More Races Population: 2010." https://www.census.gov/prod/cen2010/briefs/c2010br-13.pdf.
20. "Shades of Belonging," Pew Research Center, December 6, 2004. http://www.pewhispanic.org/2004/12/06/shades-of-belonging/.

21. National Research Council of the National Academies, *Multiple Origins, Uncertain Destinies: Hispanics and the American Future*. (Washington, D.C.: The National Academies Press, 2006), 44.
22. Lee, Jennifer and Frank D. Bean. *The Diversity Paradox: Immigration and the Color Line in 21st Century America*. (New York, NY: Russell Sage Foundation, 2010), 45.
23. Pew Research Center, "Multiracial in America," June 11, 2015. http://www.pewsocialtrends.org/2015/06/11/chapter-7-the-many-dimensions-of-hispanic-racial-identity/.
24. Pew Research Center, "U.S. Census looking at big changes in how it asks about race and ethnicity," March 14, 2014. http://www.pewresearch.org/fact-tank/2014/03/14/u-s-census-looking-at-big-changes-in-how-it-asks-about-race-and-ethnicity/.
25. Pew Research Center, "Millions of Americans Changed Their Racial or Ethnic Identity from One Census to the Next, May 5, 2014. http://www.pewresearch.org/fact-tank/2014/05/05/millions-of-americans-changed-their-racial-or-ethnic-identity-from-one-census-to-the-next/.
26. Telles, Edward and Tianna Paschel. "Who Is Black, White, or Mixed Race? How Skin Color, Status, and Nation Shape Racial Classification in Latin America," *American Journal of Sociology*. Vol. 120, No. 3, 2014, 864–907.
27. Villarreal, Andrés. "Stratification by Skin Color in Contemporary Mexico," *American Sociological Review*. Vol. 75, No. 5, 2010, 676.
28. Roth, Wendy. *Race Migrations: Latinos and the Cultural Transformation of Race*. (Stanford, CT: Stanford University Press, 2012), 20.
29. Ibid.
30. Ibid., 20.
31. Ibid., 25.
32. U.S. Census Bureau, "2010 Census Race and Hispanic Origin Alternative Questionnaire Experiment," February 28, 2013. https://www.census.gov/2010census/pdf/2010_Census_Race_HO_AQE.pdf.

PART 6

WHERE ARE WE NOW? WHERE ARE WE GOING?

THE YEAR 2020 may very well be remembered as the year that America's racial divide split open. Pick any random evening, turn on the nightly news, and you are sure to see evidence that the country seems to be coming apart at the seams.

Ultimately, if we Americans are to be said to have a social conscience, it is imperative that we ask ourselves some serious questions. Toward where are we headed? Will the wrongs of past injustices ever be righted? Will the wounds inflicted by centuries of oppression ever heal? Will the rise of a seemingly more tolerant generation, Generation Z, save us from ourselves, or have the seeds of prejudice and bigotry been planted too deeply in the American psyche? As the United States moves to a "majority-minority" nation, will things get better, or will the grip of a frightened White America only hold on to the status quo with increasing tenacity? While none of these questions can be answered with any certainty, fortunately there is a substantial body of work, particularly in the field of sociology, which has grappled with these issues.

23

A NEW RACIAL DIVIDE?

MANY SCHOLARS, perhaps most prominently, sociologist Eduardo Bonilla-Silva, have proposed that as a result of the "darkening" of the United States, there will be a "reshuffling" of the historic bi-racial, Black and White order. This will result in a tri-racial system, a process Bonilla-Silva calls "Latinization" since it's similar to the racial order of many Latin American and Caribbean nations. In this tri-racial system, Bonilla-Silva sees "Whites" at the top, an intermediary group of "honorary Whites," similar to the coloreds in South Africa in the middle, and a non-White group or the "collective Blacks" at the bottom. Included in the honorary White group would be most light-skinned Latinos, Japanese-, Korean-, Asian Indian-, and Chinese-Americans, and most Americans with a Middle Eastern background. At the bottom, the collective Black would include African Americans, dark-skinned Latinos, Vietnamese, Cambodians, Laotians, and maybe Filipinos.

While Bonilla-Silva sees skin color as being the primary driver, and there is plenty of evidence that Americans – as well as a majority of other countries on the planet – demonstrate a strong preference for lighter skin, there are abundant indicators that immigrant groups, particularly Asians, are on the path toward upward socioeconomic mobility and greater acceptance by the mainstream. However, discrimination against Blacks remains a powerful force, one that is rooted in history and awash in anachronistic stereotypes, fears, and, as all too often appears to be the case, aversion. Indeed, there are countless public opinion polls that, regrettably, indicate that there may be a unique aversion to Blacks in America.

Sociologist George Yancey predicts the change from a white/non-White dichotomy to that of a Black/non-Black divide in the United States. He argues that African Americans suffer from a unique form of alienation and found in his research that not only were Whites more accepting of Latinos and Asian Americans than Blacks, Latino and Asian Americans were more accepting of each other and Whites than they were of African Americans. For example, when asked to construct an "ideal" neighborhood, Whites, Hispanics, and Asian Americans were accepting of each other as neighbors, but drew the line once the number of Black neighbors passed a certain threshold. Yancey writes:

> Because non-Black racial groups can avoid the label of being "Black," they can eventually be given a "white" racial identity. African Americans are in a quasi-caste system by which they occupy the lowest level of social prestige in the United States, and it is in the social interests of all no-Black racial groups to keep them at the bottom.[1]

A study by sociologists Mary C. Waters and Philip Kasinitz lends support to this idea. In their research among second generation immigrants, they found that native-born Blacks and West Indians reported experiencing the most discrimination, followed by Hispanics, then Chinese, and then Russian Jews. Waters and Kasinitz conclude that in terms of prejudice, there is a predictable hierarchy based on skin color, with groups clearly of African descent experiencing the most discrimination, followed by Latinos, then Asians, with Whites reporting the least discrimination. However, they also caution that the way color is experienced is not so simple. Light-skinned respondents of "color" are often mistaken for members of another racial or ethnic group, signifying that the color-line is a fluid one. For example, among the people they interviewed, South Americans often reported being mistaken for being Italian, Greek, or Portuguese. Dark-skinned Puerto Ricans and Dominicans said they were often categorized as Black. Said one respondent: "I have to speak Spanish in order for people to know. If I don't speak, they won't notice. Maybe it's my complexion, maybe it's the way I dress. I don't know." Additionally, Dominican males, who tend to be darker, were much more likely than South American and Puerto Rican males to report problems with the police (in all groups, problems with the police were far more common for men than for women), and their perceived levels of prejudice from police more closely resembled that of African American and West Indian males.[2]

23 | A NEW RACIAL DIVIDE?

Sociologist Jessica M. Vasquez studied third generation Mexican Americans and found that in the context of sustained immigration from Mexico, dark skin becomes a frequently invoked indicator of "foreignness," and native-born Americans often assume that those of Mexican descent, particularly those with darker skin or a phenotype that marks them as "looking Mexican," are unauthorized. Others are labeled as gangsters, domestics, or unskilled workers. Said one respondent, "I think when people look at me they see my scars and the moustache ... a lot of times people get the impression that I'm a gangster or a cholo. That really bothers me because that is just totally what I'm not about." Said another:

> This lady saw me [in a bar with friends] and she said out loud, "Oh, he's mean looking." I was thrown by it. For some reason I just smiled and she was like, "Oh my god, he has a dimple." We started talking and she asked what I did and I told her [a high school career counselor]. "Oh my God, I never would have guessed." I was like, "Obviously you shouldn't judge a book by its cover." She had this image of us – Mexicans – [as] bad and mean and involved in gangs.[3]

A dark-skinned Mexican-American girl reported that she and her darker brother were treated differently at school than their blond sister. The light-skinned sister was being mentored by the high school vice principal, until she was "discovered" to be Mexican-American and not Anglo.

> My sister, she's light skinned, she looks American, but she's a Mexican-American. The Vice Principal thought she was white. They [the administration] didn't know that my brother and sister and I were related [despite sharing the same surname]. They would send information for her in English and for my brother they would send it in Spanish. She's blonde and, according to them, she's a *guera* [White woman] and he's *mexicano*, Mexican. The vice principal treated her differently [better] because she was a blonde, she was a *guera*. When they found out she was Hispanic, she was a Mexican, it wasn't the same anymore.[4]

While light-skinned Latinos are often mistaken for white, and indeed may be considered "white" in Latin American, there is ample evidence that they are treated differently by Whites upon learning that they are Hispanic. For example, a 2004 survey found that large majorities of White college students classified all Latino groups as being not white. Write two of the study's authors, sociologists Joe A. Feagin and José Cobas: "If you are an American of color, white-imposed constructions of your personal identity often crash in as you maneuver through everyday worlds, especially outside your home and community." Although many Latin Americans do identify as white, this is typically an "unacceptable choice from most Anglo Whites' perspectives," despite that "this identification would likely seem reasonable to Latin Americans and Europeans."[5]

Other studies support the idea that while "becoming white" is an option for some Latinos, it is an option limited to those with light skin. Research conducted by Tanya Golash-Boza and William Darity, in 2008, for example, confirmed that Latinos with darker skin or stereotypically Latino features experienced more discrimination and were less likely to identify as white. It's a process they call "racialized assimilation," whereby immigrants learn to adapt to the U.S. racial system. In their words:

> [Racialized assimilation] takes into account the overwhelming importance that skin color has in shaping our interactions with others. Just as our racial status can be used to predict where we live, who we will marry and our life expectancy, how immigrants are racially categorized by others will heavily influence their path of assimilation.... Hispanics will become white, others Black, and not all are likely to continue to identify as Hispanic.[6]

Yet other studies have found that people who are more fluent in English, have higher incomes, and have spent more time in the United States were more likely to opt out of existing racial identification choices and choose a separate Latino racial category.[7] According to these studies, assimilation may trump skin color as a predictor of how completely Latinos are accepted by the mainstream, particularly White Americans.

There is also evidence that different groups of Hispanics may show dissimilar assimilation patterns. Research by sociologist John Iceland on dissimilarity indices, scores which measure the relative segregation or integration of groups across neighborhoods in a city, found that over generations, Cubans and Puerto Ricans who identify as White often tend to live in neighborhoods alongside Anglos, while both White and other-race Mexicans are more likely to live with other Hispanics. At the same time, Iceland found Black U.S. born Hispanics are more segregated from non-black Hispanics than their foreign born counterparts, suggesting immigrants become acclimated to the U.S. racial hierarchy of Black and White.[8] As a result, with assimilation, Black Hispanics may come to see themselves as Black Americans.

This hypothesis was supported by Mary Waters who studied the identities of second-generation Black immigrants to the United States. Waters found that unlike their parents, who rejected African-American culture, their children embraced it as their own. She writes: "The assimilation to America that they undergo is most definitely to Black America; they speak Black English with their peers, they listen to rap music, and they accept the peer culture of their Black American friends. They are aware of the fact that they are considered Black American by others and that they can be accused of "acting white" if they don't speak Black English and behave in particular ways."[9] Said one teenager, born of Jamaican parents:

> I consider myself a Black American. When I think of a Black American I don't think of them as coming from the West Indies … I would not think of someone in a suit. I would think of a regular teenager. I would think of a regular person. I think of someone that is in style.… [By contrast, Jamaicans] dress with neon colors. Most of the girls wear gold and stuff like that.[10]

One factor that will inevitably change racial attitudes in the United States is intermarriage, and since 1967, Americans have come a long way in their views of what used to be call miscegenation, or race mixing. That year, the United States Supreme Court unanimously ruled, in *Loving v. Virginia*, that Virginia's miscegenation law banning marriage between Blacks and Whites was unconstitutional. The interracial couple involved – 17-year-old Mildred Jeter, who was Black, and her childhood sweetheart, 23-year-old White construction worker, Richard Loving – married in Washington, D.C. and returned to their home state in 1958, where they were charged with unlawful cohabitation and jailed. According to the judge in the case, Leon M. Bazile, "Almighty God created the races white, Black, yellow, malay, and red, and he placed them on separate continents … The fact that he separated the races shows that he did not intend for the races to mix." Judge Bazile sentenced the Lovings to a year in prison, to be suspended if the couple agreed to leave the state for the next 25 years.[11]

Once the prohibition on race mixing became illegal, the number of interracial marriages took off, from 150,000 in 1960 to 900,000 in 1980. By 2000, there were 3.1 million unions between people of different races, accounting for 6.2 percent of all marriages. In 2008, the percent of intermarriages increased to 7.6 percent, meaning that one in every thirteen marriages was interracial. However, there were big differences by ethnicity. When looking at just native-born Americans, the intermarriage rates for White, Black, Latino, and Asian were 7.1 percent, 17.4 percent, 52.5 percent, and 72.5 percent, respectively. In the case of Asians and Latinos, these high intermarriage rates occurred despite enormous growth in their populations, meaning a corresponding increase in the number of potential marriage partners among co-ethnics.[12]

Not only is intermarriage more common among Asians and Latinos than among Blacks, the rate at which they marry Whites is also higher. Among intermarried Asians and Latinos, about 90 percent marry Whites; only 69 percent of intermarried Blacks marry Whites. Note sociologists Jennifer Lee and Frank D. Bean, "The relatively higher intermarriage rates of Asians and Latinos indicate that not only do these groups become more receptive to intermarriage as they acculturate, but that Whites increasingly perceive them as suitable marriage partners, something that may not be occurring with Blacks".[13]

Lee and Bean found that while intermarried couples explained that their parents were generally open about them dating people of different racial or ethnic backgrounds, they drew the line when it came to marrying Blacks. Said one woman they interviewed, a 24-year-old born to a White mother and a Mexican father:

> I was never brought up to hate or dislike Black people, but if I dated a Black man, my White side of the family and Mexican side of the family would disown me. And they've made it very clear. My dad told me if I ever brought a Black guy home, he would kill him, and my grandma told me if I ever brought a Black man home that she would kill me. As long as he wasn't Black. Never said anything about any Asians or Indian or Pakistani, nothing. As long as he wasn't Black.[14]

A 26-year-old woman born to a Vietnamese mother and a White father stated:

> Yeah, they didn't like Black. My dad had a big problem about me dating Blacks in high school and right after high school. And my mom, I tried to see how she would accept me dating Black people, and she said that if I ever got married to a Black guy, I wouldn't be accepted in her house anymore. And then I said, "What about our grandchild?" and she said, "No," so I'm not really attracted to Black guys anymore.[15]

The concern of parents was perhaps best expressed by anthropologist Rich Benjamin, who wrote "Many Latino immigrants fear their children will not assimilate into the American dream, but into the rap-rhyming, booty-shaking, baby-making, welfare-chasing shiftlessness of urban Blacks. Those Latino parents frankly counsel their children to avoid the Black kids at school, fearing that the barrio will breed in them the defeat that the projects supposedly bred into Black kids."[16]

Though it is likely that these parents have come to internalize, on some level, the anti-Black aversion that has typified life in the United States, prejudice against Blacks is also common in Latin America. It is likely that this breed of discrimination has staying power. Complicating the matter is that Latin American immigrants are acutely aware that anti-Black prejudice is endemic in the United States; parents may be attempting to "protect" their children by distancing them from the racism that is so often directed at Blacks, or those seen as "acting Black."

On the other side of the coin, African Americans often tend to face stiff opposition from other Blacks when it comes to marrying "outside the race." Among African Americans who had married interracially, Lee and Bean heard about frequent objections being raised by other Blacks. Many mentioned having been accused of being "race traitors," of "weakening the race," and of "adding cream to their coffee" when they dated or married non-African Americans. This was particularly true for Black men, who are sometimes confronted with questions such as "Why are you dating her?" or "Why are you disrespecting your people?" Said one African-American man who married a White woman, "In the Black community, White is not good, you know. That is like the devil. I may walk into a restaurant with my wife and two kids, and it's like, 'You frickin' sellout!' And it's all I can do not to reach back and grab somebody's dreadlocks."[17] Writes Randall Kennedy in his book *Sellout: The Politics of Racial Betrayal*, allegations of selling out can be triggered by "marrying a White person, passing, 'acting white,' 'speaking white,' 'thinking white,' describing oneself as 'multiracial,' living in a White neighborhood, serving as a police officer or prosecutor, working as an attorney for an elite law firm, or opposing affirmative action."[18]

It remains to be seen how Hispanics will fit into the current and future racial order of the United States. African Americans have always been the one group that immigrants have historically distanced themselves from in an effort to achieve whiteness. However, as anthropologist Arlene Dávila observes, Latinos have shared African-Americans' position on the lowest rung. Like African Americans, they have been stereotyped as crime-ridden and poverty-stricken, and both share similar socio-economic statistics as far as poverty, education, and discrimination indexes. "Latinos have seldom been branded as 'model minorities,'" she notes, "as have some Asian Americans."[19] Rather, the stereotypes of Asian Americans are markedly different. Whereas Asian Americans are often viewed as intelligent, hardworking, law-abiding, and successful, Latinos are more regularly thought of as less intelligent, welfare prone, poor, and in the United States without legal status.[20]

Latinos are not the only group to find itself racialized, or even stigmatized, in a country with a Black-White history, and increasingly, a Black-White-Hispanic racial order. Sociologist Bandana Purkayashita described the challenges that second-generation Indians face in the United States. "Like other minorities," Purkayashita writes, "the inability of ... South Asian Americans to define themselves in the same racially neutral terms as their White peers, emphasizes their marginality." Her research reveals that many U.S. born South Asians encountered incidents similar to those frequently experienced by African Americans or Hispanics, being mistaken for the cleaning lady, being racially profiled, stopped by police, or encountering negative reactions from friends' parents. One of his research participants, Varsha, described what it is like being the only non-White student in an overwhelmingly white, affluent suburb:

> I think I am [not just] American because of my skin color. I mean it is a racial element, and just the way I look ... because you know when people look at you they look at your physical appearance and they look at your skin color ... Like a lot of people, they thought I'm Spanish, something like that. So it's kind of different ... I'm like, no, I'm not Spanish. And they're like, what are you? And I'm like, Indian, you know. It's so awkward to even be classified like that.[21]

In the America of post-September 11, 2001, the stereotyping of Asian Americans as "other" can be especially pernicious for those of South Asian descent, especially those who may "look Middle Eastern" or have names that "sound" Middle Eastern. In the aftermath of the attacks, Sikh males, whose religion requires them to wear turbans, were especially vulnerable, and after the 9/11 attacks, they became targets of several hate crimes. The first man killed in retaliation was a Sikh, and the killer was quoted in police reports as saying, "all Arabs had to be shot" and wanted to "slit some Iranians' throats." Radio stations provoked trouble by referring to Sikhs as "cloth heads" and "diaper heads." Purkayashta relates how many of the second generation South Asians he interviewed became fearful of attacks by Americans. One Muslim woman described feeling paralyzed with fear the first time she went to the grocery store and felt that everyone was staring at her. Many South Asian women were advised by well-meaning friends and family to stop wearing "Indian" clothes. Said one college freshman:

> People are really ignorant, and they don't bother to find out anything before they say things. Like in my senior year in high school, September 11 happened, and a couple of months later this teacher said something like all Muslims are terrorists.... Lots of students don't know any better. But a person like her that I looked up to and I respect should recognize what's going on and not label me a terrorist because I am not.[22]

However, Asian Americans, as immigrants, are generally well received by Whites, in marked contrast to Latinos. Fewer Asian Americans are in the United States without legal status, and they tend to fall much closer to Whites than to Latinos on the socioeconomic scale, surpassing Whites on many measures.

Importantly, as political scientists Marisa Abrajano and Zoltan L. Hajnal note, Whites tend to have different stereotypes of Asian Americans than they do of Latinos, at least Latino immigrants. About 61 percent of Americans are concerned that undocumented immigrants are "putting an unfair burden on U.S. schools, hospitals, and government services," and another 87 percent are concerned that immigrants "making low wages might make U.S. employers less willing to pay American workers a decent wage." Additionally, 58 percent feel that immigrants do not learn English quickly enough, and about one-third of Americans believe that Latino immigrants significantly increase crime. When given the choice between "primarily moving in the direction of integrating illegal immigrants into American society" or "in the direction of stricter enforcement against illegal immigration," almost 70 percent choose stricter enforcement. Polls also show that despite the fact that only about a quarter of the foreign-born population is undocumented, most Americans believe that the majority of immigrants are here without legal status.[23]

NOTES

1. Yancey, George. *Who Is White?: Latinos, Asians, and the New Black/NonBlack Divide.* (Boulder, CO: Lynne Rienner Publishers, 2003), 15.
2. Waters, Mary C. and Philip Kasinitz. "Discrimination, Race Relations, and the Second Generation," *Social Research.* Vol. 77, No. 1, Spring 2010, 111.
3. Vasquez, Jessica M. "Blurred Borders For Some But Not 'Others': Racialization, 'Flexible Ethnicity,' Gender, and Third-Generation Mexican American Identity," *Sociological Perspectives.* Vol. 53, No. 1, Spring 2010, 52.
4. Ibid., 53.

5. Feagin, Joe R. and José A. Cobas. *Latinos Facing Racism: Discrimination, Resistance, and Endurance.* (Boulder, CO: Paradigm Publishers, 2014), 24.
6. Golash-Boza, Tanya and William Darity Jr. "Latino Racial Choices: The Effects of Skin Colour and Discrimination on Latinos' and Latinas' Racial Self-Identifications," *Ethnic and Racial Studies.* Vol. 31, No. 5, 2008, 932.
7. Frank, Reanne, Ilana Redstone Akresh, and Bo Lu. "Latino Immigrants and the U.S. Racial Order: How and Where Do They Fit In?" *American Sociological Review.* Vol. 75, No. 3, June 2010, 384.
8. Iceland, John. *Where We Live Now: Immigration and Race in the United States.* (Berkeley, CA: University of California Press, 2009), 102.
9. Waters, Mary C. "Ethnic and Racial Identities of Second-Generation Black Immigrants in New York City," *The International Migration Review.* Vol. 28, No. 4, Winter 1994, 807.
10. Ibid., 808.
11. U.S. Supreme Court, *Loving v. Virginia.* https://www.law.cornell.edu/supreme court/text/388/1.
12. Lee, Jennifer and Frank D. Bean. *The Diversity Paradox: Immigration and the Color Line in 21st Century America.* (New York, NY: The Russell Sage Foundation, 2010), 86.
13. Ibid.
14. Ibid., 93.
15. Ibid.
16. Benjamin, Rich. *Searching for Whitopia: An Improbable Journey to the Heart of White America.* (New York, NY: Hyperion, 2009), 300.
17. Lee and Bean, 94.
18. Kennedy, Randall. *Sellout: The Politics of Racial Betrayal.* (New York, NY: Vintage, 2009), 9.
19. Dávila, Arlene. *Latino Spin: Public Image and the Whitewashing of Race.* (New York, NY: New York University Press, 2008), 162.
20. Abrajano, Marisa and Zoltan L. Hajnal. *White Backlash: Immigration, Race, and American Politics.* (Princeton, NJ: Princeton University Press, 2015), 17.
21. Purkayastha, Bandana. *Negotiating Ethnicity: Second-Generation South Asian Americans Traverse a Transnational World.* (New Brunswick, NJ: Rutgers University Press, 2005), 28.
22. Ibid., 44.
23. Abrajano and Hajnal, 31.

24

RACE, ECONOMICS, AND SOCIETY

THE ELECTIONS of 2016 brought immigration front and center, and not always in the most positive way. From the Republican nominee who launched his campaign by bashing undocumented immigrants as rapists and murderers, it was clear that there would be plenty of demagoguery and not quite as much general policy discussion as one might wish for.

The economy in 2020 has improved significantly since the economic meltdown of 2008, despite a precipitous drop with Covid-19. But there are still parts of America that feel anxious about their economic future (and present), and they see immigration, especially Mexican immigration – especially Mexican illegal immigration –, as a serious threat to their own livelihood, if not the economy of the U.S. in general. And many of those people are willing to lump all Latinos/Hispanics into the "threat" category. Those on one end of the spectrum would cut off all immigration, "build the wall, higher!" – while more benign examples are people threatened by a Latino takeover, e.g. that uncle who insists that we're going down the tubes because he's asked if he wants to press "2" for Spanish. Unfortunately, the antipathy directed at undocumented Latinos is often directed at all Latinos; this, despite that nearly two-thirds of Hispanics now living in the United States were born here.

Abrajano and Hajnal contend that fear of a Latino invasion is driven "in part by the size of the immigrant population itself, but more substantially by an immigrant threat narrative perpetuated by the media and politicians alike."[1] Their analysis found that since the mid-1990s, 66 percent of network news coverage of Latinos incorporates crime, terrorism, or unauthorized immigration, resulting in a clear link between crime and immigration in the public's imagination. A majority of White Americans view Latinos as being particularly prone to violence. Implicit attitude tests show a clear connection in the minds of Americans between Latinos and being undocumented. Concerns about undocumented immigration have also become bound up with the issue of health care. Abrajano and Hanjal contend that the public narrative is essentially one of racial threat driven by such close proximity to a sizable and growing Latino populations, writing:

> With larger numbers comes the potential for more competition for scarce resources like housing, education, welfare, jobs, and any number of other public services. Greater visibility of the immigrant population can also, in and of itself, spark stereotypes and concerns. The underlying idea is that a larger out-group increases feelings of threat – either because that threat is real or simply because it is perceived.[2]

Among Americans' concerns is that Hispanics will not assimilate, as did other immigrant groups in the past. In his 2002 book *The Death of the West*, Patrick Buchanan complained, "Mexicans not only come from another culture, but millions are of another race. History and experience teach us that different races are far more difficult to assimilate." Buchanan warns of a Mexican "Aztlan Plot" to recapture the land lost under the Treaty of Guadalupe Hidalgo, which would lead to the "Reconquista" of the American southwest; he compares Mexicans to the barbarians invading ancient Rome, referring to "the Third World invasion and conquest of America" as a "state of emergency."[3]

In a 2004 article, "The Hispanic Challenge," Harvard professor Samuel P. Huntington wrote that Hispanics, particularly Mexicans, are dividing America into "two peoples, two cultures, and two languages." He warned of Hispanics "rejecting the Anglo-Protestant values that built the American dream" and that the United States "ignores this challenge at its peril." Huffington argues that this "would not necessarily be the end of the world; it would, however, be the end of the America we have known for more than three centuries."[4]

The assertions of Buchanan and Huntington are patently false and have been dispelled by countless studies over the years. In perhaps the largest longitudinal study of its kind, sociologists Alejandro Portes and Rubén Rumbaut interviewed over 4,000 second generation teens twice, first in 1992 as freshmen and then in 1996 as seniors.

As freshman, about half the Mexicans and three-quarters of the other Hispanics preferred to speak English over Spanish. Four years later, three-quarters of the Mexicans preferred English, while the number for other Hispanics had risen well into the 90th percentile.[5] A study published in 2004 by Richard Alba of the University of Albany's Mumford Center concluded that although Hispanics are retaining their Spanish longer than earlier European immigrant groups and the Asian-Americans of today, English monolingualism is the predominate pattern by the third generation.[6] In 2012, Pew Research Center demonstrated that although only 38 percent of first generation Hispanics speak English at least "pretty well," the numbers increased to 92 percent for the second generation and 96 percent for the third. In terms of identity, 63 percent of second generation Hispanics and 69 percent of the third generation described themselves as being "a typical American."[7]

Political scientist Jack Citrin and psychologist David O. Sears developed a patriotism scale based on the level of agreement to three statements: "I am proud to be American," "I have great love for America," and "I find the sight of the flag very moving." They found that native-born Latinos expressed almost exactly the same level of attachment to the United States as Whites.[8] They conclude that "fears that more ethnic diversity in the United States will undermine patriotism seem overblown."[9] The word "overblown" seems too cautious, more like a gross understatement, based on my experience behind the focus group window.

Yet in terms of the most recent public discourse, the concern of most Americans seems to be less on the question of whether Hispanics will assimilate and more on the issue of illegal immigration. In her 2015 book, *¡Adios, America!: The Left's Plan to Turn Our Country Into a Third World Hellhole*, a work replete with one-liner zingers directed at Hispanics and liberals alike, conservative commentator Ann Coulter blasts liberals for defending undocumented Latinos: "I don't mean to be obtuse, but why is it a crisis that illegal aliens are 'living in the shadows'? ... It is not a crisis for Americans that other people have come into our country illegally and now find it uncomfortable to be living here breaking the law. It's supposed to be uncomfortable to break the law. Perhaps illegal aliens should have considered that before coming."[10]

Although Coulter speaks to conservative extremism, the success of Donald Trump in the 2016 presidential primaries seems ample evidence that in the minds of many Whites, especially Republican Whites, there is deep concern about immigration from Latin America, particularly Mexico. When Trump announced his candidacy for the Republican presidential nomination on June 16, 2015, he declared: "I will build a great wall – and nobody builds walls better than me, believe me – and I'll build them very inexpensively. I will build a great, great wall on our southern border, and I will make Mexico pay for that wall. Mark my words."[11] On July 6, he clarified his point, "What can be simpler or more accurately stated? The Mexican Government is forcing their most unwanted people into the United States. They are, in many cases, criminals, drug dealers, rapists, etc."[12]

One of the explanations of Trump's appeal may be that increasingly more Americans are being directly exposed to Hispanic immigration, and numerous studies have shown that concerns about immigrants and opposition to immigration both increase as the size of the local immigrant population grows.[13] Although the U.S. Hispanic population is still anchored in traditional settlement areas like California, Texas, New York, and Florida, Latinos are increasingly dispersing across the U.S. While the 100 largest counties of Hispanic population contain 71 percent of all Hispanics, the share of all Hispanics who live in these counties is decreasing. Demographer William H. Frey identified 145 areas where Hispanics make up less than 16 percent of the population, but had a 2000–10 growth rate of at least 86 percent, with many of these areas being in the Southeast.[14] According to Frey, nearly half of Hispanics arriving in these new destinations are foreign born, and compared to the Hispanic population as a whole are less proficient in English, less educated, and poorer.[15]

Historian Mary E. Odem documents the upheaval in suburban Atlanta, a city traditionally characterized by a Black and White dichotomy and a legacy of segregation, provoked by the growth in the foreign born population, from 47,815 in 1980 to 612,759 in 2005; over half of this staggering increase of 1,182 percent is driven by Latin American immigrants. Of the reaction by the suburban native born, Odem writes:

> Immigrant settlement has unsettled many in the suburbs. While residents worry about the social transformation of their neighborhoods and schools, local governments struggle to address the increased demands on education, transportation, and housing resources.... Local authorities have created a range of policies in education, law enforcement, housing and transportation. While some measures focus on integrating immigrants, others aim to exclude and penalize them, with the latter measures directed primarily at Latino immigrants.[16]

In the suburban community of Farmers Branch, Texas, to the northwest of Dallas, Tim O'Hare, a member of the city council, proposed making it difficult for undocumented immigrants by barring landlords from leasing units to them and penalizing employers who hired them. Also under discussion were proposals to make

English the official language of the city and having law enforcement officers ask people to demonstrate that they were in the city legally. Typical letters to the editor of the local paper included: "I grew up there and it saddens me to see what it has become. I am tired of hearing Spanish in the streets and trying to figure out if someone understands what I'm saying" and "A single-family home is for a single family, not a hotel for six or seven families."[17]

Research by Pew indicates that Americans disagree deeply over immigration policies, including how to deal with undocumented immigrants living in the U.S. and whether to build a wall along the U.S.-Mexico border, and there is a substantial – and growing – partisan divide over whether immigrants generally are a strength or burden on the country. Between 1994 and 2005, Republicans and Democrats were similar in their views of immigrants. However, beginning around 2006, their views began to diverge. That year, the partisan gap between Republicans and Democrats grew to 15 percentage points. Ten years later, the share of Democrats and Democratic-leaning independents saying that immigrants strengthen the country steadily increased, from 49 percent then to 78 percent, while the share with this view among Republicans and Republican leaners is at about 35 percent. There was similar partisan divergence in views toward building a wall along the border; 63 percent of Republicans were in favor, compared with only 13 percent of Democrats. There were also substantial generational and ethnic differences. While just 20 percent of Millennials favor a wall, 36 percent of Gen Xers, and 43 percent of Boomers favor the idea. In terms of ethnicity, 43 percent of Whites were in favor, compared with only 13 percent of Blacks and 16 percent of Hispanics.[18]

SOCIO-ECONOMIC DISPARITIES

In terms of socioeconomics, historically, Hispanics have occupied a middle position between Blacks and Whites in the United States. However, there is evidence that the relative standing of Hispanics has declined, and they have come to replace African Americans at the bottom of the class hierarchy. Sociologist Douglas S. Massey points to rising segregation levels, increased discrimination, deepening poverty, stagnating education levels, and a social safety net, which allows immigrants to fall through the holes. He contends that in one critical way, Mexicans are "much worse off than Black Americans":

> Whatever discriminatory barriers African Americans still face, they at least have the legal right to live and work in the United States. In contrast, one-fifth of all Mexican Americans lack any

legal claim on American society because they are present without authorization, and this fraction is rising rapidly. If the share of Latinos in undocumented status continues to rise, the resulting underclass will be even "better" than the one that emerged in Black inner cities during the 1980s. Not only will its members be exploited and excluded; they will be outside the law itself, deportable at a moment's notice and perhaps even at serious risk of incarceration for the felonious crime of living and working in the United States without permission.[19]

While many do point to socioeconomic gains by Latinos born in the United States, Hispanics, as a group, still lag significantly behind Whites on key measures. For instance, in 2015, the median Hispanic worker earned 72 percent of the median White worker. The median Hispanic household income was $42,500, nearly $18,000 less than that of Whites. The median net worth of Hispanic households is about one-tenth that of Whites, and Hispanic households are twice as likely to live in poverty. Only 12 percent of Latino households have access to a defined benefit pension, half the rate of White and Black households. Less than 70 percent of working-age Latino households do not own assets in a retirement account compared to 37 percent of White households.[20]

Still, despite claims by Massey, the economic situation for African Americans remains worse than that of Hispanics. In 2015, African American households had an income nearly $8,000 less than Hispanics, a household net worth of one-thirteenth that of Whites, were three times as likely to live in poverty, and had an unemployment rate of 10.1 percent, more than double that of Whites. More than half of Black families with children are headed by a single mother, compared to one-fifth of White families with children, and nearly 47 percent of families headed by a Black single mother are in poverty. One-in-10 Black homeowners who took out mortgages at the height of the housing boom eventually lost their home to foreclosure.[21]

Then there is the issue of the mass incarceration of African Americans, what Michelle Alexander calls "the new Jim Crow." According to the NAACP, Blacks now constitute nearly 1 million of the total 2.3 million incarcerated population and are incarcerated at nearly six times the rate of Whites. One in six Black men had been incarcerated as of 2001, and African Americans represent 26 percent of juvenile arrests, 44 percent of youth who are detained, 46 percent of the youth who are judicially waived to criminal court, and 58 percent of the youth admitted to state prisons. African Americans represent 12 percent of the total population of drug users, but 38 percent of those arrested for drug offenses and 59 percent of those in state prison for a drug offense. Amazingly, African Americans serve virtually as much time in prison for a drug offense (58.7 months) as Whites do for a violent offense (61.7 months).[22]

Despite these blatant structural iniquities, Americans are deeply divided in their perceptions of race and racial progress. In their 2012 paper, "The *Real* Record of Racial Attitudes," authors Lawrence D. Bobo, Camille Z. Charles, Maria Krysan, and Alicia D. Simpson synthesized data from the General Social Survey (GSS), a comprehensive survey of social trends in American life since 1972, and while the results demonstrate significant progress in terms of attitudes toward race, the data still indicate certain "enduring frictions and conflicts."

For example, in 1972, about 15 percent of Whites nationwide thought that Black and White children should attend separate schools; by 1985, so few people endorsed the segregationist response that the GSS dropped this question. Still, in 2008, 28 percent of Whites still supported an individual homeowner's right to discriminate on the basis of race when selling a home. When shown a card depicting a 15-house neighborhood with their own home in the middle and asked to indicate their preferred racial mixture, one in five Whites created an ideal neighborhood that was all white; one in four created a neighborhood with no Blacks in it, and one in three created a neighborhood with no Hispanics or no Asians. The authors note that although the overall record of GSS data "strongly points to a large and growing orbit of social and political acceptance for African Americans," they add, "despite accepting integration as a general principle and a small minority presence in schools, neighborhoods, or other public social spaces, Whites express strong social distance preferences; indeed, a racial hierarchy of association remains, with African Americans at or near its bottom."[23]

NOTES

1. Ibid., 27.
2. Ibid., 47.
3. Buchanan, Patrick J. *The Death of the West: How Dying Populations and Immigrant Invasions Imperil Our Country and Civilization.* (New York, NY: Thomas Dunne Books, 2010), 125.
4. Huntington, Samuel P. "The Hispanic Challenge," *Foreign Policy*, October 28, 2009. http://foreignpolicy.com/2009/10/28/the-hispanic-challenge/.
5. Portes, Alejandro and Rubén G. Rumbaut. *Legacies: The Story of the Immigrant Second Generation.* (Berkeley, CA: University of California Press, 2001).

6. Alba, Richard. Lewis Mumford Center for Comparative Urban and Regional Research University at Albany, "Language Assimilation Today: Bilingualism Persists More Than in the Past, But English Still Dominates," December 2004. http://mumford.albany.edu/children/reports/language_assimilation/language_assimilation_brief.pdf.
7. Pew Research Center, "When Labels Don't Fit: Hispanics and Their Views of Identity," April 4, 2012. http://www.pewhispanic.org/2012/04/04/when-labels-dont-fit-hispanics-and-their-views-of-identity/.
8. Citrin, Jack and David O. Sears. *American Identity and the Politics of Multiculturalism*. (Cambridge, UK: Cambridge University Press, 2014), 73.
9. Ibid., 87.
10. Coulter, Ann. *¡Adios, America!: The Left's Plan to Turn Our Country into a Third World Hellhole*. (Washington, D.C.: Regnery Publishing, 2015).
11. "This Is What Trump's Border Wall Could Cost US," *CNBC*. http://www.cnbc.com/2015/10/09/.
12. "Donald Trump's False Comments Connecting Mexican Immigrants and Crime," *The Washington Post*. July 8, 2015, https://www.washingtonpost.com/news/fact-checker/wp/2015/07/08/donald-trumps-false-comments-connecting-mexican-immigrants-and-crime/.
13. Abrajano and Hajnal, 47.
14. Frey, William H. *Diversity Explosion: How New Racial Demographics Are Remaking America*. (Washington, D.C.: Brookings Institution Press, 2015), 72.
15. Ibid., 76.
16. Odem, Mary E. eds. Audrey Singer, Susan W. Hardwick, and Caroline B. Brettell. "Unsettled in the Suburbs: Latino Immigration and Ethnic Diversity in Metro Atlanta," in *Twenty-First Century Gateways: Immigrant Incorporation in Suburban America*. (Washington, D.C.: The Brookings Institution, 2008), 106.
17. Brettell, Caroline B. " 'Big D': Incorporating New Immigrants in a Sunbelt Suburban Metropolis," in *Twenty-First Century Gateways*, 78.
18. Pew Research Center, "Americans' Views of Immigrants Marked by Widening Partisan, Generational Divides," April 15, 2016. http://www.pewresearch.org/fact-tank/2016/04/15/americans-views-of-immigrants-marked-by-widening-partisan-generational-divides/.
19. Massey, Douglas S. "Racial Formation in Theory and Practice: The Case of Mexicans in the United States," *Race and Social Problems*. Vol. 1, No. 1, March 2009, 25.
20. Joint Economic Committee, United States Congress, "The Economic State of the Latino Community in America," October 2015. http://www.jec.senate.gov/

public/_cache/files/2d162187-e1cc-4629-a39e-7f0853194280/jec-hispanic-report-final.pdf.

21. Joint Economic Committee, United States Congress, "Economic Challenges in the Black Community," April 14, 2015. http://www.jec.senate.gov/public/_cache/files/eb7a5e6e-db59-452e-8736-0603bef2d2c8/economic-challenges-in-the-african-american-community-4-14.pdf.

22. NAACP, "Criminal Justice Fact Sheet." http://www.naacp.org/pages/criminal-justice-fact-sheet.

23. Bobo, Lawrence D., Camille Z. Charles, Maria Krysan, and Alicia D. Simpson. ed. by Peter V. Marsden. "The *Real* Record of Racial Attitudes," in *Social Trends in American Life: Findings from the General Social Survey since 1972*. (Princeton, NJ: Princeton University Press, 2012), 38.

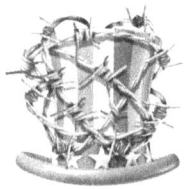

25

THE PRESENT, THE FUTURE

WHITES and non-Whites tend to be on a completely different page when it comes to perceptions of racial prejudice and racial progress. In an ironic twist, while non-Whites tend to feel that racism is alive and well in America and that progress is a slow and unsteady process, among Whites, a common narrative is that of "reverse discrimination." In the words of a respondent in a focus group I conducted, "You have African American and Hispanic dorms; I'd like to see universities start building all White dorms."

We may get a clearer picture of what's going on from a 2019 report by Pew, which showed marked differences between Blacks and Whites in their perceptions of the progress America in terms of race. According to the study, 84 percent of Blacks say African Americans are treated less fairly than Whites in their dealings with police compared with only 63 percent of Whites. Similarly, 74 percent of Blacks compared with 38 percent of Whites say Blacks are not treated as fairly as Whites when applying for a loan or mortgage; indeed, Blacks were much more likely than Whites to agree that Blacks are not treated fairly at work, in stores or restaurants, in local public schools, in getting healthcare, and when voting.[1]

During the 1960s, there was a great shift in awareness of racial issues. Though not everyone agreed that America should be proactive about narrowing the racial divide, the images of Dr. King, of riots in Watts and other cities, the image of LBJ signing civil rights legislation that was stunning in scope did have an impact on the minds of Americans and showed them that, yes, there was a racial problem. Racism is nowhere near as invidious as it was in the 1960s. That decade represented a stunning leap in terms of racial tolerance as compared with decades prior, though 2020 might indeed represent another watershed.

Many sociologists have argued that in its place has emerged a more subtle type of racism, what Bonilla-Silva calls "color-blind racism." In his research, he found that while most Whites outwardly proclaim that they don't see color, their statements were often prefaced with "Well, I'm not racist, but...." They insist that minorities are responsible for the so-called race problem we have in America, and they denounce Blacks for "playing the race card" by demanding race-based programs and for crying "racism" whenever they are criticized by Whites. He writes, "Most Whites believe that if Blacks and other minorities would just stop thinking about the past, work hard, and complain less (particularly about racial discrimination), then Americans of all hues could 'all get along.'"[2] Bonilla-Silva continues:

> Compared to Jim Crow racism, the ideology of color blindness seems like "racism lite." Instead of relying on name calling (niggers, Spics, Chinks), color-blind racism otherizes softly ("these people are human, too"); instead of proclaiming that God placed minorities in the world in a servile position, it suggests they are behind because they do not work hard enough; instead of viewing interracial marriage as wrong on a straight racial basis, it regards it as "problematic" because of concerns over the children, location, or the extra burden it places on couples.[3]

Revealing are some of the comments I received after posting a piece called "Why Do Conservatives Hate Talking About Race?" on LinkedIn. Here is one typical response:

> I don't get how I can be considered a racist for viewing everyone equal and thus not giving two shits about "race issues," yet someone can be called tolerant for continually bringing up a topic that serves to divide people on the assumption that one group is inherently racist and another a victim solely due to the color of one's skin … Jesus Christ, we all bleed red blood, and the only thing I will judge anyone on is their actions, their morals/ethics, and their integrity.… But no, I suppose that's somehow racist too.… Or is it that being truly tolerant doesn't serve a financial/political

25 | THE PRESENT, THE FUTURE

> interest for a select few who profit off of the continued strife this ridiculous issue has continued to generate?

And another:

> You mentioned Black incarceration rates. One elephant in the room that liberals evidently hate talking about is the high percentage of America's Black kids born out of wedlock and raised by single moms. Is it any wonder that so many of these kids turn into roving animals? You can't blame slavery or Jim Crow for this. When I was in school, the worst discipline cases – all white, by the way – followed this sorry pattern: no father in the home, sometimes no mother, either.[4]

Not only is there a deep aversion on the part of conservative Whites to the government taking race conscious measures to alleviate racial disparities, there is a demonstrated reluctance to talk about race at all. Following the massacre of nine African Americans by Dylann Roof in Charleston in June 2015, conservative politicians and commentators alike went to great lengths to attribute Roof's motives to anything but racism. This was in spite of the fact that he left behind a collection of racist selfies and a racist manifesto explaining his actions. "I have no choice," states part of that final section, titled "An Explanation." "I am not in the position to, alone, go into the ghetto and fight. I chose Charleston because it is [the] most historic city in my state, and at one time had the highest ratio of Blacks to Whites in the country." The manifesto declared, "Negroes have lower IQs, lower impulse control, and higher testosterone levels in general. These three things alone are a recipe for violent behavior."[5] Rick Perry, running for the GOP nomination, called the massacre an "accident" possibly caused by the overuse of prescription drugs. Presidential hopeful Rick Santorum and South Carolina Senator Lindsey Graham said it was a war on Christians. Many pundits said Roof was mentally ill. Erik Erickson, a right-winger widely followed by pundits, blamed Roof's murders on Bruce Jenner's gender reassignment.[6]

"Racism," wrote columnist Eric Boehlert, "like climate change, is denied as part of the larger conservative political reality," a point he supports with a series of poignant quotations by conservative commentators in a telling piece titled "Guns, Race, And Fox News' Pathological Denial." Bill O'Reilly announced, "We are not a racist nation.... Fair-minded Americans should be deeply offended, deeply offended that their country is being smeared with the bigotry brush." Steve Doocy declared,

345

"I don't know that Barack Obama could have been elected president if he was living in a racist nation." According to Eric Bolling, "It's getting tiring. We have a Black president, we have Black senators, we have Black heads as captains of business, companies. We have Black entertainment channels. Where – is there racism? I don't think there's racism. The only people perpetuating racism are people like this gentleman from the NAACP, are the Al Sharptons of the world. Let's move on. Let's move on."

Boehlert also points out that it is not just the pundits at Fox News who are in denial. In a 2013 interview, *Washington Post* columnist Jennifer Rubin complained that President Obama focuses too much on racism while also ignoring real problems in the Black community. Obama, she said, is not letting people "get out of this racial archaeology," so they are "held prisoners forever in a past that most Americans have never personally experienced." Peter Ferrara of the Heartland Institute, a Chicago-based conservative think tank, reported that same year that "racist attitudes" no longer "have any power or influence in American society."[7]

BLACK AMERICANS: STILL ON THE OUTSIDE

As legal scholar Randall Kennedy observes, color blindness is a fundamental idea in the modern American consciousness, offering a popular conception of that which is considered commendable racial thought and conduct. While some see it as a long range aspiration, others are in the camp of Supreme Court Justice John Roberts who said, "The way to stop discrimination on the basis of race is to stop discriminating on the basis of race," a phrase he used in the 2007 case, *Parents Involved in Community Schools v. Seattle School District No.1*, in a decision which denied school districts in Seattle and Louisville from voluntarily using racial classifications in order to achieve diversity. Roberts' statement is frequently employed by those opposed to affirmative action or other measures, which take race into account in order to remedy America's social ills.

The most widely cited statement associated with color blindness was made by Justice John Marshall Harlan in 1896, dissenting from the Supreme Court's ruling in *Plessy v. Ferguson*, which upheld the constitutionality of a Louisiana law requiring passengers of different race to occupy "equal but separate" cars on intrastate trains. Harlan stated:

> In respect of civil rights, common to all citizens, the Constitution of the United States does not ... permit any public authority to know the race of those entitled to be protected in the enjoyment of such

rights ... There is no caste here. Our constitution is color-blind, and neither knows nor tolerates classes among citizens.[8]

Importantly, as Kennedy notes, Justice Harlan offered no historical or textual support for his contention that the Constitution is color-blind, and the framers of the Fourteenth Amendment, which guaranteed equal protection of the law, declined to accept language that would have explicitly prohibited government from drawing racial lines.[9] Additionally, it is important to keep in mind the context in which Harlan was writing. Also in his dissent are the words:

> Everyone knows that the statute in question had its origin in the purpose, not so much to exclude White persons from railroad cars occupied by Blacks as to exclude colored people from coaches occupied by ... White persons ... What can more certainly arouse race hate, what can more certainly create and perpetuate a feeling of distrust between the races than state enactments which, in fact, proceed on the ground that colored citizens are so inferior and degraded that they cannot be allowed to sit in the public coaches occupied by White citizens?[10]

On the one hand are those who vehemently claim to not see color, who, ironically, tend to be the ones most opposed to actions designed to level the racial playing field and ensure that all Americans are entitled to equal opportunities. Likely, they are among the 61 percent of Whites, who, in a 2009 study by Lawrence D. Bobo and Alicia Simpson, agreed that African Americans have already achieved equality, a statement with which only 17 percent of African Americans agreed.[11] On the other hand, there are those of us who agree with another irony, one stated by Justice Harry Blackmun in his dissention in the 1978 affirmative action case *Regents of California v. Bakke*, which ruled that a university's use of racial "quotas" in its admissions process was unconstitutional, though a school's use of "affirmative action" to accept more minority applicants was constitutional in some circumstances: "In order to get beyond racism, we must first take account of race. There is no other way. And in order to treat some persons equally, we must treat them differently."[12]

It is difficult to argue that we live in a color-blind society when the experience of so many African Americans runs totally to the contrary. Take for example, the eminent sociologist William Julius Wilson, who has argued that class had supplanted race as the primary reason for the continued subordination of underprivileged Blacks.

Yet even Wilson admitted that the toxic impact of prejudice could not be completely ignored. He began his 2009 book *More Than Just Race* by writing:

> I am an internationally known Harvard professor, yet a number of unforgettable experiences remind me that, as a Black male in America looking considerably younger than my age, I am also feared. For example, several times over the years I have stepped into the elevator of my condominium dressed in casual clothes and could immediately tell from the body language of the other residents in the elevator that I made them feel uncomfortable. Were they thinking, "What is this Black man doing in this expensive condominium? Are we in danger?" I once sarcastically said to a nervous elderly couple who hesitated to exit the elevator because we were all getting off in the same floor, "Not to worry, I am a Harvard professor and I have lived in this building for nine years." When I am dressed casually, I am always a little relieved to step into an empty elevator, but I am not apprehensive if I'm wearing a tie.[13]

There may be no more telling example of the experience of Blacks, specifically male Blacks, than that given by sociologist Elijah Anderson in his book *Streetwise: Race, Class, and Change in an Urban Community*, a 10- year ethnographic study of an anonymous Eastern urban community he calls Village-Northton. Anderson deftly brings to light the racial tension that exists in American cities, the alienation of urban Blacks, and the fears that Whites often experience. Anderson writes:

> Most residents ascribe criminality, incivility, toughness, and street smartness to the anonymous Black male, who must work hard to make others trust his common decency. Pedestrians ... avert their eyes from the Black males, deferring to figures who are seen as unpredictable, menacing, and not to be provoked – predators ... Incapable of making distinctions between law-abiding Black males and others, they rely for protection on broad stereotypes based on color and gender, if not outright racism. They are likely to misread many of the signs displayed by law-abiding Black men, thus becoming apprehensive of almost any Black male they spot in public ... the fact that one is a physician or middle class or

female will not protect one from being treated as a Negro first and [anything else] second.[14]

Anderson makes amply clear that although no Black person is immune from suspicion and mistrust, these views are projected upon young Black males with particular acuteness, undermining their ability to be "taken for granted as law-abiding and civil participants in public places," often by Blacks themselves. He continues:

> In the minds of many Village residents, Black and white, the … status of the young Black male is determined by his youth, his Blackness, his maleness, and what these attributes have come to stand for in the shadow of the ghetto. In the context of racism, he is easily labeled "deviant." … Young Black males, particularly those who don the urban uniform (sneakers, athletic suits, gold chains, "gangster caps," sunglasses, and large portable radios or "boom boxes"), may be taken as the embodiment of the predator. In this uniform, which suggests to many the "dangerous underclass," these young men are presumed to be troublemakers or criminals. Thus, in the local milieu, the identity of predator is usually "given" to the young Black male and made to stick until he demonstrates otherwise, something not easy to do in circumstances that work to cut off communication.[15]

It is important to keep in mind that not all African Americans experience being Black in America in the same way. In his 2010 book, *Disintegration: The Splintering of Black America*, journalist Eugene Robinson bemoans that instead of one Black America, there are now four: a mainstream middle-class majority with a full ownership stake in American society; a large, abandoned minority with less hope than ever of escaping poverty; a small transcendent elite with enormous wealth, power, and influence; and two newly emergent groups: individuals of mixed-race heritage and recent Black immigrants who question what "Black" even means.[16]

Yet there is much in the common experience of Blacks that binds, and Robinson maintains that there is one important difference between Blacks, specifically mainstream Blacks, and that of other middle class Americans. He writes: "Despite all the progress that's been made, there's still a nagging sense of being looked down upon, of being judged, of being disrespected. What keeps this difference alive is that these suspicions aren't always paranoia. They're not always justified either, but there's enough reality behind them to keep alive a sense of separate but not-quite equal – enough to make many people seek safety, acceptance, and solidarity in numbers."[17]

The challenge of having to live daily with racial prejudice and White fear is pervasive, if not a constant for Blacks, particularly Black men. In his 2010 book about the pervasiveness of stereotypes and how they can impact the behavior and performance of people, particularly racial minorities, social psychologist Claude M. Steele chose the title *Whistling Vivaldi*, taken from the story of journalist Brent Staples, who as a young African-American graduate student at the University of Chicago learned that he could dissipate the fears of White people he encountered on the street by whistling popular songs. In Staples' words:

> I became an expert in the language of fear. Couples locked arms or reached for each other's hand when they saw me. Some crossed to the other side of the street. People who were carrying on conversations went mute and stared straight ahead, as though avoiding my eyes would save them ... I'd been a fool. I'd been walking the streets grinning good evening at people who were frightened to death of me. I did violence to them by just being. How had I missed this? ... I tried to be innocuous but didn't know how ... I began to avoid people. I turned out of my way into side streets to spare them the sense that they were being stalked ... Out of nervousness I began to whistle and discovered I was good at it. My whistle was pure and sweet – and also in tune. On the street at night I whistled popular tunes from the Beatles and Vivaldi's *Four Seasons*. The tension drained from people's bodies when they heard me. A few even smiled as they passed me in the dark.[18]

White fears and stereotypes of Blacks are not limited to the streets. Nor, as we have seen, are they limited to Blacks on the lower end of the socioeconomic spectrum. As legal scholars Devon W. Carbado and Mitu Gulati make clear in their book, *Acting White?: Rethinking Race in "Post-Racial" America*, in the workplace, Blacks are under constant scrutiny and must take great pains to project a proper "working identity," which includes how one dresses, speaks, styles one's hair; one's professional and social affiliations; who one marries or dates; one's politics and views about race; and where one lives.[19] "Talking white," for instance, is more advantageous to an employee than "talking Black," creating a constant pressure on Blacks to "work their speech" so as to reduce the likelihood that their co-workers and managers will become alienated. In order to get the job in the first place, Blacks must "whiten their resumes" and eliminate "explicit racial markers," such as activism in Black organizations or even majoring in African-American studies.[20] With the job in hand, one must take care to not be perceived as being "too Black," and employers need to be reassured that they will neither "play the race card" nor generate racial antagonism or tensions in the workplace; that they will not let White people "feel guilty about being white;" and that they will work hard to assimilate themselves into the firm's culture, by thinking of themselves as "people first and Black people second (or third or fourth)." Unlike the actors on Broadway described by Hilton Als in a March 2010 *New Yorker* article, who must "'act Black' before they're allowed to act human" at work; the pressure is always on to project an "acceptable" image.[21]

As Carbado and Gulati indicate, in order to be successful in America, the key may be in "acting like Obama" or at least the pre-presidential, pre-second term Obama. They write, "From Obama's very early public appearance at the Democratic National Convention in 2004, he seems to have understood that his political future would turn on his ability to work his identity for a White audience. He seems to have understood that he could not enact a racial performance that his White audience would perceive as being 'too Black.'"[22]

Presidential candidate Obama's style worked for then Senator Joe Biden, who described Obama as "the first mainstream African-American who is articulate and bright and clean and a nice-looking guy," prompting *Washington Post* columnist Eugene Robinson to ask, "What is it, exactly, that White people mean when they call a Black person 'articulate'?" That same week President George W. Bush had used the same word when talking about Obama. "He's an attractive guy. He's articulate," he told Fox News. Robinson writes: "Will wonders never cease? Here we have a man who graduated from Columbia University, who was president of the Harvard Law Review, who serves in the U.S. Senate and is the author of two best-selling books, who's a leading contender for the Democratic presidential nomination, and what do you know, he turns out to be articulate. Stop the presses."[23] Biden soon apologized, as would Senator Harry Reid, the Democratic majority leader, when word got out that he had predicted that Obama could become the country's first Black president because he was "light-skinned" and had "no Negro dialect, unless he wanted to have one."[24]

Fortunately, the discrimination against and racial oppression of African Americans has been made more visible in the last few years. The struggle for racial justice took center stage in 2016 when Colin Kaepernick, then a quarterback for the San Francisco 49ers, took a knee during the playing of the *Star Spangled Banner* as a way to protest racial injustice and police brutality. "I am not going to stand up to show pride in a flag for a country that oppresses Black people and people of color,"

Kaepernick said in August 2016, when the press first took notice. "To me, this is bigger than football, and it would be selfish on my part to look the other way. There are bodies in the street and people getting paid leave and getting away with murder." President Trump, then in his first year of office, said that any player who protested was a "son of a bitch" who should be fired.

A movement caught on, and the following weekend, large numbers of players took a knee. At first the NFL owners approved a new policy that would require every player to stand for the anthem or else be in the locker room while it played, though the rule was never enforced and essentially dissolved two months later after the NFL Players Association pushed back.[25] In October 2017, Kaepernick filed a grievance against the NFL, accusing owners of colluding to keep him out of the league. The NFL tried to dismiss the case, which was thrown out in arbitration, meaning the case would go to trial. On February 15, 2019, it was announced that Kaepernick had reached a confidential settlement with the NFL and withdrew the grievance.[26]

Things would change significantly in the fall of 2018. Nike unveiled an ad campaign featuring Kaepernick as an athlete taking a knee for justice, "Even if it means sacrificing everything." Faced with a tidal wave of support for Kaepernick, Jocelyn Moore, who was then the NFL's Exec VP/Communications & Public Affairs, said that the issues raised by Kaepernick "deserve our attention and action." The league soon launched its own social justice campaign including a "significant financial commitment" to issues of education and economic advancement, relationships between police and the communities they serve, and criminal justice reform.[27] The NFL would begin its reversal on May 30, 2020, following the murder of George Floyd, in a statement offering condolences to the Floyd family and unequivocally stating, "There remains an urgent need for action. We recognize the power of our platform in communities and as part of the fabric of American society. We embrace that responsibility and are committed to continuing the important work to address these systematic issues together with our players, clubs, and partners."[28] On June 6, 2020, NFL Commissioner Roger Goodell issued a statement saying, "We were wrong for not listening to NFL players earlier."

In the summer of 2020, with thousands of protestors showing their outrage over George Floyd's death and a systematic, violent racism that never seems to go away, it appears at least possible that White America might be awakening from its seeming obliviousness to the issue of racial oppression. Though racism has been a constant in American history, the oppression of African Americans has, without a doubt, been its most ugly, most deadly manifestation. And while the future football career of Colin Kaepernick is yet unknown, his legacy as a social justice trailblazer should be secure for a long time to come.

25 | THE PRESENT, THE FUTURE

AGING WHITES, DIVERSE MILLENNIALS

So. Where are we going? If one is looking for progress in racial attitudes, a good place to look is the attitudes of Millennials. To begin with, Millennials are the most diverse adult generation in U.S. history. In 2016, they were only about 56 percent white, compared with 72 percent of Baby Boomers who are white. The White percentage drops to 50 percent when looking at those age 12 and under, meaning that well before 2020 White children will become a minority.[29]

Although African Americans are increasing their share of the demographic pie by a few percentage points, the truly substantial change is being driven by Hispanics, who comprise 11 percent of the Baby Boomer population but about double that for Millennials. Of those 12 and under they represent a quarter.[30] From 2000 to 2010, the population of White children actually declined by 4.3 million, while the child population of Hispanics, Asian Americans, and those of mixed race increased by 4.8 million. At the same time, there were fewer White births than there were White children passing into adulthood. The net result is a substantial aging of the White population. In 2010, the median age for Whites was 42 years, 27.3 for Hispanics, 32.4 for Blacks, 35.4 for Asian Americans, and 19.9 for those of mixed race.[31]

There are indications that the younger generation is more racially tolerant than its elders, according to a study by Pew in 2010, with results that appear to demonstrate that times are changing. Roughly nine in 10 Millennials say they would be fine with a family member's marriage to a person of another race, which is significantly higher than older groups, particularly Americans aged 50 or older. Also, 93 percent agree with the statement "I think it is all right for Blacks and Whites to date each other." By contrast, when the first Generation Xers began to be tracked in the late 1980s, only about two-thirds agreed, though 86 percent agree today, a likely reflection of societal change. Fifty-six percent of White Millennials indicated that they have friends of different races, a full 20 points higher than White Baby Boomers.[32]

Despite this optimistic picture, even Millennials appear to have issues with race. For example, Spencer Piston, an assistant professor of political science at Syracuse University, found that 61 percent of Whites under age 30 rated Whites as more intelligent and harder-working than African Americans, just three percentage points below their older cohort. "White Millennials appear to be no less prejudiced than the rest of the White population," said Piston, "at least using this dataset and this measure of prejudice." A 2007 study, which looked at 2.5 million Implicit Attitude Tests (IATs) that were conducted over a 6-year period, tests that measure attitudes and beliefs that people may be unwilling or unable to report, found that, with the exception of those aged 60 or older, there was very little difference across generations in terms of racial prejudice.[33] However, younger respondents did show slightly lower levels of "explicit" or stated bias. Writing of the results, political analyst Sean McElwee concludes Millennials "are simply more deluded about their own beliefs."[34]

McElwee is not the only one to be complaining about the myth of Millennial exceptionalism, or at least that of White Millennials when it comes to racial tolerance. In June 2015, Scott Clement wrote an article in *The Washington Post* titled, "Millennials Are Just as Racist as Their Parents," which looked at the level of agreement with five standard measures of racial prejudice from the 2010, 2012, and 2014 General Social Survey: Blacks are lazy and less hardworking than Whites, Blacks are less intelligent than Whites, Blacks are less well-off due to a lack of motivation, I would be opposed to a relative marrying a Black person, and I would oppose living in a neighborhood that is 50 percent Black. Clement found that White Millennials expressed the least prejudice on four out of five measures in the survey, but only by a matter of 1 to 3 percentage points, not a meaningful difference. On Blacks being less intelligent than Whites, 23 percent of White Millennials agreed, four percentage points higher than their Generation X cohorts, suggesting a possible backsliding.[35]

In April 2015, following the discovery of a noose hanging from a tree at Duke University, occurring less than a week after the United States Department of Justice indicted a Georgia man for putting a noose around a civil rights statue at the University of Mississippi, *The Christian Science Monitor* ran a story asking, "Do colleges have a growing racism problem?" The piece quoted Ed Dorn, a civil rights history professor at the University of Texas in Austin: "A lot of people, even of the millennial generation, grew up believing that this country would always look a certain way, and that the people who were in charge of major institutions would always be of a certain color. But the color line is shifting, and in a few decades this will no longer be a White Man's country. That makes them uncomfortable, angry, and anxious."[36]

To what can we attribute this regression? Writer Mychal Denzel Smith may have hit on something, writing that Millennials are "fluent in colorblindness and diversity" but "illiterate in the language of anti-racism." Having grown up in the post-Civil Rights era, they have been taught that everyone is equal and, therefore, has equal opportunity for success. As a result, they see programs such as affirmative action, as another form of discrimination on par with Jim Crow segregation without believing themselves to be racist or supportive of racism.[37] According to Smith:

> [Millennials] were taught by their elders, Baby Boomers and Gen-Xers, about how to think about race and racism. The lessons Baby Boomers and Gen-Xers gleaned from the Civil Rights era is that racism is a matter of personal bigotry – racists hate people

25 | THE PRESENT, THE FUTURE

because of the color of their skin, or because they believe stereotypes about groups of people they've never met – not one of institutional discrimination and exploitation. The history Millennials have been taught is through that lens, with a specific focus on misunderstanding the message of Martin Luther King, Jr. ... Baby Boomers and Gen Xers generally decided to ignore King's diagnosis of the problem – White supremacy – and opted to make him a poster-child for a colorblind society, in which we simply ignore construct of race altogether and pray that it will disappear on its own.

Beyond the attitudes of Millennials, the actual demographic makeup of that generation and the generations to follow it, point to fundamental restructuring of American society. As demographer William H. Frey observes, there is a "sharp racial distinction" between Baby Boomers, who are mostly over the age of 50 and nearly three-quarters white, and those under the age of 35, namely, Millennials, the younger members of Generation X, and their children, who are more than 40 percent non-white. Frey writes:

> The Baby Boomers ... came of age at a moment when the United States was becoming more insular than it had been before. Growing up in mostly white, segregated suburbs, White Baby Boomers had less exposure to immigrants and foreign wars than their parents. Between 1946 and 1964, the years of the baby boom, the immigrant share of the U.S. population shrank to an all-time low (under 5 percent), and the immigrants who did arrive were largely White Europeans. Although Baby Boomers were interested in righting domestic wrongs, such as racial discrimination, and bursting glass ceilings, they did not have much interaction with people from other countries.[38]

The aging of Whites and the explosive growth of minorities, particularly Latinos at the younger end of the age spectrum, has created what Frey calls a "cultural generation gap," or in the words of author Ronald Brownstein an "intensifying confrontation between the gray and the brown." In Brownstein's words, "Like tectonic plates, these slow-moving but irreversible forces may generate enormous turbulence as they grind against each other in the years ahead."[39]

With non-Whites composing about half of the population under the age of 18, public schools are often the locus of the most intense cultural clashes. In 2012, for example, racial change was at the center of an ideological battle about history textbooks when the Texas Board of Education approved a measure requiring students to be taught not only about Martin Luther King's nonviolent philosophy during the civil-rights struggle of the 1960s but also about the Black Panthers with an emphasis on their advocacy of violence. Additionally, mention of a 1947 decision barring segregation of Mexican-American students was eliminated in the textbooks, prompting Mary Helen Berlanga, a Latina board member to ask, "Who are we kidding? These are the children that are going to be reading these materials. You want to talk about the Black Panthers in an ugly fashion? What about the Ku Klux Klan? That was a pretty nasty group. Why aren't we talking about them?" That same year, in Arizona, Governor Jan Brewer signed legislation to cut state funds for school districts offering classes deemed to encourage ethnic solidarity or promote racial resentments.[40]

Demographic shift will also lead to drastic changes in the labor force, as retiring Baby Boomers open up myriad job positions. In 2010, Whites made up 57 percent of 15-to-24 year olds, the age of those about to enter the workforce; however, they made up 75 percent of the age group on the edge of retirement, 55-to-64 year olds. Since White Baby Boomers disproportionately occupy jobs at the middle and upper ranges of the job market, the potential for racial shift there is extraordinary. In 2000, U.S. born Whites occupied nearly 80 percent of the top decile job positions, while White and Asian immigrants accounted for another 11 percent; U.S.-born Blacks and Hispanics made up only 6 percent. Conversely, nearly two-thirds of U.S.–born Blacks and Hispanics were found in the bottom-half of the labor force.[41]

As sociologist Richard Alba notes, despite socio-economic gains made by minority groups, White men still remain in the most advantaged positions, benefiting from higher levels of educational attainment, better schools, and higher earnings than other workers in the same occupational category. Alba concludes, "While the ethno-racial order of inequality may be shifting somewhat … the shifts have not eroded the privileged position of White men very much." He poignantly states that "the question that must be asked is whether more profound change is possible."[42]

When Baby Boomers retire, they will generate a heavy fiscal burden – the senior population is expected to grow by 81 percent between 2010 and 2030 – and Social Security, Medicare, and other programs will consume increasingly larger shares of federal and state budgets.[43] The burden of supporting this aging population will largely fall on the shoulders of non-Whites. As Dowell Myers, a professor of Public Policy at the University of Southern California, points out, "Growing the new base of middle-class taxpayers is closely related to building a skilled workforce. Both hinge on the crucial matter of educational attainment … Higher income taxpayers obviously can contribute more to the social support of seniors and others than can those who are not paid as well." He argues that the prospects for building a larger taxpayer base depend on two fundamental issues: ensuring that the new generation of non-Whites is highly educated and that this education translates into higher earnings and higher household income. The optimum scenario, as Myers sees it, is a virtuous cycle, whereby children and young adults receive a publicly funded, high quality education, positioning them to become high earners, home buyers, and taxpayers.[44]

However, the dynamic of an aging Boomer population, which is largely white, and an increase in the younger, largely non-white, working age populations, which is being driven by Hispanics and other immigrants, for whom dependent children is their chief financial concern, will inevitably lead to competition for fiscal resources. Writes Frey, "There is no question that the primary concern of working-age Hispanics – and to a lesser extent Asians and Blacks – will be their children rather than the older dependent population. For working-age Whites, elderly dependents will be a primary concern as well as their own future well-being as they enter their retirement years."[45]

In early summer, 2020, there are indications that the killing of George Floyd might have been the "lynching" heard around the world. In the United States, Europe, and Australia, the anger over Mr. Floyd's death has led to largely peaceful protests by day, in some cases followed by looting and violence at night. In some instances, the police have responded by using batons, tear gas, pepper spray, and rubber bullets on protesters, bystanders, and journalists. As videos of police aggression have spread, lawmakers, police officials, and judges have re-examined police department policies regarding the use of force and violence. Some American cities are cracking down on aggressive policing with an urgency like never before. On Friday, June 5, city leaders and judges in Minneapolis, Denver, and Seattle moved to rein in tactics like officers' use of chokeholds, tear gas, or rubber bullets. There have been calls across the U.S. to defund, downsize, or completely abolish police departments. "We are going to dismantle the Minneapolis Police Department," Jeremiah Ellison, a member of the City Council, said on Twitter. "And when we're done, we're not simply gonna glue it back together," he added. "We are going to dramatically rethink how we approach public safety and emergency response."[46]

It remains to be seen if the current national outrage, which seems to be a truly multiracial coalition, in many ways driven by young people, will have a lasting impact. In a sense, protests and riots over racial injustice in America is nothing new. White Americans, as I've detailed in this book, have been, throughout our country's history, fearful and even hostile toward those who might be coming to take their stuff, or even those they see as an existential threat to their way of life. Those people, whether they be Italians, Irish, Chinese, African Americans, Mexicans, have all suffered under the boot of bigotry. Too often the United States has not lived up to its highest ideals of inclusion and equality and egalitarianism.

But I don't want to end on a negative note. And I really do believe that the United States, perhaps more than any nation on earth, has the ability – maybe even the mandate – for re-invention. Race has often been a zero-sum game, but it doesn't have to be. And I don't believe it always will be.

In the aftermath of the killing of George Floyd, and the dozens of demonstrations for Black Lives Matter, one reason to have optimism about America's racial future has been the overwhelming support for Black lives demonstrated by younger Americans, particularly those belonging to Generation Z, usually defined as those born after 1996. Zoomers, as they are sometimes called, are the largest and most diverse generation in American history. They came of age in a post-9/11 world, one shaped by the War on Terrorism and the worst recession since the Great Depression. Their consciousness has been modeled by school shootings and Black Lives Matter. They are the social media generation, using platforms like Instagram, TikTok, and Twitter, rallying people to take to the streets in protest despite a global Covid-19 pandemic raging around them.

Gen Z was most visible in late June 2020, when thousands of TikTok users and fans of Korean pop music groups, in a coordinated effort, signed up for hundreds of thousands of tickets for Donald Trump's first campaign rally in Tulsa, Oklahoma, whereby people were encouraged to register online but not show up. In the end, President Trump didn't even fill the arena's 19,000-person capacity, after bragging that there were about a million RSVPs. And there's plenty of additional evidence that Gen Z might be at the vanguard of racial change. According to one survey, 90 percent of Gen Z supports Black Lives Matter, 88 percent feel that Black Americans are treated differently than others, and 78 percent have used social media to express support for their equality.

I have some hopes for the long term. I hope White Americans will finally confront the nation's past – its slavery, its genocide, its Jim Crow, its trail of tears – without defensiveness, without clenched fists. I think we can. I hope that the perception of Black men in this country changes and that something is done to stop police killings of unarmed Black men (and boys). I hope that a (still-dominant, though shrinking) White America will make peace with its diminished size and influence, and not take the "browning" of America, with its "press 2 for Spanish" and its taco trucks, as threats to what makes America great. Instead, I hope that White America will see these things as integral to what has made us into the people that we are.

25 | THE PRESENT, THE FUTURE

Barack Obama, in addition to being our first African American president, has been, on many issues including race, one of our more hopeful presidents. I prefer to believe his views on America's racial future, like what he proclaimed on September 24, 2016, during a speech at the inauguration of the Smithsonian National Museum of African American History and Culture:

> By knowing this other story, we better understand ourselves and each other. It binds us together. It reaffirms that all of us are America, that African-American history is not somehow separate from our larger American story. It is central to the American story.
>
> It reminds us that routine discrimination and Jim Crow aren't ancient history. It's just a blink in the eye of history.
>
> We should not be surprised that not all the healing is done. We shouldn't despair that it's not all solved.[47]

Racism, prejudice, exclusion, and fear have all been fundamental elements of our collective story. They have always had, and continue to have, enormous staying power. They left ugly scars on our national psyche. Yet when considered from the perspective of where we have been, over the long trajectory over time, we have made tremendous progress, albeit at times taking some giant steps backward. I have faith that we will continue to move in the direction of fulfilling the vision of equality of the Founding Fathers, however flawed this vision may have been. If indeed we are to be a great nation, then we have no other choice.

NOTES

1. "King's Dream Remains an Elusive Goal; Many Americans See Racial Disparities," Pew Research Center, August 22, 2013. http://www.pewsocialtrends.org/2013/08/22/kings-dream-remains-an-elusive-goal-many-americans-see-racial-disparities/.
2. Bonilla-Silva, Eduardo. *Racism without Racists: Color-Blind Racism and Racial Inequality in Contemporary America*. (Lanham, MD: Rowman & Littlefield Publishers, Inc., 2010), 1.
3. Ibid., 3.
4. https://www.linkedin.com/pulse/why-do-republicans-hate-talking-race-david-morse?trk=pulse_spock-articles.
5. "Dylann Roof's Racist Manifesto: 'I Have No Choice,'" June 20, 2015. https://www.washingtonpost.com/national/health-science/authorities-investigate-whether-

racist-manifesto-was-written-by-sc-gunman/2015/06/20/f0bd3052-1762-11e5-9ddc-e3353542100c_story.html.
6. "Some Republicans Can't Seem To Admit That Racism Was Behind The Charleston Murders," *Outside the Beltway*, June 15, 2015.
7. "Guns, Race, And Fox News' Pathological Denial," Media Matters for America, June 22, 2015. http://mediamatters.org/blog/2015/06/22/guns-race-and-fox-news-pathological-denial/204078.
8. *Plessy v. Ferguson*, 163 U.S. 537 (1896), https://www.law.cornell.edu/supremecourt/text/163/537.
9. Kennedy, Randall. *For Discrimination: Race, Affirmative Action, and the Law*. (New York, NY: Pantheon Books, 2013), 149.
10. *Plessy v. Ferguson*.
11. Bobo, Lawrence D. "Somewhere Between Jim Crow and Post-Racialism," *Daedalus*. Vol. 2, Spring 2011, 29.
12. *Regents of the University of California v. Bakke*, 438 U.S. 265 (1978). https://www.law.cornell.edu/supremecourt/text/438/265.
13. Wilson, William Julius. *More than Just Race: Being Black and Poor in the Inner City*. (New York, NY: W. W. Norton & Company, 2009), 1.
14. Anderson, Elijah. *Streetwise: Race, Class, and Change in an Urban Community*. (Chicago, IL: University of Chicago Press, 2013), 163.
15. Ibid., 166.
16. Robinson, Eugene. *Disintegration: The Splintering of Black America*. (New York, NY: Anchor Books, 2010), 5.
17. Ibid., 81.
18. Steele, Claude M. *Whistling Vivaldi: How Stereotypes Affect Us and What We Can Do*. (New York, NY: W.W. Norton & Company, Inc., 2010), 6.
19. Carbado, Devon W. and Mitu Gulati. *Acting White? Rethinking Race in "Post-Racial" America*. (Oxford, England: Oxford University Press, 2015), 1.
20. Ibid., 14.
21. "Underhanded," *The New Yorker*, March 15, 2010. http://www.newyorker.com/magazine/2010/03/15/underhanded.
22. Carbado and Gulati, 3.
23. "An Inarticulate Kickoff," *The Washington Post*, February 2, 2007. http://www.washingtonpost.com/wp-dyn/content/article/2007/02/01/AR2007020101495.html.
24. "Reid Apologizes for Remarks on Obama's Color and 'Dialect,'" *The New York Times*, January 9, 2010. http://www.nytimes.com/2010/01/10/us/politics/10reidweb.html?_r=0.

25. Kalef, Samer. "The NFL All but Admits That Colin Kaepernick Was Right All Along," *Slate*, June 3, 2020. https://slate.com/culture/2020/06/nfl-george-floyd-colin-kaepernick-roger-goodell-peaceful-protest.html.
26. "QB Colin Kaepernick Files Grievance for Collusion Against NFL Owners," *ABC News*, October 15, 2017. https://abcnews.go.com/Sports/qb-colin-kaepernick-files-grievance-collusion-nfl-owners/story?id=50499785.
27. Romero, Dennis. "NFL Says Issues Raised by Colin Kaepernick 'Deserve Our Attention and Action'", NBC News, September 4, 2018. https://www.nbcnews.com/news/nbcblk/nfl-says-issues-raised-colin-kaepernick-deserve-our-attention-action-n906431.
28. Kalef, Ibid.
29. Current Population Survey, February, 2016.
30. Ibid.
31. Frey, William H. *Diversity Explosion: How New Racial Demographics Are Remaking America*. (Washington, D.C.: Brookings Institution Press, 2015), 22.
32. Pew Research Center, "Almost All Millennials Accept Interracial Dating and Marriage," February 1, 2010. http://www.pewresearch.org/2010/02/01/almost-all-Millennials-accept-interracial-dating-and-marriage/.
33. Nosek, Brian A. et al. "Pervasiveness and Correlates of Implicit Attitudes and Stereotypes," *European Review of Social Psychology*, 2007, 18, 36–88. http://faculty.washington.edu/agg/pdf/Nosek%20&%20al.PCIAS.ERSP.2007.pdf.
34. "Millennials Are Less Racially Tolerant than You Think," *New York Magazine*, January 8, 2015. http://nymag.com/scienceofus/2015/01/Millennials-are-less-tolerant-than-you-think.html.
35. "Millennials are just as racist as their parents," *The Washington Post*, June 23, 2015. https://www.washingtonpost.com/news/wonk/wp/2015/06/23/Millennials-are-just-as-racist-as-their-parents/.
36. "Noose on Duke Campus: Do Colleges Have a Growing Racism Problem?" *The Christian Science Monitor*, April 2, 2015. http://www.csmonitor.com/USA/Education/2015/0402/Noose-on-Duke-campus-Do-colleges-have-a-growing-racism-problem-video.
37. Smith, Mychal Denzel. "White Millennials Are Products of a Failed Lesson in Colorblindness," *PBS Newshour*, March 26, 2015. http://www.pbs.org/newshour/updates/white-Millennials-products-failed-lesson-colorblindness/.
38. Frey, 32.
39. Brownstein, Ronald. "The Gray and the Brown: The Generational Mismatch," *National Journal*, April 18, 2012. https://www.yahoo.com/news/gray-brown-generational-mismatch-150041350.html.

40. Ibid.
41. Alba, Richard. *Blurring the Color Line: The New Chance for a More Integrated America*. (Cambridge, MA: Harvard University Press, 2009), 98.
42. Ibid., 134.
43. Frey, 34.
44. Myers, Dowell. *Immigrants and Boomers: Forging a New Social Contract for the Future of America*. (New York, NY: Russell Sage Foundation, 2007), 214.
45. Frey, 34.
46. "Global Rallies Decry Racism and Police Brutality, *The New York Times*, June 6, 2020. https://www.nytimes.com/2020/06/06/us/george-floyd-protests.html#link-12670954.
47. "Obama: African-American Museum Helps Tell Fuller Story of America," *CNN*, September 24, 2016. http://www.cnn.com/2016/09/23/politics/smithsonian-african-american-museum-obama/.

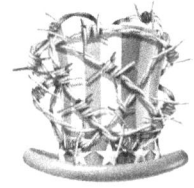

BIBLIOGRAPHY

Abrajano, Marisa and Zoltan L. Hajnal. *White Backlash: Immigration, Race, and American Politics*. Princeton: Princeton University Press, 2015.

Abrams, Charles. *Forbidden Neighbors: A Study of Prejudice in Housing*. Port Washington, NY: Associated Faculty Pr Inc. 1955.

Acosta-Belén, Edna and Carlos E. Santiago. *Puerto Ricans in the United States: A Contemporary Portrait*. Boulder, CO: Lynee Rienner Publishers, 2006.

Acuña, Rodolfo. *Occupied America: A History of Chicanos*. New York: Pearson Longman, 2002.

Adamic, Louis. "A Nation of Nations," *Pi Lambda Theta Journal*, Vol. 24, No. 4 (1946): 137–139.

Alba, Richard D. *Blurring the Color Line: The New Chance for a More Integrated America*. Cambridge: Harvard University Press, 2009.

_____. "The Twilight of Ethnicity among American Catholics of European Ancestry," *Annals of the American Academy of Political and Social Science*, Vol. 454 (1981): 86–97.

Albury, W.R. "Politics and Rhetoric in the Sociobiology Debate," *Social Studies of Science*, Vol. 10, No. 4 (1980): 519–536.

Alexander, Elizabeth. "Free Black Men," in *The New Black: What Has Changed – and What Has Not – with Race in America*, eds. Kenneth W. Mack and Guy-Uriel Charles. New York: The New Press, 2013.

Alexander, Michelle. *The New Jim Crow: Mass Incarceration in the Age of Colorblindness*. New York: The New Press, 2012.

Alim, H. Samy and Geneva Smitherman. *Articulate While Black: Barack Obama, Language, and Race in the U.S.* Oxford: Oxford University Press, 2012.

Anderson, Elijah. *Streetwise: Race, Class, and Change in an Urban Community.* Chicago: University of Chicago Press, 2013.

Anderson, Margaret L. "Whitewashing Race: A Critical Perspective on Whiteness," in *White Out: The Continuing Significance of Racism*, ed. Ashley W. Doane and Eduardo Bonilla-Silva. New York: Routledge, 2003.

Andreas, Peter. *Border Games: Policing the U.S.-Mexico Divide.* Princeton: Cornell University Press, 2009.

Arnesen, Eric. *Black Protest and the Great Migration: A Brief History with Documents.* New York: Bedford/St. Martin's, 2003.

Azuma, Eiichiro. *Between Two Empires: Race, History, and Transnationalism in Japanese America.* Oxford: Oxford University Press, 2005.

Baker, Lee D. "Columbia University's Franz Boas: He Led the Undoing of Scientific Racism." *The Journal of Blacks in Higher Education*, No. 55 (2007): 77–84.

_____. *From Savage to Negro: Anthropology and the Construction of Race, 1896–1954.* Berkeley: University of California Press, 1998.

Bald, Vivek. *Bengali Harlem and the Lost Histories of South Asian America.* Cambridge: Harvard University Press, 2013.

Balderrama, Francisco E. and Raymond Rodríguez. *Decade of Betrayal: Mexican Repatriation in the 1930s.* Albuquerque: University of New Mexico Press, 2006.

Baldwin, James. *The Fire Next Time.* New York: Vintage, 1992.

Baldoz, Rick. *The Third Asiatic Invasion: Migration and Empire in Filipino America, 1898–1946.* New York: NYU Press, 2011.

Baldwin, James. *Nobody Knows My Name.* New York: Random House Vintage, 2013. Kindle Edition.

Balz, Don and Haynes Johnson. *The Battle for America: 2008.* New York: Viking, 2009).

Banton, Michael. *Racial Theories.* Cambridge: Cambridge University Press, 1998.

Barker, Eugene C. "The Annexation of Texas," The Southwestern Historical Quarterly, Vol. 50, No. 1 (1946): 49–74.

Barone, Michael. *Shaping Our Nation: How Surges of Migration Transformed America and Its Politics.* New York: Crown Forum, 2013.

_____. *Our Country: The Shaping of America from Roosevelt to Reagan.* New York: The Free Press, 1992.

Barrett, James R. *The Irish Way: Becoming American in the Multiethnic City.* New York: The Penguin Press, 2012.

Baum, Bruce. *The Rise and Fall of the Caucasian Race: A Political History of Racial Identity.* New York: New York University Press, 2006.

Bendyshe, Thomas and Johann Friedrich Blumenbach. *The Anthropological Treatises of Johann Friedrich Blumenbach.* Ulan Press, 2012.

Benedict, Ruth. *Patterns of Culture*. Boston: Houghton Mifflin Harcourt, 1973.

Benjamin, Rich. *Searching for Whitopia: An Improbable Journey to the Heart of White America*. New York: Hyperion, 2009.

Blackmon, Douglas A. *Slavery by Another Name: The Re-Enslavement of Black Americans from the Civil War to World War II*. New York: Anchor Books, 2009.

Bliss, Catherine. *Race Decoded: The Genomic Fight for Social Justice*. Palo Alto, CA: Stanford University Press, 2012.

Boas, Franz. *Anthropology in Modern Life*. New York: Routledge Revivals, 2013.

―――. *The Mind of Primitive Man*. New York: Macmillan, 1931.

―――. "Changes in the Bodily Form of Descendants of Immigrants," *American Anthropologist*, Vol. 14, No. 3 (1912): 530–562.

Bobo, Lawrence D. "Somewhere Between Jim Crow and Post-Racialism," *Daedalus*, Vol. 2 (2011): 11–36.

Bobo, Lawrence D., Camille Z. Charles, Maria Krysan, and Alicia D. Simpson. "The *Real* Record of Racial Attitudes," in *Social Trends in American Life: Findings from the General Social Survey since 1972*, ed. Peter V. Marsden. Princeton: Princeton University Press, 2012.

Bolton, Herbert E. *The Spanish Borderlands*. New Haven: Yale University Press, 1921.

Bonilla-Silva, Eduardo. *Racism without Racists: Color-Blind Racism and Racial Inequality in Contemporary America*. Lanham, MD: Rowman & Littlefield Publishers, Inc., 2010.

Borjas, George J. "Labor Outflows and Labor Inflows in Puerto Rico," *Journal of Human Capital*, Vol. 2, No. 1 (2008): 32–68.

Brodkin, Karen. *How Jews Became White Folks and What That Says About Race in America*. New Brunswick, NJ: Rutgers University Press, 2004.

Brown, Jayna. *Babylon Girls: Black Women Performers and the Shaping of the Modern*. Durham, NC: Duke University Press Books, 2008.

Buaken, Manuel. *I Have Lived with the American People*. Caldwell, Idaho: Caxton, 1948.

Buchanan, Patrick J. *The Death of the West: How Dying Populations and Immigrant Invasions Imperil Our Country and Civilization*. New York: Thomas Dunne Books, 2010.

Buckley, Gail Lumet Buckley. *American Patriots: The Story of Blacks in the Military from the Revolution to Desert Storm*. New York: Random House, 2001.

Bulosan, Carlos. *America Is in the Heart: A Personal History*. Seattle: University of Washington Press, 2014.

Butler, Paul. "The President and the Justice: Two Ways of Looking at a Post-Black Man," in *The New Black: What Has Changed – and What Has Not – with Race in*

America, eds. Kenneth W. Mack and Guy-Uriel Charles. New York: The New Press, 2013.

Butsch, Richard. "American Movie Audiences of the 1930s," *International Labor and Working-Class History*, No. 59 (2001): 106–120.

Calavita, Kitty. *Inside the State: The Bracero Program, Immigration, and the I.N.S.* New York: Routledge, 2010.

———. "The New Politics of Immigration: 'Balanced-Budget Conservatism' and the Symbolism of Proposition 187", *Social Problems*, Vol. 43, No. 3 (1996): 284–305.

Carbado, Devon W. and Mitu Gulati. *Acting White?: Rethinking Race in "Post-Racial" America*. Oxford: Oxford University Press, 201.

Carlin, James A. *The Refugee Connection: Lifetime of Running a Lifeline*. Basingstoke, UK: Palgrave Macmillan, 1989.

Carrigan, William D. and Clive Webb. "The Lynching of Persons of Mexican Origin or Descent in the United States, 1848 to 1928," *Journal of Social History*, Vol. 37, No. 2 (2003): 411–438.

Caspari, Rachel. "From Types to Populations: A Century of Race, Physical Anthropology, and the American Anthropological Association." *American Anthropologist*, Vol. 105, No. 1 (2003): 63–74.

Chacón, Justin Akers and Mike Davis. *No One is Illegal: Fighting Racism and State Violence on the U.S. – Mexico Border*. Chicago: Haymarket Books, 2006.

Chang, Sucheng. *Asian Americans: An Interpretive History*. New York: Twayne Publishers, 1991.

Chang, Iris. *The Chinese in America: A Narrative History*. New York: Viking, 2003.

Chavez, Leo. *The Latino Threat: Constructing Immigrants, Citizens, and the Nation*. Stanford: Stanford University Press, 2013.

Chen, Yong. *Chinese San Francisco, 1850–1943: A Trans-Pacific Community*. Stanford: Stanford University Press, 2000.

Chial, Heidi. "DNA Sequencing Technologies Key to the Human Genome Project," *Nature Education*, Vol. 1, No. 1 (2008): 219.

Chomsky, Aviva. *Undocumented: How Immigration Became Illegal*. Boston: Beacon Press, 2014.

Chou, Rosalind S. and Joe R. Feagin. *The Myth of the Model Minority: Asian Americans Facing Racism*. Boulder, CO: Paradigm Publishers, 2010.

Citrin, Jack and David O. Sears. *American Identity and the Politics of Multiculturalism*. Cambridge, UK: Cambridge University Press, 2014.

Coon, Carleton S. *Origin of the Races*. New York: Alfred A. Knopf, Inc., 1962.

Coulter, Ann. ¡*Adios, America!: The Left*'s *Plan to Turn Our Country into a Third World Hellhole*. Washington, D.C.: Regnery Publishing.

Craig, Maureen A. and Jennifer A. Richeson. "On the Precipice of a 'Majority-Minority' America: Perceived Status Threat from the Racial Demographic Shift Affects White Americans' Political Ideology." *Psychological Science*, 2014, Vol. 25, No. 6 (2014): 1189–1197.

Crèvecoeur, J. Hector St. John de. *Letters from an American Farmer*. Carlisle, MA: Applewood Books, 2007.

Dana, Richard Henry. *Two Years Before the Mast*. New York: Cosimo Inc., 1965.

Daniels, Roger. *Guarding the Golden Door: American Immigration Policy and Immigrants Since 1882*. New York: Hill and Wang, 2004.

———. *Coming to America: A History of Immigration and Ethnicity in American Life*. New York: HarperPerennial, 2002.

———. *Asian America: Chinese and Japanese in the United States since 1850*. Seattle: University of Washington Press, 1988.

Darwin, Charles. *The Descent of Man*. New York: Penguin Books, 2004.

Dávila, Arlene. *Latino Spin: Public Image and the Whitewashing of Race*. New York: New York University Press, 2008.

Davis, David Brion. *Inhuman Bondage: The Rise and Fall of Slavery in the New World*. Oxford: Oxford University Press, 2008.

Dennis, Rutledge M. "Social Darwinism, Scientific Racism, and the Metaphysics of Race," *The Journal of Negro Education*, Vol. 64, No. 3 (1995): 243–252.

Dewbury, Adam. "The American School and Scientific Racism in Early American Anthropology." *Histories of Anthropology Annual*, eds. Regna Darnell and Frederic W. Gleach, Vol. 3. Lincoln, NE: University of Nebraska Press, 2007.

Dhingra, Pawan and Robyn Magalit Rodriguez. *Asian America: Sociological and Interdisciplinary Perspectives*. Cambridge, UK: Polity Press, 2014.

DiAngelo, Robin. "White Fragility." *International Journal of Critical Pedagogy*, Vol. 3, No. 3 (2011): 54–70.

Dinnerstein, Leonard. "Jews and the New Deal," *American Jewish History*, Vol. 72, No. 4 (1983): 461–476.

Dinnerstein, Leonard and David M. Reimers. *Ethnic Americans: A History of Immigration*. New York: Columbia University Press, 1999.

Doty, Roxanne Lynn. *The Law into Their Own Hands: Immigration and the Politics of Exceptionalism*. Tucson: University of Arizona Press, 2009.

Dower, John W. Dower. *War without Mercy: Race and Power in the Pacific War*. New York: Pantheon, 1987.

Duany, Jorge. "Puerto Rico: Between the Nation and the Diaspora – Migration to and from Puerto Rico," in *Migration and Immigration: A Global View*, eds. Maura I. Toro-Morn and Marisa Alicea, Westport CT: Greenwood, 2004.

_____. "Reconstructing Racial Identity: Ethnicity, Color, and Class among Dominicans in the United States and Puerto Rico, *Latin American Perspectives*, Vol. 25, No. 3 (1998): 147–172.

Dubois, W.E.B. *The Souls of Black Folk*. New York: Open Road Media, 2014.

_____. *Dusk of Dawn: An Essay toward an Autobiography of a Race Concept*. Oxford: Oxford University Press, 2014.

_____. *Health and Physique of the Negro American*. Atlanta: The Atlanta University Press, 1906.

_____. "The Study of the Negro Problems," *The Annals of the American Academy of Political and Social Science*, Vol. 11 (1898): 1–23.

Edelman, Peter Edelman. *So Rich, So Poor: Why It's So Hard to End Poverty in America*. New York: The New Press, 2012.

Edwards, A.W.F. "Human Genetic Diversity: Lewontin's Fallacy". *BioEssays*, Vol. 25, No. 8 (2003): 798–801.

Egerton, Douglas R. Egerton. *The Wars of Reconstruction: The Brief, Violent History of America's Most Progressive Era*. New York: Bloomsbury Press, 2014.

Eriksen, Thomas Hylland and Finn Sivert Nielsen. *A History of Anthropology*. London: Pluto Press, 2013.

Fanon, Frantz. *Black Skin, White Masks*. New York: Grove Press, 2008.

Feagin, Joe R. and José A. Cobas. *Latinos Facing Racism: Discrimination, Resistance, and Endurance*. Boulder, CO: Paradigm Publishers, 2014.

Fernández-Armesto, Felipe. *Our America: A Hispanic History of the United States*. New York: W.W. Norton & Company, 2014.

Fischer, David Hackett. *Albion's Seed: Four British Folkways in America*. Oxford: Oxford University Press, 1989.

Foley, Neil. *Mexicans in the Making of America*. Cambridge: Belknap Press, 2014.

_____. *The White Scourge: Mexicans, Blacks, and Poor Whites in Texas Cotton Culture*. Berkeley: University of California Press, 1997.

Fontana, Bernard L. *Entrada: The Legacy of Spain and Mexico in the United States*. Albuquerque: The University of New Mexico Press, 1994.

Frank, Reanne. Ilana Redstone Akresh, and Bo Lu. "Latino Immigrants and the U.S. Racial Order: How and Where Do They Fit In?" *American Sociological Review*, Vol. 75, No. 3 (2010): 378–401.

Franklin, John Hope. "The Two Worlds of Race: A Historical View," *Daedalus* Vol. 140, No. 1 (2011): 28–43.

_____. "Slavery and the Martial South", *The Journal of Negro History*, Vol. 37, No. 1 (1952): 51.

Franklin, John Hope and Alfred A. Moss, Jr. *From Slavery to Freedom: A History of African Americans*. New York: McGraw-Hill, Inc., 1994.

Fredrickson, George M. *Racism: A Short History*. Princeton: Princeton University Press, 2002.

_____. *The Black Image in the White Mind: The Debate on Afro-American Character and Destiny, 1817–1914*, Hanover: Wesleyan University Press, 1987.

Frey, William H. *Diversity Explosion: How New Racial Demographics are Remaking America*. Washington, D.C.: Brookings Institution Press, 2014.

Gannett, Lisa. "Racism and Human Genome Diversity Research: The Ethical Limits of 'Population Thinking.'" *Philosophy of Science*, Vol. 68, No. 3 (2001): 479–492.

Gans, Herbert J. *The Levittowners: Ways of Life and Politics in a New Suburban Community*. New York: Vintage Books, 1969.

_____. "Symbolic Ethnicity: The Future of Ethnic Groups and Cultures in America," *Ethnic and Racial Studies*, Vol. 2, No. 1 (1979): 1–21.

García, María Cristina. "Exiles, Immigrants, and Transnationals: The Cuban Communities of the United States," in *The Columbia History of Latinos in the United States Since 1969*, ed. David G. Gutiérrez. New York: Columbia University Press, 2004.

_____. *Havana USA: Cuban Exiles and Cuban Americans in South Florida, 1959–1994*. Berkeley: University of California Press, 1996.

García, Mario T. *Mexican Americans: Leadership, Ideology, and Identity, 1930–1960*. New Haven: Yale University Press, 1991.

Gates, Henry Louis Jr. and Cornel West. *The African American Century: How Black Americans Have Shaped Our Country*. New York: The Free Press, 2000.

Gates, Henry Louis and Abby Wolf. *The Henry Louis Gates, Jr. Reader*. New York: Basic Civitas Books, 2012.

Genova, Nicholas D. "Racial Formation in an Age of Permanent War," in *Racial Formation in the Twenty-First Century*, eds. Daniel Martinez HoSang, Oneka LaBennett, and Laura Pulido. Berkeley: University of California Press, 2012.

Glazer, Nathan and Daniel P. Moynihan. *Beyond the Melting Pot: The Negroes, Puerto Ricans, Jews, Italians, and Irish of New York City*. Cambridge: The MIT Press, 1970.

Golash-Boza, Tanya Maria. *Immigrant Nation: Raids, Detentions, and Deportations in Post-9/11 America*. Boulder: Paradigm Publishers, 2012.

Golash-Boza, Tanya and William Darity Jr. "Latino Racial Choices: The Effects of Skin Colour and Discrimination on Latinos' and Latinas' Racial Self-Identifications." *Ethnic and Racial Studies*, Vol. 31, No. 5 (2008): 899–934.

Goldstein, Eric L. *The Price of Whiteness: Jews, Race, and American Identity*. Princeton: Princeton University Press, 2006.

Gonzales, Alfonso. *Reform without Justice: Latino Migrant Politics and the Homeland Security State*. Oxford: Oxford University Press, 2014.

González Burchard, Esteban, Elad Ziv, Natasha Coyl., Scarlett Lin Gomez, Hua Tang, Andrew J. Karter, Joanna L. Mountain, Eliseo J. Pérez-Stable, Dean Sheppard and Neil Risch, "The Importance of Race and Ethnic Background in Biomedical Research and Clinical Practice," *The New England Journal of Medicine*, Vol. 348 (2003): 1170–1175.

Gonzalez, Juan. *Harvest of Empire: A History of Latinos in America*. New York: Penguin Books, 2011.

Gonzales, Juan L. Jr. "Asian Indian Immigration Patterns: The Origins of the Sikh Community in California." *International Migration Review*, Vol. 20, No. 1 (1986): 40–54.

Gould, Stephen Jay. *The Mismeasure of Man*. New York: W. W. Norton & Company, 1981.

Grant, Madison. *The Passing of the Great Race or The Racial Basis of European History*. Ostara Publications, 2011.

Gratton, Brian and Myron P. Guttmann, "Hispanics in the United States, 1850–1900: Estimates of Population Size and National Origin," *Historical Methods*, Vol. 33, No. 3 (2000): 137–153.

Guevarra, Rudy P. Jr. *Becoming Mexipino: Multiethnic Identities and Communities in San Diego*. New Brunswick, NJ: Rutgers University Press, 2012.

Guglielmo, Thomas A. *White on Arrival: Italians, Race, Color, and Power in Chicago, 1890–1945*. Oxford: Oxford University Press, 2003.

Gutiérrez, David G. *Walls and Mirrors: Mexican Americans, Mexican Immigrants, and the Politics of Ethnicity*. Berkeley: University of California Press, 1995.

Gyory, Andrew. *Closing the Gate: Race, Politics, and the Chinese Exclusion Act*. Chapel Hill: University of North Caroline Press, 1998.

Hamilton, Alexander, James Madison, and John Jay. *The Federalist; or The New Constitution*. White Fish, MT: Kessinger Publishing, 2010.

Handlin, Oscar. *The Uprooted: The Epic Story of the Great Migrations that Made the American People.*" Boston: Little, Brown and Company, 1973.

Harris, Fredrick. *The Price of the Ticket: Barack Obama and the Rise and Decline of Black Politics*. Oxford: Oxford University Press, 2014.

Hartman, Andrew. *A War for the Soul of America: A History of the Culture Wars*. Chicago: The University of Chicago Press, 2015.

BIBLIOGRAPHY

Hernández, Kelly Lytle. *Migra!: A History of the U.S. Border Patrol*. Oakland: University of California Press, 2010.

Hernstein, Richard J. and Charles Murray. *The Bell Curve: Intelligence and Class Structure in American Life*. New York: Simon & Schuster, 1994.

Higham, John. *Strangers in the Land: Patterns of American Nativism, 1860–1925*, (New Brunswick, NJ: Rutgers University Press, 2002.

Hine, Darlene Clark, William C. Hine, and Stanley Harrold. *African Americans: A Concise History*. Upper Saddle River, NJ: Pearson Education, 2012.

Hochschild, Jennifer, Vesla Weaver and Traci Burch. *Creating a New Racial Order: How Immigration, Multiracialism, Genomics, and the Young Can Remake Race in America*. Princeton: Princeton University Press, 2012.

Hofstadter, Richard. *Social Darwinism in American Thought*. Boston: Beacon Press, 1992.

Holli, Melvin G. "German-American Ethnic Identity from 1890 Onward: The Chicago Case," *The Great Lakes Review*, Vol. 11, No. 1 (1985): 1–11.

Hu-Dehart, Evelyn. "Chinese Coolie Labor in Cuba in the Nineteenth Century: Free Labor of Neoslavery," *Contributions in Black Studies*, Vol. 12, No. 5 (1994): 38–54.

Hull, David L. *Science as a Process: An Evolutionary Account of the Social and Conceptual Development of Science*. Chicago: University of Chicago Press, 1988.

Hunker, Henry L. "The Problem of Puerto Rican Migrations to the United States." *The Ohio Journal of Science*, Vol. 51, No. 6 (1951): 342–346.

Hunter, Margaret. "Rethinking Epistemology, Methodology, and Racism: Or, Is White Sociology Really Dead." *Race & Society*, Vol. 5 (2002): 119–138.

Huntington, Samuel P. "The Hispanic Challenge," *Foreign Policy*, No. 141 (2004): 30–45.

Iceland, John. *Where We Live Now: Immigration and Race in the United States*. Berkeley: University of California Press, 2009.

Ignatiev, Noel. *How the Irish Became White*. New York: Routledge, 1995.

Jackson, John P. Jr. and Nadine M. Weidman. *Race, Racism, and Science: Social Impact and Interaction*. New Brunswick, NJ: Rutgers University Press, 2006.

———. "In Ways Unacademical": The Reception of Carleton S. Coon's 'The Origin of Races'." *Journal of the History of Biology*, Vol. 34 (2001): 247–285.

Jackson, Kenneth T. "Federal Subsidy and the Suburban Dream: The First Quarter-Century of Government Intervention in the Housing Market," *Records of the Columbia Historical Society*, Vol. 50 (1980): 421–451.

Jacobson, Matthew Frye Jacobson. *Whiteness of a Different Color: European Immigrants and the Alchemy of Race*. Cambridge: Harvard University Press, 1999.

Jefferson, Thomas. *Notes on the State of Virginia*. New York: Penguin Classics, 1998.

Jenson, Joan M. *Passage from India: Asian Indian Immigrants in North America*. New Haven: Yale University Press, 1988.

Jones-Correa, Michael and Els de Graauw. "The Illegality Trap: The Politics of Immigration & the Lens of Illegality." *Dædalus*, Vol. 142, No. 3 (2013): 185–198.

Jordan, Winthrop D. "Historical Origins of the One-Drop Rule in the United States, *Journal of Critical Mixed Race Studies*, Vol. 1, No. 1 (2014): 1–35.

_____. *White over Black: American Attitudes toward the Negro, 1550–1812*. New York: W. W. Norton & Co Inc., 1977.

_____. *The White Man's Burden: Historical Origins of Racism in the United States*. Oxford: Oxford University Press, 1974.

Kahn, Jonathan D. "From Disparity to Difference: How Race-Specific Medicines May Undermine Policies to Address Inequalities in Health Care," *Southern California Interdisciplinary Law Journal*, 2005, Vol. 15 (105–129).

Katznelson, Ira. *When Affirmative Action Was White: An Untold History of Racial Inequality in Twentieth-Century America*. New York: W.W. Norton & Company, 2006.

Kaufmann, Eric. "American Exceptionalism Reconsidered: Anglo-Saxon Ethnogenesis in the 'Universal' Nation, 1776–1850." *Journal of American Studies*, Vol. 33 (1999): 437–457.

Kennedy, Randall. *For Discrimination: Race, Affirmative Action, and the Law*. New York: Pantheon, 2013.

_____. *The Persistence of the Color Line: Racial Politics and the Obama Presidency*. New York: Pantheon, 2011.

_____. *Sellout: The Politics of Racial Betrayal*. New York: Vintage, 2009.

Kibria, Nazli, Cara Bowman, and Megan O'Leary. *Race and Immigration*. Cambridge, UK: Polity Press, 2014.

Kinder, Donald R. and Allison Dale-Riddle. *The End of Race?: Obama, 2008, and Racial Politics in America*. New Haven: Yale University Press, 2012.

Kiser, Clyde V. "Cultural Pluralism," *Annals of the American Academy of Political and Social Science*, Vol. 262 (1949): 117–130.

Kotlowski, Dean J. *Nixon's Civil Rights: Politics, Principle, and Policy*. Cambridge: Harvard University Press, 2002.

_____. "Richard Nixon and the Origins of Affirmative Action," *The Historian*, Vol. 60, No. 3 (1998): 523–541.

Kurashige, Scott. *The Shifting Grounds of Race: Black and Japanese Americans in the Making of Multiethnic Los Angeles*. Princeton: Princeton University Press, 2008.

Ladner, Joyce A. *The Death of White Sociology: Essays on Race and Culture*. Baltimore: Black Classic Press, 1998.

Laham, Nicholas. *Ronald Reagan and the Politics of Immigration Reform*. Santa Barbara: Praeger, 2000.

Lee, Erika. *The Making of Asian America: A History*. New York: Simon and Schuster, 2015.

Lee, Erika and Judy Yung. *Angel Island: Immigrant Gateway to America*. Oxford: Oxford University Press, 2010.

Lee, Jennifer and Frank D. Bean. *The Diversity Paradox: Immigration and the Color Line in 21st Century America*. New York: Russell Sage Foundation, 2010.

Lee, Shelley Sang-Hee. *A New History of Asian America*. New York: Routledge, 2014.

LeMay, Michael C. *Illegal Immigration: A Reference Handbook*. Santa Barbara: ABC-CLIO, 2015.

Leonard, Karen Isaksen. *Making Ethnic Choices: California's Punjabi Mexican Americans*. Philadelphia: Temple University Press, 1992.

Leong, Yau Sing. "From Kwangtung to the Plantations, Farms, Stores and Beyond," in *Sailing for the Sun: The Chinese in Hawaii, 1789–1989*, ed. Arlene Lum. Honolulu: University of Hawaii Press, 1990.

Lieberman, Leonard. "The Debate over Race: A Study in the Sociology of Knowledge." *Phylon*, Vol. 29, No. 2 (1968): 127–141.

Lieberman, Leonard, Blaine W. Stevenson and Larry T. Reynolds. "Race and Anthropology: A Core Concept without Consensus," *Anthropology & Education Quarterly*, Vol. 20, No. 2 (1989): 67–73.

Logan, Enid. *"At This Defining Moment": Barack Obama's Presidential Candidacy and the New Politics of Race*. New York: New York University Press, 2011.

Logan, Rayford W. *The Betrayal of the Negro: From Rutherford B. Hayes to Woodrow Wilson*. Cambridge: Da Capo Press, 1997.

Longmore, Paul K. and Lauri Umansky. *The New Disability History: American Perspectives*. New York: New York University Press, 2001.

López, Ian Haney. *Dog Whistle Politics: How Coded Racial Appeals Have Reinvented Racism and Wrecked the Middle Class*. Oxford: Oxford University Press, 2014.

_____. "Race on the 2010 Census: Hispanics and the Shrinking White Majority," *Daedalus*, Vol. 134, No. 1 (2005): 42–52.

MacDonald, Victoria-María. "Hispanic, Latino, Chicano, or 'Other'?: Deconstructing the Relationship between Historians and Hispanic-American Educational History," *History of Education Quarterly*, Vol. 41, No. 3 (2001): 365–413.

Malik, Kenan. *The Meaning of Race: Race, History and Culture in Western Society*. New York: New York University Press, 1996.

Mandeville, Sir John. *The Travels of Sir John Mandeville: The Fantastic 14th-Century Account of a Journey to the East*. Mineola, NY: Dover Publications, 2006.

Manges Douglas, Karen and Rogelio Saenz. "The Criminalization of Immigrants and the Immigration-Industrial Complex." *Dædalus*, Vol. 142, No. 3 (2013): 199–227.

Marable, Manning. *Race, Reform, and Rebellion: The Second Reconstruction and Beyond in Black America, 1945–2006*. University Press of Mississippi, 2007.

Marks, Jonathan M. *Human Biodiversity: Genes, Race, and History*. New Brunswick, NJ: Transaction Publishers, 1995.

Massey, Douglas S. "America's Immigration Policy Fiasco," *Dædalus* Vol. 142, No. 3 (2013): 5–15.

———. "Racial Formation in Theory and Practice: The Case of Mexicans in the United States," *Race and Social Problems*, Vol. 1, No. 1 (2009): 12–26.

———. *Categorically Unequal: The American Stratification System*. New York: Russell Sage Foundation, 2007.

———. "The New Immigration and Ethnicity in the United States," *Population and Development Review*, Vol. 21, No. 3 (1995): 631–652.

Massey, Douglas S. and Karen A. Pren. "Unintended Consequences of US Immigration Policy: Explaining the Post-1965 Surge from Latin America," *Population and Development Review*, Vol. 38, No. 1 (2012): 1–29.

Massey, Douglas S. and Nancy A. Denton. *American Apartheid: Segregation and the Making of the Underclass*. Cambridge: Harvard University Press, 1998.

Massey, Douglas S., Jorge Durand, and Nolan J. Malone. *Beyond Smoke and Mirrors: Mexican Immigration in an Era of Economic Integration*. New York: Russell Sage Foundation Publications, 2003.

Masud-Piloto, Felix. *From Welcomed Exiles to Illegal Immigrants: Cuban Migration to the U.S., 1959–1995*. Lanham, MD: Rowman & Littlefield Publishers, 1995.

Mayr, Ernst. *Evolution and the Diversity of Life: Selected Essays*. Cambridge: Belknap Press, 1997.

———. *The Growth of Biological Thought: Diversity, Evolution, and Inheritance*. Cambridge: Harvard University Press, 1982.

McCaffrey, Lawrence J. "Irish America." *The Wilson Quarterly*, Vol. 9, No. 2 (1985): 78–93.

McCann-Mortimer, Patricia, Martha Augoustinos, and Amanda LeCouteur. "'Race' and the Human Genome Project: Constructions of Scientific Legitimacy," *Discourse Society*, Vol. 15, No. 4 (2004): 409–432.

McWilliams, Corey. *North from Mexico: The Spanish-Speaking People of the United States*. New York: Greenwood Press, 1968.

Melendy, H. Brett. *Asians in America: Filipinos, Koreans, and East Indians.* Boston: Twayne Publishers, 1977.

Menchaca, Martha and Richard R. Valencia. "Anglo-Saxon Ideologies in the 1920s–1930s: Their Impact on the Segregation of Mexican Students in California." *Anthropology & Education Quarterly*, Vol. 21, No. 3 (1990): 222–249.

Miller, Stuart Creighton. *The Unwelcome Immigrant, The American Image of the Chinese, 1785–1882.* Berkeley, University of California Press, 1969.

Miranda, Gloria E. "Racial and Cultural Dimensions of 'Gente de Razón' Status in Spanish and Mexican California," *Southern California Quarterly*, Vol. 70, No. 3 (1988): 265–278.

Mohl, Raymond A. "Cultural Pluralism in Immigrant Education: The International Institutes of Boston, Philadelphia, and San Francisco, 1920–1940," *Journal of American Ethnic History*, Vol. 1, No. 2 (1982): 35–58.

Montague, M.F. Ashley. *Man's Most Dangerous Myth: The Fallacy of Race.* New York: Columbian University, 1945.

Montejano, David. *Anglos and Mexicans in the Making of Texas, 1836–1986.* Austin: The University of Texas Press, 1987.

Morefield, Richard Henry. "Mexicans in the California Mines, 1848–5," *California Historical Society Quarterly*, Vol. 35, No. 1 (1956): 37–46.

Morgan, Rose M. *The Genetics Revolution: History, Fears, and Future of a Life-altering Science.* Westport, CT: Greenwood Publishing Group, 2005.

Morning, Ann. *The Nature of Race: How Scientists Think and Teach about Human Difference.* Berkeley: University of California Press, 2011.

Myrdal, Gunnar. *An American Dilemma, Volume 1: The Negro Problem and Modern Democracy.* Piscataway, NJ: Transaction Publishers, 1995.

Nelkin, Dorothy and M. Susan Lindee. *The DNA Mystique: The Gene as a Cultural Icon.* New York: W. H. Freeman & Company, 1995.

Nevins, Joseph. *Operation Gatekeeper and Beyond: The War On "Illegals" and the Remaking of the U.S. – Mexico Boundary.* London: Routledge, 2010.

Ngai, Mae M. *Impossible Subjects: Illegal Aliens and the Making of Modern America.* Princeton: Princeton University Press, 2005.

Norton, Michael I. and Samuel R. Sommers. "Whites See Racism as a Zero-Sum Game That They Are Now Losing." *Perspectives on Psychological Science*, Vol. 6, No. 3 (2011): 215–218.

Nosek Brian A. et al. "Pervasiveness and Correlates of Implicit Attitudes and Stereotypes," *European Review of Social Psychology*, Vol. 18 (2007): 36–88.

Novak, Michael. *The Rise of the Unmeltable Ethnics: Politics and Culture in the Seventies.* New York: Macmillan Publishing, Inc., 1973.

Odem, Mary E. "Unsettled in the Suburbs: Latino Immigration and Ethnic Diversity in Metro Atlanta," in *Twenty-First Century Gateways: Immigrant Incorporation in Suburban America*, eds. Audrey Singer, Susan W. Hardwick, and Caroline B. Brettell. Washington, D.C.: The Brookings Institution, 2008.

Okamura, Jonathan Y. "Bridges of Barriers: Multiracial Families and Race Relations," in *Multiethnicity and Multiethnic Families: Development, Identity, and Resilience*, eds. Hamilton McCubbin, Krystal Ontai, et al. Bloomington, IN: Xlibris, 2010.

Okihiro, Gary. *Margins and Mainstreams: Asians in American History and Culture*. Seattle: University of Washington Press, 2014.

Oliveri, Rigel C. "Between a Rock and a Hard Place: Landlords, Latinos, Anti-Illegal Immigrant Ordinances, and Housing Discrimination," *Vanderbilt Law Review*, Vol. 62, No. 1 (2009): 55–125.

Omi, Michael and Howard Winant. *Racial Formation in the United States: From the 1960s to the 1990s*. New York: Routledge, 1994.

Onwuachi-Willig, Angela. "An Officer and a Gentleman." *The New Black: What Has Changed – and What Has Not – with Race in America*, eds. Kenneth W. Mack and Guy-Uriel Charles. New York: The New Press, 2013.

Packard, Jerrold M. Packard. *American Nightmare: The History of Jim Crow*. New York: St. Martin's Griffin, 2003.

Painter, Nell Irvin. *The History of White People*. New York: W. W. Norton & Company, 2011.

Perez y González, María E. *Puerto Ricans in the United States*. Westport, CT: Greenwood Press, 2000.

Pfaelzer, Jean. *Driven Out: The Forgotten War Against Chinese Americans*. New York: Random House, 2008.

Phelan, James D. Phelan. "Why the Chinese Should Be Excluded," *The North American Review*, Vol. 173, No. 540 (1901): 663–676.

Portes, Alejandro and Rubén G. Rumbaut. *Legacies: The Story of the Immigrant Second Generation*. Berkeley: University of California Press, 2001.

Prasad, Vijay. *The Karma of Brown Folk*. Minneapolis: University of Minnesota Press, 2003.

Prewitt, Kenneth. *What Is Your Race? The Census and Our Flawed Efforts to Classify Americans*. Princeton, Princeton University Press, 2013.

Purkayastha, Bandana. *Negotiating Ethnicity: Second-Generation South Asian Americans Traverse a Transnational World*. New Brunswick, NJ: Rutgers University Press, 2005.

Raat, W. Dirk and Michael M. Brescia. *Mexico and the United States: Ambivalent Vistas*. Athens, GA: The University of Georgia Press, 2010.

Reardon, Jenny. *Race to the Finish: Identity and Governance in an Age of Genomics*. Princeton: Princeton University Press, 2004.

Robinson, Eugene. *Disintegration: The Splintering of Black America*. New York: Anchor Books, 2010.

Rodríguez, Clara E. "Counting Latinos in the U.S. Census," in *How the United States Racializes Latinos: White Hegemony and Its Consequences*, eds. José A. Cobas, Jorge Duany, and Joe R. Feagin. Boulder, CO: Paradigm Publishers, 2009.

———. *Changing Race: Latinos, the Census, and the History of Ethnicity in the United States*. New York: New York University Press, 2000.

———. "Puerto Rican Studies," *American Quarterly*, Vol. 42, No. 3 (1990): 437–455.

Rodriguez, Gregory. *Mongrels, Bastards, Orphans, and Vagabonds: Mexican Immigration and the Future of Race in America*. New York: Pantheon Books, 2007.

Roediger, David R. *Working toward Whiteness: How America's Immigrants Became White*. New York: Basic Books, 2005.

Romo, Ricardo. "Responses to Mexican Immigration, 1910–1930," in *Beyond 1848: Readings in the Modern Chicano Historical Experience*, ed. Michael R. Ornelas. Dubuque, IA: Kendall Hunt Publishing, 1993.

Rosenberg, Emily S. *A Date Which Will Live: Pearl Harbor in American Memory*. Durham, NC: Duke University Press Books, 2003.

Roth, Wendy. *Race Migrations: Latinos and the Cultural Transformation of Race*. Stanford: Stanford University Press, 2012.

Rowell, Chester H. "Chinese and Japanese Immigrants – A Comparison," *Annals of the American Academy of Political and Social Science*, Vol. 34, No. 2 (1909): 3–10.

Ruiz, Vicki L. "Nuestra América: Latino History as United States History," *The Journal of American History*, Vol. 93, No. 3 (2006): 655–672.

Rusert, Britt. "The Science of Freedom: Counterarchives of Racial Science on the Antebellum Stage," *African American Review*, Vol. 45, No. 3 (2012): 291–308.

Said, Edward W. *Orientalism*. New York: Vintage Books, 1979.

Sánchez, George J. *Becoming Mexican American: Ethnicity, Culture and Identity in Chicano Los Angeles, 1900–1945*. New York: Oxford University Press, 1993.

Sankar, Pamela. "Forensic DNA Phenotyping: Reinforcing Race in Law Enforcement," in *What's the Use of Race?: Modern Governance and the Biology of Difference*, eds. Ian Whitmarsh and David S. Jones. Cambridge: The MIT Press, 2010.

Sawyer, Mark Q. *Racial Politics in Post-Revolutionary Cuba*. Cambridge, UK: Cambridge University Press, 2005.

Schlesinger, Jr., Arthur. *The Disuniting of America: Reflections on a Multicultural Society*. New York: W.W. Norton & Company, Inc., 1998.

Schrag, Peter. *Not Fit for Our Society: Nativism and Immigration*. Berkeley: University of California Press, 2010.

Schuman, Howard, Charlotte Steeh, Lawrence Bobo, and Maria Krysan. *Racial Attitudes in America: Trends and Interpretations*. Cambridge: Harvard University Press, 1997.

Shiao Jiannbin Lee, Thomas Bode, Amber Beyer and Daniel Selvig. "The Genomic Challenge to the Social Construction of Race." *Sociological Theory*, Vol. 30, No. 2 (2012): 557–569.

Shurkin, Joel N. *Broken Genius: The Rise and Fall of William Shockley, Creator of the Electronic Age*. Basingstoke, UK: Palgrave Macmillan, 2006.

Sitkoff, Harvard and Eric Foner. *The Struggle for Black Equality, 1954–1992*. New York: Hill and Wang, 1993.

Sharkey, Patrick. *Stuck in Place: Urban Neighborhoods and the End of Progress toward Racial Equality*. Chicago: The University of Chicago Press, 2013.

Skrentny, John D. and Jane Lilly López. "Obama's Immigration Reform: The Triumph of Executive Action," *Indiana Journal of Law and Social Equality*, Vol. 1, No. 2 (2013): 62–79.

Smedley, Audrey and Brian D. Smedley. *Race in North America: Origin and Evolution of a Worldview*. Boulder, CO: Westview Press, 2011.

Snipp, C. Matthew. "Racial, Measurement in the American Census: Past Practices and Implications for the Future," *Annual Review of Sociology*, Vol. 29 (2003): 563–588.

Sohi, Seema. *Echoes of Mutiny: Race, Surveillance, and Indian Anticolonialism in North America*. Oxford: Oxford University Press, 2014.

Spickard, Paul R. "Marriages Between American Men and Japanese Women After World War II," in *Major Problems in Asian American History*, eds. Lon Kurashige and Alice Yang Murray. Boston: Houghton Mifflin Company, 2016.

Steele, Claude M. *Whistling Vivaldi: How Stereotypes Affect Us and What We Can Do*. New York: W.W. Norton & Company, Inc., 2010.

Steinberg, Stephen. *Race Relations: A Critique*. Stanford: Stanford University Press, 2007.

_____. *The Ethnic Myth: Race, Ethnicity, and Class in America*. Boston: Beacon Press, 2001.

Stepan, Nancy. *The Idea of Race in Science: Great Britain, 1800–1960*. North Haven, CT: Archon, 1982.

Stocking, George W. Jr. *Race, Culture, and Evolution: Essays in the History of Anthropology*. Chicago, University of Chicago Press, 1982.

Takaki, Ronald. *Strangers from a Different Shore: A History of Asian Americans*. New York: Back Bay Books, 1998.

_____. *A Different Mirror: A History of Multicultural America*. New York: Back Bay Books, 1993.

_____. *Pau Hana: Plantation Life and Labor in Hawaii, 1835–1920*. Honolulu: University of Hawaii Press, 1983.

Tang, Hua, Tom Quertermous, Beatriz Rodriguez, Sharon L R Kardia, Xiaofeng Zhu, Andrew Brown, James S. Pankow, Michael A. Province, Steven C. Hunt, Eric Boerwinkle, Nicholas J. Schork, and Neil J. Risch. "Genetic Structure, Self-Identified Race/Ethnicity, and Confounding in Case-Control Association Studies." *American Journal of Human Genetics*. Vol. 76 (2005): 268–275.

Tattersall, Ian and Rob DeSalle. *Race? Debunking a Scientific Myth*. College Station, TX: Texas A&M University Press, 2011.

Telles, Edward and Tianna Paschel. "Who Is Black, White, or Mixed Race? How Skin Color, Status, and Nation Shape Racial Classification in Latin America. *American Journal of Sociology*, Vol. 120, No. 3 (2014): 864–907.

Tesler, Michael and David O. Sears. *Obama's Race: The 2008 Election and the Dream of a Post-Racial America*. Chicago: University of Chicago Press, 2010.

Thomas, John F. "Cuban Refugees in the United States," *International Migration Review*, Vol. 1, No. 2 (1967): 46–57.

Tocqueville Alexis de. *Democracy in America*. Chicago: University of Chicago Press, 2012.

Torres, Héctor L., Anita O'Conor, Claudia Mejía, Yvette Camacho, and Alyse Long. "The American Dream: Racism towards Latino/as in the U.S. and the Experience of Trauma Symptoms," *Interamerican Journal of Psychology*, Vol. 45, No. 3 (2011): 363–368.

Treviño, Robert R. "Teaching Mexican American History," *OAH Magazine of History*, Vol. 19, No. 6 (2005): 18–21.

Troche-Rodriguez, Madeline. "Latinos and Their Housing Experiences in Metropolitan Chicago: Challenges and Recommendations," *Harvard Journal of Hispanic Policy*, Vol. 21 (2009): 17–33.

Tsu, Cecilia M. *Garden of the World: Asian Immigrants and the Making of Agriculture in California's Santa Clara Valley*. Oxford: Oxford University Press, 2013.

Tuan, Mia. *Forever Foreigners or Honorary Whites? The Asian Ethnic Experience Today*. New Brunswick, NJ: Rutgers University Press, 1999.

Turner, Frederick Jackson. "The Development of American Society" (1908), in *Frontiers of Historical Imagination: Narrating the European Conquest of Native*

America, 1890–1990, ed. Kerwin Lee Klein. Berkeley: University of California Press, 1999.

Vasquez, Jessica M. "Blurred Borders For Some But Not 'Others': Racialization, 'Flexible Ethnicity', Gender, And Third-Generation Mexican American Identity," *Sociological Perspectives*, Vol. 53, No. 1 (2010): 45–72.

Vecoli, Rudolph J. "The Significance of Immigration in the Formation of an American Identity," *The History Teacher*, Vol. 30, No. 1 (1996): 9–27.

———. "Return to the Melting Pot: Ethnicity in the United States in the Eighties," *Journal of American Ethnic History*, Vol. 5, No. 1 (1985): 7–20.

Villarreal Andrés. "Stratification by Skin Color in Contemporary Mexico," *American Sociological Review*, Vol. 75, No. 5 (2010): 652–678.

Võ, Linda Trinh. "The Vietnamese American Experience: From Dispersion to the Development of Post-Refugee Communities," in *Asian American Studies: A Reader*, eds. Jean Yu-Wen Shen Wu and Min Song. New Brunswick, NJ: Rutgers University Press, 2009.

Wade, Nicholas. *A Troublesome Inheritance: Genes, Race and Human History*. London: Penguin Books, 2015.

Wagner, Jennifer K., Jill D. Cooper, Rene Sterling and Charmaine D. Royal. "Tilting at Windmills No Longer: A Data-driven Discussion of DTC DNA Ancestry Tests," *Genetics in Medicine*, Vol. 14 (2012): 586–593.

Waters, Mary C. "Ethnic and Racial Identities of Second-Generation Black Immigrants in New York City," *The International Migration Review*, Vol. 28, No. 4 (1994): 795–820.

Waters, Mary C. and Philip Kasinitz. "Discrimination, Race Relations, and the Second Generation," Social Research, Vol. 77, No. 1 (2010): 101–132.

Wei, William. *The Asian American Movement*. Temple University Press, 1993.

Weiss, Richard. "Ethnicity and Reform: Minorities and the Ambience of the Depression Years," The Journal of American History, Vol. 66, No. 3 (1979): 566–585.

White, Theodore H. *In Search of History: A Personal Adventure*, (New York: Harper and Row Publishers, 1978.

Wickham, DeWayne. *Bill Clinton and Black America*. New York: The Ballantine Publishing Group, 2002.

Wilkerson, Isabel. *The Warmth of Other Suns: The Epic Story of America's Great Migration*. New York: Vintage Books, 2011.

Williams, Kim M. *Mark One or More: Civil Rights in Multiracial America*. Ann Arbor, MI: University of Michigan Press, 2008.

Williams, William Appleman. *America Confronts a Revolutionary World*, 1776–1976. New York: Morrow, 1976.

Wilson, Edward O. *Sociobiology: The New Synthesis*. Cambridge: Belknap Press, 1975.

Wilson, William Julius. *More than Just Race: Being Black and Poor in the Inner City*. New York: W.W. Norton and Company, 2010.

Winant, Howard. "Just Do It: Notes of Politics and Race at the Dawn of the Obama Presidency." *Du Bois Review*. Vol. 6, No. 1 (2009): 49–70.

Wittke, Carl. *We Who Built America: The Saga of the Immigrant*. New York, Prentice-Hall, Inc., 1948.

_____. "German Immigrants and Their Children," *Annals of the American Academy of Political and Social Science*, Vol. 223 (1942): 85–91.

Wong, K. Scott. "The Eagle Seeks a Helpless Quarry: Chinatown, The Police, and The Press, The 1903 Boston Chinatown Raid Revisited," in *Asian American Studies: A Reader*, ed. Jean Yu-Wen Shen Wu and Min Song. Rutgers: Rutgers University Press, 2009.

Woodard, Colin. *American Nations: A History of the Eleven Rival Regional Cultures of North America*. New York: Penguin Books, 2012.

Wright, Richard. *12 Million Black Voices: A Folk History of the Negro in the United States*. New York: Viking Press, 1941.

Wu, Ellen D. *The Color of Success: Asian Americans and the Origins of the Model Minority*. Princeton: Princeton University Press, 2013.

_____. "'America's Chinese': Anti-Communism, Citizenship, and Cultural Diplomacy during the Cold War." *Pacific Historical Review*, Vol. 77, No. 3 (2008): 391–422.

Wu, Frank H. *Yellow: Race in America beyond Black and White*. New York: Basic Books, 2003.

Yancey, George. *Who Is White?: Latinos, Asians, and the New Black/Nonblack Divide*. Boulder, CO: Lynne Rienner Publishers, 2003.

Young, Elliott. *Alien Nation: Chinese Migration in the Americas from the Coolie Era through World War II*. Chapel Hill: University of North Carolina Press, 2014.

Yudell, Michael. *Race Unmasked: Biology and Race in the Twentieth Century*. New York: Columbia University Press, 2014.

_____. "How Science Embraced the Racialization of Human Populations," in *Race and the Genetic Revolution: Science, Myth, and Culture*, eds. Sheldon Krimsky and Kathleen Sloan. New York: Columbia University Press, 2011.

Zangwill, Israel. *The Melting Pot*. New York: The Macmillan Company, 1923.

Zelinksy, Wilbur. *The Cultural Geography of the United States: A Revised Edition.* New York: Prentice Hall, 1992.

Zhao, Xiaojian and Edward Park (eds.). *Asian Americans: An Encyclopedia of Social, Cultural, Economic, and Political History.* Santa Barbara, CA: Greenwood, 2013.

Zhou Min. "Are Asian Americans Becoming White?" *Contexts*, Vol. 3, No. 1 (2004): 29–37.

INDEX

14th Amendment, 75, 210, 347
15th Amendment, 80
16th Street Baptist Church, 93
2004 Democratic National Convention, 66, 351
23andMe, 263
A Journey Through Texas (book), 139
A Troublesome Inheritance: Genes, Race, and Human History (book), 299
abolition, 19, 74, 81, 137, 171, 206, 269, 271
Abraham Lincoln, 3, 21
Abrajano, Marisa, 331
Abrams, Charles, 49
Acosta-Belén, Edna, 149
acting white, 108, 327, 329
Acting White? Rethinking Post in "Post Racial" America (book), 350
Adamic, Lewis, 42
Adams, John Mrs., 72
Adams, John Quincy, 11, 72, 137
affirmative action, xv, 47, 57, 97–98, 113, 115, 116, 109, 346–347, 354
African American, xi–xvi, 22, 18, 20, 37, 48–51, 72, 65–67, 75–76, 80–81, 83, 86, 91–92, 95–102, 107–111, 114, 115–121, 140, 146, 156–157, 161, 166, 188, 194, 198, 234, 263, 305, 314, 329, 339, 350–351, 359

African Ancestry, Inc., 305
Africans, 10, 69, 71, 230, 268, 318
Agassiz, Louis, 270
Age of Enlightenment, 72
Aguinaldo, Emilio, 235
Akaka, Daniel, 314
Alba, Richard D., 58, 335, 356
Alemán, Miguel, 158
Alexander, Michelle, xiii, 101, 338
Alien Registration Act, 245, 249
Alien Contract Labor Law, 206
Alien Land Law, 224
All Lives Matter, 121, 299
alleged mental illness in slaves, 270
Als, Hilton, 351
America is in the Heart (book), 238
American Anthropological Association, 283
American Apartheid: Segregation and the Making of the Underclass (book), 288
American Association of Physical Anthropologists, 283
American Community Survey, 25
American Jewish Committee, 58
American Legion Magazine, 172
American Psychological Association, 291
American revolution, 8, 11, 72–73
American School of Anthropology, 269
An American Dilemma (book), 48
Ancestry DNA, 263–264, 302

Anderson, Elijah, 348–349
Andreas, Peter, 175, 177
Anglo Protestants, 8, 11
Annals of the American Academy of Political and Social Science, 34
anti-Catholic, 17
anti-Chinese, 209, 211–213, 248
Anti-Coolie Bill, 206
anti-German, 23, 287
anti-Japanese sentiment, 220–222, 238, 244–245
anti-miscegenation laws, 70, 140, 234, 240, 327
anti-Semitism, 32–33
Anti-Terrorism and Effective Death Penalty Act, 178
Antoine, C.C., 75
Antonio de Olivares, Fray, 134
apartheid, xiv, 48, 111, 288
Applied Eugenics (book), 273
Arthur, Chester A., 212
Asian Americans, xiv, 168, 188, 197–199, 251–258, 307, 313, 324, 318, 331–335
Asian and Pacific Islander American Scholarship Fund, 197
Asiatic Exclusion League, 222, 231, 247
attacks on Filipinos, 240–241
Austin, Stephen, 137
Axelrod, David, 112
Ayres, E. Duran, 156
Azuma, Eiichiro, 218

Bai, Matt, 114
Balderrama, Francisco E., 150
Baldoz, Rick, 236, 249
Baldwin, James, xvi, 59, 284
Baltimore News, 34
Balz, Dan, 110
Bane, Mary Jo, 102
Barnett, Ross, 92
Barone, Michael, 21, 24, 31, 85
Barrett, James R., 20
Bausch, John, 25
Bean, Frank D., 328, 329

Beck, Glenn, 10
Beecher, Lyman, 17
BeerGate, 116
Benedict, Ruth, 278
Bengalis, 234
Benjamin Franklin, 7, 203
Benjamin, Rich, 328
Bernier, Francois, 267
Biddle, Francis, 24
Biden, Joe, 116, 351
BiDil, 302
Bigler, John, 207
bilingual curriculum, 23
Bill Clinton and Black America (book), 99
Bishop, Edward, 240
Black Codes, 70, 75
Black colleges, 48
Black incarceration, 11, 13, 114, 345
Black Lives Matter, 14, 2, 61, 67, 120–121, 299, 341
Black Metropolis (book), 88
Black Panther Party, 95, 356
Black Power Movement, 95, 254
Black pride movement, 56
Black Skins, White Masks (book), 283
Blackmon, Douglas A., 75
Blackmun, Harry, 347
Blavatsky, Helena Petrovna, 229
Bliss, Catherine, 301, 304
Blue Lives Matter, 121, 299
Blumenbach, Johann Frederich, 268
Boas, Franz, 37, 38, 277–283
Bobo, Lawrence D., 339, 347
Boehlert, Eric, 345–346
Boehner, John A., 190
Boeing, William, 25
Bolling, Eric, 345
Bonilla-Silva, Eduardo, xv, 323, 344
Borderers, 9
Boss William Tweed, 20
Boston Boy (book), 33
Boston International Institute, 41
Boston Pilot, 17
Boykin, A. Wade, 291–292

INDEX

Bracero Program, 158–159, 171, 173
Bradley, Tom, 110
Brewer, Jan, 189, 356
Brodkin, Karen, 51
Brown v. Board of Education, 91, 283
Brown, Hubert "Rap", 95
Brown, Jesse, 102
Brown, Lee, 102
Brown, Michael, 118
Brown, Ron, 102
Brownstein, Ronald, 355
Bryan, Jennings, 222
Buaken, Manuel, 239
Buchanan, Agnes Foster, 231
Buchanan, Patrick, 334
Bulosan, Carlos, 238
Burch, Traci, 14
Bush, George H.W., 98
Bush, George W., 99, 115, 123, 179, 181, 186, 351
Butler, Paul, 109

Cafferty, Jack, 181
Camacho, Manuel Ávila, 158
Carbado, Devon W., 350
Carmichael, Stokley, 95
Carrigan, William D., 146
Carter, Jimmy, 165, 173
Carter, Lillian, 166
Cartwright, Samuel Dr., 270
Caste system, 10, 136, 146, 291, 324
Castro, Fidel, 163–165
Catholic immigration, 7, 18, 21, 30, 58
Cavalli-Sforza, Luigi Luca, 297
Cayton, Horace, 88
Celera Gnomics, 298
Celler, Emanuel, 248–249, 251
Central American immigrants, 161, 174
Chacon, Justin Akers, 158
Chahine, Ken, 306
Chang, Sucheng, 208, 212
ChangeLab, 256
Chapman, Leonard, 172
Charles, Camille Z., 339

Chavez, Cesar, 162
Chen, Yong, 211
Chiang Kai-shek, 247
Chicago Daily News, 34
Chicago Defender, 84, 86
Chicago Tribune, 34
Chinese Exclusion Act, 30
Chinese Six Companies, 209, 214, 220, 236, 245, 248
Chisholm, Shirley, 108
Chomsky, Aviva, 171
Chou, Rosalind S., 198, 255
Christian Science Monitor, 178, 354
Churchill, Winston, 248
Citrin, Jack, 335
Civil Rights Act of 1964, 80, 94, 110
Civil rights movement, 49, 57, 80, 91–94, 108, 110, 171, 254, 283, 285, 313–314
Civil War, 7, 11, 28, 18–20, 75, 80–81, 85, 208, 269, 311
Clark, Kenneth, 288
Clark, Victor S., 149
Clement, Scott, 354
Clever, Eldridge, 95
Clinton, Bill, 99–101, 110, 175, 178, 256, 298
Clinton, Hillary, 1, 110, 113
Cobas, José, 326
Cobb, Jelani, xiv
Coca-Cola, 10
Cold War, 163–173, 250, 280
Collins, Frank, 298
color blind racism, xv, 93, 100, 113–114, 291, 207, 344, 346–347
Communist China, 250
Comprehensive Immigration Reform (CIR), 127, 185–186
Compromise of 1877, 79
Confessore, Nicholas, 192
Coolidge, Calvin, 38
Coon, Carleton S., 282–283
Cooper, Richard, 303
Cornelius, Wayne A., 179
Cortin, Juan "Cheno", 140, 148

Coulter, Ann, 335
Craig, Maureen, 19
Creating a New Racial Order (book), 14
Crowley, James Sgt., 115–116
Cuba, 76, 132, 148, 149, 163–165, 205–206, 234
Cuban Missile Crisis, 164
Cubberley, Ellwood P., 40
Cullors, Patrisse, 121
Cuomo, Andrew, 110
Curse of Ham, 71

Daly, Emma, 263
Dana, Richard Henry, 136
Daniels, Roger, 22, 24, 30, 31–32, 207, 210, 212, 213
Darity, William, 326
Darwinism, 267, 271–272, 278
Davenport, Charles Benedict, 35, 273
Dávila, Arlene, 329
Davis, David Brion, 69
Davis, Mike, 158
de facto segregation, xv, 83
de Gobineau, Comte, 18
De Long, C.E., 206
de Narváez, Pánfilo, 132
de Portola, Gaspar, 134
Dearborn Independent (newspaper), 33
Deep South, 10–11, 114
Deferred Action for Childhood Arrivals (DACA), 187, 190
Democracy in America (book), 74
Democrats, xiv, xv, 2, 21, 48, 60, 80, 93–94, 97–98, 114, 175, 186, 192, 337
Dennis, Rutledge M., 274
Denton, Nancy A., 288
Department of Homeland Security, creation of, 180
deportations, 11, 156, 180, 185–193
de Toqueville, Alexis, 74
Detroit, 67, 91, 95, 149
Diamond, John, 18
DiAngelo, Robin, 3
Dickerson, Debra, 108

Dillingham Commission, 38, 231
Dillingham, William Paul, 38
Dinnerstein, Leonard, 45, 160
discrimination in Canada, 222, 230, 232
Disintegration: The Splintering of America (book), 349
DNA testing, 263–264, 303–305, 318
DNAPrint, 304
Dobzhansky, Theodosius, 279
Dominicans, 161, 317, 324
Donelson, Andrew, 138
Doocy, Steve, 345
Dorn, Ed, 354
Doty, Roxanne Lynn, 181
double consciousness, 82
Douglas, Bill, 99
Douglas, Karen Manges, 178
Dower, John, 219
Drake, St. Clair, 88
DREAM Act, 186, 188
Dred Scott v. Sandford, 75, 270
Duany, Jorge, 161
Dubois, W.E.B., 59, 81, 82, 283
Dukakis, Michael, 98–99
Duke, David, 3, 101, 282
Dyson, Michael Eric, 116

East Indians, 205, 229
Eastern Europeans, 29, 273
Ebony, 86
Edelman, Peter, 105
Edwards, A.W.F., 298
Edwards, Steven, 181
Egerton, Douglas R., 75
Eisenhower, Dwight, 92
Elijah Muhammad, 91, 93
Ellis Island, 30–31
Emerson, Ralph Waldo, 229
English language, 40, 150, 226
English Puritans, 8
Entine, John, 301
Equal Protection Clause, 91
Equal Rights Amendment, 57
Espy, Mike, 102

INDEX

Esquire Magazine, 60
ethnic politics, 51, 58
ethnic studies, 56–57
eugenics, 35, 264
Executive Order, 4, 87
Executive Order, 102, 221–222, 245

Fanon, Frantz, 283
Farmer-Labor Party, 25
Faubus, Orval, 92, 282
Feagin, Joe R., 198, 255, 319
Federal Housing Administration (FHA), 47
Federal Times, 179
Feldman, Glenn, 115
Ferguson, Missouri, 118
Fernández-Armesto, Felipe, 132
Ferrara, Peter, 346
Ferraro, Geraldine, 113
Ferre, Maurice, 165
Filipino military service, 249
Filipinos Repatriation Act, 241
Filipinos, 201, 229
Finding Oprah's Roots, Finding Your Own (book), 305
Fischer, David Hackett, 8
Fisher, Sir Ronald, 281
Fletcher, Arthur, 313
Foley, Neil, 143, 368
Ford, Gerald, 97
Ford, Henry, 33
Ford, W.D., 91
forensic DNA, 304, 307, 377
Forever Foreigners or Honorary Whites (book), 256
Forty-Eighters, 21, 22
Fowler, Arthur E., 220
France, 7, 46, 134
Franciscan missions, 133–134
Frank, Barney, 314
Franklin, John Hope, 76, 79, 368
Fray, Junípero Serra, 134
Frazier, E. Franklin, 97
Fredrickson, George M., 70, 76
Free-stater Yankees, 26

Freedmen's Bureau, 75
freedom rides, 92
Fresno Republican, 219
Frey, William H., 259, 340, 361, 369
Fricke, Charles W., 156
Fukuzawa, Yukichi, 217

Gaines v. Missouri, 86
Galarza, Ernesto, 162
Gallup poll, 198, 252
Galton, Sir Francis, 35, 273
Gans, Herbert, 5
Garci Rodríguez de Montalvo, 132
Garcia, Maria Cristina, 169, 369
Garcia, Mario T., 167
Garmback, Frank, 118
Garner, Eric, 117–118
Garth, Thomas, 151
Garvey, Marcus, 84
Garza, Alicia, 120–121
Gates, Henry Louis Jr., 66, 83, 89, 115–116, 287, 295
Geary Act, 212
General Mills, 3
General Social Survey, 339, 341, 354
Genesis, Book of, 71
genetic differences, 281, 285, 291, 300
genetic testing, 304
Genetics and the Origin of Species (book), 279
Genomics, 293
Gentleman's Agreement with Japan, x, 217, 222, 237
George Washington, 11
German Americans, 7, 22, 23–25, 27, 38, 371
Giddon, George Robins, 270
Gil, Pedro, 241
Giuliani, Rudy, 68
Glazer, Nathan, 26, 369
GNP, 47
Goddard, Henry H., 36
Goethe C.M., 239
Golash-Boza, Tanya, 332

Gold Rush, 141
Goldstein, Eric L., 62
Gonzales, Alfonso, 186
Gonzalez, Juan, 133
Good Housekeeping magazine, 38
Gould, Stephen Jay, 269
Grace, William, 20
Grant, Madison, 43
Grant, Ulysses S., 138, 210
Gratz, Jennifer, 115
Graves, Joseph Jr., 301
Gray, Freddie, 118
Greaser Act, 139
Great Depression (1930s), 45, 86, 91, 155, 157, 358,
Great Migration, 79, 84, 86, 89, 159
Great Society, 56, 98
Groubert, Sean, 118
Grutter, Barbara, 115–116
Guglielmo, Thomas A., 33, 43
Guinier, Lani, 113
Gulati, Mitu, 350
Gutiérrez, David G., 156

H-2 temporary visa, 173
Haddon, A. C., 278
Hainal, Zoltan L., 331
Haley, Alex, 56
Haley, Nikki, 119
Hamacher, Patrick, 115
Hamill, Pete, 56
Handlin, Oscar, 8
Harlan, John Marshall, 346
Harper's Weekly, 19
Harriet Beecher Stowe, 17
Harris, Fredrick, 107
Hart-Cellars Act, 162, 171–172
Hartman, Andrew, 95, 103
Harvest of Shame (documentary), 162
Hawaiian Sugar Planters Association, 237
Hawks, John, 305
Hayes, Rutherford B., 79, 212
Hays, Benjamin K. Dr., 275
Heartland Institute, 346

Heer, Jeet, 2
Heinz, Henry J., 25
Hemings, Sally, 73
Hentoff, Nat, 33
Herman Melville, 11
Hernández, Kelly Lytle, 159, 161
Hetherington, Marc, 2
Higham, John, 34–35, 57
Hindus, 230–231, 233, 311
Hispanic culture, 132
Hispanics, 60, 102, 115, 128, 131, 132, 156–157, 163, 167, 186, 191–192, 194, 251, 299, 305, 313, 315–316, 318–320, 324, 326–327, 329–330, 333–334
Hoagland, Jim, 66
Hochschild, Jennifer, 307
Hofstadter, Richard, 272
Holli, Melvin G., 24
Home Owners' Loan Corporation (HOLC), 48
Home ownership, 60–62
homo sapient, 275
Hoover, J. Edgar, 95
Horton, Willie, 98–99
household income, 197, 338, 357
Houston, Sam, 137
How Jews Became White Folks (book), 51
How the Irish Became White (book), 18, 59
Hsu, Madeline, 254
Hu-DeHart, Evelyn, 205, 214
Hughes, Charles Evans, 86
Human Genome Diversity Project, 298
Human Genome Organization, 298
Human Genome Project (HGP), 297
Huntington, Samuel P., 339, 371
Huxley, Sir Julian, 278

I Have Lived With the American People (book), 365
Igorotte, 236
Illegal aliens, 167, 172–173, 175–176, 181, 243, 335
Immigration Act of 1965, 251, 253

INDEX

Immigration and Nationality Act (1952), 250
Immigration quota, 39, 162, 245
immigration raids, 185
Immigration Reform and Control Act, 174
Immigration Reform and Immigrant Responsibility Act, 178
Immigration Service, 30, 155,
Immigration, 46, 47, 53, 166, 168, 211, 248
Independence of the Philippines, 249
India League of America, 248
Indochinese Parole Program, 252
INS (Immigraton & Naturalization Service), 232
intermarriage, 46, 57–58, 70, 80, 83, 134, 207, 236, 240, 309, 327, 340
Internal migration, 95–97
Irish Catholic, 7, 15–16, 20
Irish, 15, 16, 17–20, 33, 35, 56, 59, 134
Isidro Ordoñez, Fray, 133
Islam, 7, 91, 93, 203
Italian, 31–36
Iyer, Vijay, 260

Jackson, Jesse, 100–102, 108, 110
Jackson, Kenneth, 49
Jamestown, 70, 132
Japanese Association of San Francisco, 222
Japanese Citizens League, 197
Japanese internment, 3, 245–246
Japanese-Americans, 24–25, 35, 246–247, 249–250, 252–255
Japanese-Korean Exclusion League, 220
Jefferson Thomas, 73–74, 203
Jensen, Arthur R., 284–285, 291
Jewish, 32–33, 58, 300
Jim Crow, xv, 47, 60, 79–86, 91, 97, 101, 112, 338, 344–345, 354, 358–359
Johnson-Reed Act, 39
Johnson, Albert, 152
Johnson, Andrew President, 75
Johnson, Haynes, 110
Johnson, Lyndon, 56, 93–96, 98, 110, 162–163

Johnson, Roswell Hill, 273
Jones Act of 1917, 159
Jones, Levar, 118
Jones, Nicholas, 315
Jones, Van, 74
Jordan, Winthrop D., 71–72

Kallen, Horace M., 41–42
Kasinitz, Philip, 324
Katznelson, Ira, 47–48
Kaufmann, Eric, 8
Keefe, Daniel J., 233
Kelly, W.F., 158
Kennedy, Anthony, 116, 189
Kennedy, Caroline, 110
Kennedy, John F., 20, 93, 94, 162, 163
Kennedy, Joseph C.G., 311
Kennedy, Randall, 113, 329, 346
Kennedy, Ted, 97, 121
Kerner Commission, 96
Kerry, John, 114
King, Martin Luther Jr., 92–95
Kiser, Clyde V., 46
Kittles, Rick, 305
Know-Nothings, 17, 21
Korean immigrants, 221, 248, 250–253
Krysan, Maria, 339
Ku Klux Klan, 79, 83–84, 151, 181, 240, 282, 356
Kurashige, Scott, 246

La Follette, Philip, 40
La Follette, Robert Jr., 40
La Follette, Robert, 40
La Gran Liga Mexicanista de Beneficiencia y Protección and the League of United Latin American Citizens (LULAC), 148
Ladner, Joyce A., 285
Lane, William Henry ("Juba"), 18
Langston, Sarah Wall, 76
Las Sergas de Esplandián (novel), 132
Latino Decisions, 60
Latson, Willliam R.C. Dr., 229–230
Lazarus, Emma, 8

Leclerc, George-Louis, the Comte de Buffon, 268
Ledyard, John, 203
Lee, Erika, 241, 256
Lee, Jennifer, 328
Lee, Robert E. Col., 140
Lee, Shelley Sang-Hee, 203, 219
Leroi, Armand Marie, 299
Letters from an American Farmer, 11
Levittown, 51–52
Lewontin, Richard, 285–287, 298–299
Liebler, Carolyn A., 316
Lindee, M. Susan, 286
Linnaeus, Carl, 268
Little Rock, Arkansas, 92, 100, 282
Little, Malcolm, 92
Loehmann, Tim, 118
Logan, Enid, 114
Logan, John R., xiii
Lomb, Henry, 25
London, Jack, 220
Longmore, Paul K., 270
Lopez, Jane Lilly, 187
Los Angeles Times, 67, 150, 157
Los Angeles, 67, 155, 225
Louisiana Purchase Exposition, 236
Loving v. Virginia, 327
Luce-Celler Act, 248–249
Luce, Clare Booth, 248
Luqman, Amina, 109
Lutheran, 21, 23

Magnuson Act, 248
Malcolm X, 92–93
Malik, Kenan, 72, 302
Man's Most Dangerous Myth: the Fallacy of Race (book), 279
Marable, Manning, 91, 93, 95
Mariel boatlift, 165–166, 173
Marketplace (radio show), 121
Marshall Plan, 46
Marshall, Ray, 173
Martin, Trayvon, 117, 120

Massey, Douglas S., 47, 171, 174, 176, 179, 288, 337–338
Mather, Kenneth, 281
Matthew, Chris, 114
Mayer, Oscar, 25
Mayr, Ernst, 278
McCaffrey, Lawrence J., 16
McCain, John, 113, 115
McCarran-Walter Act, 250
McElwee, Sean, 354
McGovern, George, 162
McKinley, William, 235
McLane, Robert, 206
McWilliams, Carey, 131, 139
Mead, Margaret, 283
Mears, John L. Dr., 211
Menchaca, Martha, 151
Menéndez de Avilés, Pedro, 132
Meredith, James, 92
mestizo, 72, 135, 145, 236, 316–317
Methodist, 9, 22, 119
Mexican labor, 141, 145–150, 158, 161, 173
Mexican lynchings, 147
Mexicans, 33–34, 127–129, 131, 138–141, 145–152, 155–157, 159–160, 162, 171–172, 178–181, 192, 218, 233, 310, 313, 317–318, 325–326, 334–335, 337, 358
middle class society, 8, 9, 16, 45, 47–49, 50–51, 56, 254–255, 288, 349, 356
Migration and Refugee Assistance Act of 1962, 163
Miles, Nelson Al, General, 149
Millard Fillmore, 18
Millennials, 15, 81, 299, 337, 353–355
Milton, William H., 83
Mineta, Norman, 314
Minority Education and Caste (book), 291
minority majority nation, xiii
minstrel, 18, 271
Minuteman Project, 181
model minority myth, 198

model minority, 198, 253–258
Molly Maguires, 17
monogenesis, 73
Montague, Ashley, 279
Montejano, David, 140
More Than Just Race: Being Black and Poor in the Inner City (book), 98
Morrison, Toni, 60, 99, 251–255, 256
Morse, Samuel F.B., 17
Morton, Samuel, 269
Moseley-Braun, Carol, 113
Moss, Alfred A. Jr., 83
Moynihan, Daniel P., 20, 96–97
mulatto, 70, 135, 161, 164, 166, 269, 311
Murray, Charles, 289–290
Murrieta, Joaquin, legend of, 148
Murrow, Edward R., 162
Muslim, 1, 61, 229, 330–331
Myers, Dowell, 356
Myrdal, Gunner, 48, 87–88

NAACP, 3, 81, 87, 91, 119, 173, 313, 338, 346
Nakagawa, Scott, 254
Napolitano, Janet, 187
Nation of Islam, 91
National Association of Latino Elected Officials, 185
National Commission for Manpower Policy, 173
National Commission on Asian American and Pacific Islander Research in Education, 197
National Defense Highway Act, 47
National Jewish Population Survey, 58
National Origins Act, 39
National Policy Institute, 2
Native American Party, 17–18
Native Americans, xvi, 17, 22, 37, 55, 73, 111, 135, 269, 292, 305, 310, 314
nativism, 7, 21–22, 34, 38, 131, 151, 220, 238
Negrito, 235–236

Neil, Charles P., 233
Nelkin, Dorothy, 286
net worth, 338
Nevins, Joseph, 176
New Deal, 45, 48–49, 88
New Netherlands, 10
New Republic, 2
New York Times, 1, 111, 114, 118, 175, 192, 254, 282, 290, 299, 302
New Yorker magazine, 99
Newton, Huey, 95
Ngai, Mae M., 155
Niagara Movement (see NAACP)
Nixon, Richard, 2, 56, 95, 97, 312
Non-Hispanic white, 2, 166–167, 313
Non-Partisan League, 25
Notes on the State of Virginia, 73
Nott, Josiah, 269
Novak, Michael, 57
Núñez Cabeza de Vaca, Álvar, 133

O'Leary, Hazel, 102
Obama, Barack, 1–2, 65–66, 99, 107–120, 185–190, 346, 351, 359
Obama, Michelle, 65, 108
Obama's "Race Speech", 66, 112, 117
octoroon, 72, 311
Odem, Mary E., 336
Ogbu, John, 291
Okamura, Jonathan Y., 314
Okihiro, Gary, 205–206
Oliver Wendell Holmes, poet, 32
Olmstead, Frederick, 139
Omi, Michael, 285
On the Origin of the Species, 271
On the Varieties of Mankind (book), 268
Onwuachi-Willig, Angela, 116
Operation Gatekeeper, 177
Operation Hold-the-Line, 176
Operation Phalanx, 186
Operation Wetback, 161–162
opium, 199, 204, 210–212
organized labor movement, 17, 37, 61, 221

Oriental religions, 229
Orientalism (book), 202
Ozawa, Takao, 225–226

pachuco gang subculture, 156–157
Packard, Jerrold M., 85
Page, Horace F., 212
Painter, Nell Irvin, 17, 19, 35, 59
Palmer, Aaron H., 207
Parker, Theodore, 19
Parks, Rosa, 92
Paschei, Tianna, 316
Patrick, Deval, 116
Patterns of Culture (book), 278
Pearce, Russell, 189
Pearl Harbor, 245–247
Pensionado Act, 237
Personal Responsibility and Work Opportunity Reconciliation Act, 102
Petersen, William, 254
Peterson, Joseph, 274
Pew Foundation, xiii
Pew research Center, 116, 191, 192–193, 197–198, 258, 315–316, 335, 337, 353
Pfaelzer, Jean, 207
Phelan, James D., 213, 224
Philadelphia Plan, 97
Philadelphia, Mississippi, 80
Philippine Commission, 235–236
Philippine-American war, 235
Phillips, John, 96
Phillips, William, 248
picture brides, 222, 224
Pierce, Charles, 61
Pinckney, Clementa Rev., 119
Piston, Spencer, 353
Platt Amendment, 149
Plessy v. Ferguson, 80, 91, 346
Plessy, Homer, 80
police violence with Black men, 113–118
Polk, James K., 138
polygenesis, 73
Ponce de Leon, Juan, 132
Popenoe, Paul, 273

Portes, Alejandro, 334
post-racial, 65–67, 73, 107, 111, 114, 350
Prasad, Vijay, 198
Prem, Karen A., 179
Presbyterian, 9, 17
private-contract emigrants, 218
Progressive Party, 25
Project RACE, 314
Proposition 177, 306
prostitution, 204, 210–211, 223
Pruitt, Kenneth, 309
Public Religion Research Institute, 60
Puerto Rico, 51, 131–132, 148–149, 159–160, 234, 317
Punjab, 230, 234
Purkayashite, Bandana, 330
Putnam, Carleton, 282, 283
quadroon, 72, 311

Quakers, 9

race card, xvi, 1, 113, 344, 351
Race Crossing in Jamaica (book), 273
race realists, 1
Race Traitor (journal), 59
Race, Culture and Evolution (book), 283
racial categories, 72, 264, 292, 312, 314, 317
Racial Formation in the United States (book), 288
racial segregation, xv, 50, 76, 84, 89, 107, 112, 152, 285, 288–289, 326–327, 339, 343–344, 355, 357
racial theories, 34, 80, 271, 285
racialized assimilation, 326
Rainbow Coalition, 101
Ramos, Jorge, 185, 187
Randolph, A. Philip, 87
Rankin, John, 47
Rasmussen poll, 114
Reader's Digest, 172
Reagan, Ronald, xvi, 57, 97–98, 173–174, 246
reapportionment, 39

INDEX

Reconstruction Act, 75, 79
Rector, Ricky Ray, 100
redlining, 49, 60
Reimers, David M., 160
Republicans, xiv–xv, 2, 48, 60, 75, 79, 100, 189–190, 193, 210, 258, 337
Reuss, Aloise, 229
reverse discrimination, 11, 115, 343
Reyes, Silvestre, 176
Rice, Tamir, 118
Richards, Samuel M., 263
Richeson, Jennifer, 19
Ripley, William Z., 22
Risch, Neil, 299, 302
Roberts, John Justice, 346
Roberts, Kenneth L., 152
Robinson, Eugene, 349, 351
Rodino, Peter, 174
Rodrigues, Raymond, 150
Rodriguez, Clara, 160
Rodriguez, Gregory, 135–136
Roediger, David, 37, 40, 49, 59
Rohrback, D.W. Judge, 238
Roldan v. Los Angeles County and the State of California, 240
Romney, Mitt, 188
Roof, Dylann, 119
Roosevelt, Franklin, 7, 33, 45, 73, 87, 241
Roosevelt, Theodore, 35, 38, 218, 221, 236
Rosenberg, Emily S., 246
Rosenzweig, Jeff, 100
Ross, Edward, 34
Roth, Wendy, 317
Rotimi, Charles, 303
Rowell, Chester H., 219
Rubin, Jennifer, 346
Rumbaut, Ruben, 334
Russians, 36, 46, 57, 58, 324
Russo-Japanese War of 1904–05, 221

Saenz, Rogelio, 178
Said, Edward, 202
Sama, Jonathan D., 32
Samuel, Terence, 111

San Francisco Chronicle, 219, 231
San Jose Mercury Herald, 241
Sanchez, George L., 152
Sanders, Bernie, 121
Santa Anna, 137
Santayana, 16
Santiago, Carlos E., 149
Satel, Sally, 302
Saturday Evening Post, 152
Sawyer, Tom, 314
Scalia, Antonin, 189
Scandinavians, 9, 303
school integration, 91, 96, 164, 282, 339
Schrag, Peter, 7, 180
Schurman, Jacob Dr., 235
Schwarzenegger, Arnold, 191
Scots-Irish, 9–10, 29
Scott, Walter, 118
Scott, Winfield, 138
Seale, Bobby, 95
Sears, David O., 335
Second War Powers Act, 249
Sedition Acts, 7, 179
Segura, Gary, 188
Select Committee on Immigration and Refugee Policy, 173
Selective Service Act, 249
Sellout: The Politics of Racial Betrayal (book), 329
Sense About Science, 264
Sensenbrenner Bill, 180
Sharpton, Al, 108, 346
Sheldon, William, 151
Shockley, William, 284
Sikhs, 230, 232, 330
Simmons, Alicia, 347
Simpson, Alan, 174
Simpson, Alicia D., 339
Simpson, J.H. Lt., 139
Singh, Gurdit, 232
Singh, Sirdar Jagit, 248
Sinhan Minbo (Korean newspaper), 221–222
Sister Souljah, 101

sit-ins, 92
skin color, 18, 37, 65, 71, 80, 93, 192, 235, 267, 269, 283, 299, 301, 316–317, 323–326, 344, 355
Skrenty, John D., 187
Slager, Michael, 118
slave codes, 70, 75
slavery, 19, 69–75, 80, 82, 85, 87, 97, 107, 137–138, 205–206, 219, 269, 304, 345
Slavic, 278
Slidell, John, 138
Smiley, Tavis, 108
Smith, Al, 20
Smith, Michael Denzel, 354
Smith, William French, 173
Snipp, C. Matthew, 312–313
social Darwinism, 272, 278
Social Security, 47–48, 98, 356
Sociobiology: The New Synthesis (book), 286, 287
Soong, May-Ling, 247
Sotomayor, Sonia Justice, 116
Southeast Asians, 233, 245, 252
Spanish names, origin of, 132
Spanish-language advertising, 9
Spanish-speaking, xv, 152–153, 164
Spencer, Herbert, 272
Spencer, Richard, 2
St. John de Crevecoeur, J. Hector, 11
Staples, Brent, 350
Statue of Liberty, 8, 162, 354
Steele, Claude M., 350
Steele, Shelby, 114
Steinberg, Steven, 11
Steinway, Henry, 25
Stepan, Nancy, 282
Stimson, Henry, 249
Stocking, George W. Jr., 279, 283
Strange Fruit: Why Both Sides are Wrong in the Race Debate (book), 302
Strauss, Levi, 25
Streetwise: Race, Class, and Change in an Urban Community (book), 348
Studebaker, John, 25

Stults, Brian J, xiii
Sumner, Charles, 210
Support our Law Enforcement and Safe Neighborhoods Act, 189
Suro, Roberto, 175
Sutherland, George Justice, 226
Swami Vivekananda, 229
Swing, Joseph, 161

Taboo: Why Black Athletes Dominate Sports and Why We Are Afraid to Talk About It (book), 301
Taft, William Howard, 235–236
Takaki, Ronald, 146, 206, 222, 224, 246
Takei George, 246
Tammany Hall, 20
Taney, Roger B., 75, 270
Task Force on Terrorism, 174
Taylor, Zachary, 138
Telemundo, 180
Telles, Edward, 316
Texas Rangers, 140
The San Diego Tribune, 175
The Alamo, 134, 140, 148
The American Party, 17
The Bell Curve: Intelligence and Class Structure in American Life (book), 289–290
The Comparative Abilities of White and Negro Children (book), 274
The Cubic Air Ordinance, 210
The Death of the West (book), 334
The Declining Significance of Race (book), 288
The Emerging Republican Majority (book), 96
The Federalist Party, 7
The Fire Next Time (book), 284
The Foreign Miners Tax, 141, 207
The History of White People (book), 59
The Inequality of Human Races (essay), 18
The Kallikak Family (book), 36
The Levittowners (book), 52
The Mind of Primitive Man (book), 37
The New Jim Crow: Mass Incarceration in the Age of Colorblindness (book), 101

INDEX

The Origin of Races (book), 282
The Passing of the Great Race (book), 36
The Portland Oregonian, 236
The Races of Europe (book), 22
The Rise of the Unmeltable Ethnics (book), 57
The Souls of Black Folk (essay), 81
The Supreme Order of the Star Spangled Banner, 17
The Travels of Sir John Mandeville (book), 201–202
The Uprooted (book), 8
The Veil, 82
The Wages of Whiteness (book), 59
Theosophical Society, 229
Thind, Bhagat Singh, 234
Thoreau, Henry David, 229
Three Strikes law, 101
Tilden, Samuel J., 79
Time magazine, 172, 247
Tometi, Opal, 121
tortilla curtain, 176
Touré, 114
Treaty of Guadalupe Hidalgos, 139, 140, 334
Treviño, Robert R., 131
tri-racial system, 323
Troche-Rodriguez, Madeline, 191
Trump, Donald, 1, 60, 122, 192, 257, 352, 358
Tuan, Mia, 256
Turner, Frederick Jackson, 10
Twitter, 2, 120
Two Years Before the Mast (book), 136
Tydings-McDuffie Act, 241
Tyler, John, 138
Types of Mankind (book), 270

U.S. Border Patrol, 150, 161
U.S. Census (history of race in), 29, 211, 264, 309, 314
U.S. Immigration and Customs Enforcement (ICE), 180
U.S. News & World Report, 284

Umansky, Lauri, 270
unauthorized immigration, 173, 176, 334
undocumented immigrants, 172, 177–178, 181, 187, 191, 193, 331, 333, 336–337
UNESCO, 280, 285, 298
United States Immigration Commission, 38, 150, 231
Univision, 185
urban ghetto riots (race riots), 55
US Census Bureau, 2, 310, 312–313, 315–316, 318
USA Patriot Act, 179

Valencia, Richard R., 151
Van Evrie, J.H., 19
Vasquez, Jessica M., 325
Vasquez, Tina, 192
Vázquez de Coronado, Francisco, 133
Vecoli, Rudolph, 8, 51, 55, 57
Venter, Craig, 298
Ventura Daily Press, 151
Veteran's Administration, 47–48
Vietnam War, 252
Villarreal, Andrés, 316
Villarreal, Danny, 305
violence against Chinese, 212
Virginia elites, 9
Voting Rights Act of 1965, 95

Wade, Nicholas, 299–300
Walker, Francis Amasa, 35
Walloons, 10
War Brides Act of 1946, 245
Warren, Earl Justice, 91
Washburn, Sherry, 283
Washington Post, 66, 101, 109, 112, 122, 236, 346, 351, 354
Waters, Mary C., 324, 327
Watts, 67, 95, 343
We Europeans: A Survey of "Racial" Problems (book), 278
Weaver, Vesla, 14
Webb, Clive, 146
Weiss, Richard, 45

Welch, Richard J., 238
West Side Story (musical), 160
West, Cornel, 83, 108
What is Your Race? The Census and Our Flawed Efforts to Classify Americans (book), 309
Wheeler, William R., 233
Whistling Vivaldi (book), 350
White fragility, 4
White nationalist, 2–3
White Trash: Race and Class in America (book), 59
White, Charles Dr., 72
White, Theodore H., 33
Whiteness studies, 59
Whitman, Walt, 42, 138
Wickham, DeWayne, 99
Wilkerson, Isabel, 80
Wilkins, Roy, 87
Williams, Jesse, 133
Williams, William Appleman, 22
Wilmore, Larry, 121
Wilson, Darren, 118
Wilson, Edward O., 286
Wilson, Pete, 177
Wilson, Thomas, 147
Wilson, William Julius, 98, 288, 347
Winant, Howard, 107, 285, 288
Winfrey, Oprah, 264, 305
Winthrop, John, 9
Wittke, Carl, 16, 19, 22, 25
Wong, K. Scott, 211
Woodward, Colin, 10
World Congress of Indigenous People, 298
World War I, 84, 158, 238, 249
World War II, 46, 85, 156, 163, 245
Wray, Matt, 59
Wright, Jeremiah Rev., 66, 111
Wright, Richard, 84
Wu, Ellen, 254
Wu, Frank H., 199

xenophobic principle, 286

Yancey, George, 324
yellow peril, 146, 199, 219–220
Yellow: Race in America Beyond Black and White (book), 199
Young, Elliott, 206
Yudell, Michael, 273
Yuji Ichioka, 223

Zangwill, Israel, 40
Zelinsky, Wilbur, 27
Zhou, Min, 198
Zimmerman, George, 117, 120
Zoot-Suit Riots, 157

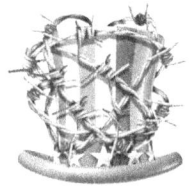

HIRE DAVID TO SPEAK

Make an impact at your next event with David as your keynote speaker.

He has spoken on a variety of topics ranging from multicultural marketing, inclusion in business and the workplace, and the history of race and racism in the United States.

David is a compelling presenter, as he draws on a wealth of knowledge and experience in multicultural markets and with multicultural Americans.

OTHER BOOKS

Multicultural Intelligence: Eight Make-or-Break Rules for Marketing to Race, Ethnicity, and Sexual Orientation.

Kissinger and the Yom Kippur War

LISTEN TO THE *RACE TALK* PODCAST

Race Talk is the podcast where race is front and center. I interview sociologists, demographers, activists, marketers, and historians about race and racism in order to garner a clearer understanding of where we've been, where we are, and where we are going.

ABOUT THE AUTHOR

DAVID R. MORSE combines his love of history and deep knowledge about multicultural communities in both his professional and personal lives. He is President and CEO of New American Dimensions, a market research company focused on Hispanic, African American, Asian American, and LGBTQ Americans, and a professor of history. A social justice activist, he is a frequent speaker on multicultural markets and is known for having worked with some of the most successful organizations in America in developing marketing and inclusion strategies focused on multicultural Americans.

He holds a Master of International Management degree from Thunderbird, The American Graduate School of Global Management, a Master of Arts from California State University, Los Angeles in History, and a Bachelor of Arts degree from the University of New Hampshire, where he studied Psychology and Japanese Studies. His books include *Multicultural Intelligence: Eight Make-Or-Break Rules for Marketing to Race, Ethnicity and Sexual Orientation* and *Kissinger and the Yom Kippur War*.

www.ingramcontent.com/pod-product-compliance
Lightning Source LLC
Chambersburg PA
CBHW071951110526
44592CB00012B/1052